Autodesk® 3ds Max® 2019 Fundamentals

Learning Guide
Mixed Units - 1st Edition

AUTODESK.
Authorized Publisher

ASCENT - Center for Technical Knowledge®
Autodesk® 3ds Max® 2019
Fundamentals
Mixed Units - 1st Edition

Prepared and produced by:

ASCENT Center for Technical Knowledge
630 Peter Jefferson Parkway, Suite 175
Charlottesville, VA 22911

866-527-2368
www.ASCENTed.com

Lead Contributor: Renu Muthoo

ASCENT - Center for Technical Knowledge is a division of Rand Worldwide, Inc., providing custom developed knowledge products and services for leading engineering software applications. ASCENT is focused on specializing in the creation of education programs that incorporate the best of classroom learning and technology-based training offerings.

We welcome any comments you may have regarding this learning guide, or any of our products. To contact us please email: feedback@ASCENTed.com.

Contents

Preface ix

In this Guide xi

Practice Files xv

Chapter 1: Introduction to Autodesk 3ds Max 1-1

   1.1   Overview 1-2

   1.2   Visualization Workflow 1-4

   1.3   The Autodesk 3ds Max Interface 1-6

        Welcome Screen 1-6

        Interface 1-7

   1.4   File Commands 1-30

        Create New Scenes 1-30

        Open and Save Files 1-31

        Preferences 1-32

        Setting the Project Folder 1-34

   1.5   Configure Paths 1-36

   1.6   Display Drivers 1-38

   1.7   Viewport Display and Labels 1-39

        General Viewport 1-39

        Point Of View 1-40

        Shading Viewport 1-41

        Per-View Preference 1-42

   Practice 1a Organizing Folders and Working with the Interface 1-45

   Practice 1b Autodesk 3ds Max Quickstart 1-57

   Chapter Review Questions 1-65

   Command Summary 1-67

Chapter 2: Autodesk 3ds Max Configuration 2-1

2.1 Viewport Navigation 2-2
    Viewport Navigation Toolbar 2-2
    Viewport Navigation Toolbar (Camera Viewport) 2-4
    Viewport Navigation Using the ViewCube 2-4
    Viewport Navigation Using the SteeringWheel 2-5

2.2 Viewport Configuration and Settings 2-6
    Viewport Configuration 2-6
    Viewport Setting and Preferences 2-9

Practice 2a Viewport Configuration and Navigation 2-11

2.3 Object Selection Methods 2-16

Practice 2b Selection Methods 2-20

2.4 Units Setup 2-27

Practice 2c Working with Units Setup 2-29

2.5 Layer and Object Properties 2-30
    Layers Toolbar 2-30
    Layer Explorer 2-30
    Layer Properties 2-32
    Object Properties 2-33
    Display Panel 2-35

Practice 2d Layer and Object Properties 2-36

Chapter Review Questions 2-41

Command Summary 2-43

Chapter 3: Assembling Project Files 3-1

3.1 Data Linking and Importing 3-2
    Linking vs. Importing 3-2
    Editing Linked Data 3-3
    Importing 3-3
    Merging Autodesk 3ds Max Scene Files 3-4
    Civil View 3-4

Practice 3a Ground Surfaces using Civil View 3-7

3.2 Linking Files 3-13
    Linking DWG Files 3-13
    Linking FBX and RVT Files 3-14
    Manage Links Options 3-14
    File Link Settings: DWG Files 3-16
    File Link Settings: Revit Files (RVT or FBX) 3-22

Practice 3b Linking an AutoCAD DWG 3-24

Practice 3c Linking and Reloading Autodesk Revit File 3-32

3.3   **References** **3-38**
     External References (XRef) 3-38
     Data Management and Asset Tracking 3-38

Practice 3d XRef and Merge Objects **3-40**

Chapter Review Questions **3-46**

Command Summary **3-47**

Chapter 4: Basic Modeling Techniques **4-1**

4.1   **Model with Primitives** **4-2**

Practice 4a Modeling with Primitives **4-4**

4.2   **Modifiers and Transforms** **4-8**
     Modifiers 4-8
     Transform Tools 4-9

Practice 4b Modeling with Modifiers and Transforms **4-13**

4.3   **Sub-Object Mode** **4-24**
     Working in Sub-Object Mode 4-24
     Geometric Edits through Sub-objects 4-25
     Geometric Sub-Objects 4-26
     Smoothing 4-26
     Caddy Display for Edit Poly Modifier 4-27

Practice 4c Modeling with Edit Poly in Sub-Object Mode **4-29**

4.4   **Reference Coordinate Systems and Transform Centers** **4-34**
     Reference Coordinate Systems 4-34
     Transform Centers 4-36

4.5   **Cloning and Grouping** **4-37**
     Cloning 4-37
     Grouping 4-38

Practice 4d Modeling with Coordinate Systems **4-40**

Practice 4e Cloning and Grouping **4-42**

4.6   **Polygon Modeling Tools in the Ribbon** **4-47**

Practice 4f (Optional) Poly Modeling Using the Ribbon **4-48**

4.7   **Statistics in Viewport** **4-63**

Chapter Review Questions **4-65**

Command Summary **4-67**

Chapter 5: Modeling From 2D Objects **5-1**

5.1   **3D Modeling from 2D Objects** **5-2**

Practice 5a Drawing Lines **5-4**

5.2   **The Lathe Modifier** **5-11**

Practice 5b Creating a Candlestick 5-12

5.3   2D Booleans 5-14

Practice 5c 2D Booleans 5-15

5.4   The Extrude Modifier 5-20

5.5   3D Boolean Operations 5-23

Practice 5d Extrude Walls and Create Wall Openings 5-28

5.6   Using Snaps for Precision 5-36

Practice 5e Creating a Door with Snaps 5-40

5.7   The Sweep Modifier 5-46
      Sweep Parameters 5-47

Practice 5f Sweeping the Wall Baseboard 5-49

Chapter Review Questions 5-55

Command Summary 5-57

Chapter 6: Materials 6-1

6.1   Understanding Materials and Maps 6-2
      Introduction to Materials 6-2
      Material Components 6-3

6.2   Material Shaders 6-6
      Shader (Specific) Basic Parameters 6-7

6.3   Managing Materials 6-10
      Slate Material Editor Interface 6-10

Practice 6a Introduction to Materials 6-19

6.4   General Materials 6-28
      Physical Material 6-28
      Multi/Sub- Object Materials 6-31
      Additional General Materials 6-32

6.5   Scanline Materials 6-34

6.6   Autodesk Materials 6-36

6.7   Assigning Maps to Materials 6-38

Practice 6b Working with Standard Materials and Maps 6-41

Practice 6c Working with Multi/Sub-Object Materials 6-52

6.8   Opacity, Bump, and Reflection Mapping 6-62
      Opacity Mapping 6-62
      Bump Mapping 6-63
      Reflection Mapping 6-63

Practice 6d Texture Mapping with Physical Material 6-64

6.9 **Arnold Materials** **6-71**

Practice 6e Working with Arnold Materials **6-74**

Practice 6f Materials that Create Lighting **6-80**

6.10 **The Material Explorer** **6-83**

6.11 **Scene Converter** **6-85**

Chapter Review Questions **6-89**

Command Summary **6-91**

Chapter 7: Mapping Coordinates and Scale **7-1**

7.1 **Mapping Coordinates** **7-2**
Mapping Controls in Slate Material Editor 7-3
MapScaler Modifier 7-4
UVW Map Modifier 7-5

Practice 7a Applying Mapping Coordinates **7-6**

Practice 7b Mapping a Large Scale Image **7-10**

7.2 **Mapping Scale** **7-14**
Explicit Map Scaling 7-14
Continuous Map Scaling 7-15

Practice 7c Assigning Map Scales **7-17**

7.3 **Spline Mapping** **7-23**

Practice 7d Spline Mapping **7-24**

Chapter Review Questions **7-30**

Chapter 8: Introduction to Lighting **8-1**

8.1 **Local vs. Global Illumination** **8-2**
Default Illumination 8-2
Local Illumination 8-2
Global Illumination 8-3
Types of Lights 8-4

8.2 **Standard Lighting** **8-5**
Common Parameters 8-6

8.3 **Types of Standard Lights** **8-8**
Omni Lights 8-8
Spotlights 8-8
Directional Lights 8-10
Fill Lights 8-11
Skylight 8-11

Practice 8a Standard Lighting for an Interior Scene **8-12**

8.4 **Shadow Types** 8-26
    Common Shadow Parameters 8-28
    Shadow Map Parameters... 8-29
    Ray Traced Shadows 8-30
    Advanced Ray-Traced Shadows................................ 8-30

Practice 8b Working with Shadow Parameters 8-32

Chapter Review Questions 8-35

Command Summary 8-37

Chapter 9: Lighting and Cameras 9-1

9.1 **Photometric Light Objects** 9-2
    Photometric Light Types 9-2
    Templates Rollout 9-3
    General Parameters Rollout...................................... 9-3
    Distribution (Photometric Web) Rollout 9-4
    Shape/Area Shadows Rollout 9-6
    Intensity/Color/Attenuation Rollout........................... 9-8

Practice 9a Working with Photometric Lights 9-10

9.2 **Arnold Lights** 9-20

Practice 9b Working with Arnold Lights 9-23

9.3 **Cameras** 9-27
    Physical Camera 9-28
    Target and Free Camera Parameters 9-30

9.4 **Background Images** 9-34
    Aspect Ratio... 9-36
    Safe Frames 9-37

Practice 9c Cameras and Background Images 9-40

Chapter Review Questions 9-50

Command Summary 9-51

Chapter 10: Exposure Control, Daylight, and Rendering 10-1

10.1 **Exposure Control** 10-2
    Exposure Control Methods.. 10-2
    Logarithmic Exposure Control Parameters 10-4
    Physical Camera Exposure Control 10-5

10.2 **Daytime Lighting** 10-6
    Sun Positioner Daylight System................................ 10-6
    Sunlight and Skylight System................................... 10-8

Practice 10a Lighting with Sun Positioner 10-12

10.3 **Rendering Options** 10-18
    Common Options 10-19

Common Tab 10-21
Renderer Tab 10-22

10.4 Arnold Renderer **10-23**
Arnold Renderer Tab 10-24
System Tab 10-26
Archive Tab 10-27
Diagnostics Tab 10-28
AOV Settings Tab 10-28
Image Based Lighting 10-28

Practice 10b Working with Arnold Renderer **10-30**

Practice 10c Image Based Lighting in Arnold Renderer **10-36**

10.5 Scanline Renderer **10-42**
Single vs. Double-Sided in Scanline Rendering 10-45

10.6 ART Renderer **10-49**

Practice 10d Working with Scanline Rendering Options **10-51**

10.7 State Sets **10-59**

10.8 The Print Size Wizard **10-63**

Practice 10e Using the Print Size Wizard **10-64**

Chapter Review Questions **10-66**

Command Summary **10-68**

Chapter 11: Animation **11-1**

11.1 Animation and Time Controls **11-2**
Time Configuration 11-6
Progressive Display and Adaptive Degradation 11-10

11.2 Walkthrough Animation **11-13**

Practice 11a Creating a Turntable Animation **11-16**

Practice 11b Keyframing a Camera Animation **11-25**

Practice 11c Creating a Walkthrough Animation **11-32**

11.3 Animation Output **11-37**

Practice 11d Creating Animation Output **11-40**

Chapter Review Questions **11-45**

Command Summary **11-47**

Appendix A: Optional Topics **A-1**

A.1 Getting Help with Autodesk 3ds Max **A-2**

A.2 Compact Material Editor **A-6**

A.3 Architectural Materials **A-9**

A.4   Object Substitution A-11

Practice A1 Substituting the Parking Lot Light Poles A-12

A.5   Creating Hierarchies A-15

Practice A2 Create Hierarchies A-16

Practice A3 Create an Assembly Animation....................................... A-19

A.6   Customizing the User Interface A-21

Practice A4 Customizing the User Interface....................................... A-23

Command Summary A-27

Appendix B: Optional Practices B-1

Practice B1 Create Additional Extrusions B-2

Practice B2 Making a Chair Base by Lofting Objects B-5

Practice B3 Shadow Study Animation B-11

Appendix C: Autodesk 3ds Max Certification Exam Objectives C-1

Index Index-1

Preface

The *Autodesk® 3ds Max® 2019: Fundamentals* learning guide provides a thorough introduction to the Autodesk 3ds Max 2019 software that will help new users make the most of this sophisticated application, as well as broaden the horizons of existing, self-taught users. The guide instructs you on how to effectively use the software interface and navigate through the scenes. It explores the creation of 3D objects and how to bring in objects from other software such as Autodesk Revit, AutoCAD, and Civil 3D. Additionally, it teaches you to prepare the scenes for renderings by adding materials, lights, and cameras. Finally, the guide covers an understanding of various renderers included with the software as well as image creation and animation techniques.

The practices in this learning guide are primarily geared towards real-world tasks encountered by users of the Autodesk 3ds Max software in the Architecture, Interior Design, and Civil Engineering industries.

Advanced topics, such as character modeling, character animation, and rigging, are not covered in this learning guide.

Topics Covered

- Autodesk 3ds Max Interface and Workflow

- Assembling Files by importing, linking, or merging

- 3D Modeling with Primitives and 2D objects

- Using Modifiers to create and modify 3D objects

- Materials and Maps

- Autodesk 3ds Max Lighting

- Working with Cameras and Exposure Control

- Rendering using various renderers such as Scanline, ART, and Arnold

- Animation for Visualization

Prerequisites

- Access to the 2019 version of the software. The practices and files included with this guide might not be compatible with prior versions.
- Experience with 3D modeling is recommended.

Note on Software Setup

This guide assumes a standard installation of the software using the default preferences during installation. Lectures and practices use the standard software templates and default options for the Content Libraries.

Students and Educators can Access Free Autodesk Software and Resources

Autodesk challenges you to get started with free educational licenses for professional software and creativity apps used by millions of architects, engineers, designers, and hobbyists today. Bring Autodesk software into your classroom, studio, or workshop to learn, teach, and explore real-world design challenges the way professionals do.

Get started today - register at the Autodesk Education Community and download one of the many Autodesk software applications available.

Visit www.autodesk.com/education/home/

Note: Free products are subject to the terms and conditions of the end-user license and services agreement that accompanies the software. The software is for personal use for education purposes and is not intended for classroom or lab use.

Lead Contributor: Renu Muthoo

Renu uses her instructional design training to develop courseware for AutoCAD and AutoCAD vertical products, Autodesk 3ds Max, Autodesk Showcase and various other Autodesk software products. She has worked with Autodesk products for the past 20 years with a main focus on design visualization software.

Renu holds a bachelor's degree in Computer Engineering and started her career as a Instructional Designer/Author where she co-authored a number of Autodesk 3ds Max and AutoCAD books, some of which were translated into other languages for a wide audience reach. In her next role as a Technical Specialist at a 3D visualization company, Renu used 3ds Max in real-world scenarios on a daily basis. There, she developed customized 3D web planner solutions to create specialized 3D models with photorealistic texturing and lighting to produce high quality renderings.

Renu Muthoo has been the Lead Contributor for *Autodesk 3ds Max: Fundamentals* since 2010.

In this Guide

The following images highlight some of the features that can be found in this guide.

Practice Files

Link to the practice files

Practice Files

The Practice Files page tells you how to download and install the practice files that are provided with this guide.

Chapter 1

Getting Started

Learning Objectives for the chapter

Chapters

Each chapter begins with a brief introduction and a list of the chapter's Learning Objectives.

1.3 Working with Commands

Starting Commands

The main way to access commands in the AutoCAD software is to use the Ribbon. Several of the file commands are available in the Quick Access Toolbar or in the Application Menu. Some commands are available in the Status Bar or through shortcut menus. There are additional access methods, such as Tool Palettes. The names of all of the commands can also be typed in the Command Line. A table is included to help you to identify the various methods of accessing the commands.

When typing the name of a command in either the Command Line or Dynamic Input, the **AutoComplete** option automatically completes the entry when you pause as you type. It also supports mid-string search by displaying all of the commands that contain the word that you typed, as shown in Figure 1–12. You can then scroll through the list and select a command

Figure 1–12

You can also click ✎ *(Customize) to display the Input Settings for the AutoComplete feature.*

To set specific options for the **AutoComplete** feature, right-click on the Command Line, expand Input Settings, and select from the various options, such as the ability to search for system variables or to set the delay response time, as shown in Figure 1–13

Figure 1–13

If you need to stop a command, press <Esc> to cancel. You might need to press <Esc> more than once.

As you work in the AutoCAD software, the software prompts you for the information that is required to complete each command. These prompts are displayed in the drawing window near the cursor and in the Command Line. It is crucial that you read the command prompts as you work, as shown in Figure 1–14

Instructional Content

Each chapter is split into a series of sections of instructional content on specific topics. These lectures include the descriptions, step-by-step procedures, figures, hints, and information you need to achieve the chapter's Learning Objectives.

Side notes

Side notes are hints or additional information for the current topic.

© 2015, ASCENT - Center for Technical Knowledge®   1–9

Practice 1c   Saving a Drawing File

Practice Objectives

- Open and save a drawing
- Modify the Automatic Saves option.

Estimated time for completion: under 5 minutes

In this practice you will open a drawing, save it, and modify the **Automatic saves** option, as shown in Figure 1–51.

Figure 1–51

1. Open **Building Valley-M.dwg** from your class files folder

2. In the Quick Access Toolbar, click 🖫 (Save). In the Command Line, _QSAVE displays indicating that the AutoCAD software has performed a quick save.

3. In the Application Menu, click `Options` to open the Options dialog box.

4. In the Open and Save tab, change the time for Automatic save to 15 minutes.

Practice Objectives

Practices

Practices enable you to use the software to perform a hands-on review of a topic.

Some practices require you to use prepared practice files, which can be downloaded from the link found on the Practice Files page.

Chapter Review Questions

1. How do you switch from the drawing window to the text window?
   a. Use the icons in the Status Bar.
   b. Press <Tab>.
   c. Press <F2>.
   d. Press the <Spacebar>.

2. How can you cancel a command using the keyboard?
   a. Press <F2>.
   b. Press <Esc>.
   c. Press <Ctrl>.
   d. Press <Delete>.

3. What is the quickest way to repeat a command?
   a. Press <Esc>.
   b. Press <F2>.
   c. Press <Enter>.
   d. Press <Ctrl>.

4. To display a specific Ribbon panel, you can right-click on the Ribbon and select the required panel in the shortcut menu.
   a. True
   b. False

5. How are points specified in the AutoCAD Cartesian workspace?
   a. X value x Y value

Chapter Review Questions

Chapter review questions, located at the end of each chapter, enable you to review the key concepts and learning objectives of the chapter.

Command Summary

The Command Summary is located at the end of each chapter. It contains a list of the software commands that are used throughout the chapter, and provides information on where the command is found in the software.

Autodesk Certification Exam Appendix

This appendix includes a list of the topics and objectives for the Autodesk Certification exams, and the chapter and section in which the relevant content can be found.

Practice Files

To download the practice files for this guide, use the following steps:

1. Type the URL shown below into the address bar of your Internet browser. The URL must be typed **exactly as shown**. If you are using an ASCENT ebook, you can click on the link to download the file.

Address bar

http://www.ASCENTed.com/getfile?id=fotsifotsy

File   Edit   View   Favorites   Tools   Help

2. Press <Enter> to download the .ZIP file that contains the Practice Files.

3. Once the download is complete, unzip the file to a local folder. The unzipped file contains an .EXE file.

4. Double-click on the .EXE file and follow the instructions to automatically install the Practice Files on the C:\ drive of your computer.

   Do not change the location in which the Practice Files folder is installed. Doing so can cause errors when completing the practices.

http://www.ASCENTed.com/getfile?id=fotsifotsy

Stay Informed!

Interested in receiving information about upcoming promotional offers, educational events, invitations to complimentary webcasts, and discounts? If so, please visit:

www.ASCENTed.com/updates/

Help us improve our product by completing the following survey:

www.ASCENTed.com/feedback

You can also contact us at: *feedback@ASCENTed.com*

Introduction to Autodesk 3ds Max

The Autodesk® 3ds Max® software is a modeling, rendering, and animation package used for the visualization and presentation of scenes. Projects can be created and modeled in the software or files from other software packages can be linked/imported for use in the software. A solid understanding of the interface, configuration settings, and the workflow used to create, render, and animate models enable you to visualize your models prior to building the final design.

Learning Objectives in this Chapter

- Identify the various data sources that can be imported into and then output from the Autodesk 3ds Max software.
- Understand the common workflow process to plan your visualization projects.
- Understand the various components of the interface.
- Set the preferences for the scene.
- Set the project folder to organize all of the files in the project.
- Set the path locations of reusable data files and reconfigurable items.
- Identify the display drivers available with the software.
- Identify the viewport display labels and the various options available in them.

1.1 Overview

The Autodesk® 3ds Max® software is a modeling, rendering, and animation package used for design visualization. It can be used to create high-quality 3D models, single-frame still renderings of virtually any size (including large-format presentation graphics), and desktop animations.

Input Into Autodesk 3ds Max

You can create geometry directly in the 3ds Max software or import it from multiple data sources, including the following:

- **AutoCAD® drawing files (.DWG, .DXF):** Including objects created in AutoCAD vertical applications, such as the AutoCAD® Architecture and AutoCAD® Civil 3D® software.

- **Autodesk® Revit® Architecture designs:** Linked into the Autodesk 3ds Max software using .RVT files or the exported .FBX or .DWG files. The Autodesk® Revit® Structure and Autodesk® Revit® MEP software can also be imported using .DWG.

- **AutoCAD® Civil 3D® (VSP3D):** Using **Autodesk Civil View**, you can import files from various civil design programs.

- **Autodesk® Inventor® files (.IPT, .IAM):** The Autodesk Inventor software must be installed on the same machine as the Autodesk 3ds Max software to import these files.

- **3D Studio Mesh format (.3DS):** A common data format used when transferring between 3D applications.

- Autodesk® Alias® .Wire files and the Autodesk® Showcase® .APF (Autodesk Packet File).

- LandXML and DEM data files.

- **Adobe Illustrator (.AI):** The Autodesk 3ds Max software only supports the Adobe Illustrator 88 software.

Vector Data

The input data formats are considered to be vector data. Graphics displayed from vector data formats are defined by point locations and mathematical formulas. Since their data is defined mathematically, vector graphics can be redrawn or regenerated at different scales or from different 3D viewpoints. The Autodesk 3ds Max software file format (.MAX file) is also a vector data file.

Output from Autodesk 3ds Max

Autodesk 3ds Max software stores its data in vector-based .MAX files, used to generate raster images as final products. These images, called *renderings*, can be configured as simple illustrations or fully realized photorealistic images. The most common Autodesk 3ds Max animations are created by combining a series of individually-rendered raster images into a desktop animation file (e.g., Windows .AVI or QuickTime .MOV).

Raster Data

Raster graphics consist of a grid of colored points called pixels Pixels are viewed at a resolution at which they cannot be identified individually, and instead are permitted to present a unified image, as shown in Figure 1–1.

Figure 1–1

The Autodesk 3ds Max software is also used to create raster images or raster based animations (Autodesk 3ds Max renderings). Raster image renderings must be recreated (re-rendered) if the point-of-view is animated or otherwise changed. Common raster file formats include .JPEG, Windows bitmap (.BMP), and .TIFF files. They can also be used as input into the Autodesk 3ds Max software to supplement the vector geometry as follows:

- Scanned or digital photographs of a proposed construction site can be used as a background image.

- Images that illustrate material texture, such as wall coverings, wood grain, or a scratched metal surface.

- Image files created in other computer graphic applications can be used as signs, posters, or company logos.

1.2 Visualization Workflow

Each visualization project can be very different from the next, but most follow a common general workflow. A suggested approach to plan your visualization project is as follows.

1. Setting Goals and Expectations

Every project should start with a clear understanding of the deliverables and expectations.

- Determine viewpoints, animation paths, lighting conditions, etc. before modeling.
- Sketch a mock-up storyboard to agree on the content and scope of an animation.
- Incorporate resolution time in your time estimates. Simple oversights and design problems are often found during the visualization process.

2. Scene Creation and Modeling

The next step is to gather data together into scenes (.MAX files).

- Create a project folder to store all of your data and source material, such as site photos, textures, drawings, scans, in the appropriate locations.
- Import or link 2D or 3D data into one or more scene files, when it is available from other design applications.
- Merge together or externally reference scene files when a project requires multiple scene files.
- Add modeled geometry at this stage. The **Graphite Modeling** tools have many new features for creating new geometry on the surfaces of imported files.

3. Material Design

Materials define how surfaces display and how light interacts with them. Often the next step is to configure the surface characteristics using the Material Editor. It is recommended that you consider the lighting and rendering as materials might need to be coordinated with renderers and lights.

- Detail materials to help simplify the geometry. For example, you do not need to model the grout along a brick wall. Material definitions, such as bump mapping, can add the appearance of depth.

- Fine-tune the material properties, as required, to make them realistic.
- Lighting and materials are often adjusted together, but it can be useful to have a first draft of your materials completed before adding lights.

4. Lighting Design

For realistic results, the 3D models need light sources to illuminate the objects.

- There are different approaches to lighting scenes in the Autodesk 3ds Max software, some are more straightforward and some are more technical.
- Most scenes might require lighting adjustments.

5. Configuring Rendered Views and Animations

Once your model, materials, and lights have been initially configured, you can focus on the final output.

- The length of any animations, their frame rate, and the required time display should be assigned first.
- Camera objects can then be positioned to set up both single-frame still renderings and animations.
- Objects are animated and animated details such as clouds blowing through the sky, pedestrians on the sidewalks, etc. can then be added.
- The rendering options should be configured at this stage.

6. Testing and Final Adjustments

Test the rendering and adjust the model, materials, and lights to achieve the required results. Note that computer processing of the renderings can be very time-consuming, especially for long animations or large still renderings.

7. Post Production

You can add details to your final renderings outside the Autodesk 3ds Max software using third-party image editing programs (Adobe Photoshop or Adobe AfterEffects) and other video post-production software (Autodesk Combustion). Usually, the finished animation segments are mixed with actual video footage, voice-over narration, background sound effects, and music in a different software (such as Apple's Final Cut Pro, or another video editing and assembly tool).

1.3 The Autodesk 3ds Max Interface

To launch the Autodesk 3ds Max software, use one of the following methods:

- Double-click on ![icon] (3ds Max) on your desktop.

- Click **Start** in the Windows Task Bar and select **All Programs>Autodesk>Autodesk 3ds Max 2019> 3ds Max 2019**.

Welcome Screen

When you launch the software, a Welcome screen displays, as shown in Figure 1–2. It presents a slide show moving through various pages showcasing the software and tips for navigation. On the Next steps slide, it has options for opening the help documentation and connecting you to the online community page where you can find tutorials and resources on 3ds Max. It also enables you to connect to an online page where you can download the sample files and watch 1-minute startup videos.

- To prevent the Welcome Screen from displaying every time you launch the Autodesk 3ds Max software, clear the **Show this Welcome Screen at startup** option.
- You can close the Welcome Screen by clicking ![x].
- You can open the Welcome Screen at any time during the current session by selecting **Welcome Screen** in the Help menu.

Figure 1–2

Interface

The Autodesk 3ds Max software consists of a main modeling window, called the *viewport*, which is surrounded by interface tools and panels. Figure 1–3 shows an example of a model created using various modifiers in the Command Panel, to display the different interface features.

*For printing purposes, the UI color scheme used in the figures is **ame-light** (Menu bar: Customize>Custom UI and Defaults Switcher> UI schemes).*

- By default, the scene is set as one viewport/four equal viewports that display the model at different viewing angles.

- You can toggle between the four viewport displays or one maximized viewport (as shown in Figure 1–3), by clicking

  ![icon] (Maximize Viewport) or pressing <Alt>+<W>.

- The active viewport displays a yellow border. Clicking in empty space in a viewport makes it active.

Figure 1–3

1. User Account menu

The User Account menu can be used to log into your Autodesk account and manage licenses for your Autodesk products.

- Expand the Sign In drop-down list and select **Sign In**. You are prompted to login using your Autodesk ID or you can create an ID by selecting **Create Account**, as shown in Figure 1–4.

- Once you have logged in, your sign in name displays in the User Account menu.

Sign in

Email or Username

NEXT

NEW TO AUTODESK? CREATE ACCOUNT

Figure 1–4

2. Menu Bar

The Menu Bar is located below the 3ds Max title bar and contains working commands that are grouped together in the menu titles, as shown in Figure 1–5 for **Create>Standard Primitives** menu. The software provides two menu bars: the default menu bar and the Alt menu bar.

Figure 1–5

The menus in the default menu bar are described as follows:

File	Contains file management tools for opening a scene, saving your work, and setting preferences to work in the software.
Edit	Contains undo and redo functions, transform tools (Move, Scale etc.), object selection options, and delete functions.
Tools	From this menu, you can open all the various Explorers (Scene Explorer, Layer Explorer etc) that are used in the software. It also contains the **Mirror**, **Array**, **Align**, and **Measure Distance** options along with the **Snap** and **Grid** settings and options.
Group	Contains tools to create and edit Autodesk 3ds Max group objects and attach/detach objects.
Views	Contains features, such as preset viewport views, viewport display options, and ViewCube and SteeringWheel options.
Create	Contains options that enable you to create objects, such as 3D geometry, 2D shapes, cameras, and lights. The creation tools are grouped based on the type of objects created, such as Standard primitive objects, compound objects, Light objects, camera objects, etc.

Modifiers	Contains sub-menus categorized by the available modifiers.
Animation	Contains common features used when creating animations.
Graph Editors	Contains several Track View features. Track View offers advanced controls for animations.
Rendering	Contains functions for rendering, such as setting up the scene environment, advanced lighting controls, and output image resolution.
Civil View	Contains features that can be used for displaying the contents of a scene created in a civil design program and to create visualizations of civil engineering projects. It offers support for various civil design programs, including the AutoCAD® Civil 3D® software. If you are opening Civil View for the first time, you need to initialize it and set the system units, country resource kit, and start mode.
Customize	Contains features for customizing the user interface, setting up the drawing units, and setting the overall Autodesk 3ds Max default options.
Scripting	Contains tools for working with the MAXScript programming language used by the Autodesk 3ds Max software.
Content	Links you to the Autodesk App Store, where the Autodesk 3dx Max Asset Library is available for download along with various other apps.
Arnold	Contains options for Arnold renderer, which is a physically-based ray/path tracing renderer. It is geared towards rendering complex scenes for animation and visual effects.
Help	The **Help** menu connects you directly to the Autodesk 3ds Max Help documentation, Tutorials, Learning Resources etc on the *autodesk.com* website. You can also link to 3ds Max Learning Channel on YouTube and #ds Max communities such as *AREA*.

Alt Menu Bar

You can display the Alt Menu Bar by selecting **Alt Menu and Toolbar** in the Workspaces drop-down list. The Alt Menu Bar contains various menus: **File**, **Objects**, **Edit**, **Modifiers**, **Animation**, **Simulate**, **Materials**, **Lighting/Cameras**, **Rendering**, **Scene**, **Civil View**, **Content**, **Publish**, **Scripting**, **Customize**, and **Help**.

- The commands and functions are organized as menu items, with submenus containing the relevant commands.

Hint: Global Menu Search

You can search for any menu command or action using the global menu search method. Press <X> to open the Search actions edit box at the cursor location and enter the name of the command or action that you want to use. As you enter the first letter of the command, a list of matching actions displays, as shown in Figure 1–6. Select an option in the list or continue entering letters to display a more specific list of actions. To clear the search action, click the red **X** icon in the upper right corner of the *Search* edit box. To exit the search feature, click in an empty space or press <Esc>.

Figure 1–6

3. Quad Menu

The Quad menus (shown in Figure 1–7) are a series of context-sensitive menus that open when selecting and right-clicking on one or more objects in the viewport. The commands display in different quadrant areas and each quad menu can have a maximum of four quadrant areas, as shown in Figure 1–8.

- Quad menus also display when nothing is selected.

- Different quad menus display when <Ctrl>, <Alt>, or <Shift> are combined with right-clicking.

display
Viewport Lighting and Shadows ▶
Isolate Selection
End Isolate
Unfreeze All
Freeze Selection
Unhide by Name
Unhide All
Hide Unselected
Hide Selection
State Sets ▶
Manage State Sets...

transform	
Move	☐
Rotate	☐
Scale	☐
Select	
Select Similar	
Clone	
Object Properties...	
Curve Editor...	
Dope Sheet...	
Wire Parameters...	
Convert To:	▶

Figure 1–7

transform	coordinates
Freeze Transform	World
Freeze Rotation	View
Transform To Zero	Screen
Rotation To Zero	Parent
	Local

pose	set
Set Pref Angles	Set Keyframe
Assume Pref Angles	Show Trajectories Toggle
Set as Skin Pose	Delete Selected Animation
Assume Skin Pose	Reaction Manager...
	Dope Sheet...
	Curve Editor...

Figure 1–8

4. Main Toolbar

The Main Toolbar (shown in Figure 1–9) is visible by default and contains tools for some of the most commonly used options. These include the **Selection**, **Transforms**, **Snap**, and **Rendering** tools.

Figure 1–9

- The Main Toolbar can extend beyond the interface and some of the tools are not visible on the screen. To slide the buttons left or right, hover the cursor over the gray empty area until the cursor changes into a Pan cursor (hand icon), hold the left mouse button, and drag.

- If the Main Toolbar is not visible, you can display it by selecting **Customize>Show UI>Show Main Toolbar**.

- You can float and dock the Main toolbar to a different location in the interface window. Hover the cursor over the handle (double lines) located along the left end of the Main toolbar. The cursor changes into a move icon, as shown in Figure 1–10. Drag and relocate the Main toolbar anywhere on the screen. You can also drag it along the left, right, or bottom of the interface window to dock it. Once you drag the Main toolbar along the side of the screen, a placement bar displays, as shown in Figure 1–10. Drop the Main toolbar when the placement area displays to dock it along that side of the viewport.

When you hover the cursor over a handle, a tooltip with the name of the interface item displays.

Figure 1–10

- You can also dock or float the Main toolbar by hovering the cursor over its handle, then right-clicking and selecting either **Dock>Right**, **Dock>Left**, or **Float** as shown in the Figure 1–11.

Figure 1–11

- You can break the Main toolbar into modular pieces and then float or dock the modular groups to different locations in the interface. To make the Main toolbar modular, in the Workspaces selector drop-down list, select **Main Toolbar - modular**, as shown on the left in Figure 1–12. The division lines are changed into Handles (double lines), which are located along the left side of each modular group, as shown on the right in Figure 1–12. Drag and drop to relocate or dock each module separately to different locations.

Figure 1–12

- You can revert back to the standard Main toolbar by selecting **Default** in the Workspace selector drop-down list.

- Selecting **Modular-mini** in the in the Workspaces selector drop-down list, displays a smaller version of the Main toolbar and the Menu Bar, containing the frequently used tools, as shown in Figure 1–13.

Figure 1–13

5. Toolbars

By default, the toolbars (except the Main toolbar) do not display. Right-click on the gray empty space of a docked toolbar including the Main toolbar or right-click on the title bar of an open toolbar to open the **Customize Display** menu (shown in Figure 1–14) where you can select the required toolbar name to display it. The toolbar has a handle along its left side, as shown for the MassFX toolbar. As with other interface components, you can float or dock the toolbars, using their respective handles.

MassFX toolbar

Handle

Figure 1–14

6. Workspace Selector

The Workspace selector (shown in Figure 1–15) enables you to manage and switch between different interface setups.

- You can create a custom interface setup that contains commonly used toolbars, menus, quad menus, viewport layout settings, ribbon tools, and hotkeys for commands and save them as workspaces.

Figure 1–15

- **Manage Workspaces:** Opens the Manage Workspaces dialog box, in which you can add new workspaces, edit workspaces, and delete workspaces.

- **Alt Menu and Toolbar:** Displays an alternate menu in the menu bar with Scene Explorer docked under the Command Panel.

- **Design Standard:** Displays an alternate ribbon containing commonly used features along with help and other learning resources in the ribbon.

- **Main Toolbar - modular:** Displays the Main toolbar in the modular form which can be broken into smaller groups.

- **Modular - mini:** Displays an alternate Main toolbar containing a limited number of commonly used tools.

- **Default:** Reverts back to the standard menu bar.

7. Command Panel

The options in the lower portion of each panel are grouped into rollouts. You can expand and collapse the rollouts by clicking on the title bar of the rollout, or the +/- signs (or downward/sideward facing arrows).

The Command Panel enables you to efficiently create, edit, and manage the settings of 3D objects. It contains six different panels or tabs, each with a different appearance and function. Figure 1–16 shows the *Object Type* rollout in the Create panel (+).

Figure 1–16

- If the list of rollouts are extensive and extend beyond the bottom of the interface, pan the list up and down by holding and dragging the mouse button in the Command Panel.

- By default, the Command Panel is docked along the right side of the viewport window. You can dock or float the Command Panel by hovering the cursor over the top handle (edge) of the Command Panel I, then right-clicking and selecting either **Dock>Right**, **Dock>Left**, or **Float** as shown in the Figure 1–17.

Figure 1–17

- You can also use the Command Panel handle to drag and drop it to dock or float it.

✛ Create Panel

The Create panel enables you to interactively create objects in the Autodesk 3ds Max software and contains the following categories of object types:

⬤	**Geometry** is 3D objects.
▣	**Shapes** are 2D objects.
💡	**Lights** are used to illuminate the scene.
🎥	**Cameras** are objects that provide scene views.
📐	**Helpers** are non-rendering tools that help with layout or work with other objects, such as a distance measuring tape object.
≋	**Space warps** are non-renderable objects that deform or otherwise influence the geometry of other objects. They are used to create ripples and waves, using forces such as wind and gravity.
⚙	**Systems** contains the Sunlight and Daylight Systems, Biped, and the controls for some 3rd party plug-ins.

⌐ Modify Panel

The Modify panel shows the selected object's parameter values, a list of modifiers added to an object, and the parameters that apply to them.

- Modifiers are geometric modifications and additional property controls that can be added to objects, as required.

- Object and modifier parameters can be changed at any time after the object's creation, if the Modifier Stack remains intact.

- The Modifier List drop-down list contains all of the modifiers that can be applied to the current selection.

- The Modifier Stack lists the modifiers that have been applied to an object. Figure 1–18 shows the Modifier Stack of a circle that was edited, extruded, and tapered into a 3D column shaft.

- The Modify panel is blank if no object is selected or if more than one object is selected.

Figure 1–18

Hierarchy Panel

The Hierarchy panel contains controls for objects that are linked together into hierarchies, such as for mechanical equipment with interconnected parts.

Motion Panel

The Motion Panel contains sophisticated motion controls for animating.

Display Panel

The Display panel contains object-level visibility controls, enabling you to hide or unhide objects individually or by category, independent of the layer settings.

Utilities Panel

The Utilities panel contains a number of miscellaneous utilities as follows:

Perspective Match Utility	Helps match the position and field of view of the camera in your 3D scene to the perspective photographic background image.
Collapse Utility	Removes the modifiers from an object's stack, turning the object into an editable mesh or poly.
Color Clipboard Utility	Stores color swatches for copying from one map or material to another.
Measure Utility	Lists the surface area and volume of objects.
Motion Capture Utility	Enables you to animate virtual objects with the real-time movement of the mouse or they input device.
Reset XForm Utility	Removes rotation and scale values of an object, applying them to the XForm modifier gizmo.
MAXScript	Accesses a scripting language that can be used to automate repetitive functions or build new tools and interfaces.
Flight Studio Utility	Enables you to open and manage the open Flight models.
More...	Provides access to a complete list of Utilities, including the controls for many 3rd party plug-in applications.

8. Modeling Ribbon

The Modeling ribbon (shown in Figure 1–19) provides easy access to polygon modeling tools, including the editing and modification tools used at sub-object level. The ribbon contains most of the commonly used tools that are also found in the Command Panel's Modify panel (at the Edit Poly sub-object level).

*If the ribbon is not displayed, in the menu bar, select **Customize> Show UI>Show Ribbon**. You can also click (Toggle Ribbon) in the Main Toolbar or select **Ribbon** in the Customize Display shortcut menu.*

Figure 1–19

The ribbon contains five tabs: *Modeling*, *Freeform*, *Selection*, *Object Paint*, and *Populate* that are further subdivided into various panels that are context dependent. All of the tools are grouped based on context and are placed in separate panels.

- For example, the *Modeling* tab contains the tools used for modeling and are grouped in the Polygon Modeling panel, Modify Selection panel, Edit panel, etc. Each of the panels has a set of related tools and commands present for easy access. For example, the Polygon Modeling panel contains tools used for **Edit Poly** modifier, as shown in Figure 1–20.

Figure 1–20

- The ribbon is docked under the Main Toolbar and might be minimized to the panel tiles. Click ⊡ to maximize the ribbon.

- The display of the tabs and panels can be controlled by right-clicking on the ribbon and select the options in the menu, as shown in Figure 1–21.

Figure 1–21

- If you are continuously using the options from a panel, you can click ⌺ in the expanded panel to lock it.

Hint: Design Workspace

The Design Workspace Ribbon contains the commonly used 3ds Max commands and features grouped together in tabs, as shown in Figure 1–22. It can be started by selecting **Design Standard** in the Workspaces selector drop-down list.

Figure 1–22

The various tabs included are:

- **Get Started**: Commands for starting a new scene, opening an already saved scene, and linking geometry and files from other 3D data software. It also contains commands for customizing the software and accessing to learning resources.

- **Object Inspection**: Commands used to control the display of objects in viewports and also explore the geometry in the scene.

- **Basic Modeling**: Tools for creating new geometry in the scene.

- **Materials**: Tools for creating, managing, and editing the materials.

- **Object Placement**: Tools for moving, placing and editing geometry. You can also open Civil View from this tab.

- **Populate**: Tools for adding animated or idle people to a scene.

- **View**: Commands to add cameras and control the viewport display.

- **Lighting and Rendering**: Tools for adding lights and creating renderings of the scene.

9. Scene Explorer

The Scene Explorer (shown in Figure 1–23) lists all of the objects that are present in a scene in the form of a tree structure, along with each object's properties displayed in a tabular form.

- By default, the Scene Explorer is docked along the left side of the viewport. You can float it or dock it to top, bottom, left, or right by right-clicking on its handle and selecting the required option.

- You can also drag and drop the Scene Explorer by its handle to float or dock it.

- It is a modeless dialog box that can remains open while you are working in the scene.

- You can open and manage the Scene Explorer from the Tools menu bar.

Figure 1–23

- A default Scene Explorer is included for each workspace and can be saved with a specific name with that workspace.

- The objects can be toggled to be displayed either as hierarchies (⬚) or as layers (≋).

- Objects and layers can be nested to any depth. Use the arrow next to the name to expand or collapse the group.

- You can perform actions and modifications such as sorting, filtering, selecting, renaming, hiding, and freezing objects, directly in the Scene Explorer.

- You can drag and drop objects and layers to reorganize the groups.

- A toolbar is provided along the left edge of the Scene Explorer that enables you to list only those objects that belong to a particular category. There are tools for various categories such as ⬤ (Display Geometry), ◼ (Display Cameras), ☀ (Display Lights), etc. When the tool for a category is active (i.e., displays with a blue background), the objects belonging to that category are listed. The ▤ (Display All) tool lists all of the different categories of objects. To only list the objects belonging to the category that you need, use ◼ (Display None) to clear any existing selections, and then select the required display category.

- To easily find and select an item, use the *Search* field.

10. Status Bar

The Status Bar (shown in Figure 1–24) found along the bottom left and center of the interface contains the following elements:

	None Selected		X: 402.695	Y: -477.52	Z: 0.0	Grid = 100.0
Welcome to M:	Loading...					Add Time Tag

Figure 1–24

MAXScript Mini-Listener	Enables you to enter commands and receive feedback (MaxScript commands)
Status Line	Identifies the number of objects selected
Prompt Line	Prompts for the next action or input that is required.
(Isolate Selection Toggle)	Zooms the current selection in the active viewport while temporarily hiding unselected objects in all viewports (except the **Camera** viewport). This enables you to work on the required object without the other objects getting in your way. You can also access this command by selecting Tools>Isolate Selection or pressing <Alt>+<Q>.
(Selection Lock Toggle)	Toggles a lock to prevent you from changing your current selection between options. Pressing the space bar toggles this on or off.
or (Absolute/Offset Transform Mode Toggle)	Enables you to toggle between Absolute mode (which sets the coordinates in the world space) and the Offset transform mode (which transforms the objects relative to its coordinates).
Transform Type In	Enables you to review and adjust transform values for the X, Y, and Z coordinates.
Grid Setting Display	Controls the distance between grid lines. Select Tools>Grids and Snaps>Grid and Snap Settings to open the dialog box. Use the *Home Grid* tab to adjust the spacing. To toggle the Grid on or off, press <G>.
(Adaptive Degradation Toggle)	Enables you to toggle adaptive degradation on or off. Right-click to open the Viewport Configuration dialog box in the *Display Performance* tab (the Adaptive Degradation tab is for legacy drivers). You can improve the viewport quality progressively and set the resolution for the texture display (for nitrous drivers). It also contains options for controlling adaptive degradation.
Time Tag	Enables you to add or edit time tags, which are labels describing specific points of an animation.

11. Viewport Layouts tab bar

The *Viewport Layouts* tab bar is a vertically, expandable bar containing a list of viewport layouts that can be selected to quickly change the layout of the viewports, as shown in Figure 1–25.

- For a new scene, only one layout tab is available. Once you have saved additional viewport layouts, they are listed along with the default one. In Figure 1–25, the *Viewport Layouts* tab bar displays the default layout and three additional viewport layouts that were saved.

Figure 1–25

- Click ▶ (as shown in Figure 1–26), to open the available standard viewport layouts for selection and customization. Once you have selected a layout, it is listed in the tab bar with any previously saved layouts. The viewports display as the new layout.

Figure 1–26

- To customize a preset layout, select it from the preset layouts, move the boundaries by clicking and dragging them to new positions, set the required *Point of View* and *Shading* modes, and then save the custom viewport layout. Save it by right-clicking on the new custom tab and selecting **Save Configuration as Preset**. Set its name by entering a new name in the edit box. The newly saved viewport configuration is saved along with the scene for easy retrieval in a later session.

- To display or hide the tab bar, right-click in an empty area of the Main Toolbar, and toggle the **Viewport Layout Tabs** option.

Hint: Interface Item customize menu

The interface items that can be docked/floated (Main toolbar, Command Panel, Ribbon, Scene Explorer, Time Slider, and Viewport Tabs Bar) contain a shortcut menu that can be used to display or hide these interface elements. To display the menu, right-click on the handle of the interface item, as shown for Command Panel in Figure 1–27. A checkmark next to an item indicates that it displays in the interface.

Figure 1–27

12. Viewport Navigation Tools

The navigation tools are discussed in detail later in the learning guide.

The navigation tools (shown in Figure 1–28), are located in the lower right corner of the interface and contain tools for navigating and displaying objects in the viewports. The tools are dependent on the active viewport.

Figure 1–28

1.4 File Commands

The **File** menu provides access to the file commands used for saving, opening, or creating new scenes, import/ export options, and preferences, as shown in Figure 1–29. Some of the commands have sub-menus that contain additional options, as shown for the **New** command in Figure 1–30.

Figure 1–29

Figure 1–30

Create New Scenes

The commands in the **File>New** menu (shown in Figure 1–30) are described as follows:

- **New All:** Opens a new empty scene from scratch. If there are unsaved objects drawn on the screen, the software prompts you to save or discard the changes first and then opens a new scene.

- **Keep Objects:** Keeps all the objects in the scene without any hierarchy.

- **Keep Object and Hierarchy:** Keeps all the objects with hierarchal links between the objects intact.

- **New from Template:** Opens the Create New Scene dialog box, which contains five standard start-up templates for creating a new empty scene, as shown in Figure 1–31. These templates contain built-in settings (rendering, environment, lighting, units, etc.) optimum for that particular type of scene. The **Open Template Manager** option enables you to create new templates or modify the existing ones.

Figure 1–31

Open and Save Files

You can open and save scenes using various commands in the **File** menu.

- The **Open** command opens an already saved .MAX file and the **Open Recent** option opens a file from the list of recently opened files.

- The **Reset** option enables you to clear all data from the already opened file.

- Use **File>Save** to save a scene as a .MAX file and it overwrites the currently open file. The **File>Save As** opens a Save File As dialog box, where you can save the file as a .MAX (current software version or three previous versions) or .CHR file in the required location. If you save it under a different name, the newly saved file remains open. If you are using the **Save** command to save an unnamed file for the first time, the option works as **Save As**.

- The **Save Copy As** option enables you to save the current open file with a different file name and save a separate copy of it without overwriting the last saved version of the file. The currently open file remains open.

Preferences

The Preference Settings dialog box (shown in Figure 1–32) contains tabs that control the display and operational settings at the program level. To open the dialog box, select **File> Preferences** or **Customize>Preferences**.

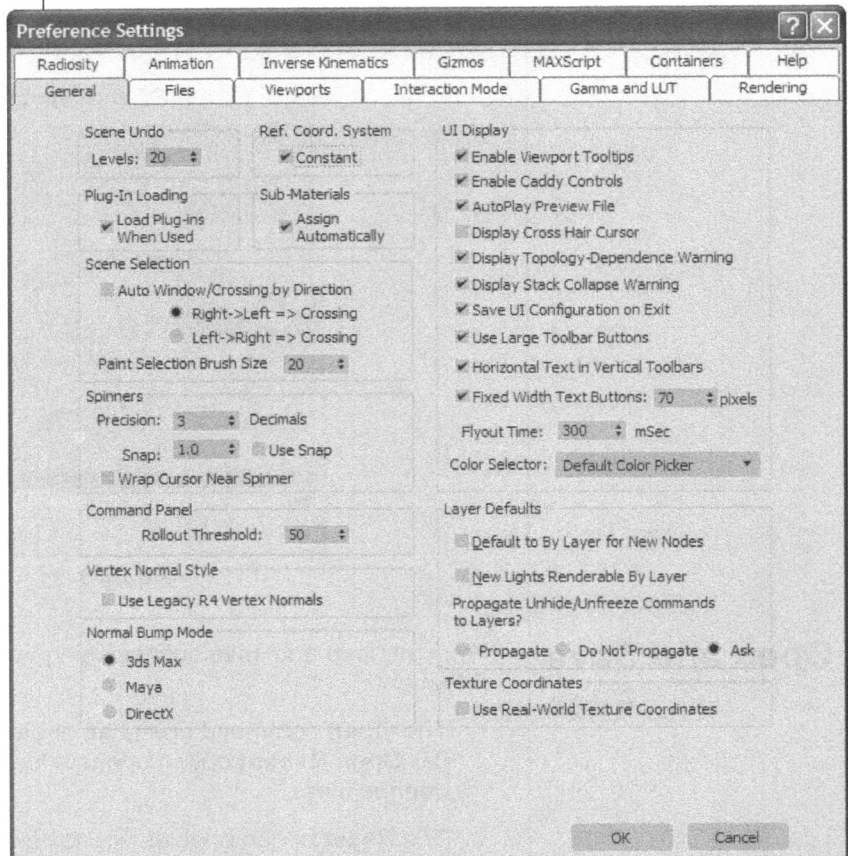

Figure 1–32

The various tabs available are described as follows:

General tab	Controls the interface settings, such as Number of Scene Undo steps (levels) that are saved, settings for the transform center, user interface display options, etc.
Files tab	Contains options for file handling, such as Automatic backup save settings.
Viewports tab	Contains options for viewport settings, highlighting options for selection and preview, and setting the display drivers.
Interaction Mode tab	Sets how the mouse and keyboard shortcuts are going to behave. You can set the mouse shortcut behavior to match with earlier releases of 3ds Max or Maya.
Gamma and LUT tab	Sets the compatibility options with respect to other Autodesk programs for a consistent display of colors among various programs
Rendering tab	Controls the rendering settings, such as the ambient light default color settings.
Animation tab	Controls the various animation settings. You can assign the sound plug-ins and controller defaults.
Inverse kinematics tab	Sets the Applied IK (for accuracy) and Interactive IK (for real-time response) settings.
Gizmos tab	Sets the display and behavior of the Transform gizmos.
MAXScript tab	Sets the various features used for the MAXScript editor, such as what font and font size to use.
Radiosity tab	Controls the radiosity settings in viewports and if the light levels with radiosity are saved with a file or not.
Containers tab	Controls the Status and Update settings in viewports.
Help tab	Controls where the help documentation is accessed from. By default, help is accessed through the Autodesk.com website. Alternatively, you can download the documentation locally and then specify its installation path in the *Help* tab.

Hint: Gamma and LUT Settings Mismatch

Gamma and LUT Settings are saved with the defaults for the current file based on the current UI. Opening or merging a scene, whose file gamma or LUT settings are different from the gamma and LUT settings of the system in which it is being opened, causes the Mismatch dialog box to open, as shown in Figure 1–33. It provides you with options to use the current settings or adopt the file settings.

Figure 1–33

Setting the Project Folder

Setting a project folder enables you to better organize all of the files for a project. By default, the project folder is set to your local *../3dsmax* folder. Once the project folder is created, a series of subfolders (e.g., scenes, render output) are generated. The project folder is maintained when the Autodesk 3ds Max software is restarted. In the **File>Project** menu (as shown in Figure 1–34) various options are provided that enable you to create and set the project folder.

Figure 1–34

- The file path of the current project folder displays at the top of the **Project** submenu. Clicking on the path opens the Configure User Path dialog box where you can change the folders for scenes, image, material libraries, etc.

- You can reset the project folder by selecting **File>Set Active Project**. This opens the Set Active Project dialog box, which displays the drives and folders in your system. Select a folder to use for the project.

- Select **Create Empty** to open the Choose a folder dialog box, where you can create a new project folder without a folder structure.

- Select **Create Default** to create a new project folder with a default folder structure using the Choose a folder dialog box.

- Select **Create from Current** to create a new project folder based on the folder structure that you select in the Choose a folder dialog box.

- The **Recent Projects** option lists the previously opened projects and you can select one to make it current.

1.5 Configure Paths

Projects can use external files such as fonts, image maps for materials, IES (Illuminating Engineering Society) data files for lights, etc. The locations of these and other required data files are identified in the Configure System Paths and Configure User Paths dialog boxes. These dialog boxes can be opened by selecting **Customize>Configure System Paths/Configure User Paths**. The Configure User Paths dialog box can also be opened in the **File>Project** menu.

Configure System Paths

The Configure System Paths dialog box (shown in Figure 1–35) stores paths to data files and contains the following tabs:

Figure 1–35

System	Paths used for additional buttons, macros, scripts and startup scripts, and temp files.
3rd Party Plug-Ins	Default paths to search for add-on application data (some standard functions and 3rd party products).

Configure User Paths

The Configure User Paths dialog box (shown in Figure 1–36) stores items that might be reconfigured for different users or for different projects. The User path settings are saved as a path configuration (.MXP) file. The dialog box has the following tabs:

Figure 1–36

File I/O	Paths used to locate files for options such as open, save, export, etc.
External Files	Paths to external data files such as image maps, IES files, etc.
XRefs	Paths that are searched to find externally referenced objects and scene files.

- Since multiple workstations often make use of the same data files, it is often helpful to create shared network locations for these files (especially when network rendering).

- Relative paths are used to help prevent *missing external files* problems when sharing or moving files from one location to another. In the Configure User Paths, all of the paths are preceded with a dot and backslash (.\) indicating a relative path.

- You can use the Configure User Paths dialog box to change hard-coded absolute paths from earlier versions to Relative paths. Select the path and click Make Relative.

1.6 Display Drivers

The Nitrous Direct3D 11 driver is the default and recommended display driver, but you can change to the other Nitrous drivers or legacy drivers. Nitrous Direct3D 9 is set as the default driver if the graphics card or operating system on your system does not support Nitrous Direct3D 11.

To open the Preference Settings dialog box, select **Customize> Preferences** or **File> Preferences**. In the *Viewports* tab, and in the *Display Drivers* area, click **Choose Driver**. Then, select the required driver in the Display Driver Selection dialog box, as shown in Figure 1–37. If you change the display driver, you need to close and reopen the software for the changes to take effect.

You can also change the graphics driver outside the software (if it is not open) using the Windows Start menu. Select Windows **Start>All Programs> Autodesk>Autodesk 3ds Max 2019> Change Graphics Mode**. *This launches the software and provides the option of selecting the display driver.*

Figure 1–37

The following display drivers are available:

- **Nitrous Direct3D 11:** The Nitrous Direct 3D 11 driver requires Direct 3D 11.0. This driver takes advantage of video card features (when available), and provides high quality realistic viewport display options and faster rendering times. The visual display is render quality and supports unlimited lights, shadows, tone mapping, etc. The Nitrous driver also enables you to display your scenes in stylized images (pencil, acrylic, ink, etc.) in the viewports.

- **Nitrous Direct3D 9:** The Nitrous Direct 3D 9 driver requires Direct3D 9.0. It works in the same way as the Direct3D 11 driver.

- **Nitrous Software:** The Nitrous Software driver has similar capabilities to the other nitrous drivers, but the hardware support is not required and it might be slower during rendering.

The **OpenGL** *and* **Direct3D** *options are useful if your system supports those forms of hardware acceleration. Experiment with these options to determine the best option for your workstation.*

- **Legacy Direct3D:** The Direct3D driver supports data culling and works well for the high-color displays.

- **Legacy OpenGL:** The OpenGL driver works well for hardware acceleration, including geometry acceleration and rasterization acceleration. You cannot display shadows or ambient occlusion in viewports while using this driver.

1.7 Viewport Display and Labels

Geometry opens in the software through one or more viewports, which can be configured to show objects from different viewing angles and with different viewport shading modes.

The *Viewport* label menus (shown in Figure 1–38) display in the upper left corner of each viewport. Note that the four labels are only available for the Nitrous displays, while the legacy driver display shows only three labels.

[+] [Perspective] [User Defined] [Default Shading]

Figure 1–38

General Viewport

Click on **[+]** to open the *General Viewport* label menu, as shown in Figure 1–39. It includes the ability to display grids, the ViewCube, and the SteeringWheels. It also contains tools for the **xView** functionality, which enables you to show statistics and diagnose problems in polygonal geometry such as overlapping faces, unwelded vertices, or face normal orientation issues.

	Restore Viewport	Alt+W
	Active Viewport	▶
	Disable Viewport	D
✓	Show Grids	G
	ViewCube	▶
	SteeringWheels	▶
	xView	▶
	Create Preview	▶
	Configure Viewports...	
	2D Pan Zoom Mode	

Figure 1–39

Point Of View

The *Point of View* label displays the name of the view projection (i.e., Perspective, Orthographic) that is being shown in the viewport. Clicking on this *Viewport* label opens the *Point of View* label menu (shown in Figure 1–40), which enables you to change the view type.

The three most common view types are:

- **Perspective View:** This view displays what is seen with human vision and uses vanishing points to make distant objects appear to recede from view. The most realistic output is shown through perspective views or the camera view, as shown in Figure 1–41.

*You can also change the view using the shortcut keys that are listed next to the type in the label menu (e.g., <T> for **Top**, <B> for **Bottom**, etc.).*

Figure 1–40

Figure 1–41

- **Orthographic (Axonometric Rotated) View:** Orthographic views (shown in Figure 1–42) do not use vanishing points or convergence; therefore objects do not seem to recede over distance. You can think of Orthographic views as being similar to Isometric views (Isometric views are special cases of Axonometric views where the axes are equally inclined to the screen).

You might find Orthographic views easier to navigate (especially when zooming with a mouse wheel), but the rendered output often does not display as realistic as from a perspective view.

[+] [Orthographic] [Standard] [Edged Faces]

Figure 1–42

- **Other Views:** The **Left**, **Right**, **Top**, **Bottom**, **Front**, and **Back** views are all types of predefined views, which show a 2D projection of the model.

Shading Viewport

The *Shading Viewport* label provides options to change the shading display methods used in the viewport, such as **High Quality**, **Standard**, **Performance**, and **DX Mode** (as shown in Figure 1–43). In addition to shading, this menu contains tools for the **Lighting and Shadows**, and display of materials with textures and maps.

[+] [Top] [Standard] [Wireframe]

High Quality   Shift+F3
✓ Standard
Performance
DX Mode

Lighting and Shadows   ▶
Materials   ▶

Viewport Global Settings
Per-View Presets

High Quality   **Standard**   **Performance**

Figure 1–43

Per-View Preference

The *Per-View Preference* label menu (shown in Figure 1–44) displays the visual style methods for a view, such as **Default Shading**, **Facets**, **Bounding Box**, **Clay**, etc. You can select different edge modes and with the selected shading method. This menu also contains tools for various **Stylized** options, **Lighting and Shadows**, and **Viewport Background**. You can use the **Display Selected** options to control the display of selected geometry in shaded viewports.

Figure 1–44

Some of the visual style modes (using the Standard shading viewport display) are shown in Figure 1–45.

Default shading *Default shading & Edged Faces* *Flat Color & Edged Faces*

Wireframe *Hidden Line* *Bounding Box*

Figure 1–45

- The **Default Shading** mode displays the object as smooth with Phong shading being applied to it.

- The **Facets** option always displays the geometry as faceted even if the **Smooth** modifier or Smoothing have been applied to the object. This enables you to precisely locate the edges in the model and makes it easier to work with the geometry.

- The **Bounding Box** option is useful when scenes are extremely complex and software performance is an issue. Alternatively, in this situation, individual objects can be set to view as bounding boxes through Object Properties.

- In the **Flat Color** mode, lighting effects are disabled and the object displays with just the color.

- The **Hidden Line** option improves the Wireframe display by hiding the lines that are on the backside of the objects.

- The **Edged Faces** option overlays a wireframe over any other visual style, such as Default shading, Facets, Clay, and others.

- The **Clay** option displays the geometry in a terracotta color without any material or texture color.

- The **Stylized** menu options enables you to display objects with a variety of effects that are non-photorealistic, as shown in Figure 1–46.

Graphite   *Color Pencil*   *Pastel*

Figure 1–46

Hint: Legacy Driver Display Labels

The legacy driver display shows only three labels:

- The *General Viewport* label and the *Point of View* label contains the same menu options as for the nitrous drivers.

- The *Shading Viewport* label has menu options pertaining to the legacy drivers, as shown in Figure 1–47.

Figure 1–47

Practice 1a

Organizing Folders and Working with the Interface

Practice Objectives

- Set the project folder and configure User Paths.
- Create Viewport Layouts and navigate the graphic user interface
- Modify an object using the Command Panel and using the Scene Explorer.

In this practice, you will work with the Autodesk 3ds Max software by setting the project folder to organize the files in the project. You will also configure the user paths to set the folders. You will then create different Viewport layouts by changing the viewing angles and different shading modes. You will also navigate the graphic user interface. To complete the practice you will open a file and modify the objects using different interface components.

For printing purposes, the UI color scheme used for this practice is **ame-light** (Menu bar: Customize>Custom UI and Defaults Switcher>ame-light in UI schemes list), and the *Theme* in the *Colors* tab has been set to **Light** in the Customize User Interface dialog box.

Task 1 - Set the Project Folder.

1. Install the practice files by launching the self-extracting .EXE file. Ensure that the files are located in the *C:\Autodesk 3ds Max Fundamentals Practice Files* folder.

2. Launch the Autodesk 3ds Max 2019 software.

   - If a Welcome Screen displays, clear the **Show this Welcome Screen at startup** option and close the Welcome Screen.
   - If it is already running, reset the program by selecting **Reset** in the **File** menu. This closes the current file and opens a new blank file. If an unsaved scene is open, you might be required to save or discard the changes to the scene. Click **Don't Save**. Click **Yes** to reset the file.

*Selecting from the menu bar will be referred to in the **File>Project> Create from Current** format in the learning guide.*

3. In the **File** menu, hover the cursor over **Project** and note the folder path at the top of the submenu. It is the current project folder based on your local settings.

4. In the Project submenu, select **Create from Current**.

5. In the Choose a folder dialog box, navigate to C: and select the *Autodesk 3ds Max Fundamentals Practice Files* folder.

6. Click **Select Folder**.

7. Select **File>Project** to open the submenu again. Note that **C:\Autodesk 3ds Max Fundamentals Practice Files** displays at the top of the submenu, as shown in Figure 1–48.

Figure 1–48

Task 2 - Setting Preferences.

*Alternatively, you can also select **Customize> Preferences**.*

1. In the menu bar, select **File>Preferences**. The Preference Settings dialog box opens.

2. In the *General* tab, in the *Ref. Coord. System* area, select **Constant**, as shown in Figure 1–49. This enables the Transform types to use the same Reference Coordinate System.

Figure 1–49

3. In the *Layer Defaults* area, verify that **Default to By Layer for New Nodes** is cleared, as shown in Figure 1–50. Click **OK**.

Layer Defaults

Default to By Layer for New Nodes

New Lights Renderable By Layer

Propagate Unhide/Unfreeze Commands to Layers?

Propagate   Do Not Propagate   Ask

Figure 1–50

Task 3 - Configure the User Paths.

*Alternatively, you can also select **File> Project> Configure User Paths**.*

1. Select **Customize>Configure User Paths** to open the Configure User Paths dialog box. Note that the Project Folder is set to the current active folder (*C:\Autodesk 3ds Max Fundamentals Practice Files*).

2. Verify that the *File I/O* tab is selected. In the list, select **Materials** and click **Modify**. In the Choose Directory for Materials dialog box, browse to *C:\Program Files\Autodesk\ 3ds Max 2019\materiallibraries*. Click **Use Path** (You might have to click **Use Path** again until you are back in the Configure User Paths dialog box). The path displays as shown in Figure 1–51.

Configure User Paths

File I/O | External Files | XRefs

Project Folder

C:\Autodesk 3ds Max Fundamentals Practice Files

Animations	.\sceneassets\animations
Archives	.\archives
AutoBackup	.\autoback
BitmapProxies	.\proxies
CFD	.\sceneassets\CFD
Downloads	.\downloads
Export	.\export
Expressions	.\express
Images	.\sceneassets\images
Import	.\import
Materials	..\Program Files\Autodesk\3ds Max 2019\materiallibraries
MaxStart	.\scenes
Photometric	.\sceneassets\photometric

Modify...

Make Relative

Make Absolute

Figure 1–51

3. In the Configure User Paths dialog box, select the *External Files* tab and click **Add**.

The paths are searched in order from top to bottom, so moving a custom path to the top saves time when searching for files.

4. In the Choose New External Files Path dialog box, navigate to C:\Autodesk 3ds Max Fundamentals Practice Files and double-click on the folder. (Or you can just select it and click **Use Path**). Double-click on the *Maps* folder and click **Use Path**. Verify that you have returned to the Configure User Paths dialog box. This enables all of the folders under the main folder to be searched for missing external files.

5. In the Configure User Paths dialog box, verify that the Maps new path is still selected and click **Move Up**. Continue clicking **Move Up** until the new path is at the top of the list, as shown in Figure 1–52.

Figure 1–52

6. Select the *XRefs* tab and verify that the *..\scenes* folder displays, which points to the practice files folder (C:\Autodesk 3ds Max Fundamentals Practice Files).

7. Click **OK** to exit the Configure User Paths dialog box.

Task 4 - Setting a Viewport Layout.

1. Select **File>Open**.

2. In the Open File dialog box, note that the *\scenes* folder in the practice files folder is already set, as shown in Figure 1–53. Select the file **Interface.max** and click **Open**.

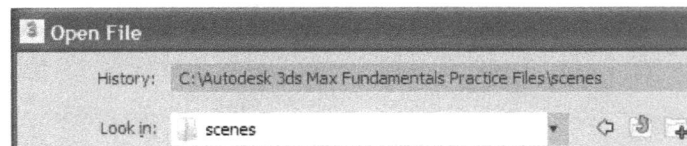

If you have created something in the current scene, you might be prompted to save or discard any changes.

If a dialog box opens prompting you about a File Load: Mismatch for Gamma & LUT settings, click **OK** to accept the default values.

Figure 1–53

If the ribbon is covering the top portion of your model, minimize it by clicking ⏷.

3. The model should display similar to that shown in Figure 1–54. Note that it opens in one maximized viewport layout, which was previously saved with the scene.

4. Verify that the *Viewport Layout* tab bar and the Scene Explorer are displayed and docked along the left side of the viewport.

5. Verify that in the InfoCenter, the *Workspaces* is set to **Default**.

6. In the Scene Explorer toolbar, click ■ (Display None) to clear all the categories. Note that the object list is empty.

7. Click 🗐 (Display All) to activate all the different categories of objects. All of the selected tools have a blue background, indicating that they are active. Note the three main objects that make up the model are listed, as shown in Figure 1–54.

Figure 1–54

• The file can be zoomed out by rolling the middle mouse button to display the complete model in the viewport.

8. In the Viewport Layouts tab bar, click to expand the Standard Viewport Layouts panel. Select the layout, as shown in Figure 1–55 (second row, second column).

- Note that the model displays in three viewport layouts and the newly selected layout is added to the tabs list, as shown in Figure 1–56.

| Figure 1–55 | Figure 1–56 |

9. Note that a yellow border displays around the **Top** viewport, indicating that it is the active viewport. In this viewport, click on **[Wireframe]** (*Per-View Preference* label) to display the menu.

10. Select **Stylized>Graphite**, as shown in Figure 1–57. Note the change in the display of objects in this view only.

11. Click on **[Top]** (*Point of View* label) and select **Right**, as shown in Figure 1–58. Alternatively, you can press <R> to display the **Right** view of the object.

Figure 1–57

Figure 1–58

12. Use the mouse wheel to zoom out so that the complete model displays in this viewport. While holding the middle mouse button, drag the cursor to pan the objects so that they are centrally located in the viewport.

13. Click in empty space in the lower right viewport (**Left** view). Note that the yellow border now displays around this viewport, indicating that it is the active viewport.

*Clicking on **[Left]** (Point of View label) and selecting **Perspective** in the drop-down list will be referred to set the Left [Point of View] label.*

14. Set the following by clicking the respective labels and selecting the required option from each menu:

    • **Left** *Point of View* label: **Perspective**
    • **Wireframe** *Per-View Preference* label: **Default Shading**

15. Press <Z> to zoom in to the objects in this viewport.

16. Activate the top right viewport, ensure that the *Point of View* is set to **Front** and change the *Wireframe [Per-View Preference]* to **Clay**.

17. Use the middle mouse button to pan and zoom to display the objects in this view.

    • The objects and the viewport layout should look similar to those in Figure 1–59.

Figure 1–59

Task 5 - Modifying the objects using the Command Panel.

1. In the Viewport Layout tab bar, select the initial layout that existed with the scene, as shown in Figure 1–60. The objects display in a single viewport in the **Perspective** view with the **Default Shading** Visual Style.

2. In the Command Panel, select the Create panel (+), if required (active by default), as shown in Figure 1–61.

Figure 1–60   **Figure 1–61**

3. Select the **Geometry** category by clicking ● (Geometry), if required (active by default). The different types of geometry that you can create are listed here.

4. In the Command Panel, select the Modify panel ( ). The panel is empty as no objects are currently selected.

5. In the Main Toolbar, click (Select Object), if required.

Names only display in the tooltip when the cursor is hovered over an unselected object. Once the object has been selected, its name displays in the Modifier Stack.

6. In the viewport, hover the cursor over the cyan (blue) object to display its name, **Ionic Column Shaft**. Click the object to select it. The **Ionic Column Shaft** is highlighted in the Scene Explorer, indicating that it is selected. The name and modifiers that have been applied display in the Command Panel. The Status Line at the bottom of the viewport, displays **1 Object Selected**, as shown in Figure 1–62.

Figure 1–62

7. In the Command Panel, next to the object name **Ionic Column Shaft**, select the color swatch. Select a different color and click **OK** to change the color of the column shaft.

8. In the Modifier Stack, the list of modifiers that have been used on the column shaft display as shown in Figure 1–63. Click ⊙ (eye) next to the **Taper** modifier to toggle the taper off and then on again and note the effect on the object. Leave it on.

9. In the Modifier Stack, select the **Extrude** modifier. In the Warning dialog box, click **Hold/Yes** to continue.

You can adjust parameters at any level of the Modifier Stack. To change the parameter, enter the value in the Amount edit box or use the spinners ⬍.

10. The **Extrude** parameters display in the rollouts. Note that the *Amount* displays the height of the shaft. Change it to **440.0** (as shown in Figure 1–64) and press <Enter>. The column shaft is extended and touches the top. The modifiers above the extrude are automatically reapplied to the object with its new height.

Figure 1–63

Figure 1–64

Task 6 - Using the Scene Explorer.

1. In the Scene Explorer, note an arrow besides the objects **Capitol** and **Base,** indicating that each have a group of objects inside it. Click on the arrow besides **Capitol** to expand the group and note the different objects sorted in a hierarchical fashion, as shown in Figure 1–65.

Figure 1–65

2. Click in empty space in the viewport to clear the selection. Note that the Command Panel is empty as there are no objects currently selected. Also note that nothing is highlighted in the Scene Explorer.

3. In the viewport, hover the cursor over the top gray square portion of the object. It displays the name as **[Capitol] Plinth Mesh**, as shown in Figure 1–66.

Figure 1–66

4. As the ▦ (Select Object) is already active, click on **[Capitol] Plinth Mesh** in the viewport to select it. The complete object is selected although, the Plinth Mesh is just the top square portion.

5. Click in empty space in the viewport to clear the selection.

6. In the Scene Explorer, click on 👁 for **Plinth Mesh** and note that the top most square object of the Capitol is hidden in the viewport, as shown in Figure 1–67.

Figure 1–67

7. Similarly, in the Scene Explorer, click on 👁 for **Volute Face Mesh** and **Volute Ridge Mesh** and note that only the inner cylindrical object remains visible, as shown in Figure 1–68.

Figure 1–68

8. In the Scene Explorer, click on ▢ (grayed out eye) for the three hidden sub objects to make them visible again.

*Selecting **File>Save** overwrites the existing file. If you are saving an unnamed file for the first time, these options work as **Save As**.*

9. Select **File>Save As** and save your work as **MyInterface.max**.
   - When you save a file, note that it is being saved to the practice files ...\scenes folder.

Practice 1b

Autodesk 3ds Max Quickstart

Practice Objective

- Create primitive objects and apply basic animation to a primitive object.

In this practice, you will model and animate a teapot driving through a city of pyramids. This practice will introduce you to the Autodesk 3ds Max interface and workflow fundamentals. Many of the commands used In this practice, are discussed later in the learning guide.

Many of you will probably never need to animate a teapot driving through a city of pyramids. This practice is designed to introduce you to interactive 3D modeling and animation, and working with the interface.

Task 1 - Create Primitive Objects.

If an unsaved scene is open, you might be required to save or discard any changes to the scene.

1. Select **File>Reset** to start a new file. Click **Yes** in the confirmation dialog box.

2. In the Command Panel, verify that the Create panel (➕) and ⬤ (Geometry) are selected (active by default). Also, ensure that the **Standard Primitives** sub-category displays.

Alternatively, use <Alt>+<W>.

3. Verify that the **Perspective** viewport is active (yellow border).

   Maximize it (single viewport) by clicking 🔲 (Maximize Viewport) in the Navigation toolbar, found in the lower right corner of the interface.

4. In the *Object Type* rollout, click **Pyramid** to activate it, as shown in Figure 1–69.

Figure 1–69

If the Scene Explorer is not displayed, select **Tools>Scene Explorer** *and then dock it.*

Eyeball the size of the pyramid.

5. Near the center of the grid, click and drag to create the base for a pyramid, as shown in Figure 1–70. Release the mouse button and continue to move the cursor up to set the height of the pyramid. When your pyramid displays correctly (similar to that shown in Figure 1–71), click to end the creation process. In the Scene Explorer, note that a highlighted geometry is listed with the name **Pyramid001,** indicating that it is selected.

Figure 1–70   **Figure 1–71**

To make any changes, the object should be selected.

Your objects will be of different colors than those shown in the figures.

6. In the Command Panel, in the *Name and Color* rollout, click the **Color** swatch to the right of the pyramid name (**Pyramid001)**, select a different color in the Object Color dialog box and verify that **Assign Random Colors** is selected. This enables you to create objects with different colors automatically. Click **OK**. Note that the swatch color changes and the pyramid color changes in the viewport.

7. In the Navigation toolbar, click ![icon] (Maximize Viewport) or use <Alt>+<W>. Note that the pyramid displays in four equal viewports with different viewing angles.

The transform tools are discussed in detail, later in the learning guide.

8. You might need to move the pyramid to the upper left quadrant of the home grid. In the Main Toolbar, click

   ![icon] (Select and Move). In the **Top** view (upper left viewport), right-click to make it active with the object still selected.

   • Clicking in a viewport makes it active, but loses the selection of objects. To maintain the selection of objects, right-click to activate the viewport.

9. Click and hold the yellow square (anywhere along the two outer edges when the cursor displays as a move cursor) of the Transform gizmo, as shown in Figure 1–72. While holding the object, drag it to the new location (upper left quadrant). Leave the gizmo once the object is at the correct location.

Figure 1–72

10. In the *Object Type* rollout, click **Pyramid** again. In the **Top** viewport, click and drag to create the base for another pyramid on the lower side of the main grid line, opposite to the first one. Release the mouse button and continue to move the cursor up to set the height of the pyramid. Because you are in the **Top** viewport, the height of the pyramid is not displayed. You can visually note the height in other three viewports in which the height displays. Once the pyramid displays as required, click to complete the command.

You can create objects in any viewport, but the orientation of the objects depends on the viewport created. Note that their creation is also displayed interactively in other viewports.

11. Similarly, create a number of pyramids on the home grid. Create a row of pyramids in one direction and a few others to create a street corner in the pyramid city, as shown in Figure 1–73. Try to keep all of the pyramids in the grid visible in the **Perspective** viewport. You can organize them as shown in Figure 1–73, by moving them in the **Top** viewport

using ⊕ (Select and Move) in the Main toolbar.

Figure 1–73

To display all of the pyramids in a viewport, use the middle mouse wheel to zoom in and out and press, hold, and drag it to pan.

12. Once the required number of pyramids have been created, right-click in empty space or press <Esc> to exit the **Pyramid** command.

13. Make the **Perspective** viewport active and maximize the viewport by clicking ▣ (Maximize Viewport) or use <Alt>+<W>. You can click anywhere in empty space to clear a selected object and activate the viewport.

14. In the Create panel (+)> ● (Geometry), in the *Object Type* rollout, click **Teapot** to activate it.

15. In the lower left area of the **Perspective** viewport, click and drag to create a teapot, as shown in Figure 1–74.

Figure 1–74

Task 2 - Add Basic Animation.

Animation controls are discussed in detail later in the learning guide.

1. The Animation controls are located on the left of the Navigation tools at the bottom of the screen. Click **Auto Key**, as shown in Figure 1–75. Once you click it, the Auto Key, time slider bar, and border around the active viewport (**Perspective** viewport) are highlighted in red.

Figure 1–75

2. Along the bottom of the viewport, click and hold the time slider (0/100 button). Drag the time slider button in the red slider bar until the frame indicator displays **30/100** ( ) and the blue marker is on 30 in the track bar, as shown in Figure 1–76.

Figure 1–76

A selected object has a blue boundary and the cursor gizmo attached with it.

3. Click on the teapot, if not already selected. Verify that

 (Select and Move) is still highlighted (blue background), If not, right-click and select **Move** in the quad menu, as shown in Figure 1–77 or simply click in the Main Toolbar.

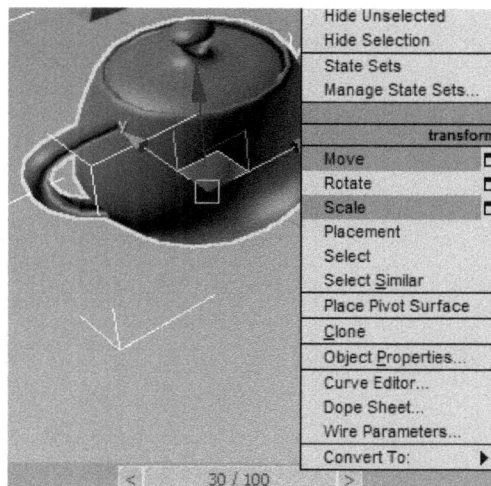

Figure 1–77

4. Move the cursor over the X axis (red arrow) of the Move gizmo so that it displays in yellow. Hold and drag to move the teapot in the X direction, as shown in Figure 1–78. Move it to midway between the original position and the intersection of the home grid.

Figure 1–78

5. Click and drag the time slider again to read **60/100**.

6. Move the teapot in the X direction till it reaches the intersection of the horizontal street, as shown in Figure 1–79.

Figure 1–79

7. Click and drag the time slider to read **90/100**. Move the teapot in the Y direction (left, green arrow) till it reaches the end of the horizontal street, as shown in Figure 1–80.

Figure 1–80

- The track bar below the time slider now has four red boxes (as shown in Figure 1–81) indicating that the keyframes have been set at frames 0, 30, 60, and 90.

Figure 1–81

8. In the Animation Controls (|◄◄ ◄‖ ► ‖► ►►|) located near the bottom right of the screen, click ► (Play). The teapot is now animated in the viewport, moving through the pyramid city. Click ‖ (Stop Animation) to stop the animation.

9. You can add a rotation to the teapot. Drag the time slider to frame **60**.

10. Verify that the teapot is selected. Right-click on the teapot and select **Rotate** in the quad menu. The Rotation Transform gizmo displays on the teapot.

11. In the Status Bar, along the left of the animation controls, in the **Z** *Transform Type-in* field, enter <90> and press <Enter>, as shown in Figure 1–82. The teapot is rotated and the spout is pointing to the left.

Figure 1–82

- At frame 60, the time slider now displays a red and green box indicating both rotation and position keys.

12. Play the animation using ▶ (Play). Click ∎ (Stop) to stop the animation. You can also view the animation by dragging the time slider back and forth. This is called *scrubbing* the time slider.

13. To only rotate the teapot after frame 45, add a keyframe rotation of **0** at frame 45. Play the animation to view the changes.

14. Toggle off **Auto Key** mode by clicking the red **Auto Key**.

15. Click in empty space to clear the object selection.

16. Select **File>Save As** and save your work as **MyPyramidCity.max**. Verify that it is being saved in the ...*scenes* folder.

- You can also open **Pyramidcity.max** from the practices files folder to compare with a similar type file. You can play the animation and select the teapot to check the various keys.

Chapter Review Questions

1. Which of the Autodesk 3ds Max interface components contains 🔒 (Selection Lock)?

   a. Modeling Ribbon

   b. Status Bar

   c. InfoCenter

   d. Command Panel

2. Which menu or drop-down list enables you to break the Main toolbar into modular pieces?

   a. Workspace selector drop-down list

   b. Quad menu (shortcut menu)

   c. **Customize** menu

   d. *General Viewport* label menu

3. Which of the following tabs are part of the Modeling ribbon? (Select all that apply.)

   a. Freeform

   b. Display

   c. Utilities

   d. Modeling

4. In the Configure User Paths dialog box, which tab stores the location of the files for open, save, export, etc.?

   a. *XRefs* tab

   b. *System* tab

   c. *External Files* tab

   d. *File I/O* tab

5. Which display driver does not require hardware support?

   a. Nitrous Direct3D 11

   b. Nitrous Direct3D 9

   c. Nitrous Software

6. Which of the following is not a **Stylized** menu option?

   a. **Color Pencil**

   b. **Graphite**

   c. **Shaded**

   d. **Pastel**

Command Summary

Button	Command	Location
+	Create panel	• **Command Panel**
N/A	New	• **Menu Bar:** File>New>New All
N/A	Open	• **Menu Bar:** File>Open
N/A	Preferences	• **Menu Bar:** File>Preferences
N/A	Project Folder	• **Menu Bar**: File>Set Project Folder
	Ribbon	• **Main Toolbar** • **Customize:** Show UI>Show Ribbon
N/A	Save	• **Menu Bar:** File>Save
N/A	Save As	• **Menu Bar:** File>Save As
N/A	Scene Explorer	• **Tools:** Scene Explorer

Autodesk 3ds Max Configuration

The Autodesk® 3ds Max® software layout and unique to other Autodesk products. Becoming familiar with its navigation tools, viewing the model in the viewport, and how to work with the model in the interface is an important step to efficiently create a visualization project.

Learning Objectives in this Chapter

- Move around in a scene using the various navigation tools.
- Set the layout and viewport configuration settings.
- Select objects using the object selection tools.
- Assign and change units in a scene.
- Group similar objects together in a layer and adjust layer properties.
- Modify the display settings of layers and objects.

2.1 Viewport Navigation

Navigation tools are used to change the point of view in viewports. Perspective, User, and Orthographic views (non-camera views such as Top, Front, etc.) share common viewport controls. The navigation tools are different in the non-camera and camera views.

Viewport Navigation Toolbar

The navigation tools (shown in Figure 2–1) are available in the lower right corner of the interface.

Figure 2–1

- When selected, the tool button is highlighted. Press <Esc> or select another tool to toggle a selected tool off.

- Several buttons contain an arrow symbol in the lower right corner, which you can hold to expand a flyout.

Zooming with the mouse wheel in a perspective view might not work in all scenes due to roundoff issues. If you are unable to zoom, click ⬚ (Zoom Extents) and use

⌕ (Zoom) instead of the mouse wheel.

⌕	**Zoom:** When this tool is active, click, hold, and drag the cursor to zoom in or out of the active viewport.
⌕	**Zoom All:** Activate and then click and drag to zoom in or out simultaneously in all viewports.
⬚ / ⬚	**Zoom Extents/Zoom Extents Selected:** Zooms to the extents of all visible objects/selected objects only in the active viewport.
◈ / ◈	**Zoom Extents All/Zoom Extents All Selected:** Zoom to the extents of all visible objects/selected objects only in all viewports.
⬚	**Zoom Region** (zoom window) in the active viewport.
▷	**Field of View**: This is a flyout option in Zoom Region, available only in **Perspective** or **Camera** view. It adjusts the perspective of the view, similar to changing the focal length of a camera. Even small changes to the Field of View setting can cause large distortions. To reset, enter a default field of view value of **45 degrees** in the Viewport Configuration dialog box.
✋	**Pan View:** Hold in a viewport and drag to pan your objects. You can also hold and drag the middle mouse wheel to pan.

	2D Pan Zoom mode: A flyout option in Pan View, available in **Perspective** and **Camera** views only. It enables you to zoom/pan on objects in a viewport that are not located in the rendering frame. The camera remains unchanged when you are panning and zooming in the **Camera** viewport.
	Walk Through: A flyout option in Pan View, available in **Perspective** and **Camera** views only. Click and hold while moving the cursor to change where you are looking. Use the arrow keys to walk forward, back, and to the side. Move up or down by pressing <Shift>+<Up> or <Down>. To speed up a movement hold <]> (right bracket) while moving, and slow down movement by pressing <[> (left bracket).
	Orbit, **Orbit Selected,** and **Orbit SubObject**: Enables you to rotate the view by clicking and dragging inside or outside a trackball. Dragging inside the trackball causes the view to rotate around the scene, while dragging outside causes the view to twist in place. Click and drag on the boxes that display along the trackball to constrain the rotation to a single axis.
	Orbit Point of Interest: The point of interest is set as the point of rotation around which the view is rotated.
	Maximize Viewport: Toggles between the display of multiple viewports and the display of a single maximized viewport. Keyboard shortcut is <Alt>+<W>.

Hint: Switching Maximized Viewports

When you maximize to a single viewport from a multi-viewport layout, you can switch to any other available viewport while in the current maximized viewport display. In the maximized viewport display, hold <Win> (the Windows logo key, which might also be the <Start> key) and then press <Shift> (do not hold <Shift>). An overlay opens displaying all of the available viewports and the currently maximized viewport highlighted with a yellow border, as shown in Figure 2–2. While holding <Win>, press <Shift> repeatedly to highlight the next viewport option and release <Win> to maximize the highlighted viewport.

Figure 2–2

Viewport Navigation Toolbar (Camera Viewport)

Camera viewports show what is visible to the camera object based on its Field of View. Similar to other viewports, camera viewports can be directly navigated, but some of the controls are slightly different, as shown in Figure 2–3.

Figure 2–3

- Note that most of these controls actually move the camera or target object.

	Dolly Camera is similar to **Zoom**. The flyout contains options to dolly (move) the camera, the target, or both along the camera's directional axis.
	Perspective is a combination of **Field of View** and **Dolly** that attempts to maintain the same scene composition while changing the camera's Field of View.
	Roll Camera rotates a camera along the axis of its view.
	Orbit Camera rotates a camera around the target position similar to **Orbit**. The flyout option (**Pan Camera**) rotates the target around the camera instead.
	Truck Camera is similar to Pan when used in a **Camera** view.

Viewport Navigation Using the ViewCube

The ViewCube (shown in Figure 2–4) is a navigation tool and by default, it displays in the top right corner of each viewport indicating the orientation of the scene. The ViewCube is activated by hovering the cursor over it in the active viewport.

- Selecting any of the ViewCube faces or edges, causes the viewport to immediately swing around to that view. You can also select the ViewCube and drag the mouse to quickly rotate the Viewport.

- When the ViewCube is active, the **Home** icon becomes visible near the top left corner. Clicking the **Home** icon resets the viewport.

Figure 2–4

*The ViewCube tool options can also be accessed in the **Views** menu.*

- Clicking on the menu button or right-clicking on the ViewCube provides you with additional options (shown in Figure 2–4) that enable you to set the current view as Home, Orthographic, Configure etc.

- Selecting the **Configure** option, opens the Viewport Configuration dialog box in the *ViewCube* tab. It contains options to show/hide the ViewCube, control its size and display, control what happens when dragging on the ViewCube, and displaying the compass below the ViewCube.

Viewport Navigation Using the SteeringWheel

The SteeringWheel (shown in Figure 2–5) is another navigation tool and it can be toggled on by pressing <Shift>+<W> or **Views>SteeringWheels>Toggle SteeringWheels**. When toggled on, it gets attached to the cursor.

- It provides instant access to zoom/pan, orbit, etc. The **Rewind** feature is unique to this tool and provides a thumbnail of all of your previous views. It also enables you to visually select any of them to return to that view. Press <Shift>+<W> to toggle the SteeringWheel on and off. You can also press <Esc> to hide its display.

*The Steering wheel tool options can also be accessed in the **Views** menu.*

Figure 2–5

2.2 Viewport Configuration and Settings

Viewport Configuration

The layout and display settings of your viewports can be set through the Viewport Configuration dialog box. In the *Viewport* label, click [+] (*General* label) to display the label menu and select **Configure Viewports**, as shown in Figure 2–6. Alternatively, select the *Shading Viewport* label>**Viewport Global Settings**.

Figure 2–6

If you have selected one of the legacy display drivers (Direct 3D or OpenGL), the Rendering Method tab displays.

The Viewport Configuration dialog box opens and contains tabs which differ based on the selected display driver. By default, the Viewport Configuration dialog box opens with the *Display Performance* tab active. Some of the tabs that are available in the Viewport Configuration dialog box are described in the following section. The remaining tabs are discussed throughout the learning guide, as required.

Layout tab

You can also set up multiple viewport layouts and switch between them by selecting the saved tabs in the Viewport Layouts tab bar.

The *Layout* tab in the Viewport Configuration dialog box (shown in Figure 2–7) enables you to set the size and shape of viewports and its view type. Select one of the preset viewport layouts to select a view type.

Figure 2–7

SteeringWheels tab

The *SteeringWheels* tab (shown in Figure 2–8) enables you control the properties of the Steering Wheel such as displaying them as Big or Mini Wheels and setting their respective sizes and opacity. You can also set the options for tools, such as the **Zoom** tool and the **Orbit** tool.

Figure 2–8

ViewCube tab

Similar to the *SteeringWheels* tab, the *ViewCube* tab has options for controlling the display of the ViewCube. You can control its size, what it displays when selected, and the position of the compass.

Statistics tab

The *Statistics* tab enables you to customize the display of various statistics for the selected geometry or the complete scene. In the viewports, you can display the number of polygons in a scene, number of triangular faces, number of edges, number of vertices, etc. The statistics can be displayed on the screen, near the left hand corner of the active viewport by selecting **Show Statistics in Active View** in the dialog box. You can also display statistics by selecting **Show Statistics** in the *General Viewport* label menu>**xView** or by pressing <7>.

Background tab

The *Background* tab (shown in Figure 2–9) enables you to set an image, environment map, or animation as the background of your active viewport or all viewports.

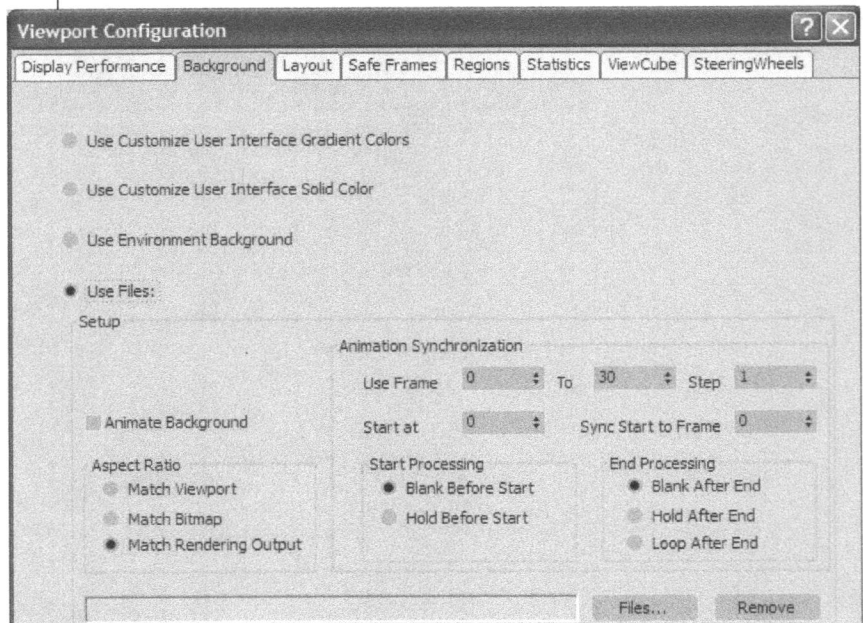

Figure 2–9

Viewport Setting and Preferences

You can control the viewport display of the models in the Viewport Setting and Preference dialog box, as shown in Figure 2–10. To open the dialog box, in the viewport, click the *Shading Viewport* label and in the label menu select **Per-View Presets**, as shown in Figure 2–10. Alternatively, select *Per-View Preference* label menu>**Per-View Preference**.

Figure 2–10

The Viewport Setting and Preference dialog box contains two tabs: *Per-View Presets* and *Per-View Preferences*. The *Per-View Presets* tab (shown in Figure 2–11), has the following options:

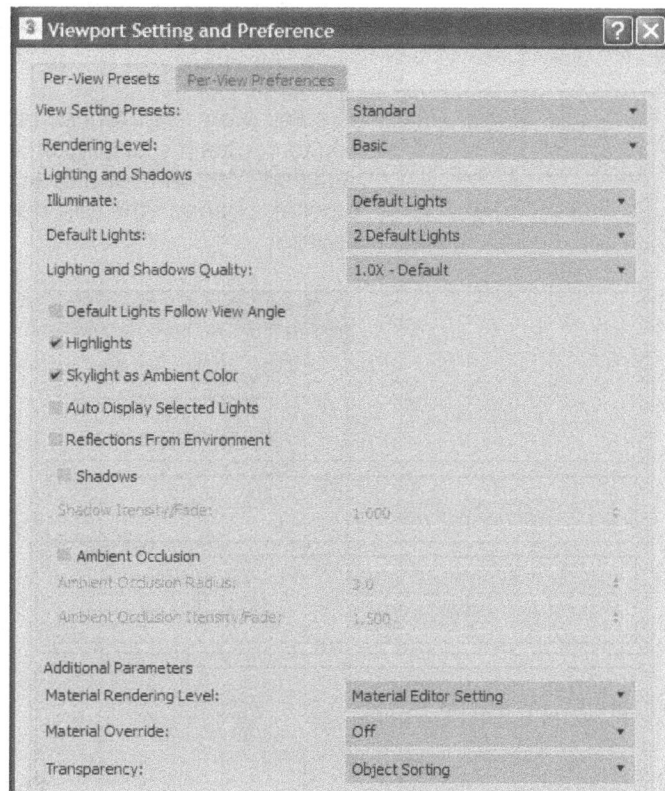

Figure 2–11

- You can create and add a user-defined view setting preset to the list of choices. Note, however, that you can have only one user-defined view setting, and you cannot change the four existing presets (i.e., High Quality, Standard, Performance or DX mode).

- The **Default Lights** are used to illuminate the viewports, providing even illumination. You can select **1 Default Light** or **2 Default Lights**.

- The **Default Lights Follow View Angle** option tracks changes to the position of the viewport using two default lights.

- The **Skylight as Ambient Color** option causes the skylights to emit ambient color and not cast shadows.

- The **Shadows** options renders the scene with shadows and the **Ambient Occlusion** helps improve the display of shadows.

- The *Additional Parameters* area contains settings for various material-related options, such as Material override and Transparency.

The *Per-View Preferences* tab (shown in Figure 2–12) enables you to control the display of selected objects in a specific viewport. You can set a selection to display using a selection bracket, or shade the selected faces/objects with or without edges.

Figure 2–12

Practice 2a

Viewport Configuration and Navigation

Practice Objectives

- Set the configuration of the viewport.
- Move around a scene using different navigation tools.

In this practice, you will set various configuration option for an exiting viewport layout. You will then move around a scene and experiment with changing the camera position by using navigations tools such as **Zoom**, **Orbit**, **Pan View** and other **SE Camera** options.

1. Select **File>Open** to open the Open File dialog box. If you were working in the software, you might be prompted to save or discard any changes to the scene.

    - In the Open file dialog box, note that the *C:\Autodesk 3ds Max Fundamentals Practice Files\scenes* folder is set, because you have already set the Project Folder. If you did not set the path to the practice files folder, return to Chapter 1 and complete Task 1 to Task 3 in *Practice 1a: Organizing Folders and Working with the Interface*. You are required to set the project folder only once.

*If a dialog box opens prompting you about a Mismatch, click **OK** to accept the default values.*

2. In the Open File dialog box, select **Navigation.max** and click **Open**.

    - If the Viewport Layout tab bar is not displayed, right-click in an empty space of the Main Toolbar, clear and select the **Viewport Layout Tabs** option, and then dock it.
    - The file opens the objects in four equal sized viewports. Along the left edge of the interface, in the Viewport Layouts tab bar, note that the file has been saved with two different viewport layout configuration.

Alternatively, select the required viewport layout in the Viewport Configuration dialog box>Layout tab.

3. To create another layout, in the Viewport Layouts tab bar, click ▶ to expand the Standard Viewport Layouts panel. Select the layout shown in Figure 2–13.

Figure 2–13

- The pillar objects display in the **3 X 1** viewport layout and another layout tab is added to the Layouts tab bar.

4. Note that the **Top** viewport is the active viewport (it displays a yellow border). In the Navigation toolbar, note the available navigation tools are for the **Orthographic** view, as shown in Figure 2–14.

Figure 2–14

*Click and hold **Zoom Extents All** to open the flyout and select the required button.*

5. The complete objects are not displayed in the viewports. In the Zoom Extents All flyout, click ⬩ (Zoom Extents All) to zoom to the extents of all of the objects in all of the viewports.

6. Click on empty space in the **Front** viewport to activate it.

*If the Scene Explorer is not displayed, select **Tools>Scene Explorer** and then dock it.*

7. In the Scene Explorer, select **Base** to select the base objects in all the viewports, as shown in Figure 2–15.

Figure 2–15

8. In the Zoom Extents All flyout, click ![icon] (Zoom Extents All Selected). Note that you are zoomed to the extents of the selected objects (Base) in all of the viewports.

9. With the **Base** still selected, in the Zoom Extents All flyout, click ![icon] (Zoom Extents All). The viewports zoom to the extents of all of the objects in all of the viewports.

10. Right-click in empty space in the **Left** viewport. Note that the **Left** viewport becomes active and the base object remains selected.

11. Click in empty space in the **Top** viewport to make it active. Note that this also clears the selection.

12. Hover the cursor over the left edge of the **Perspective** viewport. The cursor displays as a two-sided arrow. Click and drag the arrow horizontally to the right to resize the viewports, as shown in Figure 2–16.

Figure 2–16

13. Click in the **Perspective** view to make it active. In the Viewport navigation tools, click ![icon] (Maximize Viewport Toggle) to maximize the active viewport. Select the toggle again to return to the four viewport arrangement. Alternatively, press <Alt>+<W> to toggle between the maximized single viewport and multiple viewports. Leave the **Perspective** viewport maximized.

*You must hold <Win>
continuously for the
overlay to display.*

14. Hold <Win> (windows logo or the <Start> key) continuously
    and press <Shift> once. An overlay displays all of the
    available viewports in the layout, as shown in Figure 2–17.
    With <Win> still pressed, press <Shift> repeatedly to cycle
    through all of the viewports. When [Left] [Standard] is
    highlighted (as shown in Figure 2–17), release <Win> to
    maximize the viewport.

Figure 2–17

15. Select the **[Left]** *Point of View* label. In the label menu, select
    Cameras>SE Camera, as shown in Figure 2–18, to display
    the **Camera** view.

Figure 2–18

   • Note that the navigation tools are different in a camera
     viewport, as shown in Figure 2–19.

Figure 2–19

16. Click [icon] (Maximize Viewport Toggle) to toggle to the four viewport display.

17. Click [icon] (Zoom Extents All). Note that the **SE Camera** (lower left viewport) does not change because the non-camera navigation tools do not affect the camera views.

18. Click in the **Perspective** view to make it active and note how the navigation tools change.

19. Click in the **SE Camera** viewport to make it active.

20. Click [icon] (Orbit Camera) and use it in the **SE Camera** viewport to orbit the camera. In the other viewports, note that the camera object is moving simultaneously as the pillar object moves in the camera viewport.

21. Experiment with changing the camera position using [icon] (Roll Camera) and [icon] (Dolly Camera).

You can use the mouse wheel to zoom in and out in a viewport and hold and drag the middle mouse button to pan.

22. In the **Perspective** viewport, practice navigating with the **Zoom**, **Zoom All**, **Orbit**, and **Pan View** options.

23. Close the file without saving.

2.3 Object Selection Methods

Working with modifiers and other functions requires you to select objects accurately, using various methods. The recommended method is to click on the required geometry in one of the

viewports to select it. It uses the ▨ (Select Object) tool in the Main Toolbar which is active by default.

Selection Preview

In the Nitrous viewports, hovering the cursor over an object displays a yellow outline for that object. This enables you to easily determine the object that is going to be selected. Once you click on an object a blue outline displays indicating the selection, as shown in Figure 2–20.

Figure 2–20

The highlighting can be controlled in the Preference Settings dialog box>*Viewports* tab, as shown in Figure 2–21.

Figure 2–21

Scene Explorer

If the Scene Explorer is not displayed, click

(Scene Explorer) in the Min toolbar or select **Tools>Scene Explorer**. *Dock the Scene Explorer.*

Being a modeless interface component, you can have the Scene Explorer open while working in the viewports.

- The Scene Explorer can be used to easily select objects. If you know the name of the object, locate it in the tree list and select it, as shown in Figure 2–22. It gets selected in the viewports interactively. Use <Ctrl> to click on multiple objects in the list to select them together.

Figure 2–22

- You can use the Scene Explorer toolbar to list only those objects that belong to the particular type and then select it.

  Use (Display None) first to clear all the selected categories, and then select the tools for the required categories to list only the objects belonging to that category.

- To easily find and select an item you can use the *Find* field in the Scene Explorer. Enter the initial letters to select only the objects that begin with the entered letters

- In the **Display** menu, verify that the **Display Children**, **Display Influences**, and **Display Dependants** are cleared for all the objects to be displayed in the list.

Main Toolbar

A variety of selection tools are provided in the Main Toolbar, as shown in Figure 2–23.

Figure 2–23

Select by Name tool

(Select by Name) opens the Select From Scene dialog box (shown in Figure 2–24), which enables you to select one or more objects. It is a modal version of the Scene Explorer, and therefore works the same way as the Scene Explorer. However, the only difference is that after selecting objects in the list of the dialog box, you must click **OK** to close the dialog box in order to continue working with the selection.

Figure 2–24

Select Object tool

(Select Object) enables you to select objects and to drag selection regions inside your viewports depending on the selected Region selection type.

- You can add to your current selection if you select or drag a region while holding <Ctrl>. You can remove items from the selection with <Alt>.

- You can also select with the **Move**, **Rotate**, **Scale**, and **Place** tools.

- You can access **Select** in the quad menu.

- If one of the **Transform** tools is active, you can click

  (Select Object) or press <Q> to activate select objects.

  If (Select Object) is already active, press <Q> repeatedly to cycle through the various Region selection types.

Rectangular Selection Region

(Rectangular Selection Region) in the Main Toolbar enables you to draw the shape of your selection region. The default is a rectangular region. There are also flyout options for **Lasso**, **Paint**, **Circular**, and **Fence** selections, as shown in Figure 2–23. Paint selection is particularly useful when you have thousands of objects or vertices that need selecting.

Window/Crossing

/ (Window/Crossing) enables you to define the *Window Selection Region* (only objects completely within the region are selected), or the *Crossing Region* (objects within or crossing the boundary are selected) as the selection toggle.

Edit Menu

The **Edit** menu also has a number of important selection options including **Select All**, **Select None**, **Select Invert**, **Select Similar**, **Select Instances**, and **Select By** (e.g., **Color**). These options also work in Sub-object mode.

Layer Explorer

(Layer Explorer) (in the Main Toolbar) lists and selects objects directly from the Layer Explorer.

Edit Named Selection Sets

(Edit Named Selection Sets) (in the Main Toolbar) enables you to create and edit named selection sets. Named Selection Sets are different than layers, in that an object can be in many different named selections. An object can only be on one layer, making Named Selection Sets more flexible.

Practice 2b

Selection Methods

Practice Objective

- Select objects using **various** selection tools.

In this practice, you will select objects in a scene using the Window and Crossing selection tools. You will also use the Scene Explorer and Select from Scene dialog box to select objects.

You must set the paths to locate the External files and Xrefs used in the practice. If you have not done this already, return to Chapter 1 and complete Task 1 to Task 3 in *Practice 1a: Organizing Folders and Working with the Interface*. You only have to set the user paths once.

*If prompted that there is a File Load: Mismatch, click **OK** to accept the default values.*

1. Select **File>Open** to open the Open File dialog box. If you were working in the software, you might be prompted to save or discard any changes to the scene. Open **Selection Methods.max**.

2. Click in an empty space in the **Perspective** viewport to make it active.

3. Maximize the **Perspective** viewport to fill your screen by clicking (Maximize Viewport Toggle) or by pressing <Alt>+<W>.

*Depending on how you rotate the viewing angle, it might be difficult to select a specific object. Setting the viewport shading to **Wireframe Override** can make it easier to select.*

4. In the viewport, click on the left most parking lot light pole. Note that it is selected as a blue outline encloses the object and all the face edges of the geometry are highlighted as white, with white bounding brackets enclosing the geometry.

5. Hover the cursor on the other parking lot light pole and note that it is highlighted with a yellow outline indicating the selection preview as shown in Figure 2–25.

Previewed (yellow outline)

Selected (blue outline)

Figure 2–25

6. Click on the **[Edged Faces]** *Per-View Preference* label and select **Per-View Preference** in the label menu. The Viewport Setting and Preferences dialog box>*Per-View Preferences* tab opens. Select **Display Selected with Edged Faces** and clear all of the other options, as shown in Figure 2–26. Ensure that **Apply to All Views** (near the bottom of the dialog box) is cleared. Click **OK**.

Figure 2–26

- In the viewport, note how the white bounding brackets are no longer displayed.

7. Open the Viewport Setting and Preference dialog box again. In the *Per-View Preferences* tab, select **Selection Brackets** and **Edge Faces**. Click **OK**. The selection brackets and edged faces display.

8. In the Menu bar, select **Edit>Select None** or click in empty space to clear your selection.

9. In the Main Toolbar, verify that the *Window/Crossing* toggle is set to [icon] (Crossing), the *Selection Region* is set to [icon] (Rectangular), and that [icon] (Select Object) is selected. Starting in a blank area, near the top left corner of the farther parking lot light, click and drag the cursor diagonally down to create a rectangular crossing region around the light pole, as shown in Figure 2–27. Once you let go, the crossing window will select several other objects in the background, in addition to the light pole.

    *   In the Status bar, near the bottom left of the screen, note the number of objects selected.

Figure 2–27

10. Click in empty space to clear the selection.

11. Toggle the **Selection/Crossing** toggle from [icon] (Crossing) to [icon] (Window). Click and drag the selection region around the light pole again.

   - In the Status bar, note that you selected fewer objects than before, but some additional objects are still selected.

If the Scene Explorer is not displayed, click

[icon] *(Scene Explorer) in the Main toolbar or select **Tools>Scene Explorer**.*

12. In the Scene Explorer toolbar, click [icon] (Display None). Note that the list is empty.

13. In the Scene Explorer toolbar, click [icon] (Display All). Note that the list of objects is very long as all the different categories of objects are listed.

14. In the Scene Explorer toolbar, click [icon] (Display None) and then click [icon] (Display Geometry) to display all of the geometry objects in the scene. Note that some objects are highlighted (as shown in Figure 2–28), indicating that they are selected in the viewport.

Figure 2–28

15. Click in empty space in the viewport to clear the selection.

16. In the Main Toolbar, click ⬛ (Select by Name) to open the Select From Scene dialog box.

The Select From Scene dialog box is similar to the Scene Explorer.

17. The objects listed depend on the selection tools that are toggled on in the toolbar in the dialog box. In the toolbar, click

    ⬛ (Display None) to clear any selection group. Verify that

    ⬛ (Sort by Hierarchy) is selected, as shown in Figure 2–29.

Figure 2–29

18. In the Select From Scene dialog box, click ⬛ (Display Shapes), as shown in Figure 2–30. This enables you to filter the number of items listed in the dialog box so that you can easily select the required items.

Figure 2–30

19. Using <Ctrl> or <Shift>, select all of the **Block:Light Pole - Single** shapes. Click **OK** to close the dialog box. Note that the two single lights are selected in the viewport.

20. Click in empty space in the viewport to clear the selection.

21. In the Scene Explorer toolbar, click ■ (Display None) and click ▣ (Display Shapes). Expand the tree list by clicking on the arrow left of the Site Model, as shown in Figure 2–31.

Figure 2–31

22. Select the first **Block:Light Pole - Single**. Note that this light pole is not visible in the viewport.

23. Select the second **Block:Light Pole - Single** and continue selecting from the list. The third **Block:Light Pole - Single** selects the light pole in the view, as shown in Figure 2–32.

Figure 2–32

24. In the list, click again on the highlighted entry to convert it into an edit box and rename it to **Block:Light Pole - Front Left** and then click anywhere. Note that the newly-named entry moves above **Block:Light Pole - Single,** as shown in Figure 2–33, as the list is sorted in ascending order.

Figure 2–33

25. Select **File>Reset**. Click **Don't Save** and click **Yes** to close the current file without saving it.

2.4 Units Setup

Each scene file is based on a unit of measurement called the System Unit Scale. You can change and assign the units settings using the Units Setup dialog box. Select **Customize> Units Setup** to open the Units Setup dialog box, as shown in Figure 2–34. In the dialog box, click **System Unit Setup** to open the System Unit Setup dialog box, as shown in Figure 2–35.

Figure 2–34   **Figure 2–35**

- For efficient viewport rendering, the Autodesk 3ds Max software might incur round off errors to very large and very small numerical values, as displayed by the slider bar in the System Unit Setup dialog box. These round off errors become problematic when the geometry is located further away from the center of the virtual universe.

- The Autodesk 3ds Max Help recommends that you center scene geometry close to the origin and not have any significant details smaller than one system unit. (For example, a unit scale of meters might not be appropriate for architectural work. Instead, you might consider using a **System Unit Scale** of inches, millimeters, or centimeters.) It is recommended not to make changes to the System Unit Scale unless there is a viewport problem due to very small or large models.

- Assign the unit scale before adding any geometry to the scene. Changing the System Unit Scale later does not rescale the existing objects. (To rescale objects, use the **Rescale World Units** utility in the Command Panel's Utilities panel ( ).

- Selecting **Respect System Units in Files** enables individual scene files that have different Unit Scales assigned to them to be scaled when merging them together.

The Display Unit Scale does not need to match the System Unit Scale.

- The *Display Unit Scale* area defines the units to be displayed by the interface when measuring coordinates and distances.

- When the *Display Unit Scale* is set to **Feet w/Fractional Inches** or **Feet w/Decimal Inches**, the **Default Units** option identifies how a distance is read if a value is entered without a unit designation (' or ").

- If the current System Unit Scale does not match that of a file that is opened, you are warned with the Units Mismatch dialog box, as shown in Figure 2–36. It is recommended to select **Adopt the File's Unit Scale**, unless you specifically want to change the Unit Scale of the file being opened.

File Load: Units Mismatch

The Unit Scale of the file does not match the System Unit Scale.

File Unit Scale: 1 Unit = 1.0000 Feet

System Unit Scale: 1 Unit = 1.0000 Inches

Do You Want To:

○ Rescale the File Objects to the System Unit Scale?

◉ Adopt the File's Unit Scale?

OK

Figure 2–36

Practice 2c

Working with Units Setup

Practice Objective

- Assign and set up units in a scene.

In this practice, you will setup units for the projects.

1. In the Menu Bar, select **File>Reset** and click **Yes** in the confirmation dialog box.

If an unsaved scene is open, you might be required to save or discard the changes to the scene.

2. Select **Customize>Units Setup** to open the Units Setup dialog box. Click **System Unit Setup**.

3. In the System Unit Setup dialog box, in the *System Unit Scale* area, verify that *1 Unit* = is set to **1.0** and to **Inches**. Click **OK**.

4. You are returned to Units Setup dialog box. Select **US Standard**, and then select **Feet w/Fractional Inches** and **1/8** in the respective drop-down lists, as shown in Figure 2–37.

5. Set the following, as shown in Figure 2–37:
   - *Default Units:* **Inches**
   - *Lighting Units*: **American**

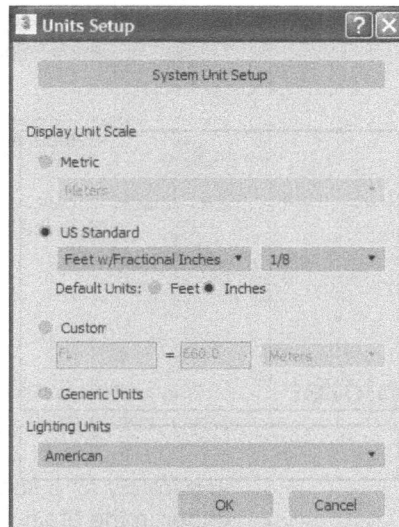

Figure 2–37

6. Click **OK** to close the Units Setup dialog box.

7. Select **File>Save As** to save your work as **MyUnits Setup.max**. Verify that it is being saved in the ...*scenes* folder.

2.5 Layer and Object Properties

It is convenient to group similar objects into layers to modify these objects' properties and control their visibility together.

Layers Toolbar

By default, the Layers toolbar does not display. To display it, right-click on a blank space in the Main Toolbar and select **Layers,** as shown in Figure 2–38. You can also select the toolbar from the Interface Item customize menu, which displays by right-clicking on the handle of the interface menu item. The toolbar enables you to set an active layer by selecting it from the drop-down list. Additionally, it contains various layer specific tools.

Figure 2–38

	Opens the Layer Explorer.
	Creates a new layer.
	Adds selected objects to the current layer.
	Selects all objects in the current layer.
	Sets the current layer to the layer of a selected object.

Layer Explorer

In the Scene Explorer, click (Sort by Layer) to display it as a Layer Explorer. If you want to display the Layer Explorer separately as a floating window, click (Layer Explorer) either in the Main Toolbar or in the Layers toolbar, or select **Tools>Layer Explorer**. This version of Scene Explorer has tools and functions specific to layers, as shown in Figure 2–39.

Figure 2–39

- View all of the objects on a layer by expanding the layer and clicking the arrow beside it. Right-clicking on an object in the list enables you to select and/or change its **Object Properties**.

- Click ▨ (gray layer icon) next to a layer to make the layer active. An active layer displays the ≋ (blue layer icon).

Tools in the Layer Explorer

You can create and adjust layers using the tools in the Layer Explorer toolbar.

⊕	Creates a new layer and makes it the active layer. Using this button in the Layer Explorer automatically moves selected objects to a new layer. If no objects are selected, an empty layer is created.
≋	Moves selected objects to the active layer.
▤	Selects all of the objects in the selected layer.
≋	Activates the selected layer.
⊛	Hides or Unhides all of the layers. Hiding a layer makes those objects invisible in the viewports and in renderings.

Freezes or Thaws all of the layers. You can freeze or thaw an individual object or layer by clicking ✳ in the *Frozen* column. Freezing a layer (or individual object) displays those objects, but makes them unselectable. Frozen objects display as gray in the viewports, but render normally.

- The **Layers** quad menu (shown in Figure 2–40) opens by right-clicking on the name of the layer in the Layer Explorer and enables you to view and adjust other layer properties.

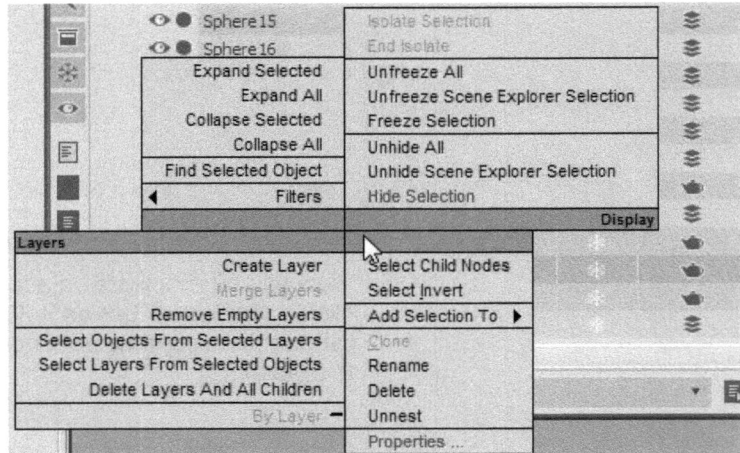

Figure 2–40

- You can also modify the display settings of one or more layers using the Layer Properties dialog box, that can be opened by selecting **Properties** in the **Layers** quad menu. Layer properties apply to all objects on that layer that do not have overrides set in their Object Properties.

Layer Properties

The Layer Properties dialog box (shown in Figure 2–41) contains two tabs:

- *General* tab: Used to set the display properties, hide and freeze options, or the rendering options of the layer.

- *Adv. Lighting* tab: Used to set the radiosity properties such as whether the layer objects can cast shadows and receive illumination.

Figure 2–41

Object Properties

Right-clicking on an object in the Scene Explorer or Layer Explorer opens the quad menu for the object, as shown in Figure 2–42. In this menu, you can quickly edit or modify the properties of an object. Using the menu to edit the Display Properties is shown in Figure 2–42.

Figure 2–42

You can modify the detailed properties of an object in the Object Properties dialog box, as shown in Figure 2–43. The Object Properties dialog box is opened by selecting **Properties** in the quad menu. Alternatively, you can right-click on an object in a viewport and select **Object Properties**.

Figure 2–43

- It lists important information about an object, such as the name of the object, how many faces it consists of, the material assigned to it, whether its properties are controlled by layer or by object, etc.

- Changes made in the Object Properties dialog box override any layer settings for that object. The *Rendering Control* area in the Object Properties dialog box enables you to change setting for casting shadows on individual objects in a layer. This is useful when you do not want an object to cast shadows, while keeping the display of the other objects.

- To override the layer properties for an object, click the appropriate **By Layer** so that it changes to **By Object**.

Display Panel

The Command Panel's Display panel (![icon]) also contains controls for hiding and freezing objects, as shown in Figure 2–44.

Figure 2–44

*A Display Floater is available in the **Tools** menu, where you can **Hide**, **Unhide**, **Freeze**, and **Unfreeze** objects.*

*You can also use the right-click on the **Display** quad menu.*

The Display panel enables you to:

• Hide all objects by category (all lights, all geometry, etc.).

• Hide or Freeze objects individually or by selecting them first.

• Unhide or Unfreeze all objects, or do so by object name. You can also freeze or hide by hit.

Practice 2d

Layer and Object Properties

Practice Objectives

- Create a new layer and move objects into a layer.
- Adjust properties of the layer and objects in the layer.

In this practice, you will create a new layer and move several objects into it. You will also set and modify the properties of the layer and of an individual object using Layer Properties and Object Properties respectively.

You must set the paths to locate the External files and Xrefs used in the practice. If you have not done this already, return to Chapter 1 and complete Task 1 to Task 3 in *Practice 1a: Organizing Folders and Working with the Interface*. You only have to set the user paths once.

Task 1 - Practice Layer Management.

*If a dialog box opens prompting you about a File Load: Mismatch, click **OK** to accept the default values.*

1. Open **Layers.max** from the ...*scenes* folder.

2. Click ▤ (Layer Explorer) in the Main Toolbar or select **Tools>Layer Explorer** to open the Layer Explorer.

3. In the Layer Explorer, next to layer **0 (default)** note the ▤ (blue layer icon) indicating that it is the active layer. Verify that the **Name (Sorted Ascending)** displays as the title heading to display the **0 (default)** at the top of the list. If it does not display as mentioned, keep on clicking on the title to cycle through different options.

4. Select the arrow beside **0 (default)** to expand it and list all of the objects on this layer.

5. Scroll down in the object list and locate the objects **Building Pad**, **Inside Curbing**, **Inside Grading**, **Outside Curbing**, **Outside Grading**, and **Parking Lot Surface**.

6. These objects are ground surfaces and part of a group called **Site XREF**. You can verify it by selecting one of these objects such as the **Building Pad** (shown in Figure 2–45) in the

   Layer Explorer. In the Scene Explorer, verify that ▦ (Sort by Hierarchy) is selected. Note that **Site XREF** is expanded and all of the objects in the group are highlighted, as shown in Figure 2–46. Scroll down and note that **Building Pad** is also listed and highlighted.

Figure 2–45

Figure 2–46

7. Zoom out in the viewport so that all the objects are visible.

If you already have objects selected, click in empty space in the viewport to clear selection.

8. In the Layer Explorer, in layer **0 (default)**, select **Site XREF**. Note that a number of objects are selected in the viewport and that **1 Group Selected** displays in the Status bar.

9. With **Site XREF** selected, in the Menu bar, select **Group>Open**. The Site XREF group is now open. Note that nothing is selected now.

   • To verify this, select **Building Pad** in layer **0 (default)**. Note that only the **Building Pad** is selected in the Scene Explorer and that a single object is highlighted in the viewport.

10. In the Layer Explorer, select the six ground surfaces by using
    <Shift> or <Ctrl>, as shown in Figure 2–47.

Figure 2–47

11. In the menu bar, select **Group>Detach**.

12. In the Layer Explorer with the six ground surfaces selected,
    click ![icon](Create New Layer). A new layer called **Layer001**
    is automatically created with the six building surfaces placed
    in it, as shown in Figure 2–48. Note that the software
    automatically sets this layer to be the current layer, which is
    indicated by ![icon](blue icon).

You can also use

![icon] *(Create New
Layer) in the Layer
toolbar, which opens a
dialog box. Verify that
**Move Selection to New
Layer** is selected and
then click **OK**.*

13. Right-click on the layer **Layer001** and select **Rename**.
    Rename the layer as **Ground Surfaces**, as shown in
    Figure 2–49.

Figure 2–48   **Figure 2–49**

14. Expand layer **Corridor and Original Surfaces|Surfaces** and
    note that there are eight ground surfaces in it. Right-click on
    this layer to open the menu and note that **Delete** is
    unavailable (grayed out), because the layer contains objects.

*You can also select
Select Child Nodes in
the right-click quad
menu.*

15. With the **Corridor and Original Surfaces|Surfaces** layer
    selected, in the Layer Explorer toolbar, click ![icon] (Select
    Children). This selects all of the objects in this layer.

*You can also select **Add Selection To>New Parent (pick)** and then select the required layer to move.*

16. In the Layer Explorer toolbar, click ![icon] (Add to Active Layer). The eight objects from the **Corridor and Original Surfaces|Surface** layer are moved to the **Ground Surfaces** layer (which is the active layer), as shown in Figure 2–50.

> ▶ ⊙ C-MARK-YELLOW-3D
>   ⊙ Corridor and Original Surfaces|Surfaces
> ▼ ⊙ ≋ Ground Surfaces
>   ⊙ ● AeccDbSurfaceTin
>   ⊙ ● AeccDbSurfaceTin
>   ⊙ ● AeccDbSurfaceTin
>   ⊙ ● Building Pad
>   ⊙ ● Corporate Drive: Asphalt
>   ⊙ ● Corporate Drive: Concrete
>   ⊙ ● Corporate Drive: Grassed Areas
>   ⊙ ● Existing Ground Surface
>   ⊙ ● Inside Curbing
>   ⊙ ● Inside Grading
>   ⊙ ● Outside Curbing
>   ⊙ ● Outside Grading
>   ⊙ ● Parking Lot Surface
>   ⊙ ● Water Surface
> ▶ ⊙ LIGHTPOLE_DOUBLE

Figure 2–50

17. Right-click on **Corridor and Original Surfaces|Surfaces** and note that **Delete** is now available. Select **Delete** to remove **Corridor and Original Surfaces|Surfaces**.

18. Select ![icon] (gray layer icon) next to layer **0 (default)** to make the layer active which toggles the icon to ![icon] (blue layer icon).

Task 2 - Set Layer and Object Properties.

Set the ground surfaces so that it does not cast shadows although they will still receive shadows. This simplification can save rendering time without significantly affecting the final output when using relatively flat ground surfaces.

1. In the Layer Explorer, select and right-click on the layer **Ground Surfaces**, and then select **Properties**.

2. In the Layer Properties dialog box, in the *Rendering Control* area, toggle off **Cast Shadows** (as shown in Figure 2–51) and click **OK**.

Figure 2–51

3. You can override this setting for one of the ground surfaces. In the Layer Explorer, in the layer **Ground Surfaces**, select and right-click on **Outside Grading**. Select **Properties** to open the Object Properties dialog box.

4. In the Object Properties dialog box, in the *Rendering Control* area, click **By Layer** so that it changes to **By Object**. Verify that **Cast Shadows** for this object is enabled and click **OK**.

5. Close the Layer Explorer.

6. Select **File>Save As**, and save your work as **MyLayers.max**.

Chapter Review Questions

1. Which tool can be used to zoom to the extents of all visible objects in all viewports?

   a. (Zoom Extents)

   b. (Zoom All)

   c. (Zoom Extents All)

   d. (Zoom Region)

2. After selecting a number of objects, which key do you press to remove items from the selection?

   a. <Shift>

   b. <Ctrl>

   c. <Alt>

   d. <Esc>

3. In the maximized viewport display, along with holding <Win>, which key do you need to press to open the viewport overlay where you can switch to a different viewport?

   a. <Shift>

   b. <Ctrl>

   c. <Alt>

   d. <Tab>

4. You should assign the unit scale before adding any geometry to the scene. Changing the **System Unit Scale** later does not rescale objects that are already present.

   a. True

   b. False

5. In the Layer Explorer, which option makes objects unselectable, but leaves them visible in the viewport and renders them normally?

   a. **Hide**

   b. **Freeze**

   c. **Render**

   d. **Radiosity**

6. In the Layer Explorer, selecting a few objects and then

clicking (Create New Layer) creates:

a. A new inactive layer that is empty.

b. A new active layer that is empty.

c. A new inactive layer that contains the selected objects.

d. A new active layer that contains the selected objects.

Command Summary

Button	Command	Location
Layers		
	Add Selection to Current Layer	• **Layers Toolbar**
	Add to Active Layer	• **Layers Toolbar** • **Layer Explorer Toolbar**
	Create New Layers	• **Layers Toolbar** • **Layer Explorer Toolbar**
	Layer Explorer	• **Main Toolbar** • **Layers Toolbar**
	Select Objects in Current Layer	• **Layers Toolbar**
	Set Current Layer to Selection's Layer	• **Layers Toolbar**
Object Selection		
	Crossing	• **Main Toolbar:** Window/Crossing Toggle
	Rectangular Selection Region	• **Main Toolbar**
	Select Object	• **Main Toolbar**
	Select by Name	• **Main Toolbar**
	Window	• **Main Toolbar:** Window/Crossing Toggle
Viewport Navigation		
	Dolly Camera	• **Viewport Navigation Toolbar (Camera Views):** Dolly Camera flyout
	Field-of-View	• **Viewport Navigation Toolbar:** Zoom Region flyout in Perspective and Camera views
	Maximize Viewport Toggle	• **Viewport Navigation Toolbar**
	Orbit Camera	• **Viewport Navigation Toolbar (Camera Views)**
	Orbit	• **Viewport Navigation Toolbar (Non-Camera Views):** Orbit flyout

	Orbit Point of View	• **Viewport Navigation Toolbar (Non-Camera Views):** Orbit flyout
	Pan View	• **Viewport Navigation Toolbar**
	Perspective	• **Viewport Navigation Toolbar (Camera Views)**
	Roll Camera	• **Viewport Navigation Toolbar (Camera Views)**
	Truck Camera	• **Viewport Navigation Toolbar (Camera Views)**
	Walk Through	• **Viewport Navigation Toolbar:** Pan View flyout in Perspective and Camera views
	Zoom	• **Viewport Navigation Toolbar (Non-Camera Views)**
	Zoom All	• **Viewport Navigation Toolbar (Non-Camera Views)**
	Zoom Extents	• **Viewport Navigation Toolbar (Non-Camera Views):** Zoom Extents flyout
	Zoom Extents Selected	• **Viewport Navigation Toolbar (Non-Camera Views):** Zoom Extents flyout
	Zoom Extents All	• **Viewport Navigation Toolbar:** Zoom Extents All flyout
	Zoom Extents All Selected	• **Viewport Navigation Toolbar:** Zoom Extents All flyout
	Zoom Region	• **Viewport Navigation Toolbar (Non-Camera Views)**

Assembling Project Files

The files used in the Autodesk® 3ds Max® software can be modeled directly in the software, referenced by linking, or directly imported from another source. Linking files enables you to incorporate objects or other scene files into the current scene by externally referencing them. Once referenced, the connection between the two files can be maintained. If files are imported, they are merged with the project and no link is established. Understanding the benefits and drawbacks of using external data helps you decide how to best reference it in a project.

Learning Objectives in this Chapter

- Understand the difference between File Linking and File Importing, and edit the linked data files.
- Combine entities from .DWG, .DXF, .FBX, and .RVT files into an active Autodesk 3ds Max scene.
- Understand how to link AutoCAD® DWG, DXF, generic FBX files, and Autodesk® Revit® RVT/FBX files.
- Create and modify presets.
- Incorporate objects or other scene files into the current scene by externally referencing them.
- Manage data using the asset tracking systems.

3.1 Data Linking and Importing

Although the Autodesk 3ds Max software has a robust 2D and 3D modeling system, it might be efficient to link or import some or all of the design data from other Autodesk software, such as AutoCAD®, Autodesk® Revit® Architecture, AutoCAD® Architecture, or Autodesk® Inventor®.

Linking vs. Importing

You can link or import files using the **File Link** and **Import** tools. You can link files such as .DWG, .DXF, .FBX, and .RVT, and import files such as Autodesk® Inventor® (.IPT, .IAM), Autodesk® Alias® .Wire, LandXML and DEM data files, and Adobe Illustrator (.AI).

- Linked geometry differs from imported geometry in that it remains connected to the source file. If the source file is edited, the Autodesk 3ds Max Scene can be updated to show those changes. Imported geometry maintains no connection to the source file.

- If a source .DWG, .DXF, .FBX, or .RVT file is likely to change (or you would prefer to make changes in the .DWG, .DXF, .FBX, or .RVT directly), then using **File Linking** might be the best way to incorporate this data into the Autodesk 3ds Max software.

- **Importing** can be used as a faster alternative to linking to bring large amounts of data into the software. Complex geometry might be faster to reimport than to update through a file link.

- File links and imports are launched from the **File>Import** in the Menu bar, as shown in Figure 3–1.

Figure 3–1

Editing Linked Data

- Linked geometry can be edited but not directly deleted from a scene file. Alternatively, the layer on which the objects are placed might be ignored during a reload, or set to **Hide** in the Layer Explorer.

- Edits applied to linked geometry (such as through modifiers) are reapplied after a link is updated. Some complex modifications might not apply as expected, so you should always review your geometry carefully after a link is updated.

- Links to drawing files are not bi-directional, so that changes you make to the data in the Autodesk 3ds Max software do not update the original .DWG, .FBX, .DXF, or .RVT file.

- In linked files that are bound, the geometry stays in the scene file as-is, but the connection to the source file is dropped.

Importing

You can export an .FBX file from the Autodesk Revit software and import it in Autodesk 3ds Max software. The FBX importer is an independent plug-in that is frequently updated. In the FBX Import dialog box, use **Web Update** to check for web updates, download the latest updates, and install them. Close 3ds Max when you do the install.

Merging Autodesk 3ds Max Scene Files

Objects already saved in Autodesk 3ds Max scenes (.MAX files) are imported into the current scene using the **Merge** option (**File>Import>Merge**). Merging files is a one-directional transfer that does not maintain any connection between the two files. Using the **Merge** option, you can either load a few objects from a scene or you can load a complete scene into the current one.

Civil View

Civil View enables you to import 3D geometry from Civil/Survey products, such as AutoCAD Civil 3D, Land Desktop, and other formats such as BentleyMX files.

Initializing Civil View

You only have to initialize Civil View once.

To use Civil View the first time, you are required to initialize it by selecting **Civil View>Initialize Civil View**. In the Initialize Autodesk Civil View dialog box that opens (as shown in Figure 3–2), you can set the *System Units* and the *Country Resource Kit* based on the civil project that you will be opening. After initializing the Civil View, you are required to exit and restart the Autodesk 3ds Max software.

Figure 3–2

Although Civil View is initialized, if the *Start Mode for Civil View* is set to **Manual**, next time you launch the Autodesk 3ds Max software, you will still be required to start Civil View. You can change this setting in the Civil View Preferences dialog box, which can be accessed by selecting **Civil View>Civil View> Preferences**, in the *General* tab of the dialog box, selecting **Automatically start Civil View?**, as shown in Figure 3–3.

Figure 3–3

Using Civil View

*   You can open the interface from the Menu bar by selecting **Civil View>Start Civil View**.

*   Once Civil View is started, you can import the required geometry by selecting **Civil View>Geometry Import** as shown in Figure 3–4.

Figure 3–4

Civil View Explorer

You can use the Civil View Explorer (shown in Figure 3–5) to access the visualization aspects of the objects in the scene. It also contains all the editing commands for the selected objects. The objects that are imported retain a link to the original source file. The civil View visualization model retains a link to the original source file and updates the model whenever a design changes.

Figure 3–5

Practice 3a

Ground Surfaces using Civil View

Practice Objective

- Open a Civil 3D data file in a scene file.

In this practice, you will open a .VSP3D file for importing ground surfaces using Civil View. You will then modify the material assignment for various ground surfaces using the Civil View Explorer.

You must set the paths to locate the External files and Xrefs used in the practice. If you have not done this already, return to Chapter 1 and complete Task 1 to Task 3 in *Practice 1a: Organizing Folders and Working with the Interface*. You only have to set the user paths once.

Task 1 - Initialize Civil View.

It is recommended that you import 3D ground surfaces from Civil/Survey products, such as AutoCAD Civil 3D or Land Desktop using the vsp3d data format.

You have to initialize Civil View once.

1. In the menu bar, select **Civil View>Initialize Civil View**. If you have already initialized Civil View, go to Step 5.

2. In the Initialize Autodesk Civil View dialog box, set the *System Units* to **Feet** because the civil project that you will be opening uses Feet as its unit of measurement. Verify that **Don't warn me about System Units again** is selected.

3. In the *Select a Country Resource Kit* area, select **US IMPERIAL** and verify that *Start Mode for Civil View* is set to **Manual**. Click **OK**. In the Information dialog box, click **OK**.

4. Exit and then restart the Autodesk 3ds Max software.

5. Select **Civil View>Start Civil View** to start Civil View.

Task 2 - Opening a Civil 3D File.

1. Open **Civil Base XRef.max** from the *...\scenes* folder. If a Mismatch dialog box opens, click **OK** to accept the default values. If prompted again, click **OK**. This is an empty scene in which the System Unit Scale has been set to **1 Unit=1.0 Feet**.

2. In the menu bar, select C**ivil View>Geometry Import>Civil 3D (VSP 3D) File**, as shown in Figure 3–6.

Figure 3–6

3. In the Civil 3D Import Panel dialog box, click **Open**. In the Select a VSP3D File dialog box, browse to the *...\import* folder in the practice files folder and open **Civil surfaces.vsp3d**.

The objects listed include surfaces, site/ grading objects, corridors, (surfaces, baselines, featurelines etc.),and point groups, etc.

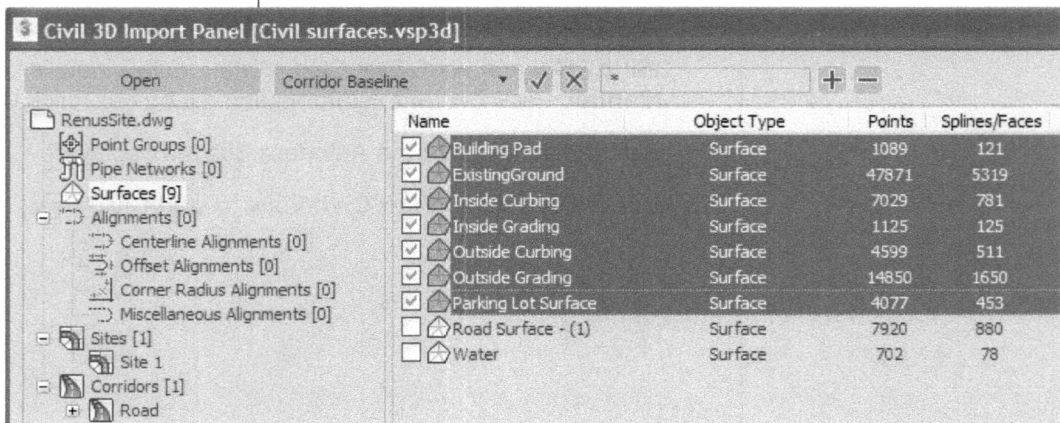

4. In the Civil 3D Import Panel dialog box, a list of objects that are in the AutoCAD Civil 3D file are listed. In the left pane, select **Surfaces [9]** to display all of the surfaces in the right pane. Select **Building Pad**, hold <Shift>, and select **Parking Lot Surface** to highlight the first seven surfaces. Select the checkbox for **Building Pad** to select all seven highlighted surfaces, as shown in Figure 3–7. You can select them individually as well.

Figure 3–7

5. You will select the corridor surfaces and the baseline. In the left pane, select **Corridors [1]** and in the right pane, click in the checkboxes for **PrimaryAccess**, **Region(1)**, **Region(2)**, and **Region(3)**, as shown in Figure 3–8.

Hinge_Cut	Corridor Feature Line	6
Hinge_Cut	Corridor Feature Line	65
☑ PrimaryAccess	Corridor Baseline	57
☑ Region (1)	Corridor Surface	306
☑ Region (2)	Corridor Surface	42
☑ Region (3)	Corridor Surface	159
Top_Curb	Corridor Feature Line	34
Top_Curb	Corridor Feature Line	6

Figure 3–8

6. Click **OK**. In the Civil View Information, click **Yes** to accept the global shift values.

7. Click **Yes** to proceed without a feature interpretation style.

It takes a few minutes to load the file.

8. The ground surfaces, building pad, corridor, and parking lot display in all of the viewports. If they are not, click ⚹ (Zoom Extents All). In the Perspective viewport, note that only the corridor displays the right surface material but the rest of the surfaces display a checkerboard material.

Right-click on the title bar and select Dock> Left.

9. In the menu bar, select **Civil View>Civil View>Civil View Explorer** to open the Civil & View Explorer. Dock it along the left side of the screen.

Task 3 - Modify Material Assignment.

1. Verify that the *Civil Explorer* tab is selected. Expand **Civil View Objects>Imported Objects**, if not already expanded. Select **Surfaces** and note that the corridor is selected in the viewports. The *Object List* rollout opens with all of the surfaces listed, as shown in Figure 3–9.

▾ **Object List**

Surfaces (10)   □

C3Dsurface-Road-Region (1)
C3Dsurface-Road-Region (2)
C3Dsurface-Road-Region (3)
C3Dsurface-C-TOPO-Building Pad

Right-click item for pop-up menu

Figure 3–9

A material is not required for the first three corridor regions.

The complete list might not be visible in the Explorer. Hover the cursor in empty space in the information area until it displays as a Pan (hand) cursor. Slide up or down, using the hand cursor or the scroll button to display all of the information.

2. Scroll or pan down to display the rest of parameters, as shown in Figure 3–10.

3. In the *Object List* rollout, select **C3Dsurface-C-TOPO-Building Pad**.

4. In the *Surface Parameters* rollout, select the *Statistics* tab and note that in the *Face Selection Sets*, in *By Material ID*, **[31] Ground Type 4** has been assigned, as shown in Figure 3–11.

Figure 3–10

Figure 3–11

5. Right-click on **[31] Ground Type 4** and select **Modify Material ID Assignment**, as shown in Figure 3–12.

Figure 3–12

6. Click **Yes** in the Warning dialog box.

7. In the Modify material channel dialog box, select [**22**] **Concrete Type 1** as shown in Figure 3–13. Click **OK**.

Figure 3–13

8. In the **Perspective** viewport, use **Zoom** and **Pan** to zoom into the building pad. Note how the new material is applied.

9. Select **Surfaces** again and in the *Object List* rollout, select **C3Dsurface-C-TOPO-Existing Ground**. In the *Surface Parameters* rollout, in the *Statistics* tab, right-click on [**31**] **Ground Type 4**, and select **Modify Material ID Assignment**. In the Warning dialog box, click **Yes**.

10. In the Modify material channel dialog box, select [**35**] **Ground Type 6** and click **OK**. In the **Perspective** viewport, note that the new ground type material is applied to the ground surface.

A material is not required for the first three corridor regions.

11. Similarly, for the other surfaces, apply the material types as follows:
   - C3Dsurface-C-TOPO-Inside Curbing: [**38**] **Concrete Type 3**
   - C3Dsurface-C-TOPO-Inside Grading: [**35**] **Ground Type 6**
   - C3Dsurface-C-TOPO-Outside Curbing: [**38**] **Concrete Type 3**
   - C3Dsurface-C-TOPO-Outside Grading: [**35**] **Ground Type 6**
   - C3Dsurface-C-TOPO-Parking Lot Surface: [**39**] **Asphalt Type 4**

You might need to undock the explorer first to close it.

12. Close the Civil View Explorer.

13. Click ![icon] (Zoom Extents All). In the **Perspective** view, the scene displays as shown in Figure 3–14.

Figure 3–14

14. Save your work as **MyCivil Base XRef.max**.

3.2 Linking Files

File Linking is used to incorporate data from other Autodesk software such as Autodesk Revit and AutoCAD into the Autodesk 3ds Max scene. If the incorporated data is changed in the originating software, the file link enables you to update those changes in the 3ds Max scene. File linking is useful when you are working on a visualization project and know that all design decisions have not yet been made. You can link files using the Manage Links dialog box that can be opened as follows:

- **File>Import>Link Revit**: Links the .RVT files from the Autodesk Revit Architecture software.

- **File>Import>Link FBX**: Links the .FBX files that can be created in the Autodesk Revit, Autodesk MotionBuilder, Autodesk Maya, and Autodesk Mudbox software.

- **File>Import>Link AutoCAD**: Links the .DWG and .DXF files from the AutoCAD software.

- You can also open the Manage Links dialog box outside of the Link commands (**File>Reference> Manage Links**) and modify the Link settings.

Linking DWG Files

In CAD data files it is common to have large numbers of objects. When linking or importing AutoCAD .DWG or .DXF files, it is efficient to combine multiple, related objects together into a single Autodesk 3ds Max object to control their display and visibility.

- When multiple entities are combined into compound Autodesk 3ds Max shapes (2D objects) and meshes (3D objects), you can still access and adjust the original geometry using the Sub-object level modifiers, such as **Edit Spline**, **Edit Mesh**, and **Edit Poly**.

- Once multiple entities are combined, you can detach objects or portions of an objects to form new ones for individual editing control.

Linking FBX and RVT Files

The Autodesk Revit and Autodesk 3ds Max software share the Autodesk Material Library materials.

- The .RVT and .FBX file format supports the import of photometric lights, both interior artificial lights and exterior daylight systems.

- Detailed .RVT and .FBX file formats can become very large in size and importing them as single files cannot be accomplished. In such cases, use a section box in the **3D View** in the Autodesk Revit software to limit the amount of the scene you are exporting.

Manage Links Options

The Manage Links dialog box (shown in Figure 3–15) contains the following tabs:

Figure 3–15

Attach Tab

The options available in the *Attach* tab are described as follows:

- **File...** enables you to open a file (.DWG, .DXF, .FBX, or .RVT) for linking. The selected filename and its path display in the File drop-down list. If the file that you selected is a .RVT file with more than one camera view, you are prompted to select a camera view.

- The Preset drop-down list enables you to select the preset settings. The Presets listed here can be created or modified using the *Presets* tab. You can set the units by selecting them in the Incoming file units drop-down list.

- **Select Layers to include** is only available with .DWG and .DXF file formats and enables you to select the layers that you want included with the drawing file.

- **Attach this file** links the selected file with the specified preset settings to the current Autodesk 3ds Max scene.

Files Tab

The *Files* tab displays a list of files that are linked to the current scene with a specific status icon.

- If the linked file has been modified, displays with the linked filename.

- indicates that the linked file is unchanged and does not have any errors.

- When a file is highlighted, the following options are available:

Reload...	When the original file has been changed, it displays the changes in the current scene.
Detach...	Use when you want to remove the link with the original file. This option removes all geometry associated with the linked file.
Bind...	Removes the link with the original file, but the geometry stays in the current scene, although the link between the original file is broken. Changes made to the original linked file cannot be reloaded.

Presets Tab

Many options are available before files are linked to your current scene. These options are configured and saved as **Presets** and can be used when linking files at a later stage. Many of these options require trial and error to find the most appropriate settings. You can link a file and then reload (or detach and relink) with different settings until you achieve the required results.

If you are linking a file for the first time, it is recommended that you create a new preset.

The *Presets* tab lists all existing presets and contains options for creating new presets, modifying existing presets, copying existing ones, renaming and deleting them. You need to select a preset for the **Modify**, **Copy**, **Rename**, and **Delete** options to be available, as shown in Figure 3–16. If no preset is selected, **Copy** is replaced by **New** and is the only available option.

Figure 3–16

Depending on the type of preset selected (.RVT, .FBX, or .DWG), clicking **Modify...** opens a specific File Link Settings dialog box, which enables you to define the way you want the geometry to be linked, what portions of the file are to be modified on **Reload**, and how the geometry is combined.

File Link Settings: DWG Files

In the Manage Links dialog box, in the *Presets* tab, selecting an AutoCAD DWG file preset and clicking **Modify...** opens the File Link Settings: DWG Files dialog box, as shown in Figure 3–17.

Figure 3–17

Basic Tab

The options available in the *Basic* tab are described as follows:

- **Weld nearby vertices** and **Weld threshold:** Welding joins together vertices of the same object that fall in the weld threshold. If the objects are joined by layer, this option removes duplicate vertices so that the adjacent 2D objects on the same layer are automatically combined into splines. Adjacent 3D objects that are welded become faces in a single mesh that share common vertices.

- **Auto-smooth adjacent face** and **Smooth-angle:** Auto-smooth enables adjacent faces in the same 3D mesh to display smooth if the angles of separation between their face normals (a directional vector perpendicular to the face) is equal to or less than the Smooth-angle. Otherwise, the adjacent faces have a faceted edge between them. This is the same smoothing process used in the Edit Mesh and Edit Poly modifiers.

You can adjust smoothing later if you still encounter smoothing issues after import.

- **Orient normals of adjacent faces consistently:** This option coordinates the face normals of linked objects. This option should be left off by default unless some faces of your 3D objects are missing after the link.

- **Cap closed splines:** It assigns an Extrude modifier to all closed 2D geometry (e.g., circles and closed polylines).

- **Texture mapping:** Texture mapping is used to locate texture maps on objects. Two options are available:

Generate coordinates on-demand	• Links objects without adding any texture mapping. • Adds the mapping when it is first called for by the software. • Enables a faster link but might cause some discrepancies.
Generate coordinates for all objects	• Adds texture mapping to all objects at the time of the link, matching any that might have existed in the original drawing file.

- **Curve steps:** This setting defines the number of segments to subdivide each 2D curve segment into if they are later extruded in the Autodesk 3ds Max software. This setting applies to circles, arcs, polyline curves, spines, and similar curved objects.

- **Maximum surface deviation for 3D solids:** This setting defines the allowed deviation distance from a parametric AutoCAD 3D curve (such as a curved AutoCAD extrusion) and the resulting Autodesk 3ds Max mesh. The lower the value, the more a 3D curve is subdivided. In the Autodesk 3ds Max software, all 3D curves must be segmented.

This value can be set as low, (0.01).

- **Include area options:** These options enable you to select the type of objects to be brought into the scene. Note that the **Lights** option only brings in Lights from AutoCAD drawings pre-2007. If you have Sun and Sky checked, a daylight system is created based on the information in the incoming DWG file from the Autodesk Revit 2009 software.

Advanced Tab

The *Advanced* tab (shown in Figure 3–18) controls the import of AutoCAD primitives and the effect of scene materials while importing.

Figure 3–18

The options available in the *Advanced* tab are described as follows:

- **Derive AutoCAD Primitives by:** Controls how AutoCAD objects are combined when linked.

Layer	Creates one object for each AutoCAD layer. Each AutoCAD block links as a single object called a VIZBlock.
Layer, Blocks as Node Hierarchy	This option preserves material assignments in linked AutoCAD blocks. It structures each as a hierarchy of objects rather than single objects.
Layer, Blocks as Node Hierarchy, Split by Material	This option works similarly to the one above but takes into account drawings that have more than one material applied to objects on the same layer. Separate hierarchies are created for each material type on each layer.
Entity, Blocks as Node Hierarchy	This option includes all non-blocks as separate, individual objects. Blocks are preserved as hierarchies, however, organized by layer.
Color	Combines AutoCAD objects by color. All objects of one color are joined in as a single object, regardless of layer.

Entity	Does not combine AutoCAD objects at all. Instead, each AutoCAD object becomes an individual object.
One Object	This option combines all AutoCAD objects into a single object.

- **Create helper at drawing origin:** Adds an origin point helper at the origin of the current coordinate system. All of the linked geometry is part of a hierarchy parented by this helper, so all of the linked objects can be repositioned as one by transforming the helper.

- **Use Extrude modifier to represent thickness:** When disabled, linking 2D AutoCAD objects with a non-zero thickness value translates the objects into the Autodesk 3ds Max software as a 3D mesh. When enabled, objects translate as 2D objects with a parametric extrude modifier. The resulting geometry is the same but when this option is enabled, the extrusion properties (such as height) can be modified after the link or imported using the modifier stack.

- **Create one scene object for each AutoCAD Architecture one:** When unchecked, AutoCAD Architecture and AutoCAD MEP objects are subdivided into separate objects by material.

- **Use scene material definitions:** When unchecked, the Autodesk 3ds Max software includes the current state of any material applied to the linked objects in the AutoCAD software. If selected and the current scene has a material with the same exact name as the AutoCAD material, the scene material is used instead.

- **Use scene material assignments on Reload:** When unchecked, the Autodesk 3ds Max software re-loads the current state of any AutoCAD materials present in the drawing file when the link is updated. When enabled, the Autodesk 3ds Max software maintains the current state of any materials in the scene file after a link is updated. Select this option if you intend to adjust linked materials in the Autodesk 3ds Max software or leave it unchecked if you intend to adjust them the AutoCAD software.

- **Selective Reload:** Enables you to reload a subset of the original file. You can select objects to reload by selecting them in the scene or by selecting them from a list. If you select **Selected in List**, and click **Linked Objects** a list opens.

Hint: Hierarchies and File Linking

Autodesk 3ds Max Hierarchies are collections of objects linked together into parent/child relationships where transform applied to a parent are automatically passed on to its children. Connecting multiple objects in a hierarchical chain can enable sophisticated animations in the Autodesk 3ds Max software, such as the motion of jointed robotic arms.

In the case of the **hierarchy** file link options, incoming AutoCAD blocks are brought into the Autodesk 3ds Max software as multiple objects so that they can maintain multiple material assignments from the AutoCAD software. The parent object itself does not have any geometry and does not render. Most modifiers (such as **Substitute**) must be applied to the objects in the hierarchy rather than the parent.

Spline Rendering Tab

The options available in the *Spline Rendering* tab (shown in Figure 3–19) enable linear objects (2D and 3D lines, polylines, etc.) to display as extruded 3D objects in the viewports or rendering. Normally, splines cannot be rendered because they do not have surface area to interact with scene lighting. These options enable splines to link into the Autodesk 3ds Max software as 3D linear objects with a cross-sectional radius or a rectangular length and width. This provides the surface area for rendering.

Figure 3–19

- If splines are to be rendered with materials then options such as smoothing, mapping coordinates, and/or real-world map size are often important.

- When enabled, all of the splines linked with this setting are renderable, and all have the same cross-section geometry.

- To make only certain 2D objects renderable (or want some to render differently than others) you could apply a Renderable Spline modifier directly to those objects after linking.

File Link Settings: Revit Files (RVT or FBX)

In the Manage Links dialog box, in the *Presets* tab, selecting an Autodesk Revit file and clicking **Modify...** opens the File Link Settings: Revit Files (RVT or FBX) dialog box, as shown in Figure 3–20. Additionally, you can also select the Autodesk FBX (Generic) file preset and click **Modify...**.This opens the File Link Settings: FBX Files dialog box, as shown in Figure 3–21. This dialog box is similar to the Autodesk Revit Files (.RVT and .FBX) but without a *Geometry* area for controlling the segments and smoothing the linked geometry.

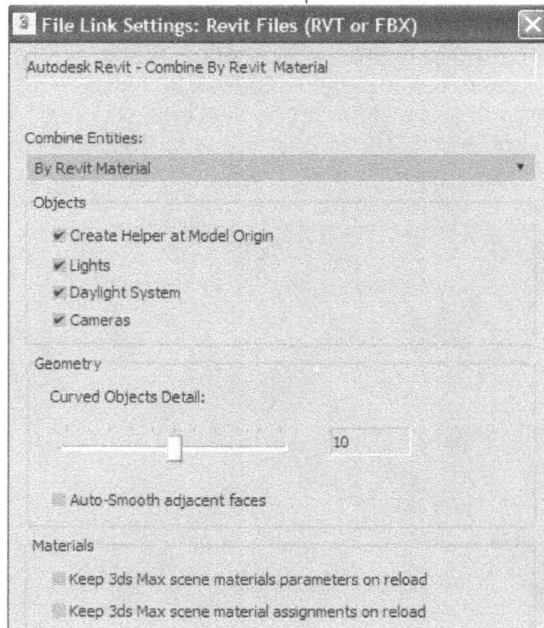

Figure 3–20

Figure 3–21

The options available in the File Link Settings: Revit Files (RVT or FBX) dialog box are described as follows:

It is recommended that you combine entities to reduce the number of objects.

- **Combine Entities** list: Enables you to select the Autodesk Revit entities that you want to combine, as shown in Figure 3–22. For example, if you select **By Revit Material**, all of the entities that have the same material are linked in the current Autodesk 3ds Max scene as a single object.

Figure 3–22

- ***Objects*** area: The selected options in this area are linked from the .RVT file to your current scene. If the .RVT file or .FBX file contains photometric lights, interior artificial lights, cameras, and exterior daylight systems, you can select the associated options in the File Link Settings dialog box.

- ***Geometry*** area: Enables you to set the number of segments for your curved entities and apply auto-smoothing to them.

- ***Materials*** area: Enables you to control the material definitions and assignment settings.

Practice 3b

Linking an AutoCAD DWG

Practice Objectives

- Create a preset to link an AutoCAD .DWG file and reposition it.
- Revise the link settings and reload the linked file.

In this practice, you will link AutoCAD geometry to represent the parking lot details, such as pavement markings and other details. You will reposition this file using the Helper object, and will create 3D markings by projecting 2D lines to the elevation of a terrain model.

You must set the paths to locate the External files and Xrefs used in the practice. If you have not done this already, return to Chapter 1 and complete Task 1 to Task 3 in *Practice 1a: Organizing Folders and Working with the Interface*. You only have to set the user paths once.

Task 1 - Link an AutoCAD .DWG File.

*If a dialog box opens prompting you about a File Load: Mismatch, click **OK** to accept the default values.*

1. Open **Civil Base.max** from the *...\scenes* folder.

2. Select **File>Import>Link AutoCAD**. In the Open dialog box, browse and open the *...\import* folder in the practice files folder. Select **3D Parking Lot Detail-Civil.dwg** and click **Open**. The Manage Links dialog box displaying the partial path, as shown in Figure 3–23.

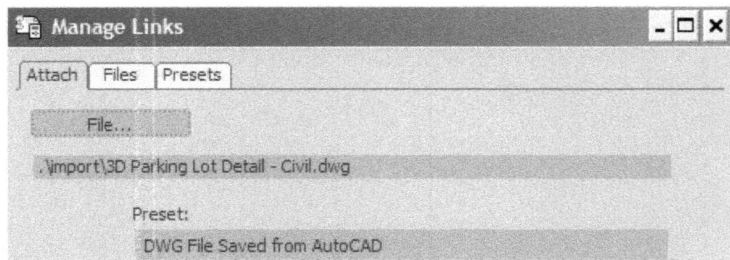

Figure 3–23

At the time of the printing of this guide, the full path of the linked file is required to display such that the software finds the file in the Manage Links dialog box.

3. To display the full path, click on **File** to reopen the Open dialog box, select **C:\Autodesk 3ds Max Fundamentals Practice Files\Import** from the History drop-down list and select the **3D Parking Lot Detail.dwg** again. Click **Open** again. The complete path should display as shown in Figure 3–24.

Figure 3–24

*If no preset is selected, only **New...** is available.*

4. Select the *Presets* tab and click **New...** to create a new link preset.

5. In the New Settings Preset dialog box, set *New Name* as **AutoCAD – Derive by Layer**. Note that the *Format* is selected as **AutoCAD Drawings**. Click **OK**.

6. In the Manage Links dialog box, select the new **AutoCAD – Derive by Layer** preset, as shown in Figure 3–25. Click **Modify...**.

Figure 3–25

*The **Create Helper at drawing origin** option adds a helper object at the origin of the linked file.*

7. In the File Link Settings: DWG Files dialog box, in the *Basic* tab, set the link options, as shown in Figure 3–26. Select the *Advanced* tab and select **Create helper at drawing origin**, as shown in Figure 3–27. Leave all other options as defaults (clear).

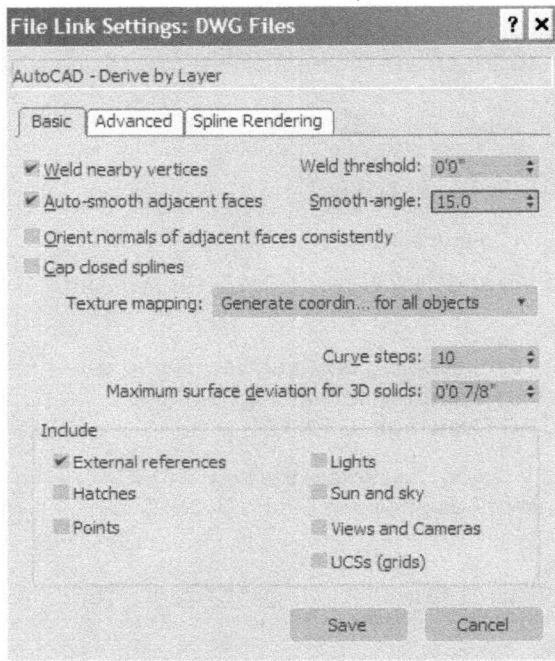

Figure 3–26

Figure 3–27

8. Select the *Spline Rendering* tab and verify that the link options are set to the defaults, as shown in Figure 3–28.

Figure 3–28

9. Click **Save**.

10. In the Manage Links dialog box, select the *Attach* tab. Set *Preset* to **AutoCAD – Derive by Layer**, as shown in Figure 3–29. Click **Select Layers to include...**.

Figure 3–29

11. In the Select Layers dialog box, select **Select from list**. Clear **0** and **DEFPOINTS** and leave all other layers as selected, as shown in Figure 3–30. Click **OK**.

Figure 3–30

12. In the Manage Links dialog box, click **Attach this file**. Close the Manage Links dialog box. Note that the parking lot details have been added to the scene, but are located far away from the origin, as shown in the **Top** viewport in Figure 3–31.

Figure 3–31

Task 2 - Relocate the Linked Geometry.

You might need to start Civil View, if it is not set to start automatically.

1. You need to move the parking lot details by the global shift values in Civil View. In the menu bar, select **Civil View>Civil View>Civil View Explorer**.

2. In the Civil View Explorer, select **Scene Settings**, as shown in Figure 3–32. In the *Scene Settings* rollout, note the *Global Import Shift* values for *X Shift* and *Y Shift (-9901)*, as shown in Figure 3–33. Close the Civil View Explorer.

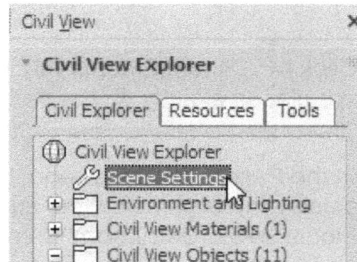

Figure 3–32   **Figure 3–33**

3. In the Main Toolbar, click ⊕ (Select and Move).

If the Scene Explorer is not displayed, select Tools>Scene Explorer and then dock it.

4. In the Scene Explorer, click (■ (Display None) and ◺ (Display Helpers)), and then select the helper object **3D Parking Lot Detail - Civil.dwg**, as shown in Figure 3–34. Note that the **User Coordinate System** icon located at the origin is selected, as shown in Figure 3–35.

Figure 3–34   **Figure 3–35**

Ensure that the feet symbol is added with the values.

5. In the Status Bar, ensure that ⊞ (Absolute Mode Transform) displays. Set the following, as shown in Figure 3–36:
   - *X* edit box: **-9901'0"**
   - *Y* edit box: **-9901'0"**

⊞ X: -9901'0" ⬍ Y: -9901'0" ⬍ Z: 0'0" ⬍

Figure 3–36

6. Press <Enter>.

7. Click ⊡. (Zoom Extents All). Note how the parking lot details are placed exactly on the parking lot surface.

In the Main toolbar, use

▤ (Select Object) to exit any command.

8. In the **Perspective** viewport, use ◉ (Orbit) to tilt the view to display the area below the surfaces, similar to that shown in Figure 3–37. Use **Zoom** to zoom into the area. Note that in addition to the 3D pavement markings, 2D line markings are imported through the link.

Figure 3–37

Task 3 - Revise the Link Settings.

In the Files tab, if the linked file has been modified, 🗅 displays.

1. Click **File>Reference>Manage Links** to open the Manage Links dialog box.

2. In the Manage Links dialog box, select the *Files* tab and note that the linked file displays 🗅, indicating that the file has not changed. Although the linked file has not changed, you can use **Reload...** to revise the link settings. Verify that **Show Reload options** is selected and click **Reload...**.

You can use:
__Reload...__ to update the file in the scene.
__Detach...__ to remove a linked drawing from the scene.
__Bind...__ to insert the drawing as is and removes the connection.

3. The File Link Settings: DWG Files dialog box opens. In the *Advanced* tab, click **Select Layers to include...**. Clear the 2D layers (**C-MARK-WHITE-2D and C-MARK-YELLOW-2D)**, and the two **LIGHTPOLE** layers, as shown in Figure 3–38.

Figure 3–38

The 2D linework should no longer display, keeping the scene smaller.

4. Click **OK** twice to close both dialog boxes. Click ✕ to close the Manage Links dialog box. In the **Perspective** viewport, note that the 2D line markings do not display any longer.

5. Save your work as **MyCivil Base.max**.

Practice 3c

Linking and Reloading Autodesk Revit File

Practice Objectives

- Link and reposition an Autodesk Revit file to the current scene.
- Reload a modified .RVT file.

In this practice, you will link a .RVT file into a 3ds Max scene. You will reposition the Revit file using the Helper object. You will then reload a modified version of the .RVT linked file to incorporate the changes made to the original Autodesk Revit file using **Reload**.

You must set the paths to locate the External files and Xrefs used in the practice. If you have not done this already, return to Chapter 1 and complete Task 1 to Task 3 in *Practice 1a: Organizing Folders and Working with the Interface*. You only have to set the user paths once.

Task 1 - Link an Autodesk Revit (.RVT) file.

*If a dialog box opens prompting you about a File Load: Mismatch, click **OK** to accept the default values.*

1. Open **Civil Base Link.max** from the ...*scenes* folder. The file contains the ground surfaces, building pad, and parking lot details.

2. Select **File>Import>Link Revit**.

3. In the Open dialog box, in the ...*import* folder, select **Revit Building-1.rvt** and click **Open**.

It might take a few minutes to load the file.

4. The Status Bar is replaced by the Loading file bar, indicating the progress of the file as it loads. Once loaded, the Select Revit View dialog box opens, as shown in Figure 3–39.

Figure 3–39

5. Select **Front Exterior 3D View** and click **OK**.

6. In the Manage Links dialog box, select the *Presets* tab. Click **New...** to create a new preset. In the New Settings Preset dialog box, set the following:
   - *New Name*: **Revit Preset**
   - *Format*: Select **Autodesk Revit (*.rvt,*.fbx)**

7. Click **OK**.

8. In the Manage Links dialog box, select **Revit Preset** and click **Modify**.

9. In the File Link Settings dialog box, do the following, as shown in Figure 3–40:
   - In the Combine Entities drop-down list, select **By Revit Category**.
   - In the *Objects* area, clear the **Lights** and **Daylight System** options.
   - In the *Objects* area, select **Create Helper at Model Origin** and **Cameras**.
   - In the *Geometry* area, set *Curved Objects Detail* to **6**.
   - In the *Materials* area, verify that **Keep 3ds Max scene materials parameters on reload** and **Keep 3ds Max scene material assignments on reload** are cleared.

*The **Create Helper at Model Origin** option adds a helper object at the origin of the linked file. Selecting and applying transforms (move, rotate, or scale) to the helper object applies the transform to the linked geometry together.*

Figure 3–40

10. Click **Save**.

11. Select the *Attach* tab. Expand the Preset drop-down list and select **Revit Preset**.

It might take a few minutes to load the file.

12. Click **Attach this file**. Note that the Autodesk Revit building and camera are loaded at the 0,0,0 location in the viewports.

13. Click ⊠ to close the Manage Links dialog box.

*If the Scene Explorer is not displayed, select **Tools>Scene Explorer** and then dock it.*

14. In the Scene Explorer, click ▪ (Display None) and ◣ (Display Helpers), if required, and then select the helper object **Revit Building-1.rvt**, as shown in Figure 3–41.

Figure 3–41

15. Right-click on the **Top** viewport to make it active and to maintain the selection. In the Main Toolbar, click ✛ (Select and Move). The Transform gizmo displays at the helper location, which is the origin of the linked Autodesk Revit file.

The position of the building pad from the origin has been calculated.

16. In the Status Bar, verify that ▦ (Absolute Mode Transform) displays. Set the following, as shown in Figure 3–42:
   - *X* edit box: **800'0"**
   - *Y* edit box: **382'0"**
   - *Z* edit box: **154'6"**

Figure 3–42

17. Press <Enter>.

18. Click ⚙ (Zoom Extents All). Note how the building is placed on the building pad.

Grid has been hidden for clarity. Press <G>.

In the Main toolbar, use

🔲 *(Select Object) to exit any command.*

19. In the **Front** viewport, use 🔲 (Zoom Region) and create a rectangular window around the building to zoom into the building. Verify that the **Standard** shading label displays. Select the **[Wireframe]** *Per View* label and select **Default Shading**. Then, select **Default Shading** again and select **Edged Faces** to define the windows and doors. The building should display similar to that shown in Figure 3–43.

Figure 3–43

20. In the **Left** viewport, select the **[Wireframe]** *Per View* label and select **Default Shading** and then **Edged Faces**.

21. Select the **[Left]** *Point of View* label, and select **Cameras>Views: Front Exterior 3D View**, as shown in Figure 3–44.

Figure 3–44

22. Use ![icon](Orbit Camera) and to display the complete building in the **Left** viewport, similar to that as shown in Figure 3–45.

23. In the **Perspective** viewport, use , and **Pan** to zoom into the building and parking lot area so that the display is similar to that shown in Figure 3–45.

Figure 3–45

Task 2 - Reload the variation of the .RVT file.

A variation to the .RVT linked file (windows have been added) has been included in the *...\import* folder.

1. In Windows Explorer, open the *...\import* folder in the practice files folder.

2. Right-click on **Revit Building-1.rvt** and select **Rename**. Rename the file as **Revit Building-1_ORIGINAL.rvt**.

3. Right-click on **Revit Building-2.rvt**, and select **Copy**. Paste a copy of this file into the same directory. Right-click on the copied file, select **Rename**, and rename the file as **Revit Building-1.rvt**. This must be the same name as the original file that was linked to indicate that the original linked file has changed.

4. Return to the Autodesk 3ds Max software. Select **File>Reference>Manage Links** to open the Manage Links dialog box.

5. In the Manage Links dialog box, select the *Files* tab. Note that ![icon] displays in front of the .RVT filename (as shown in Figure 3–46), indicating that changes have been made to the original linked file.

Figure 3–46

6. Select **Revit Building -1.rvt** (if not already selected) and click **Reload...**. The Loading file bar displays the progress.

7. In the File Link Settings dialog box that opens, in the *Materials* area, select **Keep 3ds Max scene material assignments on reload**. Click **OK**. The scene is refreshed with the new changes.

8. In the Manage Links dialog box, in the *Files* tab, the icon has changed to ⬚, as shown in Figure 3–47. This indicates that there are no differences between the original file and the linked file.

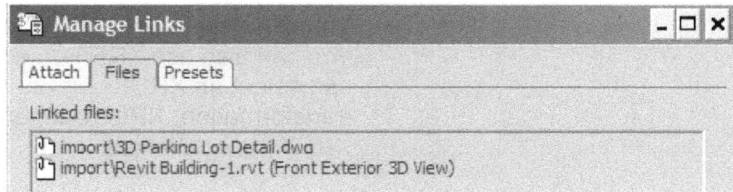

Figure 3–47

9. Close the Manage Links dialog box.

10. In the viewports, the modified building displays. More windows are added to the building, as shown in Figure 3–48.

Figure 3–48

11. Save the file as **MyCivil Base Link.max**.

3.3 References

External References (XRef)

Autodesk 3ds Max Scene files can reference data from other .MAX scene files by expanding **File> Reference>XRef Objects or XRef Scene**. The XREF data remains linked to the source (.MAX) scene file so that changes in the source file can be reflected in any scene that contains the XREF.

- External References are useful to break up large projects into more manageable pieces, permit more than one person to work on the same project at the same time in separate files, and to enable the same core scene geometry to be used in multiple files.

- **XRef Scenes** bring in the entire scene. All of the XREF objects are non-selectable and cannot be modified.

- **XRef Objects** enable you to select individual objects (or all) from an XREF scene. These objects remain selectable and modifiable in the XREF scene file.

- You can snap to XREF and use XREF objects with AutoGrid. You can also use XREF objects as alignment targets and you can select an XREF object's coordinate system for object transformation. XREF support parameter wiring and you can XREF the controllers.

- Objects in scenes (.MAX) are imported into other . MAX scenes using the **Merge** option.

Data Management and Asset Tracking

The Autodesk 3ds Max software enables you to manage your data through Data Management (DM) solutions, referred to as Asset Tracking Systems (ATSs).

- DM solutions such as the Autodesk® Vault software enables you to store scene files and any supporting data (such as material maps) in a single database repository.

- These systems can be accessed simultaneously by multiple users with different rights assigned based on their project responsibilities. Data can be checked out for editing by one individual at a time while still being referenced by other users. Users can see who is editing which portion of the project at any time.

- By centralizing the files in a DM system it is much easier to adjust paths for external files such as image maps.

- Data files can be versioned through DM solutions, so that the older versions can be readily accessed, if required.

- For more information see *Asset Tracking* in the Autodesk 3ds Max Help files. Asset Tracking is available through the **File>Reference> Asset Tracking Toggle**.

Practice 3d

XRef and Merge Objects

Practice Objective

- Link an AutoCAD .DWG file and incorporate objects from another scene file into the current scene.

In this practice, create a new scene file that will contain linked AutoCAD objects and XRef objects from the Civil Base scene. You will then merge objects into the current scene file.

You must set the paths to locate the External files and Xrefs used in the practice. If you have not done this already, return to Chapter 1 and complete Task 1 to Task 3 in *Practice 1a: Organizing Folders and Working with the Interface.* You only have to set the user paths once.

Task 1 - Assemble the Data.

If an unsaved scene is open, you need to save or discard the changes to the scene.

1. Click **File>Reset** and click **Yes** to reset the scene.

2. For this scene, set the *System Unit Scale* to **Inches**. Select **Customize>Units Setup**. In the dialog box, verify that the following is set:
   - *Display Unit Scale:* **US Standard, Feet w/ Fractional Inches**
   - *Default Units:* **Inches**
   - *Lighting Units:* **American**

3. Click **System Unit Setup**. In the System Unit Setup dialog box, set *System Unit Scale* to **Inches**. Click **OK** in both the dialog boxes.

4. Expand **File>Reference** and select **Manage Links**.

5. In the Manage Links dialog box, in the *Attach* tab, click **File....** In the ...*import* folder, select **Exterior AutoCAD Architectural Model.dwg**. Click **Open**.

*The **AutoCAD – Derive by Layer** preset was created in the **Practice: Linking an AutoCAD DWG**. Complete the above mentioned practice to create the preset if not already done so.*

6. In the *Preset* drop-down list, select **AutoCAD – Derive by Layer** and click **Attach this file**. Once the file has been loaded, close the Manage Links dialog box.
   - The AutoCAD objects were not joined together by layer. Each was subdivided by material type into different objects. Materials previously assigned in AutoCAD were preserved on these separate objects.

7. Click (Zoom Extents All) to display all of the objects in all of the viewports.

8. In the **Front** viewport, select all of the objects by creating a window around the objects. In the Main Toolbar, in the *Named Selection Sets* field, enter **exterior AutoCAD Architectural building**, as shown in Figure 3–49. Press <Enter>.

Figure 3–49

You select objects to XREF rather than the entire scene because XREF scene objects cannot be individually selected or modified.

9. Click **File>Reference>XRef Objects**. In the XRef Objects dialog box, click (Create XRef Record from File) as shown in Figure 3–50.

Figure 3–50

10. In the Open File dialog box, select **Parking Lot Detail.max** (from the ...\import folder) and click **Open**.

11. If the Units Mismatch dialog box opens, click **OK**. This rescales the XRef objects to the system units.

12. The Duplicate Material Name dialog box opens prompting you that there is an incoming material with the same name as an existing scene material. Select **Apply to All Duplicates** to keep both materials, as shown in Figure 3–51. Click **Auto-Rename Merged Material**.

Figure 3–51

13. In the XRef Objects dialog box, note that the .MAX filename displays. Click [X] to close the dialog box.

14. Click [Zoom Extents All]. Note that the Civil Base objects are located far from the origin. This is a coordinate system discrepancy and not a scale issue. The AutoCAD drawing is based in a different coordinate system and scale than the accompanying Civil drawing.

Task 2 - Coordinate the Data.

In this task you will relocate the Civil Base in the Architectural Data. To line up the data accurately you will need the exact coordinate translation and rotation. You can measure ahead of time in programs, such as AutoCAD by comparing the coordinates of points common to both files.

1. Verify that no object is selected. In the Scene Explorer, click [■] (Display None) and [🔘] (Display Object XRefs). Select all of the XRef objects in the list (use <Shift> and then select the first and last).

2. With these XRef objects selected, select **Group>Group** from the menu bar.

3. In the Group dialog box, set the *Group name* to **Site XRef** and click **OK**.

4. In the Main Toolbar, click [✛] (Select and Move). In the Reference Coordinate System, select **World**, as shown in Figure 3–52. Click [▣] (Use Transform Coordinate Center).

Figure 3–52

The translation coordinates have already been measured in AutoCAD.

5. In the Status Bar, verify that ⊞ (Absolute Mode) displays. In the *Transform Type-in* area, set the following, as shown in Figure 3–53:

   - *X:* **-197'4"**
   - *Y:* **-30'0"**
   - *Z:* **-4'11"**

   | ⊞ | X: -197'4" ⇕ | Y: -30'0" ⇕ | Z: -4'11" ⇕ |

   Figure 3–53

6. Press <Enter>.

7. In the Main Toolbar, click ▢ (Select Object) to exit the **Move** transform operation.

8. Click 🔧 (Zoom Extents All).

9. In the **Perspective** viewport, use ⬯ (Orbit Point of Interest) and click to place a point on the building and then orbit around that point. Using **Pan** and **Zoom**, zoom into the parking lot and building area (as shown in Figure 3–54), and verify that the building is located on the building pad. Although the XREF had a different Unit Scale (feet), it scaled correctly to the active scene (in inches).

Figure 3–54

10. Save your work as **MyArchitectural Scene.max**.

Task 3 - Merging Objects.

1. Select **File>Import>Merge**. In the Merge File dialog box, select **Light Poles for Project1.max** from the ...*scenes* folder. Click **Open**.

2. In the Merge dialog box, click **All**, as shown in Figure 3–55. Click **OK**.

Figure 3–55

*Merge enables both objects to have the same name, **Skip** ignores the incoming object, and **Delete Old** removes the original object.*

3. The Duplicate Name dialog box opens, prompting you that an object with the same name already exists in the scene. Select **Apply to all Duplicates** and click **Auto-Rename**.

4. The light poles display in the scene, as shown in Figure 3–56.

Figure 3–56

5. Save your work.

Chapter Review Questions

1. The following file formats can be linked to the current Autodesk 3ds Max scene:

   a. .DWG, .OBJ, .APF, .FBX

   b. .DWG, .DXF, .FBX, .RVT

   c. .DWG, .DXF, .OBJ, .RVT

   d. .DWG, .OBJ, .FBX, .RVT

2. In the Manage Links dialog box, in the *Files* tab, which of the following options do you use to remove the link with the original linked file but maintain its geometry in the current scene?

   a. **Reload...**

   b. **Detach...**

   c. **Bind...**

3. Which command do you use to combine objects from a saved Autodesk 3ds Max scene (.MAX file) into your current .MAX scene?

   a. **Import**

   b. **Link**

   c. **Open**

   d. **Merge**

4. While linking Autodesk Revit files in the current Autodesk 3ds Max scene, which of the following options are provided in the Combine Entities List? (Select all that apply.)

   a. By Revit Material

   b. By Revit Layer

   c. As One Object

   d. By Revit Camera

5. When an entire .MAX scene is brought into the current scene using **XREF Scenes**, the XREF objects are selectable but cannot be modified.

   a. True

   b. False

Command Summary

Button	Command	Location
⊞	**Absolute Mode**	• **Status Bar**
N/A	**Civil View**	• **Menu Bar:** Civil View
N/A	**Asset Tracking**	• **Menu Bar:** File>Reference
N/A	**Import**	• **Menu Bar:** File>Import
N/A	**Link AutoCAD**	• **Menu Bar:** File>Import
N/A	**Link FBX**	• **Menu Bar:** File>Import
N/A	**Link Revit**	• **Menu Bar:** File>Import
N/A	**Manage Links**	• **Menu Bar:** File>Reference
N/A	**Merge**	• **Menu Bar:** File>Import
	Select by Name	• **Main Toolbar**
	Select Object	• **Main Toolbar**
	Use Transform Coordinate Center	• **Main Toolbar**
N/A	**XRef Objects**	• **Menu Bar:** File>Reference
N/A	**XRef Scene**	• **Menu Bar:** File>Reference

Basic Modeling Techniques

Autodesk® 3ds Max® is a rendering and animation software that allows for objects to be directly modeled in the software. Modeling can be accomplished using Primitive Objects or Polygon Modeling tools that are further manipulated using Modifiers and Transforms to move, rotate, and scale them. Additionally, sub-object modes can be used to further modify and control the resulting objects.

Learning Objectives in this Chapter

- Identify the various primitive objects provided with the software.
- Apply changes to the model geometry using modifiers.
- Move, rotate, scale, and place objects, and constrain the movement of the Transform tools.
- Modify objects at a sub-object level.
- Work with various coordinate systems and transform systems.
- Create copies of the same object using various Clone options and create a single unit by grouping multiple objects together.
- Create and modify objects using the Polygon modeling tools.
- Review the status of the overall model and display information about the scene, such as polygon count, number of vertices, etc.

4.1 Model with Primitives

The Autodesk 3ds Max software enables you to create and adjust 3D geometry by creating a complex model from simple 3D objects called primitives, as shown in Figure 4–1.

Figure 4–1

- All various types of already built objects (i.e., Standard Primitives, Extended Primitives, Compound Objects, etc.) are listed in the Command Panel, Create panel (➕)>

  ● (Geometry), as shown in Figure 4–2. Each of these categories consists of a group of objects that can be modeled and modified to create simple or complex objects.

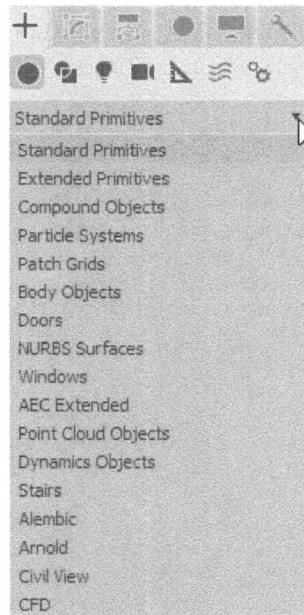

Standard Primitives
Standard Primitives
Extended Primitives
Compound Objects
Particle Systems
Patch Grids
Body Objects
Doors
NURBS Surfaces
Windows
AEC Extended
Point Cloud Objects
Dynamics Objects
Stairs
Alembic
Arnold
Civil View
CFD

Figure 4–2

- You can model the selected 3D object directly in the viewport by using the mouse to locate and specify the starting point and then dragging the mouse to pick the other locations (length, height, etc.).

- You can also enter the precise values in the edit boxes of the *Keyboard Entry* rollout in the Command Panel (as shown in Figure 4–3), and then click **Create**. You can either enter the values or use the spinner arrows to increase or decrease the values. After entering a value in a field, click in another field or press <Enter> to assign the values to the object.

- To modify a created object, use the *Parameters* rollout in the

  Modify panel ( ), as shown in Figure 4–4. Using the *Keyboard Entry* rollout to enter different values creates another object and does not modify the existing one.

Create objects

Figure 4–3

Modify objects

Figure 4–4

- You can also create geometry by modeling with modifiers, creating loft compound objects, or creating a 3D terrain from 2D contour objects.

Practice 4a

Modeling with Primitives

Practice Objective

- Create primitive objects by using standard primitives and the modify the object.

In this practice, you will model the base for the parking lot light fixtures by modeling the object using a standard primitive and then modifying its parameters using the Modify panel in the Command Panel.

You must set the paths to locate the External files and Xrefs used in the practice. If you have not done this already, return to Chapter 1 and complete Task 1 to Task 3 in *Practice 1a: Organizing Folders and Working with the Interface*. You only have to set the user paths once.

If a dialog box opens prompting you about a File Load: Mismatch, click OK to accept the default values.

1. Open **Modeling with Primitives.max**. It is an empty base scene file.

2. Click in the **Top** viewport to make it active. The orientation of the object being created depends on the active viewport. For this practice, you will create the cylinder with its height in the Z-axis direction.

3. In the Command Panel, verify that the Create panel (+) >

   (Geometry) is selected with **Standard Primitives** displayed in the drop-down list, as shown in Figure 4–5. In the *Object Type* rollout, click **Cylinder**.

Figure 4–5

The 0,0,0 location corresponds to the default axes (center of the active grid) of the construction plane. Any value entered for X,Y, and Z, offsets the object by that number in the specified direction.

You can enter the values in their respective fields or use the spinner arrows to increase or decrease the values. After entering a value in a field, click in another edit field or press <Enter> to assign the values to the object.

4. Click on the *Keyboard Entry* title bar to expand the rollout. Leave the X, Y, Z coordinates at **0'0"**. The software places the base center of the cylinder at 0,0,0, location. Set the following, as shown in Figure 4–6:

   • *Radius*: **1'0"**
   • *Height*: **3'0"**

Figure 4–6

5. Click **Create**. Note that a cylinder is created and is displayed in all viewports.

Hint: Creating Objects

After creating an object, you cannot change the parameters in the *Keyboard Entry* rollout. Changing the parameters in the *Keyboard Entry* rollout and clicking **Create** adds a second object. If you created another object, in the Main Toolbar, click

⤺ once to undo the creation of the second object. Use the

Modify panel ( ) to change the parameters.

---

6. In the Zoom Extents All flyout, click (Zoom Extents All) to display the base more clearly. Note that it zooms into the cylinder in all of the viewports.

7. With the cylinder still selected, in the Command Panel, select the Modify panel ( ). At the top of the modifier list, in the *Name* field, rename the object from *Cylinder001* to **LP Base**.

8. In the *Parameters* rollout, set the following, as shown Figure 4–7. Note the effect on the geometry:
   - *Radius*: **1'6"**
   - *Height Segments*: **1**
   - *Cap Segments:* **1**
   - *Sides*: **20**

Figure 4–7

The object colors are random and your objects can be of a different color than shown in the figure.

9. Select the Create panel (+) and in the *Object Type* rollout, click **Box** to create the anchor base plate. In the *Keyboard Entry* rollout set the following, as shown in Figure 4–8:
   - *X:* **0'0"**
   - *Y:* **0'0"**
   - *Z:* **3'0"**
   - *Length*: **1'4"**
   - *Width:* **1'4"**
   - *Height*: **0'2"**

The **X, Y, Z** values create the center of the base of the box at the 0,0,3 location, which is the top of the cylinder (the height of the cylinder is 3'-0").

10. Click **Create**. A box is created on top of the **LP Base** cylinder, as shown in Figure 4–8.

Figure 4–8

11. With the box still selected, select the Modify panel ( ) and rename the *Box001* as **LP Anchor Base**.

12. Save your work as **MyLight Pole.max**.

4.2 Modifiers and Transforms

The Autodesk 3ds Max software includes various modifiers and transforms that enable you to modify your geometry. They are described as follows:

Modifiers	• Adds geometric and property alterations to objects such as Extrude, Taper etc.
	• Listed in the Modifier Stack and their parameter values are available for adjustment afterwards.
Transforms	• Transforms are used to translate and scale objects in the scene.
	• Initiated by selecting the required buttons in the Main Toolbar or by using the Transform modes in the right-click quad menu.
	• Conducted by accessing a transform mode and entering new values, or graphically transforming objects on the screen.
	• Applied to objects after basic parameters and modifiers have been taken into account (except world-space modifiers). For example, if you scale a box, the **Length** parameter shown in the Modifier Stack does not take into account the effects of the scale transform.

- An object can have any number of modifiers, but only has a single set of transform values at any time.

- Transforms and almost all object and modifier parameters can be animated. For example, a walkthrough animation can be created using Move Transform to move the camera, its target, or both.

Modifiers

Any object that you create can be modified using the modifiers in the Modifier List, as shown in Figure 4–9. This list is located in

the Command Panel's Modify panel ( ) on top of the Modifier Stack.

- Click the down arrow to display the list and use the scroll bar to navigate through the complete list of modifiers.

- The modifiers in the Modifier drop-down list are placed in groups and then listed alphabetically.

- If you know the name of the modifier, you can enter the first letter to jump to that part of the selection list.

- Once a modifier is applied, it displays in the Modifier stack as shown in Figure 4–10.

- The Modifier stack lists modifiers in reverse historical order. In Figure (right side), *Taper* modifier is applied after the *Extrude* modifier.

- The parameters of the objects and modifiers are always accessible through the Modifier stack, irrespective of their position in the stack.

Figure 4–9   Figure 4–10

Transform Tools

The Transform tools are available in the Main Toolbar, as shown in Figure 4–11.

Figure 4–11

The available Transform tools are described as follows:

✛	**Select and Move**
↻	**Select and Rotate**
	Select and Scale: Scaling has three flyout options: ▪(Uniform), ▪ (Non-uniform), and ▪ (Squash). • **Non-uniform:** Enables you to scale one or two axes independently. • **Squash**: Enables you to do the same, but scaling one or two axes applies a simultaneous opposite scaling to the other(s). The Scale Transform gizmo also has the tools for Non-uniform scaling.
	Select and Place / Select and Rotate: Enables you to locate and position/locate and rotate an object with respect to the surface of another object. Right-click on **Select and Place** and use the Placement Settings dialog box (as shown in the image below) to customize how the objects are aligned. Right-clicking on **Select and Rotate** opens the same dialog box with the Rotate option selected.

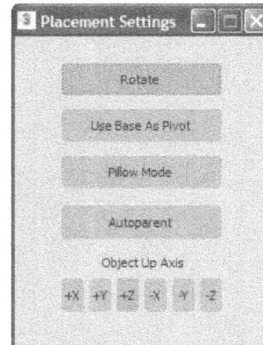

- **Rotate:** Enables you to click and drag an object to rotate around the local axis that is specified with the object Up Axis.
- **Use Base As Pivot:** Constrains the base of the object as the contact point with the surface of another object. By default, the pivot point of the object is used as the contact point.
- **Pillow Mode:** Enables you to move the objects around each other, but restricts them from intersecting. Useful when moving the object over uneven surfaces.
- **Autoparent:** Automatically links the object that is being placed as a child of the object it is being placed on, creating a hierarchical relationship.
- **Object Up Axis:** The selected up axis is used as the local axis on the object that is being moved.

Hint: XForm Modifier with Scale

To avoid problems in animation, it is recommended that you do not to use the Scale transform directly on objects. Instead, apply an XForm modifier to the objects and then **Scale** the XForm gizmo.

To display a toolbar, right-click anywhere on an empty space in the Main Toolbar and select the required toolbar.

- Transforms can be constrained to one or two axes by selecting one of the buttons in the Axis Constraints toolbar, as shown in Figure 4–12. However, it is more common to use the gizmos or the keyboard shortcuts to constrain the transforms. This toolbar is hidden by default.

- When a transform mode is active, a Transform gizmo displays (as shown in Figure 4–13) on the selected object on the screen.

Figure 4–12

Move   Rotate   Scale

Figure 4–13

- Clicking and dragging over the gizmo enables you to perform the transform interactively on the screen. You can also constrain the transform by highlighting an axis handle on the gizmo before clicking and dragging.

- You can change the display size of the transform gizmo interactively in the viewport. Pressing <-> decreases its display size while as pressing <=> increases its display size.

- You can apply a transform accurately by entering (or using spinners) the required transform values in the *Transform Type-In* area, in the Status Bar, as shown in Figure 4–14.

X: 50.0   Y: -32.0   Z: 11.0

Figure 4–14

- In the Main Toolbar, right-click on **Transform** to open its Transform Type-In dialog box, as shown in Figure 4–15 for the Move transform. The Transform Type-In dialog box can be also be accessed by clicking ☐ (Settings) in the right-click quad menu, as shown in Figure 4–16.

| Figure 4–15 | Figure 4–16 |

- Transform modes remain active until they are canceled by either clicking (Select Object) in the Main Toolbar or by pressing <Q>.

- Click (Select Object) after you have finished a transform to avoid accidentally moving, rotating, or scaling objects while making selections.

Practice 4b

Modeling with Modifiers and Transforms

Practice Objectives

- Create a 2D shape and then extrude it into a 3D object.
- Create primitive solids dynamically and modify objects.
- Transform objects to place them at the right location.

In this practice, you will refine the parking lot lighting fixture by creating a 2D shape and then extruding it to create a 3D object. You will create primitive objects dynamically in the viewport and then modify the objects using various modifiers in the Command Panel. You will also use Transforms (**Move**, **Rotate**, and **Place**) to place the created objects in the correct scene positions.

You must set the paths to locate the External files and Xrefs used in the practice. If you have not done this already, return to Chapter 1 and complete Task 1 to Task 3 in *Practice 1a: Organizing Folders and Working with the Interface*. You only have to set the user paths once.

Task 1 - Extrude and Adjust the Light Pole.

Modeling 3D geometry from 2D shapes is discussed in detail later in the learning guide.

To create the rectangular light pole, create a 2D cross-section shape and then extrude it into a 3D object. This approach is another way to create 3D geometry.

1. Open **Modeling with Modifiers and Transforms.max**.

2. Make the **Top** viewport active. In the Create panel (+),

   click ![Shapes icon] (Shapes) to create 2D objects. Verify that *Splines* displays in the drop-down list and click **Rectangle**, as shown in Figure 4–17.

Figure 4–17

The corner radius fillets the corners of the rectangle.

3. In the Command Panel, expand the *Keyboard Entry* rollout and set the following:
   - *X*: **0'0"**
   - *Y*: **0'0"**
   - *Z*: **3'2"**
   - *Length*: **0'6"**
   - *Width*: **0'6"**
   - *Corner Radius*: **0'1"**

4. Click **Create**. A 2D rectangle is created on top of the base plate.

The modifiers in the Modifier drop-down list are placed in groups and then listed alphabetically. Use the scroll bar to navigate through the list.

5. With the rectangle still selected, select the Modify panel

   ( ). Expand the Modifier List (click down arrow) and select **Extrude** in the *OBJECT-SPACE MODIFIERS* category. Note that **Extrude** is listed in the Modifier Stack above the **Rectangle** entry, as shown in Figure 4–18.

Figure 4–18

6. Rename the object *Rectangle001* as **LP Pole**.

7. In the *Parameters* rollout, set *Amount* to **15'0"** and leave the other parameters as the defaults. Note that the rectangle is extruded and becomes a rectangular-shaped pole.

The object colors are random and your objects can be of a different color than shown in the figure.

8. In the **Perspective** viewport, use **Zoom** and **Pan** to get a closer look at the light pole, as shown in Figure 4–19. Note how much detail the light pole's fillet adds to the model.

Figure 4–19

Hint: Simple Models

If the object is to be used only as a background item, you should remove any unnecessary detail. Keeping models simple reduces the file size and speeds up software performance and rendering times.

Although the Extrude modifier is listed directly above the Rectangle object in the Modifier Stack, the rectangle's parameters are still accessible and can be changed anytime.

9. With the **LP Pole selected**, in the Modify panel ( ), in the Modifier Stack, select **Rectangle**. It is highlighted in blue. In the *Interpolation* rollout, change *Steps* to **2** and press <Enter>, as shown in Figure 4–20. The fillet divisions are reduced, as shown in Figure 4–21.

Figure 4–20

Figure 4–21

10. Save your work as **MyLightPole01.max**.

Task 2 - Taper the Light Pole.

Use the scroll bar to navigate to Taper near the bottom of the list.

1. In the Modifier Stack, select **Extrude** (so that the next modifier *Taper* is applied after it). In the Modifier List, select **Taper**. Note that the *Taper* displays above the *Extrude* in the Modifier Stack, as shown in Figure 4–22. The Modifier Stack lists modifiers in reverse historical order.

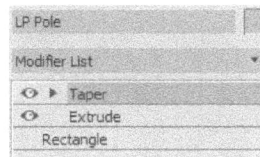

Figure 4–22

2. With **Taper** selected, in the *Parameters* rollout, set *Amount* to **-0.5** and press <Enter>. You can still adjust the original **Rectangle** and **Extrude** parameters by selecting them in the Modifier Stack.

3. Click ⬚ (Zoom Extents All) to see all of the objects in the viewports. Note the taper on the pole towards the top.

4. Save your work incrementally as **MyLightPole02.max**.

Task 3 - Create the Fixture Housing and Globe.

1. In the **Perspective** viewport, zoom in so that the LP Base object displays. Additionally, maximize the **Perspective** viewport.

2. In the Create panel (+)> ● (Geometry), in the Standard Primitives drop-down list, select **Extended Primitives** as a sub-category. In the *Object Type* rollout, click **ChamferCyl**.

You do not have to be accurate because you will modify the dimensions later.

3. In the **Perspective** viewport, next to the base (LP Base), click and drag the left mouse button to size the radius to roughly **2'0"** (Note the *Parameters* rollout in the Command Panel where the Radius changes interactively as you move the cursor). After releasing the mouse button, move the cursor up the screen slightly to give the cylinder a height of approximately **1'0"**. Click a second time to set the cylinder height and complete the object creation process. The object should display as shown in Figure 4–23.

Figure 4–23

4. With the **ChamferCyl** object still selected, in the Command Panel, select the Modify panel ( ). Name the object **LP Fixture Housing** and modify the parameters, as shown in Figure 4–24.

5. In the Create panel (+), verify that (Geometry) is selected. In the drop-down list, select **Standard Primitives.** In the *Object Type* rollout, click **Sphere** to create the fixture's globe. Click and drag anywhere on the screen to size a sphere of approximately **1'0"** in radius. Select the Modify panel ( ) and assign the parameters, as shown in Figure 4–25.

A value of 0.5 for the hemisphere creates half a sphere.

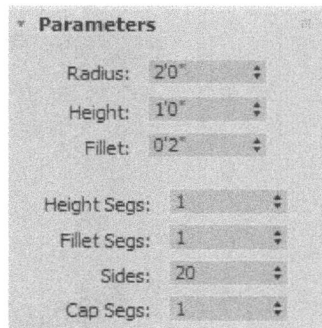

Parameters	
Radius:	2'0"
Height:	1'0"
Fillet:	0'2"
Height Segs:	1
Fillet Segs:	1
Sides:	20
Cap Segs:	1

Parameters	
Radius:	1'0"
Segments:	10
	✔ Smooth
Hemisphere:	0.5
● Chop	Squash
	Slice On
Slice From:	0.0

| Figure 4–24 | Figure 4–25 |

6. Select **Squash**. This option generates more faces and creates a smoother appearance.

7. Rename the hemisphere **LP Fixture Globe**.

8. Save your work incrementally as **MyLightPole03.max**.

Task 4 - Use Transforms to Position Objects.

---

1. Select the **LP Fixture Housing** (the chamfered cylinder) and in the Main Toolbar, click (Select and Move).

2. In the Main Toolbar, set the *Reference Coordinate System* to **World** and click [icon] (Use Pivot Point Center), as shown in Figure 4–26.

Figure 4–26

3. The Move gizmo displays for the object, as shown in Figure 4–27. Move the fixture housing by clicking and dragging the gizmo's axis handles and plane handles. By default, the gizmo displays at the object's pivot point, located at the bottom center for this object.

Figure 4–27

*The [icon] (Absolute Mode) toggles with [icon] (Offset Mode). If the values are entered in **Offset Mode**, they are added to the current coordinates. This option is useful if you want to move an object a certain distance from the current position.*

4. To position the object correctly, verify that [icon] (Absolute Mode Transform Type-In) displays in the Status Bar. Set the following in the type in edit boxes, as shown in Figure 4–28:
   - *X*: **0'0"**
   - *Y*: **-6'0"**
   - *Z*: **19'0"**

Figure 4–28

5. Click ![icon](Zoom Extents All) to display all of the objects in the viewports. In the **Left** viewport, note that the **LP Fixture Housing** (the chamfered cylinder) has now moved to the top right side of the light pole assembly.

6. As the **Move** transform and **Absolute Mode** are already active, select **LP Fixture Globe** (hemisphere) and enter the same X, Y, Z coordinates as you did for LP Fixture Housing (*X:* **0'0"**, *Y:* **-6'0"**, *Z:* **19'0"**). The half globe moves inside the fixture housing.

7. With the half globe still selected, in the Main Toolbar, click

   ![icon](Select and Rotate).

8. In the Status Bar, note that the *X, Y, Z Transform Type-In* fields display the current rotations of **0**. Set *X* to **180** and note the position of the globe is inverted.

9. Toggle **Maxmize** to the four viewport view. The object should display as shown in Figure 4–29 in the **Left** viewport.

Figure 4–29

10. Click ![icon](Select Object) or press <Q> to end the **Rotate** transform to avoid rotating objects accidentally.

11. Save your work incrementally as **MyLightPole04.max**.

Task 5 - Use Additional Transforms to Place Objects.

You will create a nut and bolt group and place it on the top surface of the anchor plate.

1. In the **Perspective** viewport, zoom into LP Base (base cylinder).

2. In the Create panel (+), ensure that ● (Geometry) and **Standard Primitives** as a sub-category is selected. In the *Object Type* rollout, click **Cylinder**.

3. In the **Perspective** viewport, click and create a cylinder smaller than the base object.

4. With the new cylinder selected, select the Modify panel (⌒). Rename the new cylinder as **LP Nut** and assign the parameters shown in Figure 4–30.

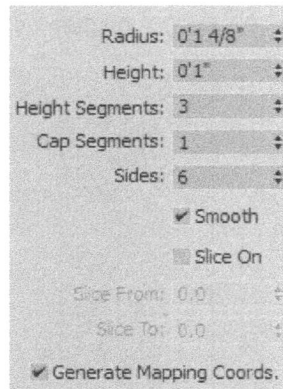

Radius:	0'1 4/8" ↕
Height:	0'1" ↕
Height Segments:	3 ↕
Cap Segments:	1 ↕
Sides:	6 ↕
	☑ Smooth
	▨ Slice On
Slice From:	0.0 ↕
Slice To:	0.0 ↕
☑ Generate Mapping Coords.	

Figure 4–30

5. With **LP Nut** still selected, click ⬈ (Zoom Extents All Selected) so that it is zoomed in on all the viewports.

6. Click in the **Top** viewport to activate it and clear the selection.

7. In the Command Panel>Create (+)> ● (Geometry), verify that **Standard Primitives** is selected. In the *Object Type* rollout, click **Cylinder**, and in the **Top** viewport create a small cylinder next to LP Nut.

8. With the new cylinder selected, select the Modify panel ( ). Rename the new cylinder as **LP Bolt** and assign the parameters, as shown in Figure 4–31. The bolt displays as shown in Figure 4–32.

▼ **Parameters**

Radius: 0'0 6/8"
Height: -0'0 3/8"
Height Segments: 2
Cap Segments: 1
Sides: 20
☑ Smooth
☐ Slice On
Slice From: 0.0
Slice To: 0.0
☑ Generate Mapping Coords.
☑ Real-World Map Size

Figure 4–31   **Figure 4–32**

9. With **LP Bolt** selected, in the Main Toolbar, click (Select and Place).

10. In the **Perspective** viewport, click and hold over the selected **LP Bolt** object. While holding, drag it over the **LP Nut** object. Note that when you move the **LP Bolt** object along the sides of the **LP Nut** object, it automatically flips on its side, as shown in Figure 4–33. Drag the selected **LP Bolt** object along the top surface of the **LP Nut** object and note how it flips so that its base touches the top surface. Place the **LP Bolt** object at the approximate center of the **LP Nut** object, as shown in Figure 4–34.

Figure 4–33

Figure 4–34

11. Click ![Select Object icon] (Select Object) in the Main Toolbar to exit the Placement command.

12. Select both the **LP Nut** and the **LP Bolt** objects (<Ctrl>) and select **Group>Group**. In the Group dialog box, name the grouped object as **LP Anchor** and click **OK**.

13. Activate the **Perspective** viewport (if not already active) and click ![Maximize Viewport Toggle icon] (Maximize Viewport Toggle), or use <Alt>+<W> to maximize the viewport.

14. Zoom and pan so that you can clearly see the **LP Anchor** group and the **LP Anchor Base**, as shown in Figure 4–35.

Figure 4–35

15. In the Main Toolbar, click ![Select and Place icon] (Select and Place). Click and hold on the **LP Anchor** group and then drag it on top of the LP Anchor Base plate object. Place the **LP Anchor** group near one of the corners of the plate, as shown in Figure 4–36.

   • Note that the group object is placed halfway inside the LP Anchor Base object.as shown in Figure 4–37.

Figure 4–36   **Figure 4–37**

16. In the Main Toolbar, right-click on ![icon] (Select and Place). In the Placement Settings dialog box, select **Pillow Mode** to activate it.

17. Click on the **LP Anchor** group object and slightly move it. Note how its base now touches the top surface of the anchor plate. Place it in one of the corners, as shown in Figure 4–38. Close the Placement Settings dialog box.

Figure 4–38

*It might be easier to copy the object in the **Top** viewport.*

18. Hold <Shift> and then click and drag a copy of the **LP Anchor** group object to place it near the next corner of the plate. Click **OK** in the Clone Options dialog box.

19. While still holding <Shift>, place two more copies of the objects at the other corners of the plate. A total of four **LP Anchor** group objects should now be placed at the four corners of the anchor plate, as shown in Figure 4–39.

Figure 4–39

20. Save your work incrementally as **MyLightPole05.max**.

4.3 Sub-Object Mode

Many of the objects and modifiers available in the Autodesk 3ds Max software contain sub-objects that can be independently adjusted through transforms and special modifier controls. These sub-objects are adjusted through a special Autodesk 3ds Max state called Sub-object mode. For example, the **Taper** modifier in the column has Gizmo and Center sub-objects (as shown in Figure 4–40) that can be adjusted to position the Taper.

Figure 4–40

Working in Sub-Object Mode

Sub-object mode is activated through the Modifier Stack. You can expand the modifier by clicking ▶ (arrow) next to the object or modifier that has sub-objects, then clicking the sub-object level to be adjusted.

- You can only have one object selected to enter the Sub-object mode. When Sub-object mode is active, the sub-object level (or the modifier name if the sub-object list has not been expanded) is highlighted in blue (with the default user interface settings).

- You cannot clear the currently selected object while in Sub-object mode. Therefore, to edit another object you must first exit Sub-object mode. To do so, click the level of the Modifier Stack presently highlighted to toggle it off.

Geometric Edits through Sub-objects

*You can also use the **Polygon Modeling** tools in the ribbon to perform modeling and use modifiers with the **Edit Poly** technique.*

A whole range of explicit geometric changes can be made through Sub-object mode.

*   Objects imported into the Autodesk 3ds Max software often take the shape of **Editable Splines** or **Editable Meshes**. These have sub-object controls that can be edited directly. For example, a group of vertices in an Editable Mesh can be selected, moved, or deleted separate to the rest of the geometry.

*   Many Autodesk 3ds Max objects can also have the controls applied to them through an **Edit Spline** modifier (for 2D objects) or an **Edit Mesh** or **Edit Poly** modifier (for 3D objects). This includes geometry linked to AutoCAD drawings that list only as *Linked Geometry* in the Modify panel.

*   Figure 4–41 shows an example of a Box that is being edited geometrically by lowering two of its vertices with the **Move** transform.

Figure 4–41

*   The **Edit Mesh** modifier is best for objects based on a triangular mesh, such as triangulated terrain models.

*   The **Edit Poly** modifier is best for objects with faces of more than three vertices, such as rectangular objects.

*   To easily review and make changes, it is recommended to adjust objects through their core parameters (such as the length, width, and height of a primitive) and standard modifiers. When required, you can use Spline, Mesh, and Poly for editing.

*   A single hotkey can be used to easily and quickly toggle between the various sub-object levels. This speeds up your overall modeling workflow. To use this, to hover the cursor over the required sub-object level and press the hotkey.

Geometric Sub-Objects

The Editable Spline, Editable Mesh, and Editable Poly objects (and any other object with an Edit Spline, Edit Mesh, or Edit Poly Modifier applied to it) share a number of common Sub-object modes. These are described as follows:

	Vertex: The individual 3D points that define an object (Edit Spline, Edit Mesh, or Edit Poly).
	Segment: A single line or curve segment of an Editable Spline.
	Spline: A series of one or more connected Editable Spline segments. Segments are considered connected if they share a common vertex.
	Edge: The linear segments connecting vertices with Edit Mesh or Edit Poly. Three edges are shown in the button.
	Face: The triangular surface area defined by three edges (Edit Mesh only).
	Border: A series of edges that define an opening in an Editable Poly (only).
	Polygon: Enables you to work with coplanar faces (Edit Mesh) or a defined polygon (Edit Poly).
	Element: Enables you to work with all of the faces or polygons that form a contiguous whole (Edit Mesh or Edit Poly).

Smoothing

One of the most important properties controlled at the face or polygon sub-object level is smoothing. Figure 4–42 shows the same geometry without and with smoothing applied.

Figure 4–42

- The Autodesk 3ds Max software can have two adjacent faces appear to be smooth or faceted. When smoothed, faces display smooth but the software does not adjust the actual geometry.

- Smoothing is controlled by smoothing groups. Each face or polygon can be a member of up to 32 smoothing groups. If two adjacent faces share a common smoothing group, the software attempts to blend the surfaces together to disguise the edge that separates them.

- Figure 4–43 show an example of the smoothing groups for the selected faces that controls polygon smoothing groups (in Edit Mesh and Edit Poly). When some but not all selected faces fall into a particular smoothing group, that group's box is shown without a number.

Figure 4–43

- Alternatively, the **Auto Smooth** feature automatically places adjacent selected faces into smoothing groups if their normal vectors have an angle of separation equal to or less than the Auto Smooth angle.

Caddy Display for Edit Poly Modifier

The caddy display (shown in Figure 4–44) enables you to enter values on the screen for various modifiers at the Edit Poly sub-object level. The modifications are dynamically updated and reflected in the model.

- To dynamically view and update the changes, you can type the values in the edit boxes or you can hold and drag the spinner arrows.

- Click ⊘ to accept the change or ⊕ to accept the change and continue in the same modifier.

Figure 4–44

- The caddy interface can be accessed through:

  - **Modeling ribbon**: Hold <Shift> and select the sub-object level modifier tool or click the down arrow next to the modifier and select the required setting, as shown for the Bevel modifier in Figure 4–45.

Figure 4–45

  - **Command Panel**: Click ▢ (Settings) next to the sub-object level modifier option. This enables you to enter the values while performing the operation.

- The caddy interface display is controlled by the **Enable Caddy Controls** option in the Preference Settings dialog box>*General* tab>*UI Display* area, as shown in Figure 4–46. By default, this option is selected.

Figure 4–46

Practice 4c

Modeling with Edit Poly in Sub-Object Mode

Practice Objective

- Modify objects at a sub-object level.

In this practice, you will add some detail to the concrete base of the light pole by chamfering (beveling) the outside top of the cylinder and then add smoothing to it.

You must set the paths to locate the External files and Xrefs used in the practice. If you have not done this already, return to Chapter 1 and complete Task 1 to Task 3 in *Practice 1a: Organizing Folders and Working with the Interface*. You only have to set the user paths once.

1. Open **Edit Poly in Sub-Object Mode.max**.

2. In the **Perspective** viewport, select **LP Base** and click

   (Zoom Extents Selected). Use (Zoom) and

   (Orbit) to display the base object similar to that shown in Figure 4–47.

Figure 4–47

3. In the Modify panel ( ), select **Edit Poly** from the Modifier List. Click ▶ (arrow sign) for Edit Poly to display its Sub-object modes. Select **Polygon** to activate the Sub-object mode at the Polygon level. The highlighting in the Modifier Stack indicates that you are in the Polygon Sub-object mode, as shown in Figure 4–48.

Figure 4–48

Hint: Using Modeling Tools in the Ribbon

You can also perform all of the commands using the **Polygon Modeling** tools in the Modeling ribbon. With the object selected, select the *Polygon Modeling* tab in the *Modeling* tab, in the ribbon. In the drop-down list, select **Apply Edit Poly**

Mod, as shown in Figure 4–49. Click ☐ for **Polygon** sub-object level. Note that the selections that you make in the ribbon are reflected in the Command Panel and vice-versa.

Figure 4–49

4. Select the polygon at the top of the cylinder, as shown in Figure 4–50. The selected polygon tuns red.

Figure 4–50

5. Creating a 1" bevel will raise the cylinder top by 1". In preparation, you will first lower the top of the cylinder by that same 1". In the Main Toolbar, click ✛ (Select and Move). Note that the Move gizmo only displays for the selected polygon.

6. In the Status Bar, click ⊞ (Absolute Mode Transform) to toggle it to ⌐ (Offset Mode Transform) and set *Z* to **-0'1"**. Press <Enter>. The cylinder geometry is adjusted by moving the polygon down.

7. Right-click to activate the **Left** viewport (keeping the polygon selected) and zoom into the base area. Note that the base is not touching the base plate anymore, as shown in Figure 4–51.

*The rollouts in the Command Panel might extend below the display window. To scroll, hover the cursor over an empty gray area until it displays as a **Hand** icon, then hold and drag the cursor up or down to locate the required rollout.*

8. In the Command Panel, scroll down and locate the *Edit Polygons* rollout. Expand the *Edit Polygons* rollout and next to **Bevel**, click ▢ (Settings), as shown in Figure 4–52.

Figure 4–51

Figure 4–52

In the caddy display, when you select the edit box, its icon displays as a spinner and the edit name (Height or Outline) displays in addition to the modifier name (Bevel) at the top. You can enter new values in the edit box or use the spinner to change the values.

9. The caddy display opens on the screen, in the **Left** viewport. Hover the cursor over the ⬚ *Height* edit box and set its value to **0'1"** and an ⬚ *Outline* of **-0'1"**, as shown in Figure 4–53. Click ✓. Verify that the caddy display closes and the base is beveled, as shown in Figure 4–54.

Figure 4–53   **Figure 4–54**

10. To make the newly created faces smooth you will adjust the smoothing groups. While still in Polygon Sub-object mode, in the menu bar, expand **Edit** and select **Select All** to select all of the polygons in the base object.

11. In the Command Panel, scroll down and locate the *Polygon: Smoothing Groups* rollout. Click **Clear All** to remove the existing smoothing. Set the *AutoSmooth angle* to **30**, as shown in Figure 4–55. Click **Auto Smooth**.

Figure 4–55

12. To end Sub-object mode, in the Command Panel>Modifier Stack, click the **Polygon** highlighted in blue to clear the selection.

13. To display the effect of the smoothing change, in the **Perspective** viewport, clear the object selection by clicking anywhere in empty space. The 30 degrees angle enabled the newly created faces to smooth across each other, but the faces are not smoothed with the top of the cylinder, as shown in Figure 4–56. This is the chamfered appearance that was originally intended. A larger smoothing angle enables the chamfered faces between the top and sides to smooth out.

*To display the smoothing effect, toggle off **Edged Faces** in the Viewport Shading label, if it is enabled.*

Figure 4–56

14. In the Main Toolbar, click ![icon] (Select Object) to end the Move Transform mode as a precaution to avoid moving objects accidentally while making further selections.

15. Save your work as **MyLightPole06.max**.

4.4 Reference Coordinate Systems and Transform Centers

All geometry in the Autodesk 3ds Max software is referenced to a base coordinate system called the Home Grid.

- You can create your own coordinate systems by creating and locating grid objects, available in the Helpers Category in the Create panel.

- You can also create objects in the Auto-grid mode, which creates a temporary 3D Grid aligned to the object directly under the crosshairs. The **AutoGrid** option can be found in the Create panel, in the *Object Type* rollout, as shown Figure 4–57. If you hold <Alt>, the AutoGrid remains available for future use. If you use AutoGrid without any key pressed, the grid disappears after object creation.

Figure 4–57

Reference Coordinate Systems

The current Reference Coordinate System might differ depending on which view you are in and which transform is active. It is recommended that new users stay in the **World** system to avoid confusion from changing axis labels. By default, the Reference Coordinate system is set to **View**.

- In the Main Toolbar, the options listed in the Reference Coordinate System drop-down list (shown Figure 4–58) control how transform values are read. Note that a single grid is active at any one time.

Figure 4–58

- In the **World** coordinate system the X, Y, and Z axes are interpreted based on the Home Grid, even if a user-defined grid is active. To use the coordinates of the active user-defined grid instead, select the **Grid** option.

- In the **Screen** coordinate system the X-axis is always measured along the bottom of the viewport, the Y-axis is always measured along the side, and the Z-axis is measured perpendicularly out of the screen.

- The **View** system is a combination of **World** and **Screen**. In an orthographic view, the **Screen** system is used, while in other views the **World** system is used.

- The **Local** system considers the coordinate system of the selected object. Note that only the Z axis of the object is considered, which can cause unpredictable changes along the X and Y axis.

- The **Grid** system is based on the currently active grid and uses its coordinate system.

- The **Working** option enables you to use the Working Pivot. It is a temporary modeling pivot tool you create from the Hierarchy panel's *Pivot* tab. Generally you need to assign a hotkey to **Use Working Pivot** and **Edit Working Pivot** to make them functional tools.

- The **Local Aligned** option is used with sub-objects in an editable mesh or poly. It calculates all three (X,Y,Z) axes by using the coordinate system of the selected object. It can be used when multiple sub-objects need to be adjusted at the same time.

- The **Pick** option enables you to pick any object in the viewport or from a list and use the reference coordinate system of that object as the reference for transforms. You can use XRef objects with the **Pick** option.

Transform Centers

Transforms are applied through a Transform Center point indicated by the Transform gizmo. The Transform Center options are available in the Main Toolbar, in the Transform Center flyout, as shown Figure 4–59.

Figure 4–59

Pivot Point Center: Transforms are applied through each selected object's pivot point. Pivots often default to the bottom center or geometric center of objects. Pivot points can be adjusted through controls in the Hierarchy panel. Select this option if you want to rotate many objects, each around its own center.

Selection Center: Transforms are applied through the geometric center of all selected objects.

Transform Coordinate Center: Transforms are applied through the origin point of the current Reference Coordinate System. For example, if you wanted to rotate objects around their individual pivot points about the World Z-axis, you would select the World Coordinate System and Pivot Point Transform Center. Alternatively, to rotate all of the objects around the origin, you would do the same with the Transform Coordinate Center.

- The Transform Center might automatically change depending on whether one or multiple objects are selected, and on the active transform.

- The Reference Coordinate System and Transform Center can be held using **Constant** in the Preference Settings dialog box, in the *General* tab, as shown in Figure 4–60.

Figure 4–60

4.5 Cloning and Grouping

Cloning

In Autodesk 3ds Max, objects can be duplicated using the **Clone** option (**Edit>Clone**), which opens the Clone Options dialog box, as shown in Figure 4–61.

Figure 4–61

Copy	Makes an independent copy without a dynamic link to the source object.
Instance	Makes the duplicate and original Instances of each other. Changes made to any Instance automatically update all Instances, including changes to Modifiers, property changes, and material assignments (except for Transforms).
Reference	A one-directional link where changes made to the original object affect the duplicate. You can apply Modifiers to the Reference without affecting the Source object.

- To access the **Clone** command, an object should be selected first, otherwise it remains grayed out.

- You can also clone an object by holding <Shift> while transforming through a click and drag on the Transform gizmo. In this procedure, you have an additional option for specifying the number of copies you want to make, which are arrayed at the same Transform value.

- The *Controller* area in the Clone Options dialog box applies to objects in a group or hierarchy.

- Objects that are instanced or referenced display with the Modifier Stack text in bold type. Instancing or referencing can be disabled by right-clicking on the item in the Modifier Stack and selecting **Make Unique**.

Grouping

Grouping enables multiple objects to be treated as a single unit, for selection and transforms. The various grouping options are available in the **Group** menu, as shown in Figure 4–62.

Figure 4–62

Group	Creates a group out of all of the currently selected objects. Groups can have other groups inside them (nested groups).
Ungroup	Dissolves any selected groups back into their constituent objects.
Open/Close	Enables you to select, modify, and transform individual group members as if they were not in a group. The group is still defined; however, it can be Closed to treat the objects as a single unit again.
Open Recursively	Enables you to select, modify, and transform individual members at any level in a group. The group is still defined. Use the **Close** command to restore the original group.
Attach	Enables you to add another object to a group. First select the objects to be attached, then select the **Attach** option in the **Group** menu. When prompted, select a closed group to which to add the objects.
Detach	Enables you to remove selected objects from a group. You must first open the group to select the objects to be detached.
Explode	Dissolves the selected groups and any groups nested inside them.
Assembly	Special case object grouping that are intended for creation of lighting assemblies called luminaires, and for character assemblies.

- Groups are located in the Command Panel's Modify panel, with group name in bold type, and a blank Modifier Stack. The Modifier Stack of individual group members displays if it is opened.

- Groups can be copied, instanced, and referenced.

- It is recommended not to use grouping on objects that are linked into a hierarchy and then animated.

Practice 4d | Modeling with Coordinate Systems

Practice Objective

- Create an object and modify the parameters.

In this practice, you will add the Light Pole Mounting Arm to the Light Pole model by creating the model and modifying the parameters.

You must set the paths to locate the External files and Xrefs used in the practice. If you have not done this already, return to Chapter 1 and complete Task 1 to Task 3 in *Practice 1a: Organizing Folders and Working with the Interface*. You only have to set the user paths once.

*If a dialog box opens prompting you about a File Load: Mismatch, click **OK** to accept the default values.*

1. Open **Modeling with Coordinate Systems.max**.

2. Activate the **Front** viewport, if required.

3. Use a combination of **Zoom** and **Pan** to zoom into the top portion, as shown in Figure 4–63. If the Grid is showing in the **Front** view, in the *Viewport* label, click [+] and select **Show Grids** to clear it. Alternatively, you can press <G> to toggle the grid on or off.

4. In the Create panel (+)> ● (Geometry), click **Box**. Use the cursor to create a small box near the top of the light pole with approximate dimensions for *Length*, *Width*, and *Height*, as shown in Figure 4–64.

Figure 4–63   Figure 4–64

The object creation orientation depends on the viewport in which it is being created.

5. With this box still selected, in the Modify panel ( ), in the *Parameters* rollout, set the following, as shown in Figure 4–65:

   - *Name:* **LP Mounting Arm**
   - *Length*: **0'3"**
   - *Width*: **0'3"**
   - *Height*: **4'6"**
   - *Height Segs*: **6**

6. In the **Perspective** view, use a combination of **Zoom**, **Pan**, and **Orbit** to zoom into the **LP Mounting Arm**, as shown in Figure 4–65. Since you created the box in the **Front** viewport, the height of the box is measured perpendicular to the view, in this case along the world Y-axis.

Figure 4–65

7. With the LP Mounting arm selected, click (Select and Move). In the Status Bar, set the transform mode to

   (Absolute mode) and set the location of the mounting arm with the Z value at **18'0"**, as shown in Figure 4–66.

Figure 4–66

8. In the Modifier List, select **Bend** to curve the arm to the housing. In the Parameters, set the following:

   - *Bend Angle*: **30** degrees
   - *Direction*: **-90** degrees

   Note that the arm is bent and extended.

9. Save your work as **MyLightPole07.max**.

Practice 4e

Cloning and Grouping

Practice Objectives

- Create a single unit of multiple objects.
- Clone an instance of the group and modify it.

In this practice, you will complete the model of the light pole using Cloning and Groups. You will first create a single unit by grouping multiple objects. You will then clone an instance of a group and modify the instance so that the original object is modified as well.

You must set the paths to locate the External files and Xrefs used in the practice. If you have not done this already, return to Chapter 1 and complete Task 1 to Task 3 in *Practice 1a: Organizing Folders and Working with the Interface*. You only have to set the user paths once.

1. Open **Cloning and Grouping.max**.

If the Scene Explorer is not displayed, select ***Tools>Scene Explorer***

or click 🗔 *(Toggle Scene Explorer) in the Main Toolbar.*

2. In the Scene Explorer, (⬛ (Display None) and ⬤ (Display Geometry) to display the scene geometry only. Select **LP Fixture Globe**, **LP Fixture Housing**, and **LP Mounting Arm** (use <Ctrl> to select multiple items), as shown in Figure 4–67. Note that the three items are selected in the viewports.

3. In the menu bar, select **Group>Group** to combine the three objects together into a single, selectable unit. In the Group dialog box, name the group **LP Fixture**, as shown in Figure 4–67. Click **OK**.

Figure 4–67

4. In the Scene Explorer, note that the group name is identified with the ▣ symbol and the geometry objects displayed under it, as shown in Figure 4–68. In the Scene Explorer, select the group **LP Fixture** and note that all the three objects are selected in the viewport. Similarly, select **LP Fixture Globe** in the Scene Explorer and note that the three objects are still selected in the viewports, as shown in Figure 4–68.

Figure 4–68

5. In the Scene Explorer, select the group **LP Fixture** and then in the menu bar, select **Group>Open**. The group remains intact but a pink bounding box encloses the group objects indicating that it is an open group. Here, you can select, manipulate, and transform the three component objects individually.

6. With one or more of the group components selected, in the menu bar, select **Group>Close**. The pink bounding box is cleared with all of the group objects selected, indicating that it is treated as a single object and that the components cannot be modified separately.

7. With the **LP Fixture** group selected, in the menu bar, select **Edit>Clone**.

8. In the Clone Options dialog box, in the *Object* area, select **Instance** (if not already selected) leaving all other options at their default values, as shown in Figure 4–69. Click **OK**.

   - The original and the copy now directly overlay each other. Note that in the Scene Explorer, another group with the name **LP Fixture001** is created.

Figure 4–69

9. In the Scene Explorer, select **LP Fixture001**.

10. In the Main Toolbar, click (Select and Rotate).

11. The position of the Transform gizmo is dependent on the Reference Coordinate System and the active **Use Transform**. In the Main Toolbar, in the Reference Coordinate System, select **Parent**, as shown in Figure 4–70.

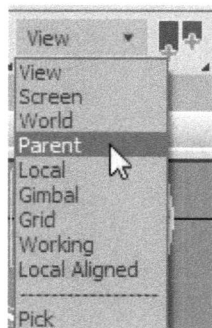

Figure 4–70

12. In the Use Transform flyout, click (Use Pivot Point Center). Note in the **Top** viewport that the Rotate transform gizmo is in the center of the group, as shown in Figure 4–71. This rotation will not place **LP Fixture001** in the correct position.

13. In the Use Transform flyout, click [icon] (Use Transform Coordinate Center). In the **Top** viewport, note that the Rotation gizmo moves to the base of the selected group, as shown in Figure 4–72.

Figure 4–71	**Figure 4–72**

14. Right-click in the **Front** viewport to activate it and keep the selection of **LP Fixture001** intact.

15. In the Status Bar, in the *Transform Type-In* area, set Z to **180.0** (as shown in Figure 4–73) to rotate **LP Fixture001** by **180°** about the Z axis. Press <Enter>.

Figure 4–73

- The cloned group is moved opposite to the original group, as shown in the Left viewport in Figure 4–74.

Figure 4–74

16. Click ![icon](Select Object) to end the Rotate transform mode.

17. To verify that the groups are instanced, with **LP Fixture001** selected, select **Group>Open**. A pink bounding box displays around the group.

18. In the Scene Explorer, select **LP Fixture Housing001**.

19. In the Modify panel (![icon]), in the *Parameters* rollout, reduce the *Height* from **1'0"** to **0'8"**. Both Fixture Housings update and have reduced height as shown in Figure 4–75.

Figure 4–75

20. Select **Group>Close** to close **LP Fixture001**.

21. Save your work as **MyLightPole08.max**

4.6 Polygon Modeling Tools in the Ribbon

The Autodesk 3ds Max software is a powerful environment for creating a variety of 3D models. The box modeling technique, also called polygon modeling or mesh modeling, is an interactive method for creating vertices, edges, faces, and surfaces in a free form way.

- Box modeling can be performed using either the **Edit Mesh** or **Edit Poly** modifiers, or be converted to an **Editable Mesh** or **Editable Poly** object. Any of these methods give you the access to the sub-object levels required to do this type of modeling.

- The **Edit Poly** modifier is a commonly used modeling technique, although you can convert the object to an editable mesh or editable poly object and discard the modifier. You can also use the **Edit Mesh** modifier which is the most stable.

- The Modeling ribbon (*Modeling* tab) provides easy access to polygon modeling tools, including the editing and modification tools used at sub-object level. The ribbon contains many of the commonly used tools that are present in the Command Panel's Modify panel, at the Edit Poly sub-object level. In the *Modeling* tab, the polygon modeling and modifying tools are organized into panels.

- By default, the ribbon can be minimized to the panel tiles by clicking ⬒ and can be docked under the Main Toolbar. By default, **Minimize to Panel Titles** is set in the drop-down list, as shown in Figure 4–76. Click ⬓ to maximize the ribbon. You can also set the ribbon to be minimized to tabs or Panel Buttons by selecting the respective option in the drop-down list.

*If the ribbon is not displayed, in the Menu Bar, select **Customize> Show UI>Show Ribbon** or click*

*(Toggle Ribbon) in the Main Toolbar or by select **Ribbon** in the Interface Item menu.*

Figure 4–76

Practice 4f

(Optional) Poly Modeling Using the Ribbon

Practice Objective

- Create and modify a model using the box modeling technique.

In this practice, you will learn to create a model using some of the tools and techniques of box modeling. You will also use the **Edit Poly** modifier and the modifier tools available in the ribbon.

Task 1 - Model the Armchair.

1. Start an empty file by selecting **File>Reset**.

2. In the Create panel (+)> ● (Geometry), click **Box** in the *Object Type* rollout to activate the **Box** tool.

3. In the **Perspective** viewport, near the center of the grid, create a box of any size by clicking and dragging to define the length and width of the rectangle. Click and continue moving the mouse upwards to define the height.

The model is created in any color.

4. Initially, you use the *Parameters* rollout in the Create panel to enter the values. After completing a command, you will use the Modify panel (⌐) to edit the values. Set the following:
   - *Length*: **4'2"**
   - *Width*: **2'9"**
   - *Height*: **0'10"**

Press <Enter>. In the **Perspective** viewport, the box should look similar to that shown in Figure 4–77.

Figure 4–77

5. Name the object **armchair**.

6. To display the edges more clearly, change the display mode to wireframe by selecting the *Per-view Preference* label and selecting **Wireframe Override**.

7. Press <G> to hide the grid.

8. If the Modeling ribbon is only displaying Panel titles, click ⊡ (Show Full Ribbon).

9. Verify that the *Modeling* tab is active. Ensure that the armchair model is selected. Expand the Polygon Modeling panel and select **Apply Edit Poly Mod**, as shown in Figure 4–78. This adds an **Edit Poly** modifier to the armchair model. This is also displayed in the Command Panel. Note

   that the Modify panel (🗺) is already open and that the Modifier Stack displays the **Edit Poly** modifier, as shown in Figure 4–79.

Figure 4–78

Figure 4–79

10. In the Modeling panel of the ribbon, click ◁ (Edge) to activate Edge Selection, as shown in Figure 4–80. Alternatively, you can press <2> to select it. Expand the **Edit Poly** modifier in the Modifier Stack and note that **Edge** is already selected (highlighted in blue).

Figure 4–80

11. In the Navigation toolbar, click [icon] (Zoom Extents All Selected) and using **Pan** and **Zoom** fill the viewport with the box. Maximize the **Perspective** viewport.

12. Hold <Ctrl> and select the upper two long edges, as shown in Figure 4–81. The selected edges display in red.

Figure 4–81

13. Hold <Shift>, and in the ribbon, in the Loops panel, click

    [icon] (Connect) to open the **Connect Edges** caddy display.

In the Caddy display, hover the cursor on the edit box to display the option in its title.

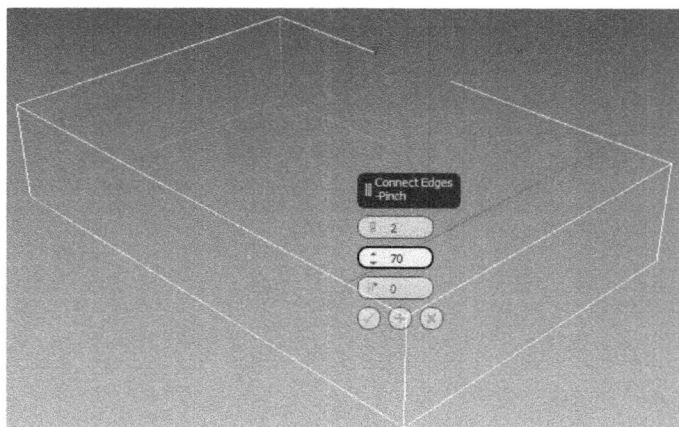

14. In the Connect Edges caddy display, set *Segments* to **2** and *Pinch* to **70**. Press <Enter> (leaving *Slide* as **0**). Note that two new edges are created along the two short edges, as shown in Figure 4–82.

Figure 4–82

Use ⊕ (Apply and continue) when you need to continue in the same tool. If you want to use another tool, use

⊘ (OK) to exit the caddy display.

15. If your *Pinch* edit box is still highlighted (white) with the cursor in the edit box, you are required to exit it first. Press

    ⊕ (Apply and continue) and note that two more edges are created along the longer edge.

    • To create a new set of segments, if ⊕ highlights, then you need to click ⊕ once to apply and continue.

    • If it does not highlight, then you need to click ⊕ twice, first to exit the *Pinch* edit box and then to place a new set of segments along the long edge of the box.

Pinch moves the lines in opposite directions, while Slide moves both of them in the X-direction

16. Leave the *Segments* at **2**. Use the spinner arrows to change the *Pinch* and *Slide* values and move the new edges towards the back of the armchair (which looks like a rectangle), as shown in Figure 4–83. You can drag their slider arrows in either direction viewing the changes dynamically. The values of *Pinch* and *Slide* are approximately **-30** and **-180** respectively. Press <Enter> each time if you enter a new value in the edit box, to see how it affects the lines. Click

    ⊘ (OK) to accept the changes and exit the caddy display.

Figure 4–83

17. In the Modeling panel, click ☐ (Polygon), or press <4> to change the sub-object selection level from *Edge* to **Polygon**. Alternatively, select **Polygon** in the **Edit Poly** modifier in the Modifier Stack. In the viewport, right-click and select **Select**. Hold <Ctrl> and select the two polygons along the shorter side of the box, as shown in Figure 4–84.

Figure 4–84

18. In the Modeling ribbon, in the Polygons panel, hold <Shift> and click ☐↑ (Extrude) to open the **Extrude Polygons** caddy display. Set *Height* to **0'2"**, as shown in Figure 4–85. Then, click ⊘ to apply the change and exit the caddy display.

Figure 4–85

19. In the Polygons panel, hold <Shift> and click (Bevel) to open the **Bevel** caddy display. Set the following, as shown in Figure 4–86:

- *Height*: **0'1"**
- *Outline*: **-0'1"**

20. Click ⊘ to apply and accept the changes.

Figure 4–86

The shortcut for Orbit is <Alt> + middle mouse button.

*You might need to right-click in empty space to exit the **Orbit** command first and then select the polygon.*

21. In the Navigation toolbar, click 🖱 (Orbit) to orbit in the **Perspective** viewport so that you can see the back of the armchair.

22. Select the long, thin rectangle at the top (along the longer end) for the back of the chair. In the Polygons panel, hold <Shift> and click 📦 (Extrude). In the **Extrude Polygons** caddy display, set *Height* to **0'5"** (as shown in Figure 4–87) and press <Enter>. Click ⊘ to exit the caddy display.

Figure 4–87

23. With the polygon still selected, in the Polygons panel, hold

<Shift> and click ⬜ (Bevel) to access the Bevel caddy display. Bevel up the back of the chair, as shown in Figure 4–88. Do not to bevel too much or the edges will overlap. The values are approximately **0'7"** for *Height* and

-0'2" for *Outline*. Click ⊘ to exit the caddy display.

Figure 4–88

*Use 🔄 (Orbit) or hold <Alt> and use the middle mouse button to orbit in the **Perspective** viewport for a better view around the object.*

24. In the Main Toolbar, click ✛ (Select and Move) and move the selected polygon backwards along the X-axis, as shown in Figure 4–89 (It might be easier to move the polygon in the **Top** viewport). Orbit the viewport to view the design.

Figure 4–89

Alternatively, click

[Edge icon] *(Edge) in the Modeling panel or select* **Edge** *in the Modifier Stack.*

Use [Orbit icon] (Orbit) or hold <Alt> and use the middle mouse button to orbit in the **Perspective** *viewport for easy access for clicking the edges at the back side.*

25. Press <2> to change to the **Edge** selection level. If some edge(s) have already been selected, click in an empty area in the viewport to clear the selection.

26. In the Modify Selection panel, click [icon] (Ring Mode) at the bottom of the panel (Ensure that you select **Ring Mode** and not **Ring**). This enables to select a ring of edges when a single edge is selected.

27. Select one of the long edges at the top of the chair back. Because the **Ring Mode** is toggled on, all of the other edges along the first edge are selected and display in red.

28. In the Modify Selection panel, click [icon] (Ring Mode) again to toggle it off.

29. In the Modify Selection panel, click [icon] (Shrink Ring) to clear one edge on either side of the ring. Alternatively, you can hold <Alt> and select one edge in front and one edge in the back to remove them from the selection. Only six edges should be selected, as shown in Figure 4–90.

Figure 4–90

30. In the Loops panel, hold <Shift> and click ⊞ (Connect). In the **Connect Edges** caddy display, reset the Pinch and Slide to 0, set the segments to **21** and press <Enter>. This adds 21 vertical segments, as shown in Figure 4–91. Click ⊘ (OK) to exit the caddy display.

Sometimes clicking ⊕ does not work correctly when you need to continue in the same modifier. You can use ⊘ and then reopen the modifier.

Figure 4–91

31. Hold <Shift> and click ⊞ (Connect) to open the **Connect Edges** caddy display. Change the *Segments* to **3** and press <Enter>. This adds three rows of horizontal segments between two horizontal edges along the armchair back. Click ⊘ to exit the caddy display.

32. Clear the selection by clicking in empty space.

33. Maximize the **Left** viewport. Use the **Zoom** and **Pan** tools to fill the viewport with the model.

34. In the Modeling ribbon, in the Polygon Modeling panel, click ⬚ (Vertex) or press <1>.

Click ↩ (Undo) if you selected the wrong vertices.

35. Click ✛ (Select and Move) and using a selection rectangle, select only the middle vertices in the top row leaving four vertices on each side unselected, as shown in Figure 4–92.

Figure 4–92

- The row of vertices selected display in red.

36. Maximize to display all of the four viewports. In the **Perspective** view, orbit around and verify that you have selected the correct row (only the top most row) of vertices.

37. In the Command Panel, note that you are in the Modify panel with the Modifier Stack indicating that you are at the **Edit Poly>Vertex** level. Expand the *Soft Selection* rollout and select **Use Soft Selection**. A rainbow color displays. The Red/Yellow/Orange/Green vertices will be affected by the selected transform (e.g., **Move**), while the Dark Blue vertices remain unaffected. You can change the Falloff values to add or remove vertices from the affected/unaffected group. Using the spinners in *Falloff,* note that decreasing the falloff changes the cyan colored vertices to a dark blue. Set the *Falloff* similar to that shown in Figure 4–93. Note that the resulting model might differ from that shown.

Figure 4–93

You can change the size of the Transform gizmo using the <->(hyphen) and <=> (equal sign).

38. Use ✛ (Select and Move) and move the vertices up by moving the gizmo along the Z-axis, to create the curved chair back, similar to that shown in Figure 4–94. Note that while moving the vertices, the dark blue vertices remain unaffected.

Figure 4–94

Hint: Assign Hotkey

You can assign a hotkey to interactively adjust the Soft selection falloff and pinch in the viewport. To do this, assign a hotkey to **Edit Soft Selection Mode**. Refer to **To edit a soft selection** in the Autodesk 3ds Max Help.

39. In the Modifier Stack, select **Edit Poly** to toggle off the sub-object selection

*Alternatively, you can click the **Viewport Shading** menu and select **Realistic** and **Edged Faces**.*

40. Click anywhere in empty space in the **Perspective** viewport to clear the selection. Press <F3> to toggle from *Wireframe* to **Default Shading** mode and press <F4> to toggle on **Edged Faces** mode. The model displays similar to that shown in Figure 4–95.

41. Press <F4> to end the **Edged Faces** mode and display the model using the **Default Shading** mode. In the *Display Method* label menu, select **High Quality**, as shown in Figure 4–96. Note that there are some problems with smoothing and that the chair looks faceted.

Figure 4–95

Figure 4–96

42. Select the chair and in the Modifier Stack or ribbon, select **Polygon** or press <4> to access the **Polygon** sub-object level.

43. In the Command Panel, scroll down and expand the *Polygon: Smoothing Groups* rollout. Press <Ctrl>+<A> to select all of the polygons, and click **Auto Smooth** in the rollout, as shown in Figure 4–97.

Figure 4–97

44. Click in empty space in the viewport to clear all of the selections. Note that the faceted problem has been fixed, as shown in Figure 4–98.

Figure 4–98

Task 2 - Apply Geometric Smoothing.

In this task you will add Geometry Smoothing using the **MSmooth** operation.

1. In the **Perspective** view, select the chair, if not already selected. In the Modeling ribbon, in the Polygon Modeling panel, click ☐ (Polygon), or press <4>.

2. Press <Ctrl>+<A> to select all of the polygons. If they are completely displayed in red, press <F2> to only display the faces in a red outline (edges).

You can add divisions to the seat portion of the chair for the MSmooth modifier to have a smoother effect. Use the Slice modifier to add divisions.

3. In the Modeling ribbon, in the Subdivision panel, hold <Shift> and click ⊞ (MSmooth). **Msmooth** changes the geometry by adding density to the mesh, as shown in Figure 4–99.

Figure 4–99

4. Click ✓ to exit the caddy display.

5. Save the file as **My Armchair.max**.

Task 3 - Using Freeform tools. (Optional)

If you have time, you can soften the model using the **Freeform** tools.

1. In the *Polygon Modeling* tab, click ▢ (Polygon), if it is not selected. Press <Ctrl>+<A> to select all of the polygons.

2. Select the *Freeform* tab, as shown in Figure 4–100.

Figure 4–100

3. In the Paint Deform panel, click ⊕ (Shift).

4. When you start this command, a Shift Options panel displays on the screen. Also note that the cursor displays as two circles in the active viewport, specifying the brush size. Set the values shown in Figure 4–101.

In the Main Toolbar,

click ↰ (Undo) if you moved the wrong vertices.

5. Right-click to activate the **Left** viewport (with the selection on) and hover the cursor (two circles) near the back middle of the chair. Click and drag the cursor (2 circles) to stretch the back upward, as shown in Figure 4–102.

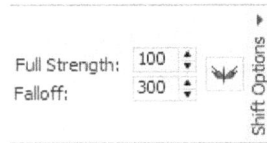

Full Strength: 100
Falloff: 300

Figure 4–101

Figure 4–102

Task 4 - Optimize the Mesh.

The shape of the chair has been softened. Now you need to reduce the polycount so the file can be used efficiently. The **ProOptimizer** modifier will achieve this.

1. Select the **Edit Poly** modifier in the stack to disable Sub-object mode. In the Modifier drop-down list, select **ProOptimizer**, as shown in Figure 4–103.

2. In the Command Panel, in the *Optimization Level* rollout, click **Calculate**. Change the *Vertex %* to **22**. Use the spinner to move it up or down as shown in Figure 4–104. Keep watching the viewport. The statistics display in the rollout.

Figure 4–103   Figure 4–104

3. Save your work as **Myarmchair_softened.max**.

> **Hint: Using Optimize and MultiRes Modifiers**
>
> The **Optimize** and **MultiRes** modifiers are both accessed from the Modifier List. They can be used to reduce the number of vertices and polygons.
>
> • **Optimize:** Reduces the model geometry, but does not critically change the appearance of the model.
>
> • **MultiRes**: Reduces the model geometry and enables you to specify the exact vertex count to be used for reduction. This modifier should be used if you have to export the models to other 3D applications because it maintains the map channels.

4.7 Statistics in Viewport

While Box modeling it is recommended to frequently review the status of your model. You can expand **File>Summary Info** to get details about the file. You can also **Show Statistics** directly in the viewport by, clicking **[+]>xView>Show Statistics**. The total number of polygons, vertices, and Frames Per Second display in the viewport (as shown in Figure 4–105), and are dependent on the options selected in the Viewport Configuration dialog box. Alternatively, press <7> to toggle the statistics display in the viewport on and off, in the active viewport.

Figure 4–105

The statistics options can be controlled by selecting **Views> Viewport Configuration** and in the *Statistics* tab of the Viewport Configuration dialog box, as shown in Figure 4–106. Here, you can customize the display (e.g., **Polygon Count**, **Triangle Count**, **Edge Count**, **Vertex Count**, etc.).

Figure 4–106

Hint: Low Polygon Count

When designing, it is recommended to keep the **Polygon Count** or **Triangle Count** as low as possible to speed up rendering and viewport performance. If you are creating real time models, this impacts the interactive viewport navigation and playback speed.

Performance might be improved if you keep this off when not in use.

• You can toggle the view of the statistics on and off, as required.

Hint: Use Summary Info

Sometimes **Show Statistics** does not give correct results. To check the information, expand **File>Summary Info** and then compare the Vertex/Face/Poly count displayed there.

Chapter Review Questions

1. Which of the following are the **Transform** tools in the Autodesk 3ds Max software? (Select all that apply.)

   a. **Move**

   b. **Stretch**

   c. **Trim**

   d. **Scale**

2. Which of the following do you press to change the size (shrink and enlarge) of the Transform gizmo?

   a. <-> and <+>

   b. <+> and <=>

   c. <-> and <=>

   d. </> and <+>

3. Which **Transform center** option do you select if you want to rotate many objects, each around its own center?

   a. (Pivot Point Center)

   b. (Selection Center)

   c. (Transform Coordinate Center)

4. Which clone option creates a one-directional link in which changes made to the original object affect the duplicate, but the modifiers applied to the duplicate do not affect the source object?

   a. **Copy**

   b. **Instance**

   c. **Reference**

5. In addition to the **Polygon Modeling** tools, the *Modeling* tab in the Ribbon contains the commonly used tools from which panel of the Command Panel?

   a. Modify panel ( )

   b. Hierarchy panel ( )

   c. Display panel ( )

   d. Utilities panel ( )

6. Which key on the keyboard can be used as a shortcut to toggle the statistics display in the viewport on and off?

   a. <1>

   b. <3>

   c. <5>

   d. <7>

Command Summary

Button	Command	Location
	Ribbon (Graphite Modeling Tools)	• **Main Toolbar** • **Customize**>Show UI>Show Ribbon • **Interface Item Menu**: Ribbon
	Select and Move	• **Main Toolbar** • **Edit**>Move
	Select and Place	• **Main Toolbar** • **Edit**>Placement
	Select and Rotate	• **Main Toolbar** • **Edit:**>Rotate
	Select and Uniform Scale	• **Main Toolbar**: Scale flyout • **Edit**>Scale
	Select and Non-uniform Scale	• **Main Toolbar**: Scale flyout
	Select and Squash	• **Main Toolbar**: Scale flyout
	Use Pivot Point Center	• **Main Toolbar**: Transform Center flyout
	Use Selection Center	• **Main Toolbar**: Transform Center flyout
	Use Transform Coordinate Center	• **Main Toolbar**: Transform Center flyout

Modeling From 2D Objects

In addition to Primitive Objects or Polygon Modeling tools, models in the Autodesk® 3ds Max® software can also be created using 2D shapes that are subsequently used to generate 3D geometry. Tools such as Lathe, Extrude, and Sweep Modifiers enable you to create 3D geometry from a 2D shape.

Learning Objectives in this Chapter

- Create 2D shapes, such as lines and closed shape objects.
- Revolve a profile around an axis using the Lathe modifier.
- Add and subtract shapes using the 2D Boolean operations.
- Add depth to a 2D shape to create 3D geometry using the Extrude modifier.
- Combine two or more 3D objects to generate a third 3D object by performing Boolean operations on their geometry.
- Modify shapes and geometry with precision using various snap modes.
- Create 3D geometry based on a 2D section that follows a series of spline segment paths using the Sweep modifier.

5.1 3D Modeling from 2D Objects

The Autodesk 3ds Max software enables you to create 2D shapes in the form of splines and NURBS, and using various modifiers, to create organic smooth curved surfaces from the shapes. Shapes can be created using ![icon] (Shapes) in the Command Panel's Create panel (![icon]), as shown in Figure 5–1. The splines consist of:

Although the software includes 2D tools, Autodesk 3ds Max is not a drafting application.

- Basic shapes (Splines): **Line**, **Rectangle**, **Ellipse**, etc.

- Extended Splines: **WRectangle**, **Channel**, **Angle**, etc.

Figure 5–1

The software enables you to draw lines and curves in a freeform interactive manner by clicking points in the viewport. Lines can be drawn to create three kinds of shapes: open, closed, and self-intersecting.

You cannot draw a 2D line that forks or branches.

- Closed shapes can also be created using other shape object types, such as Rectangle, Ellipse, Ngon, or Text.

- Open shapes and self-intersecting shapes can be extruded to create 3D objects, but these objects have mixed face normals. Some faces do not render and might not be visible in the viewport.

- The **Edit Spline** modifier: Enables you to apply edits such as trim, extend, fillet, and chamfer to 2D objects.

- The **Extrude** modifier: Enables you to create 3D objects by extruding closed shapes. The outside of these objects is visible and renderable from all sides. All face normals point away from the center of the object.

- The **Lathe** modifier: Enables you to create 3D objects by using on open shapes where a profile is revolved.

- The Transform Type-In functionality: Enables you to achieve precision using snaps and vertices, which can be shifted after placement.

The **Line** tool has two basic drawing techniques:

Method 1

You can draw straight line segments by clicking and moving the cursor repeatedly. This method does not create any curves at first. All of the vertices created are Corner type. After clicking to set the vertices, you select the line vertices individually or in sets and then change their type from Corner to **Bezier** or **Smooth** to create curves.

> **Hint: Preventing Self-intersecting Shapes**
>
> If you draw too quickly when drawing using Method 1, the program might translate your motions into press and drag, and self-intersecting shapes can be inadvertently drawn. To prevent this, in the Create panel's *Creation Method* rollout, change the drag type to **Corner**. In doing so, you are not able to drag curves interactively.

Method 2

Draw curves directly by clicking, holding, and dragging to create **Bezier** vertices rather than **Corner** vertices. This is a faster method but harder to control, since you are defining the curve on both sides of the vertex in a single move. Holding <Alt> while dragging enables you to define the curve on the leading side of the vertex, introducing an angle between the vertex handles.

*You cannot create **Bezier** vertices by clicking, holding, and dragging if both the Initial Type and Drag Type have been set to **Corner** in the Creation Method rollout, in the **Line** tool.*

- Using either method, these curved segments are created out of smaller straight line segments. Increasing the segments makes the curve smoother. The *Steps* value in the *Interpolation* rollout sets the number of segments.

- Drawing while holding <Shift> also draws straight lines and perpendicular lines.

- Press <Backspace> to undo the last drawn vertex in a line.

Practice 5a

Drawing Lines

Practice Objectives

- Create an open and closed 2D shape.
- Move the location of a vertex and change the shape of a curve.

In this practice, you will create, open, and close 2D shapes using the **Line** command. You will then move the location of a vertex and change the shape of a curve using the Bezier handles. Finally, you will create a candlestick model using the 2D shapes drawn.

You must set the paths to locate the External files and Xrefs used in the practice. If you have not done this already, return to Chapter 1 and complete Task 1 to Task 3 in *Practice 1a: Organizing Folders and Working with the Interface*. You only have to set the user paths once.

Task 1 - Drawing 2D lines.

*If a dialog box opens prompting you about a File Load: Mismatch, click **OK** to accept the default values.*

1. Reset the scene.

2. Maximize the **Front** viewport from the layout overlay using <Shift> and <Win>, if you are already in another maximized viewport. If you are maximizing from the four viewport screen, use ▣ (Maximize Viewport) or press <Alt>+<W>.

3. Press <G> to hide the grid.

4. In the Command Panel>Create panel (✛), click

   ⬚ (Shapes). Note that **Splines** is preselected in the list, as shown in Figure 5–2.

Figure 5–2

5. In the *Object Type* rollout, click **Line**.

*Closed shapes and open shapes are both used in creating 3D objects. Modifiers, such as **Extrude**, **Lathe**, and **Surface**, can be used to build 3D surfaces based on 2D shapes.*

6. In the **Front** viewport, draw a saw-tooth pattern line, as shown in Figure 5–3. Click to set the first point, move the cursor to the next location of the point and click to place the second point. The first line displays. Continue the pattern. Right-click to end, once you have placed the last line. An open shape is created.

Figure 5–3

7. With the line still selected, delete the lines by pressing <Delete>.

8. Still in the **Line** command, repeat the drawing process to create a closed shape, similar to that shown in Figure 5–4. Click to set each point and for the last point, click on the starting point (yellow vertex) to close the shape. In the Spline dialog box, click **Yes** to close the shape. Right-click in the empty space to exit the command. Do not delete this shape.

Figure 5–4

9. To draw curved lines, in the *Object Type* rollout, click **Line**. Then, in the *Creation Method* rollout, set the *Drag Type* to **Bezier**, as shown in Figure 5–5.

Figure 5–5

10. Click to set the first point, move the cursor, then click, hold, and drag to create a Bezier curve running through the second point. Each time you click, hold, and drag, the curve extends through the new point. This draws a curve, but it is difficult to control, since dragging affects the curve on both sides of the point at the same time. Draw a curved line similar to the one shown in Figure 5–6. Right-click to exit the command and press <Delete> to delete to this curved line.

Figure 5–6

11. Right-click in empty space to exit the **Line** command.

12. Select the closed shape that was previously created. In the

   Command Panel, select the Modify panel (   ). Click ► in the Modifier Stack to expand **Line**. Select **Vertex** at the sub-object level, as shown in Figure 5–7.

Figure 5–7

13. In the viewport, select the vertex at the top left of the saw tooth pattern. The selected vertex displays in red. Right-click and select **Bezier** in the tools 1 quadrant of the quad menu. Note that the vertex corner is replaced by a Bezier curve and that the Bezier handles display.

14. In the Main Toolbar, click ✛ (Select and Move). The Transform gizmo displays with the bezier handles. Click and drag the red vertex (or use the yellow plane on the interior of the gizmo) to move the curve to another location. Click and drag either handle end (green square) to modify the curve shape, as shown in Figure 5–8. The handle movement is constrained by the Transform gizmo usage. Note that dragging one handle moves the other handle simultaneously.

Figure 5–8

Hint: Transform Gizmo Size

<-> (hyphen) and <=> (equal sign) can be used to decrease or increase the size of the Transform gizmo. If the Transform gizmo handles extend beyond the vertex handles, you might have trouble moving the vertex handles.

If you move the Transform gizmo in one axis, the movement of the bezier handles is constrained to that axis. To have the handles move freely, select the yellow square of the gizmo to have movement in the XY-axes. This can also be controlled using the Axis Constraints toolbar.

15. Hold <Shift> and move one of the handles. This changes the command to **Bezier Corner** and enables you to break the continuity of the curve to manipulate the handles on one side of the curve separately from the other, as shown in Figure 5–9. Right-click on the red vertex and select **Reset Tangents** to return the original curve shape. To return to **Bezier**, right-click on the red vertex and select **Bezier** again in the quad menu.

Figure 5–9

Task 2 - Using 2D Shapes to draw a candlestick model.

In this task you will draw a model of a candlestick. A reference photo (**Candlestick_pewter.jpg**) of an actual candlestick as shown in Figure 5–10, is located in the ...\Maps folder.

1. In the Modifier Stack, select **Line** to exit sub-object selection mode. Select the previously drawn closed shape and any other lines that you might have drawn and delete them using <Delete>.

2. In the Create panel, click (Shapes) and click **Line**. In the *Creation Method* rollout, in the *Drag Type* area, select **Corner**.

Holding <Shift> creates straight lines at a 90 degree angle (vertical direction) and 180 degree angle (horizontal direction).

3. Start at the bottom right (the yellow vertex indicates the start point) and click to place the first line vertex, as shown in Figure 5–11. Hold <Shift>, move the cursor left, and click to draw the base of the candlestick. Still holding <Shift>, move the cursor up to draw the long straight vertical line segment, and then click to place the vertex. Release <Shift> and continue clicking and drawing in a clockwise direction.

• Press <Backspace> to undo the points if you make a mistake.

| **Figure 5–10** | **Figure 5–11** |

4. Continue to place approximately 16 points and close the shape by clicking over the first point. Click **Yes** and then right-click to exit the **Line** command. The shape should look similar to the one shown in Figure 5–11.

The vertices turn red at selection.

5. With the shape selected, in the Modify panel ( ), in the Modifier Stack, expand **Line** and select the **Vertex** sub-object level. Hold <Ctrl> and select the four vertices, as shown in Figure 5–12.

Figure 5–12

6. Right-click and select **Bezier** in the quad menu. This changes all the four vertices to **Bezier** vertices with handles.

7. Adjust the handles of each vertex using ✥ (Select and Move) to obtain a shape similar to that shown in Figure 5–13. Move the vertices and handles individually to get a shape similar to that shown in Figure 5–14.

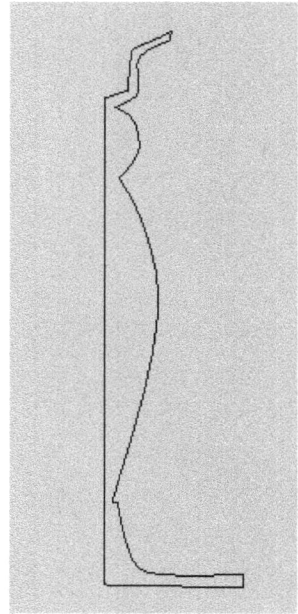

Figure 5–13   **Figure 5–14**

8. After completing the shape, click on **Line** in the Modifier Stack to exit the sub-object level and click anywhere in the viewport to clear the selection.

9. Save your work as **MyCandlestickProfile.max**.

10. For comparison, you can open the file **Candlestick_Profile.max**. Then, close it without saving. You will use the file in the *Practice 5b*.

5.2 The Lathe Modifier

The **Lathe** modifier enables you to create a 3D object by revolving a profile (2D shape) around an axis. It can be accessed in the Modifier List, in the Modify panel ( ) in the Command Panel.

How To: Create a 3D Object Using the Lathe Modifier

1. Select a profile (usually a line object).
2. Apply a **Lathe** Modifier.
3. Adjust the axis of revolution.
4. Adjust the alignment of the axis with the profile.

Practice 5b

Creating a Candlestick

Practice Objective

- Revolve a 2D shape around its axis.

In this practice, you will resolve a 2D shape around its axis, using the **Lathe** modifier to create the solid geometry for the candlestick.

You must set the paths to locate the External files and Xrefs used in the practice. If you have not done this already, return to Chapter 1 and complete Task 1 to Task 3 in *Practice 1a: Organizing Folders and Working with the Interface*. You only have to set the user paths once.

*If a dialog box opens prompting you about a File Load: Mismatch, click **OK** to accept the default values.*

1. Open **Candlestick_Profile.max**.

2. Maximize the **Front** viewport.

3. Select the profile. In the Modify panel ( ), in the Modifier Stack, verify that the **Line** is highlighted and that no sub-object level is highlighted.

4. In the Modifier List, select **Lathe**. The profile revolves around a center point, but the alignment is off, as shown in Figure 5–15.

*Sometimes, lathed objects display inside-out. If something looks wrong with your candlestick, use the **Flip Normals** option in the Parameters rollout.*

5. In the *Parameters* rollout, in the *Align* area, click **Min**. The candlestick should now display as shown in Figure 5–16.

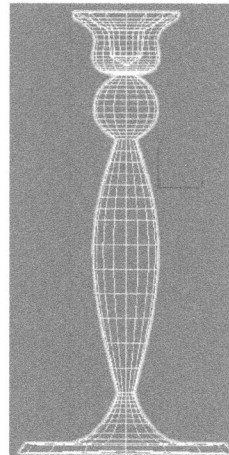

Figure 5–15   Figure 5–16

6. In the Modifier Stack, expand **Lathe** and select **Axis**. Using

   ✛ (Select and Move), move the X-axis to display the candlestick in various positions.

7. In the Main Toolbar, click �);(Undo) or press <Ctrl>+<Z> to undo the axis moves.

8. Select **Lathe** (highlighted) to exit the Sub-object mode. Maximize the viewport to display the four viewports.

9. Assign a color to the geometry by selecting the candlestick first, selecting the color swatch next to the **Line** name, and selecting a color in the Object Color dialog box.

10. In the **Perspective** viewport, use 🪐 (Orbit) and examine the geometry, as shown in Figure 5–17.

Figure 5–17

11. Save your work as **MyCandlestick.max**.

5.3 2D Booleans

2D Boolean operations enable you to create shapes by combining drawn lines and shapes. Using the **Edit Spline** modifier, you can add or subtract shapes at the sub-object level. The **Edit Spline** modifier enables you to convert a shape to an editable spline

- 2D Boolean operations (Union, Subtraction, Intersection) are available in the Spline sub-object level, in the *Geometry parameters* rollout, as shown in Figure 5–18.

- Before using a boolean operation, all shapes that are to be combined must be part of a single shape. The **Attach** and **Attach Mult.** options (Spline sub-object level, *Geometry parameters* rollout) enable you to combine multiple shapes into a single shape.

- When drawing shapes, if you clear the **Start New Shape** option in the *Object Type* rollout (as shown in Figure 5–19), all of the subsequent shapes that you create become part of a single shape. If you already have a shape selected, anything you draw becomes part of that shape. By default, the **Start New Shape** option is selected before you start drawing any shapes.

Figure 5–18

Figure 5–19

- No history is associated with 2D Boolean operations and you are not able to retrieve the various Boolean components after saving.

Practice 5c

2D Booleans

Practice Objective

- Modify a shape using 2D Booleans.

In this practice, you will add and subtract rectangles using 2D Booleans to change the shape of the profile for the candlestick.

You must set the paths to locate the External files and Xrefs used in the practice. If you have not done this already, return to Chapter 1 and complete Task 1 to Task 3 in *Practice 1a: Organizing Folders and Working with the Interface*. You only have to set the user paths once.

Task 1 - Creating and Attaching Shapes.

*If a dialog box opens prompting you about a File Load: Mismatch, click **OK** to accept the default values.*

1. Open **Candlestick.max**.

2. Maximize the **Front** viewport and zoom to the extents of the objects.

3. Select the candlestick. In the Modify panel ( ), in the Modifier Stack, click (eye) next to the **Lathe** to toggle the **Lathe** modifier off. The line profile and the **Lathe** axis displays in the viewport.

4. In the Create panel (+), click (Shapes).

5. Click **Rectangle**. Draw four rectangles intersecting the right edge of the profile, similar to that shown in Figure 5–20.

Figure 5–20

6. Right-click to cancel the command and click to clear the selection.

7. Select the candlestick profile. Open the Modify panel (![icon]), and in the Modifier Stack, select **Line**.

8. Scroll down and in the *Geometry* rollout, click **Attach Mult**.

A blue background in the button means it is active.

9. In the Attach Multiple dialog box, click ![icon] (Display Shapes) to activate it, if not already active. Select all of the four rectangles and click **Attach**. All of the rectangles become part of the candlestick profile spline object.

Task 2 - Applying Boolean Operations.

1. In the Modifier Stack, select the **Spline** sub-object in the **Line** object and select the candlestick profile in the viewport. The selected profile displays in red and the rectangles remain white (unselected).

2. In the *Geometry* rollout, scroll down and click **Boolean** to activate it. Verify that ![icon] (Union) is already active.

3. In the viewport, hover the cursor over the topmost rectangle, and note that the cursor displays as a Union cursor (![icon]). Select the topmost rectangle and then select the second rectangle. Note that in each case, the profile is extended to the right to include part of the rectangle, and the inner part of the rectangle is discarded.

4. In the Command Panel, with **Boolean** still active, click ![icon] (Subtraction) to activate it. Hover the cursor over the third rectangle to display the cursor as a Subtraction cursor (![icon]).

5. Select the third rectangle and then select the last rectangle. For these shapes, the rectangle is subtracted from the candlestick.

   • Note that the top two rectangles create a rim (Union), and the bottom two create an inscribed groove (Subtraction), as shown in Figure 5–21.

Figure 5–21

6. In the Modifier Stack, select **Lathe**, and then click
   (grayed out eye) next to **Lathe** to toggle it on.

7. Press <Alt>+<W> to return to four viewports. Activate the
   Perspective viewport and review the results in **Default
   Shading** display mode. The two rims and two grooves are
   created in the candle stick, as shown in Figure 5–22.

Figure 5–22

8. Save your work as **MyCandlestick01.max**.

Task 3 - Modifying Shapes.

1. Select the candlestick, if required. In the Modify panel
   ( ), select **Line** and **Vertex** sub-objects.

2. In the **Front** viewport, select one of the vertices in the first rim
   that you created, as shown in Figure 5–23.

3. In the Modifier Stack, click (Show end result on/off
   toggle), as shown in Figure 5–24. This tool enables you to
   see the object as an end product.

Figure 5–23

Figure 5–24

4. Move the selected vertex in the **Front** viewport and note the
   change in the **Perspective** viewport. You are now sculpting
   the candlestick in real time, as shown in Figure 5–25.

Figure 5–25

5. In the Modifier Stack, select **Line** to exit the sub-object level.

6. Save your work as **MyCandlestick01.max**.

5.4 The Extrude Modifier

The **Extrude** modifier enables you to add depth to a 2D shape to create 3D geometry. As with other modifiers, the Extrude modifier is available in the Modifier List, in the Command Panel's

Modify panel ( ), as shown in Figure 5–26.

Figure 5–26

Capping area

The capping options are located in the *Parameters* rollout, in the *Capping* area, as shown in Figure 5–26.

* Capping only applies to closed extruded shapes. Open shapes can be extruded but they cannot be capped.

- Closed shapes often do not cap if they cross themselves or if they have more than one vertex at the same location.

- You can also extrude with a height of **0** to create a flat surface. In this situation, only the start or end cap is required.

- Figure 5–27 shows **various** capping options.

Original Shape   *No Capping*   *Cap Start*   *Cap End*

Figure 5–27

- **Morph** capping type linearly interpolates across the vertices to create the cap, as shown in Figure 5–28. This option creates less geometry and is the default setting.

- **Grid** capping type breaks down the cap into a repeating grid of vertices, in square shapes, as shown in Figure 5–29. The grid method enables more complex modeling on the surface of the cap, but adds a great deal of geometry.

Figure 5–28   **Figure 5–29**

Output area

The *Output* area options controls the kind of object that is derived if you simplify (collapse) the object. It is recommended to select the default **Mesh** option. **Patch** and **NURBS** options are used to create complex curved geometry.

Mapping Coordinates

The options for mapping coordinates and real-world map sizing are described with materials.

- For surfaces that have tiled, repeating textures of a specific size (e.g., carpeting, wall surfaces, metal, etc.) select **Generate Mapping Coords** and **Real-World Map Size**.

- For surfaces meant to show textures that are scaled explicitly (e.g., signs, labels, company logos, paintings, computer screens, etc.) you might use **Generate Mapping Coords option,** but the **Real-World Map Size** option can be cleared.

- Select **Generate Material IDs** to apply a different material to the sides, start, and end cap through a Multi/Sub-object material.

- Selecting **Use Shape IDs** assigns material IDs that have been applied to the segments of the spline that you extruded.

Extruding Nested Splines

When linked or imported geometry is merged together (such as by layer with the weld option) or, when 2D objects become attached to form complex splines, these objects are called **nested splines**. When extruding a nested spline (as shown in Figure 5–30), the enclosed areas form solid masses and can be used for modeling wall systems and similar geometry.

Figure 5–30

5.5 3D Boolean Operations

Boolean operations enable you to graphically bring together two 3D objects to generate a third 3D object. This is an intuitive way to create complex geometry from simple 3D primitives and extruded 2D shapes.

The Boolean objects are available in the Create panel (+), by clicking ● (Geometry) and selecting **Compound Objects** in the drop-down list. You can select the required Boolean object in the *Object Type* rollout, as shown in Figure 5–31.

Figure 5–31

The three types of Boolean objects that can be created, are described as follows:

Boolean compound object	Combines two 3D objects to generate a third 3D object by applying a logical operation. The Boolean compound object offers improved stability.
ProBoolean compound object	Similar to the Boolean compound object, this option has more advanced functionality and alternate workflow.
ProCutter compound object	Enables you to separate objects into pieces so that you can use them in dynamic simulations.

Boolean Operations

The original objects are referred to as **Operands** and the final result is a **Boolean** object. The operands can be combined in three ways, as shown in Figure 5–32:

- By subtraction of one from the other.

- By finding the intersection where their geometries overlap.

- By the union of the two together.

Original Operands   *Subtraction*   *Intersection*   *Union*

Figure 5–32

- Boolean operations can be nested where the results of one operation can be used as input to the next. **ProBooleans** offer superior methodology when creating objects with multiple operands. It enables you to reorder and change the operations interactively.

- Boolean operations can be animated, this is often a technique used to reveal or hide geometry in a presentation.

Boolean Explorer

The Boolean Explorer can help you to keep track of the various operands that are being used, as shown in Figure 5–33. The Boolean Explorer is only available with the Boolean compound object.

Figure 5–33

- To open the Boolean Explorer, in the *Boolean Parameters* rollout, click **Open Boolean Explorer**.

- Whenever you add an operand, it displays in the Boolean Explorer.

- If you change the order of the operands, the change is reflected in the Boolean Explorer.

Adjusting Boolean Results

The results of a Boolean operation can be adjusted dynamically by making changes to the operands' parameters or modifier stack. This dynamic update requires that operands be identified as a reference or instance on creation (or an extracted operand is selected to be an instance).

- The original operands can be maintained for editing after the fact or they can be reconstituted (extracted) from the Boolean result later on.

- The practical application of adjusting Boolean results is best left for Intermediate course material.

Best Practices

Boolean operations are known to produce unexpected results if the operand geometries had certain issues such as: gaps, irregular face normals, did not overlap each other, etc. It is recommended to avoid the following issues whenever possible:

- Avoid coplanar operands, whenever possible, to minimize Boolean complexity.

- Boolean operations expect water-tight geometry. If the geometry does not cleanly define a volume, the Boolean might not work, as shown in Figure 5–34.

Figure 5–34

Collapsing Booleans

When an object has been sufficiently modeled with Boolean operations you can leave the result as a Boolean object or simplify (collapse) it to a mesh.

- To collapse a Boolean object to an editable mesh, in the Modifier Stack, right-click on the Boolean and select **Convert to: Editable Mesh** or **Convert to: Editable Poly**.

- If you are using a Boolean result as an operand for another Boolean operation and are not getting the expected results, it might help to convert the original Boolean object to an editable mesh before the second operation. It is recommended to use ProBooleans if you have multiple operands.

- Boolean objects that originate from linked AutoCAD geometry might react unpredictably after an updated DWG link.

- Many other kinds of 3D objects besides Booleans can be collapsed to a mesh to simplify them.

- Once an object is converted to a mesh, it loses all of its parametric controls. Therefore, converted Boolean objects cannot be updated by editing instanced operands or a file link update.

If you select a selective reload and avoided the layers used to create your Booleans, any connected Boolean objects would be removed from the scene.

Hint: Controlling Edge Line Visibility

After a Boolean or other complex operation, there might be missing or unnecessary edge lines in a wireframe or default shading viewport rendering mode. To easily read the geometry on the screen, only certain edges across your 3D object are visible.

To display the edges, right-click on the object and select **Object Properties**. In the *Display Properties* area, clear the **Edges Only** option. The **Edges Only** option is available in the **By Object** mode, as shown in Figure 5–35. Then, click **By Layer** to toggle it to **By Object**.

Display Properties

- See-Through
- Display as Box
- Backface Cull
- ✔ Edges Only
- Vertex Ticks
- Motion Path

By Object

Figure 5–35

Alternatively, in the Modify panel, add an **Edit Mesh** modifier to your object and select **Edge** Sub-object mode. In the **Edit** menu, select **Select All**. In the *Surface Properties* rollout, click **Invisible** to make all edges invisible. Click **Auto Edge** to only show the edges with 24°+ separation. To get required results on curved objects (including curved walls), you might have to enter different separation angles.

Practice 5d

Extrude Walls and Create Wall Openings

Practice Objective

- Add depth to a 2D spline to create 3D walls and openings in 3D walls.

In this practice, you will extrude walls from a spline to create 3D walls. You will then refine the walls by creating openings for a corridor and doors, using the **Extrude** modifier. Additionally, you will use **ProBoolean** objects to graphically subtract two objects from the walls.

You must set the paths to locate the External files and Xrefs used in the practice. If you have not done this already, return to Chapter 1 and complete Task 1 to Task 3 in *Practice 1a: Organizing Folders and Working with the Interface*. You only have to set the user paths once.

Task 1 - Extrude the Walls.

*If a dialog box opens prompting you about a File Load: Mismatch, click **OK** to accept the default values.*

*If the Scene Explorer is not displayed, select **Tools>Scene Explorer** or click* ▦ *(Toggle Scene Explorer) in the Main Toolbar.*

1. Open **Spline Walls Bound.max**.

2. In the Scene Explorer toolbar, click ▪ (Display None) and click 🔲 (Display Shapes). Select **Layer:VIZ-1-Walls** and note that the 2D lines for the walls (cyan colored shapes) are selected in the viewport.

3. In the Command Panel, select the Modify panel (⬚). The name **Layer:VIZ-1-Walls** displays in the Command Panel and it is an **Editable Spline**.

4. In the Modifier List, select **Extrude**. In the *Parameters* rollout, set *Amount* to **11'0"** (the height of the first floor walls), as shown in Figure 5–36. Press <Enter>.

Figure 5–36

The missing wall sections eventually contain curtain walls.

5. Click (Zoom Extents All). Only the areas enclosed by the wall linework are extruded, as shown in Figure 5–37.

Figure 5–37

Task 2 - Creating the Subtraction Operands.

1. In the Main Toolbar, click ▣ (Layer Explorer). In the Layer
   Explorer, select the two layers **VIZ-1-Booleans-Doors** and
   VIZ-1-Boolean-Soffit. Right-click on any of the selected
   layer and click **Select Child Nodes**, as shown in
   Figure 5–38. These layers contain closed polylines that
   define the openings to be created. Note that these layers are
   selected as well.

Figure 5–38

2. To avoid a coplanar face along the floor, first move these
   objects below the floor level. In the Main Toolbar, click

   ✛ (Select and Move). Set coordinate system to **World** and

   click ▮▮ (Use Transform Coordinate Center), as shown in
   Figure 5–39.

Figure 5–39

3. In the Status Bar, in the *Transform Type-In* area, activate

   ![icon] (Offset Mode Transform), enter **-1'0"** in the *Z* field, and press <Enter>.

4. In the Main Toolbar, click ![icon] (Select Object).

5. Click anywhere in empty space to clear the selection. In the Layer Explorer, highlight only the layer **VIZ-1-Boolean-Soffit**. Right-click on the selected layer and click **Select Child Nodes**. This layer contains a single polyline defining an opening in one of the walls.

6. In the Command Panel>Modify panel (![icon]), verify that the name **Layer:VIZ-1-Boolean-Soffit** displays in the panel.

7. In the Modifier List, select **Extrude**. In the *Parameters* rollout, set *Amount* to **9'0"** and press <Enter> (this is **8'** + the **1'** that was just used to lower the object). The first subtraction operand (8'0") is created, as shown in Figure 5–40.

Figure 5–40

8. Repeat Steps 5 to 7 for **VIZ-1-Booleans-Doors**. Select the child layer of **VIZ-1-Booleans-Doors** and extrude it with an *Amount* of **8'0"**. The four 7'0" subtraction operands are created, as shown in Figure 5–41.

Figure 5–41

Task 3 - Creating the Wall Openings.

1. In the Layer Explorer, select **VIZ-1-Walls.** Right-click on the selected layer and click **Select Child Nodes**.

2. In the Create panel (+)> ● (Geometry), select **Compound Objects** in the drop-down list, as shown in Figure 5–42. Click **ProBoolean** to convert the wall system into a Boolean object. The selected walls (**VIZ-1-Walls)** are now your Operand A.

3. In the *Pick Boolean* rollout, verify that **Move** is selected and click **Start Picking**.

4. In the *Parameters* rollout, in the *Operation* area, verify that **Subtraction** is selected, as shown in Figure 5–43. This subtracts **Operand B** (the soffit opening) from **Operand A** (the walls).

Figure 5–42

Figure 5–43

5. In the viewport, select the Boolean Soffit extrusion (**VIZ -1-Boolean Soffit**, the 9'0" operand that was created first). The volume contained by the Soffit object is removed from the walls, as shown in Figure 5–44.

6. Click any of the **VIZ-1-Boolean-Doors** objects to complete the second ProBoolean subtraction operation. The volume contained by the Doors object is also removed from the walls, as shown in Figure 5–44.

Figure 5–44

7. Click **Start Picking** to end the ProBoolean operation.

8. The ProBoolean operation has the ability to change the way the faces are built in the object using the Quadrilateral Tessellation function. In the Layer Explorer, with the **VIZ-1-Walls** highlighted, right-click on **VIZ-1-Walls** and select **Properties**. In the Object Properties dialog box, verify that the *Name* displays as **Layer:VIZ-1-Walls**. In the *Display Properties* area, click **By Layer** to toggle it to **By Object**. Clear **Edges Only** and click **OK**.

9. Press <F4> to display the edges of the newly created faces, as shown in Figure 5–45. Note the way long triangular faces are created on some of the walls.

Figure 5–45

10. In the Command Panel>Modify panel ( ), note that the **ProBoolean** displays in the Modifier Stack. Expand the *Advanced Options* rollout (collapse *Pick Boolean* and *Parameters* rollouts). In the *Quadrilateral Tessellation* area, select **Make Quadrilaterals**, as shown in Figure 5–46. Note how the geometry changes. There are no long triangular faces, as shown on the right in Figure 5–47.

Figure 5–46

Figure 5–47

11. Increase the *Quad Size %* to **10.0**. This modifies the geometry so that the polygons are bigger, as shown in Figure 5–48.

Figure 5–48

12. You can collapse the **ProBoolean** to a simple mesh. In the Modifier Stack, right-click on **ProBoolean** and select **Editable Poly**.

13. Save your work as **MySpline Walls Bound.max**.

5.6 Using Snaps for Precision

Snaps enable you to create, move, rotate, and scale objects with precision and are activated using the buttons in the Main Toolbar, as shown in Figure 5–49. Press <S> to toggle Snaps on and off while drawing lines, creating primitives, or transforming objects.

Figure 5–49

The available Toggle options are described as follows:

	3D Snap: This mode snaps to objects in 3D. It is the default option.
	2.5D Snap: This mode snaps to a projection of the selected point at elevation 0 on the current grid.
	2D Snap: This mode enables you to snap to points at elevation 0 on the current grid.
	Angle Snap: This mode enables you to set rotational values (such as a Rotate Transform amount) in angle increments.
	Percent Snap: This mode enables percentile-based values (such as a Scale Transform amount) in percent increments (5%, 10%, etc.).
	Spinner Snap: This mode causes all spinner controls to increment at a set value with a single click. Transform and a host of parameter values can be adjusted by spinners ( ).

- Snap settings, such as the increment values for angle and percent snap, can be set in the *Options* tab of the Grid and Snap Settings dialog box, as shown in Figure 5–50. You can access the dialog box by right-clicking on **2D**, **2.5D**, **3D**, **Angle**, or **Percent Snap**, from **Tools>Grids and Snaps> Grid and Snap Settings**, or by holding <Shift> and right-clicking anywhere in the viewport and selecting **Grid and Snap Settings** in the quad menu.

- The active snaps are selected in the *Snaps* tab of the Grid and Snap Settings dialog box, as shown in Figure 5–51.

Figure 5–50

Figure 5–51

- You can activate snaps by selecting buttons in the Snaps toolbar (hidden by default), as shown in Figure 5–52. Right-click on an empty space in any interface item and select **Snaps** in the menu to open the Snaps toolbar.

Figure 5–52

- You can also activate snaps in the **Snaps** quad menu. Hold <Shift>, right-click anywhere in the viewport, and select **Standard**, as shown in Figure 5–53.

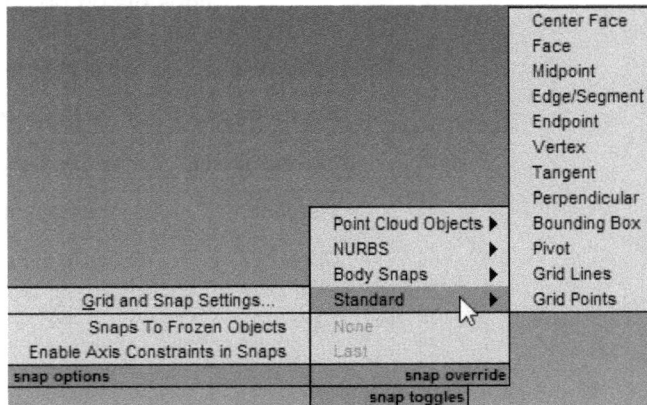

Figure 5–53

- The toolbar contains buttons for the most common snap settings. These are described as follows:

	Grid Points: Snaps to grid intersections.
	Pivot: Snaps to the pivot point of an object.
	Vertex: Snaps to vertices on splines, meshes, or similar geometry.
	Endpoint: Snaps to the vertices at the end of a spline segment, mesh edge, or similar geometry. Similar to Vertex except that not all vertices are at the endpoints of spline segments and mesh edges.
	Midpoint: Snaps to the middle of spline segments, mesh edges, or similar geometry.
	Edge/Segment: Snaps to anywhere along spline segments, mesh edges, or similar geometry.
	Face: Snaps anywhere on the surface of a face.
	Snap to Frozen Objects: Enables other snaps to reference frozen objects.
	Snaps Use Axis Constraints: Forces result along the selected axis constraints set in the Axis Constraints toolbar.

- The following additional snaps are available in the Snap and Grid Settings dialog box and the **Snaps** quad menu.

Grid Lines	Snaps to anywhere along a grid line.
Bounding Box	Snaps to the corners of an object's bounding box.
Perpendicular	Snaps perpendicularly to a spline segment.
Tangent:	Snaps tangent to a curved spline segment.
Center Face	Snaps to the center of triangular faces.

By default, these snapping methods are not directly available in the software interface and are required to be added to the toolbar.

- The two additional snap functions available in the Autodesk 3ds Max software are described as follows:

	Ortho Snapping: Forces a transform in the horizontal or vertical directions based on the active grid.
	Polar Snapping: Forces results to the angle increment set in the Grid and Snap Settings dialog box.

- You can snap to XRef objects just like any other object.

Practice 5e

Creating a Door with Snaps

Learning Objective

- Create doors at precise locations using snaps.

In this practice, you will add a door to an opening, using snaps to position it precisely.

You must set the paths to locate the External files and Xrefs used in the practice. If you have not done this already, return to Chapter 1 and complete Task 1 to Task 3 in *Practice 1a: Organizing Folders and Working with the Interface*. You only have to set the user paths once.

*If a dialog box opens prompting you about a Mismatch, click **OK** to accept the default values.*

1. Reset the scene and open **Creating a Door.max**.
   - The scene contains extruded walls with openings and extruded carpet and tile areas. A camera has also been added.

2. Maximize the **Perspective** viewport.

3. In a **Perspective** viewport, use 🔍 (Zoom) and 🪐 (Orbit) to display the west side of the model (where the space for the outer door is located), as shown in Figure 5–54. Verify that the **Perspective** viewport displays as Default **Shading with Edged Faces**.

Figure 5–54

4. Using ⌕ (Zoom) and 🖐 (Pan), zoom into the doorway opening (as shown in Figure 5–55) to display the points for snapping.

Figure 5–55

5. In the Main Toolbar, click ³ᵖ (3D Snaps) to activate it. In the Command Panel, verify that Create panel> ● (Geometry) is open. Expand the Standard Primitives drop-down list, and select **Doors**.

Hint: Create Window and Door Objects

By default, Autodesk 3ds Max Doors and Windows are created by:

- **Clicking and dragging:** To define the width of the door/ window.

- **Releasing and picking:** A point to define the depth of the wall opening.

- **Releasing and picking:** A point to define the height of the opening.

---

*You can also press
<Shift> and right-click to
open the **Snaps** quad
menu and select
Standard>Endpoint.*

6. In the *Object Type* rollout, click **Pivot** to start the door creation process, as shown in Figure 5–56.

7. Right-click on the Interface Item menu to open the Snaps toolbar. Click (Snap to Endpoint Toggle), as shown in Figure 5–57.

Figure 5–56

Figure 5–57

8. Hover the cursor at the bottom left corner of the door opening. Note that when the cursor hovers over the endpoint (corner), it snaps to that point and a small yellow square (endpoint marker) displays, as shown in Figure 5–58.

Figure 5–58

9. Click and hold at this point and then while still holding, drag the cursor over to the lower right corner. Once it snaps to the lower right corner (as shown in Figure 5–59), release the mouse button to define the width of the door.

- If you have difficulty with this, change the orientation of the **Perspective** viewport, as shown below. You might also want to change to Wireframe display.

Layer:VIZ-1-Floor-Tile

Figure 5–59

10. Move the cursor to the back corner of the door opening and click (not click and drag) to define the depth of the opening, as shown in Figure 5–60.

Figure 5–60

11. Move the cursor to the upper right corner of the door opening and click (not click and drag) to define the height, as shown in Figure 5–61. Sometimes this is difficult to do, depending on the angle of your view. You can toggle off the Snap by pressing <S>, then adjust the height using the *Parameters* rollout.

Figure 5–61

12. Select **Display geometry** in the Scene Explorer and verify that the **PivotDoor** object is still selected. In the Command Panel, select the Modify panel (⌐). In the *Parameters* rollout, select **Double Doors**. Set the *Open* angle to **45**, as shown in Figure 5–62. In the *Leaf Parameters* rollout, in the *Panels* area, select **Beveled**. Note that in the viewport, the door will change to double doors with beveled panels and will be open at a **45°** angle, as shown in Figure 5–62.

Figure 5–62

13. Set the *Open* angle to **0°** to display the panels as closed.

14. Save your work as **MyCreating a Door.max**.

Hint: Holes in Walls using Window and Door Objects

When you use Autodesk 3ds Max Wall objects combined with Window or Door objects, you can automatically create holes for the doors and windows using snaps to align them in place. If you create the door or window away from the wall, you can move it so it intersects with the wall. Use **Select and Link** to link the door or window to the wall to automatically create the hole. You can use Edge snap to align the doors with the walls.

The advantage is that if you move the door or window, the hole moves with it. However, this functionality only works when you create Autodesk 3ds Max wall objects and it is not available when you are extruding linked geometry.

5.7 The Sweep Modifier

The Sweep modifier is a simple and effective option to create 3D geometry based on a 2D section that follows a series of spline segment paths.

- This modifier can create 3D pipe networks, curbing, moldings, and similar types of geometry, very quickly.

- Sweeps are created by adding the Sweep modifier to the path, followed by adjusting cross-section settings and other parameters in the Modify panel.

- You can select a predefined cross-section shape such as, boxes, pipes, tees, and angles, or you can use a custom shape.

- Although this functionality is also available through the Loft compound object, the Sweep modifier is easier to configure.

To use the Sweep modifier, select a spline and then in the Modify panel ( ), select **Sweep** from the Modifier List. Figure 5–63 shows an example of a wall baseboard created using the Sweep modifier.

Figure 5–63

Sweep Parameters

Section Type

In the *Section Type* rollout, you can select the type of profile that you want to sweep along the spline segments.

- If you selected **Use Built-In Section**, a list of precreated cross-sections is available as your profile, as shown in Figure 5–64. The **Angle** is the default cross-section.

Figure 5–64

- You can select **Use Custom Section** to use a custom shapes as your section. You can either create your section in the current scene or obtain it from another .MAX file.

Interpolation

In the *Interpolation* rollout, you can control the smoothness of the cross-section by adding or removing vertices.

- Steps can be set to **0** for cross-section shapes that have sharp edges (no curves). Otherwise this value should be kept low to reduce complexity. The two options available are described as follows:

Optimize	Groups the supplemented vertices closer to the corners rather than evenly along the shape.
Adaptive	Tessellates (break into segments) curves in the section shape. Select Adaptive results in a wireframe rendering mode to reduce complexity

Parameters

In the *Parameters* rollout, you can control the size and shape of the predefined cross-sections.

Sweep Parameters

In the *Sweep Parameters* rollout, you can control the placement and orientation of the cross-section shape along the path object.

- If a sweep result is backwards or upside down, use the two mirroring options to correct it. The options available are described as follows:

Offset	This option enables you to shift the horizontal and vertical position of the sweep geometry away from the spline path
Angle	This options rotates the section relative to the plane. The spline path is drawn as defined by its pivot point.
Smooth Section/ Smooth Path	Selecting these options enables you to make the object smooth, even if the path object or shape are not smooth. In the case of the swept wall baseboard, the section is smoothed to make the cross-section display as filleted, not because the baseboard follows the angled corners of the wall.
Pivot Alignment	This options enables you to anchor the cross-section shape to the path based on the shape's pivot point.
Banking	This option rotates a cross-section shape assigned to a 3D path, similar to an airplane rolling during a turn.

Practice 5f

Sweeping the Wall Baseboard

Practice Objective

- Create a wall baseboard by extruding a precreated cross-section along a selected spline.

In this practice, you will create a vinyl baseboard object around the walls using the **Sweep** modifier.

You must set the paths to locate the External files and Xrefs used in the practice. If you have not done this already, return to Chapter 1 and complete Task 1 to Task 3 in *Practice 1a: Organizing Folders and Working with the Interface*. You only have to set the user paths once.

Task 1 - Sweep the path.

*If a dialog box opens prompting you about a Mismatch, click **OK** to accept the default values.*

1. Open **Sweep Modifier.max**.
   - The scene contains the extruded walls and main door in the closed position. A camera has also been added.

2. Open the Layer Explorer (Main Toolbar> ▤ (Layer Explorer). Select and right-click on **VIZ-1-Floor Baseboard Path**. In the quad menu, select **Select Child Nodes**. This layer contains a series of lines and polylines that define the base of the wall with gaps at the openings. Close the Layer Explorer. The **VIZ-1-Floor Baseboard Path** is still selected.

*You can also right-click in the viewport and select **Isolate Selection** in the quad menu.*

3. In the Status Bar, click ▦ (Isolate Selection Toggle) to only display the selected sweep path (2D line). Click anywhere in the **Perspective** viewport to clear the selection. Zoom in so that the path (lines) display as shown in Figure 5–65.

Figure 5–65

4. In the **Perspective** viewport, click on the 2D line to select it.

You can also create a custom profile to be swept along the sweep spline.

5. In the Command Panel, select the Modify panel ( ). The name **VIZ-1-Floor Baseboard Path** displays. In the Modifier List, select **Sweep**. The **Sweep** modifier displays in the Modifier Stack. In the **Perspective** viewport, zoom in on the left side baseboard. Note that the lines have extruded along an angled cross-section, as shown in Figure 5–66. The shape of the extrusion depends on the selected *Built In Selection* in the *Section Type* rollout. The **Angle** type is the default selection, as shown in Figure 5–67.

| Figure 5–66 | Figure 5–67 |

6. In the *Interpolation* rollout, set *Steps* to **0**. (Since all of the wall corners are square, there are no curves required to interpolate along the path.)

7. In the *Parameters* rollout, set the values shown in Figure 5–68. This shape is meant to create a baseboard with minimal detail. In the viewport, note how the baseboard detail changes.

8. The angle is still facing outward (in the wrong direction). In the *Sweep Parameters* rollout, select **Mirror on XZ Plane** to reverse the angle face. Clear **Smooth Path** (all of the corners are square and should not display as rounded). Anchor the **Pivot Alignment** option by clicking ⬑ in the lower right corner. This option creates the 3D geometry object by sweeping the lower left corner of the baseboard cross-section along the baseboard path. Select **Gen. Mapping Coords.** and **Real-World Map Size**, as shown in Figure 5–69.

Sweep Parameters

☑ Mirror on XZ Plane
☐ Mirror on XY Plane

X Offset: 0'0"
Y Offset: 0'0"
Angle: 0.0

☑ Smooth Section
☐ Smooth Path

Pivot Alignment:

Align Pivot

☑ Banking
☐ Union Intersections
☑ Gen. Mapping Coords.
☑ Real-World Map Size
☑ Generate Material IDs
  ☑ Use Section IDs
  ☐ Use Path IDs

Parameters

Length: 0'6"
Width: 0'0 4/8"
Thickness: 0'0 2/8"

☐ Sync Corner Fillets

Corner Radius 1: 0'0"
Corner Radius 2: 0'0 1/8"
Edge Radii: 0'0"

Figure 5–68   **Figure 5–69**

9. In the Status Bar, click (Isolate Selection Toggle) again to clear it. The walls and other geometry are now displayed.

10. In the **Front** viewport, select the **Front** *Point of View* label and select **Cameras>Camera002-Door**. This displays the door from the inside. Select the *Per-View Preference* label and select **Default Shading** and **Edged Faces**. Note that the baseboard runs along the entire wall, including across the door, as shown in Figure 5–70.

Figure 5–70

Task 2 - Modify the path.

1. Maximize the **Camera002-Door** viewport.

2. Click anywhere on the baseboard to select it. In the Modify

   panel ( ), verify that *Name* displays **Layer:VIZ-1-Floor Baseboard Path**.

3. In the Modifier Stack, in Editable Spline, select **Vertex**. In the viewport, note that the baseboard is not displayed because you have selected an option before the **Sweep** modifier.

4. In the *Geometry* rollout, click **Refine**.

5. In the Main Toolbar, clear the Snap. In the viewport, click on the spline to place a vertex on either side and outside of the door frame, as shown in Figure 5–71. Once the two vertices have been placed, click **Refine** again to clear it.

Figure 5–71

6. In the Modifier Stack, in Editable Spline, select **Segment**. In the viewport, click on the segment between the two vertices, n front of the door. It displays as a red line, as shown in Figure 5–72.

Figure 5–72

7. With the segment selected, press <Delete> to remove the segment.

8. In the Modifier Stack, select **Sweep**. In the viewport, note that the baseboard has been modified and does not pass in front of the door, as shown in Figure 5–73.

Figure 5–73

9. Maximize to open the four viewports display.

Task 3 - Merging objects.

1. Select **File>Import>Merge**. In the Merge File dialog box, select **Interior Furnishings and Detail.max**. Click **Open**. In the Merge dialog box, click **All** at the bottom left to select all of the objects and click **OK**.

2. In the **Perspective** viewport, select the **Perspective** *Point of View Viewport* label and select **Cameras>Camera001 – Lobby1**. This changes the display to look through the newly merged **Camera – Lobby1**, as shown in Figure 5–74.

Figure 5–74

3. Select **Edit>Select None** to clear the object selection.

- Note that the desk, chairs, and other furnishings are AutoCAD 3D blocks. The curtain walls, stairs, and doors are examples of architectural objects that can be created. Save your work as **MySweep Modifier.max**.

Hint: Precreated Objects

Instead of modeling all of your scene content from scratch, look for royalty-free or low-cost objects posted on the Internet. Consider 3D blocks from other software, such as AutoCAD, Autodesk Revit, AutoCAD Civil 3D, or directly from manufacturer's web sites.

Chapter Review Questions

1. While editing a spline at the vertex sub-object level, which tool enables you to manipulate the handles on one side of the curve separately from the other handle?

    a. **Bezier**

    b. **Bezier Corner**

    c. **Smooth**

    d. **Smooth Corner**

2. To combine shapes using the 2D Boolean operations, which sub-object level in the **Edit Spline** modifier should be selected?

    a. Vertex

    b. Segment

    c. Spline

3. The **Capping** option in the **Extrude** modifier applies to both open and closed shapes.

    a. True

    b. False

4. The Boolean Explorer is available with which type of 3D Boolean object?

    a. Boolean compound object

    b. ProBoolean compound object

    c. Procutter compound object

5. Which **Sweep** modifier option in the *Sweep Parameters* rollout rotates a cross-section shape assigned to a 3D path?

    a. **Offset**

    b. **Angle**

    c. **Banking**

    d. **Pivot Alignment**

6. Which of the following Snap mode enables you to snap to points at elevation **0** on the current grid?

a. (Angle Snap)

b. (3D Snap)

c. (2.5D Snap)

d. (2D Snap)

Command Summary

Button	Command	Location
3	3D Snap	• **Main Toolbar:** Snaps flyout
2.5	2.5D Snap	• **Main Toolbar:** Snaps flyout
2	2D Snap	• **Main Toolbar:** Snaps flyout
	Angle Snap	• **Main Toolbar**
	Isolate Selection	• **Status Bar** • **Quad Menu**
	Layer Explorer	• **Main Toolbar** • **Layers Toolbar**
N/A	Merge	• **Menu Bar:** File>Import>Merge
	Offset Mode	• **Status Bar**
	Percent Snap	• **Main Toolbar**
	Shapes	• **Command Panel:** *Create* panel • **Menu Bar:** Create>Shapes
	Snap to Edge/ Segment	• **Snaps Toolbar**
	Snap to Endpoint	• **Snaps Toolbar**
	Snap to Face	• **Snaps Toolbar**
	Snap to Frozen Objects	• **Snaps Toolbar**
	Snap to Grid Point	• **Snaps Toolbar**
	Snap to Midpoint	• **Snaps Toolbar**
	Snap to Pivot	• **Snaps Toolbar**
	Snap to Vertex	• **Snaps Toolbar**
	Snaps use Axis Constraints	• **Snaps Toolbar**

Materials

To create a realistic visualization, materials are used to more accurately represent the model as a realistic real-world design. The Autodesk® 3ds Max® software provides material libraries that can be used to assign materials to objects in a scene or to create and customize materials. Materials control such attributes as color, texture, transparency, and a host of other physical properties that you can adjust to create a realistic representation of the model.

Learning Objectives in this Chapter

- Understand the role of materials and maps in visualization.
- Control the various attributes of a material using various shaders, components, and maps.
- Display and manage all of the materials used in a scene using the Material Explorer.
- Use various types of Standard materials and control the parameters of the material shaders.
- Assign bitmaps or procedural maps to replace the shader parameters in materials.
- Control transparency, embossed or pitted appearance, glass or mirror effect on objects using various mapping techniques.
- Working with Arnold materials.

6.1 Understanding Materials and Maps

Introduction to Materials

Materials can be used to create believable visualizations and to dress up geometry so that it resembles objects in the real world. Materials control how light interacts with surfaces in 3D models. If an object is shiny it reflects the light, however, if transparency is applied, the light passes through the object.

- Materials use Maps to paint the surfaces with all types of textures to resemble the actual construction materials for your design.

- Different material types use different material shaders to generate their work. Shaders are algorithms that create the image. Each shader has its own set of parameters.

Materials and Renderers in the Autodesk 3ds Max Software

Materials are deeply interconnected with the renderers. Regardless of which renderer is used, the rendering process is similar for all material types. In the 3D visualization process, to create an image in the viewport or in a image file, a *renderer* is employed. The viewport display uses an interactive viewport renderer, however the image is created using an *image* (production) renderer. The renderer determines what the pixel's RGB (red, green, blue) values are in the image based on the material assignments.

- In the Autodesk 3ds Max software, you can use the Scanline, Quicksilver, VUE File, ART renderer, or Arnold as image renderers. You can set the appropriate renderer in the Render Setup dialog box. in the Main toolbar, click

  (Render Setup) and select the required renderer in the Renderer list.

- Depending on the selected image renderer, the materials displayed in the material list vary.

- To create an image render of a view, use (Render Production) in the Main toolbar. You are required to use

  (Render Production) throughout the practices in this chapter.

- The viewport renderer can use Nitrous Direct 3D 11 (default), Nitrous Direct3D 9, Nitrous Software, Legacy Direct3D, or Legacy OpenGL graphics drivers to create the real-time interactive display.

- The viewport provides a frame around the image and the output resolution determines the number of pixels to be created in that frame. The renderer then examines the geometry in the scene, first looking at the face normals, removing the faces whose normals face away from the camera (face normals are directional vectors perpendicular to the surface of the face). The remaining faces are z-sorted, the faces in front covering up the ones further away.

- Once the faces are determined, the color, transparency, shininess, texture, reflection, bumpiness, and other values are defined based on the material type, shaders, and map channels.

- The visible faces are calculated using the UVW mapping coordinates and the scene illumination. This determines RGB values, which are applied to the pixels in the image.

Material Components

Materials have several fundamental components. Standard materials have channels that determine the color applied in the calculation based on the lighting interaction. The components available are described as follows:

- The *Diffuse* channel represents those faces that are receiving illumination.

- The *Ambient* channel paints the faces that are in darkness, and it contributes color to all faces in the scene.

- The *Specular* channel determines color based on shininess and lighting information.

- The Shininess is controlled by various parameters, such as **Specularity** and **Glossiness**. Shininess also plays a part in reflection and refraction.

- A Transparency quality is determined by *opacity* values, which can have advanced features such as *falloff* and *additive* or subtractive behavior.

- Materials are defined by maps and other physical properties (diffuse, ambient, shininess, etc.).

Maps

Maps are the key components when working with materials. Maps are based on either 2D image files (bitmaps) or are formula-based, computer-generated images called procedural maps. Some maps can be configured as composites or adjustments to other maps.

- Materials can include multiple maps to serve different purposes.

- Map also serve in other roles, such as an environment background or a lighting projection.

When a material containing a map is applied to an object, mapping coordinates are required for the software to render correctly.

- Maps cannot be applied directly to objects in a scene; instead, they are assigned to materials. These materials are then directly applied to objects, as shown in Figure 6–1.

Figure 6–1

- Two of the most commonly used maps types are **diffuse color** and **bump**.

Diffuse Color	Defines the color of objects under normal lighting.
	- Digital or scanned photographs can be used as Diffuse Color maps.
	- The figure below is a brick image map (left) and a rendering of an object with a brick material that uses it (right).
Bump maps	Make objects appear to have texture without modifying object geometry.
	- Bump maps are used to describe indentations, relief, and roughness.
	- In bump maps the lighter-colored areas display projected away from the surface while the darker areas display recessed.
	- The figure below displays a brick bump map (left) and a rendering of an object with a brick material that uses it (right).
	- You can apply both the diffuse and bump map to a single object.

- In addition to these two map types, the Autodesk 3ds Max software can use maps to control many different material parameters that might vary across a surface, including shininess, transparency, and more.

6.2 Material Shaders

Material Shaders are complex algorithms that describe how light interacts with surfaces. The material color, highlights, self-illumination, and many other features are dependant on the material shaders.

- In Standard materials, the shader type is selected through the *Shader Basic Parameters* rollout, as shown in Figure 6–2.

Figure 6–2

The standard shader types are described as follows:

	Anisotropic	Shader for materials with elliptical highlights, such as hair, glass, or brushed metal.
	Blinn	General purpose shader for shiny, smooth objects with soft, circular highlights. Blinn is the default shader for Standard materials.
	Metal	Shader for luminous metallic surfaces.
	Multi-Layer	Enables two sets of anisotropic controls for complex or highly polished surfaces.
	Oren-Nayar-Blinn	A variation of the Blinn shader that provides additional controls for matte surfaces, such as fabric or terra cotta.

	Phong	Related to the Blinn shader, also used for shiny, smooth surfaces with circular highlights. The Phong shader generates harder, sharper (often less realistic) highlights than Blinn.
	Strauss	For metallic and similar surfaces, Strauss offers a simpler interface than the Metal shader.
	Translucent Shader	Enables you to control translucency, which is the scattering of light as it passes through the material. Appropriate for Semi-transparent materials, such as frosted glass.

Shader (Specific) Basic Parameters

Each material shader has a unique combination of parameters (as shown in Figure 6–3) that can be controlled.

Figure 6–3

- Most of these parameters can be replaced by a map when their values are not constant across the surface. For example, a Diffuse Color Map can be used to replace a single diffuse color for a brick material.

- Colors can be selected by picking on the color swatch next to a color parameter, which opens the interactive Color Selector.

Ambient Color	The color of a material under ambient (background) lighting. It can be assigned globally and through standard lights set to cast ambient light. Ambient and diffuse colors can be locked at the same values, if required.
Diffuse Color	The color of a material under direct lighting. This is the base color of a material (outside of highlights).
Specular Color	The highlight color of a material. It is calculated automatically for the Metal and Multilayer shaders.
Self-Illumination	Values greater than 0 cause materials to appear to be illuminated, but surfaces with this material do not illuminate other objects. This parameter is useful for materials used in light fixtures. Self-illuminated objects do not automatically glow. Glows must be assigned as a special effect (**Rendering>Effects**).
Opacity	The percentage measurement of opacity, the opposite of transparency. Materials that have 0% opacity are completely see-through. For example, a typical clear glass material could have an Opacity between 0-10%.

- Many shader properties relate to highlights, the bright areas caused by the specular reflection of a light source on the surface of an object.

- Parameters relating to *Specular Highlights* are listed next to a highlight curve that shows a graphical representation of these settings. Not all of the parameters are available for each shader type. The *Specular Highlights* parameters for Blinn are shown in Figure 6–4.

Figure 6–4

- The *Specular Highlights* parameters for Anisotropic shaders are shown in Figure 6–5.

Figure 6–5

Specular Level	A relative measurement of the overall highlight intensity.
Glossiness	A relative measurement of the overall size of highlights. The more glossy an object, the smaller and more intense the highlights.
Soften	A relative measurement used to soften the edges of highlights.
Anisotropy	Defines the elliptical shape of Anisotropic highlights, where 0 = round and 100 = a very tight ellipse.
Orientation	Defines the degrees of rotation for an Anisotropic highlight.

6.3 Managing Materials

Materials are managed through the Material Editor (Slate or Compact). The Slate Material Editor has the Material/Map Browser included with it whereas the Compact Material Editor has an option for accessing the Material/Map Browser.

- Use the Slate Material Editor to design and build materials.

- Use the Compact Material Editor to apply existing materials.

Slate Material Editor Interface

The Slate Material Editor is a graphical interface for listing, creating, modifying, and assigning different kinds of materials. It enables you to graphically create and modify complex materials by wiring the maps and materials to different channels of the parent material. It also enables you to edit and modify the parameters of already created materials. In the Main Toolbar, in the Material flyout, use ![icon] (Slate Material Editor) to open the Slate Material Editor, as shown in Figure 6–6.

Figure 6–6

The interface of the Slate Material Editor has the following main areas:

Material/Map Browser

The Material/Map Browser area (shown in Figure 6–7) contains an extensive list of predefined materials and maps. You can use the predefined materials directly or as a base for modifying them to get the required material effect.

You can also select ***Rendering>Material Editor>Slate Material Editor***. *Pressing <M> opens the last material editor that was used.*

Figure 6–7

*You can also open the Material/Map Browser independent of the Material Editor by selecting **Rendering> Material/Map Browser** in the menu bar.*

- The Browser displays by default, but you can temporarily close it by clicking **X** in the title bar. You can open it by selecting **Tools>Material/Map Browser** in the Slate Material Editor's menu bar (as shown in Figure 6–8) or by pressing <O> when the Slate Material Editor is the active window.

- At the top of the Material/Map Browser, click ▼ to open the drop-down list (options menu), as shown in Figure 6–9. It contains options that enable you to control the display of the libraries, materials, maps, and other groups of materials. It also enables you to create and manage new custom libraries and groups.

Figure 6–8

Figure 6–9

The materials and maps listed in the Material/ Map Browser are dependent on the active image renderer.

- The *Search by Name* box enables you to enter the first few characters of the material/map name to display the list of materials/maps that you want to use.

- The materials in the Browser are organized in the form of libraries and groups. The groups are organized on the basis of their attributes such as Maps, Materials, etc and are further divided into subgroups (For example, **Materials>General**). Each library or group has a +/- sign, to expand or contract, along with its heading.

- The *Materials* and *Maps* groups contain the type of materials and maps that can be used as templates for creating custom materials and maps.

- The *Controller* group contains the animation controllers that can be used for material animation.

- The Autodesk Material Library contains Autodesk materials, which are shared between various Autodesk applications, such as AutoCAD, Inventor, and Revit. The library displays when the active production renderer is set to the **ART** renderer or **Quicksilver Hardware** renderer.

- All of the materials used in the scene are listed in the *Scene Materials* group. A solid wedge shaped red band displayed with a scene material name indicates that the **Show Shaded Material In Viewport** option has been selected.

- The materials listed in the Browser are dependent on the type of renderer currently in use. To see all of the materials independent of the renderer, select **Show Incompatible**

  option in the Material/Map Browser drop-down list (click ▼ to open the options menu).

Active View

The Active View is an area in the Slate Material Editor that displays the expanded view of materials with all its elements shown as nodes, as shown in Figure 6–10. You can graphically create and modify complex materials by wiring their nodes together, and further edit their parameters through this view.

Figure 6–10

You can also double-click on the material in the Map/Material Browser to automatically place it on the View1 sheet.

- To display a material in the active view (*View1*, by default), drag the material from the Map/Material Browser and then drop it on the *View1* sheet. These are called nodes.

- Once the material node is loaded on the active view, the title bar with a preview icon is displayed and the list of various channel slots are listed, as shown in Figure 6–10. You can wire each of these slots to another map or material. On the left side, each node has a number of input sockets (small circles) for each slot. On the right side of each node is a single output socket. These can be wired to the sockets of other material. If a map or material is wired to a channel, the slot displays in green. This material, with its input sockets wired, becomes the parent material and the materials and maps that are wired to the slots become the children. You can further wire the children to other materials to create complex material trees.

- You can also right-click in an empty area of the active view to open a menu containing options for selecting any material/ map/controller listed in the Material/Map Browser.

- The main material node has a blank output socket on the right side that can be used to assign this material to geometry in the viewport. Click and hold the output socket and drag the cursor on to the object. A temporary wire displays indicating that you are assigning the material. Assigning material in this way ignores already selected objects or geometry in the viewport.

- You can use the scroll wheel to zoom in or zoom out on the nodes in the *View1* sheet. Hold the scroll wheel to pan around in the sheet.

- You can also delete wires to cut the connection between the parent material and the child material. To delete a wire, select it and press <Delete>.

- If a white dashed line displays as a border around a node, its Parameter Editor displays in the active view.

- The color of the title bar of the node indicates the type of material.

Blue node	Indicates that it is a material.
Green node	Indicates that it is a Map.
Yellow node	Indicates that it is a Controller

- A diagonal line dividing the title bar into two colors (red and blue) indicates that the **Show Shaded Material In Viewport** option is selected for that material.

- Right-clicking on a title bar of a node displays a specific shortcut menu containing the options for managing that material or map. The options enable you to control the display and how you want the preview to be displayed on the active sheet. It also enables you to organize the material nodes and their children more efficiently.

- You can select multiple material/map nodes together, then right-click to open the combined menu and use the options for all of the nodes at the same time.

- You can toggle between a large and small material preview icon by double-clicking on the icon in the node title bar.

- The outline of a preview icon indicates whether the material is assigned or not (hot or cold) to objects in the viewport.

No white boundary around the icon indicates that the material is not used in the scene and is cold.

Outlined white triangles at the four corners indicate the material is hot and is being used in the scene. Modifying this material interactively displays the modifications in the scene.

Solid white triangles at the four corners indicate the material is applied to the currently selected object on the scene.

- Additional sheets can be added to the View area by right-clicking on the default *View1* tab and selecting **Create New View**. Using this menu, you can also rename and delete your views. Once multiple sheets exist, you can select the appropriate tab to active it.

Hint: Active View

To organize your working space, it is recommended that you delete any unused materials from the active view. Deleting a material from the active view does not delete the material from the Scene materials list. You can drag and drop (or double-click) the material back to the active view.

- After you have created and applied materials to a scene, the *View* sheets are saved with the .MAX file. When you open the file again, the sheets display the saved material nodes.

Navigator Window

The Navigator window, which displays by default, provides a quick layout of the nodes in the active sheet, as shown in Figure 6–11. It can be used to pan around in the active view by dragging the outlined red box. The colored nodes indicate the same concepts as that of a sheet. A red and blue node indicates that the **Show Map In Viewport** option is selected for that material.

Figure 6–11

Parameter Editor

You can modify a material or a map by adjusting their parameters. Double-click on the material's title bar heading to display the Parameters, as shown in Figure 6–12. A white dashed line border displays around the node indicating that its Parameter Editor is displayed. The parameters are grouped in rollouts and you can click **+** on the rollout name bar to expand the rollout and access its parameters. You can rename the material by entering a new name in the *Name* field of the Parameter Editor.

Figure 6–12

Floating the Parameter Editor and hiding the Navigator can help reduce the footprint of the Slate Material Editor on the screen.

- As with any other window, you can move, dock, float, or close the Parameter Editor. To float the Parameter Editor, drag its header outside the Slate Material Editor. To dock it again, double-click on its header.

Toolbar

The Slate Material Editor includes a toolbar (shown in Figure 6–13) at the top left corner of the window and contains the following tools.

Figure 6–13

(Select Tool)	Enables you to select a material node in the Active View. It is the tool that is selected by default.
(Pick Material from Object)	Enables you to pick a material that is assigned to an object in the scene and display it in the active view.
(Put Material to Scene)	Enables you to update objects having an older material whose copy has been edited after it was applied.
(Assign Material to Selection)	Enables you to assign a selected material to selected objects in the viewport.
(Move Children)	Enables you to move the complete material tree when you move the parent material node in the Active View. Clearing this tool, moves the Parent individually and extends the wires as you move the parent
(Show Shaded Material in Viewport)	Enables you to display the maps for the active material. This is helpful when you are modifying the map in the *View* sheet, you can see the changes interactively in the viewport. You do not have to render to see the map changes.
/ (Lay Out All-Vertical/ Horizontal)	Enables you to organize all of the material nodes and their children in the *View* sheet either vertically or horizontally.
(Lay Out Children)	Enables you to lay out the children of the currently selected node without changing the position of the parent node.
(Material/Map Browser) (Parameter Editor)	Enable you to control the display of these tools in the Slate Material Editor.
(Select by Material)	Enables you to select objects based on the active material.

Menu Bar

The Slate Material Editor displays a menu bar along the top of the window (shown in Figure 6–14) that contains commands for various actions related to materials.

Figure 6–14

Modes	Enables you to toggle between the two editors (Slate and Compact).
Material	Enable you to select a material by picking it from the object in the viewport, by selecting an object in the viewport, or selecting all of the materials used in the scene. You also have the options for assigning materials.
Edit	Enables you to edit the active view and update the preview windows.
Select	Provides different selection options that can be used in the active view.
View	Provides different zoom and pan options and contains options for the layout of the nodes in the active view.
Options	Enables you to further manage the Slate Material Editor.
Tools	Controls the display of the Material/Map Browser, Parameter Editor, and Navigator.
Utilities	Provides the render and object selection options and contains options for managing the materials.

Practice 6a

Introduction to Materials

Practice Objectives

- Load a material library in the Slate Material Editor.
- Create and edit a new material and assign it to objects in the scene.

In this practice, you will assign previously created materials to different objects on the scene. You will then create, edit, and assign new materials to objects in the scene using the Parameter Editor of the Slate Material Editor.

You must set the paths to locate the External files and Xrefs used in the practice. If you have not done this already, return to Chapter 1 and complete Task 1 to Task 3 in *Practice 1a: Organizing Folders and Working with the Interface*. You only have to set the user paths once.

Task 1 - Assigning materials in the Slate Material Editor.

*If a dialog box opens prompting you about a Mismatch, click **OK** to accept the default values.*

1. Open **Intro to Materials and Rendering.max**.
   - The Light pole model displays in the viewport.

2. In the Main Toolbar, in the Material flyout, click (Slate Material Editor) to open the Slate Material Editor. Alternatively, you can select **Rendering>Material Editor> Slate Material Editor**.

If you start a new scene file, no materials are listed in the View1 sheet.

3. In the Slate Material Editor, in the *View1* sheet, four materials nodes display as shown in Figure 6–15. Note that all the materials used in the scene are listed in the *Scene Materials* group (bottom of the list) in the Material/Map Browser.

Figure 6–15

A blue node indicates that it is a material, a green node indicates that it is a Map, and a yellow node indicates that it is a Controller.

- A diagonal line dividing the title bar into two colors (red and blue) indicates that the **Show Map In Viewport** option is selected for that material

4. Click in an empty space in the *View1* sheet, and using the scroll wheel on your mouse, zoom into the nodes. Hold the scroll wheel to pan around to see the details of each node. The red bounding box in the *Navigator* area can also be dragged around to quickly access specific areas in the *View1* sheet.

5. Using Zoom and Pan, locate the **Concrete** material (second material node from the top).

6. Move and size the Slate Material Editor in the Drawing window so that you can see both the Material Editor and the model in the viewport window side by side.

You can close the Navigator and Parameter Editor to create more space for displaying the nodes in the active sheet.

7. In the **Concrete** material, click and hold ⬜ (material output socket) on the right side. Drag and drop the **Concrete** material from the *View1* sheet directly to the LP Base object in the viewport window, as shown in Figure 6–16. A temporary wire displays in *View1* indicating that you are assigning the material. (Dragging in this way ignores which objects or geometry are currently selected in the model.) The material is assigned to the object and displays in the viewport.

Figure 6–16

Dragging materials in highly complex scenes can be challenging. Instead, you can select objects, select material, and use ⬚ (Assign Material to Selection).

8. Using the Scene Explorer, select the groups **LP Fixture** and **LP Fixture01** (each group contains housing, globe, and mounting arm). You can also select them directly in the viewport.

9. In the Slate Material Editor, in the *View1* sheet, locate **Metal_Grey_Plain** (the first material node). Right-click on the title bar of the material and select **Assign Material to Selection**. The material is applied to all of the objects in the two **LP Fixture** groups.

> **Hint: Group Objects**
>
> To assign a material to individual objects in a group, select the group, select **Group>Open**, and then select the individual object in the group. Then, assign materials to individual parts in the group.

10. Click in the empty space to clear the selection. Orbit around in **Perspective** viewport to see the globes.

11. You can also assign materials directly from the Material/Map Browser. Scroll to the bottom of the Material/Map Browser and expand the **Scene Materials** category, if required, as shown in Figure 6–17. Click and drag **Illuminated Lens** to one of the LP Globe objects in the model. This method only assigns the material to the object on which you are dropping the material.

12. Drag and drop the **Illuminated Lens** material to the other LP Globe object in the model, as shown in Figure 6–17.

Figure 6–17

13. Assign the **Metal_Grey_Plain** material to the LP Base Plate and LP Pole objects using any of the assigning materials method.

14. Orbit and zoom into all objects in the viewport. In the Main Toolbar, click ![teapot icon] (Render Production) to render the scene. The scene is rendered, as shown in Figure 6–18. Close the Render window.

A gradient background was added for visual clarity.

Figure 6–18

- The globe material was made to look as if it is illuminated, but it does not actually add any light to the scene.

15. Save the file as **MyLightPoleMaterials.max**.

Task 2 - Working with Materials.

When you are starting a new scene or working in an existing scene you will have to create new materials or edit existing materials. In this task, you will be able to use the Slate Material Editor to create and work with materials.

1. The Material/Map Browser of the Slate Material Editor contains an extensive list of predefined materials that you can use directly or use them as a base for creating your custom materials. You can also import your own material library. Scroll through the list of materials that are available in the list.

2. At the top of the Material/Map Browser, click ![down arrow icon] to open the **Materials/Map Browser Options** menu.

If the material libraries were not installed, there will be no files in the project folder in the \materiallibraries subdirectory.

3. In the **Materials/Map Browser Options** menu, select **Open Material Library**. The Import Material Library dialog box opens in the *materiallibraries* subdirectory. If required, browse to the path under the root installation (usually *C:\Program Files\ Autodesk\3ds Max 2019*) and open the *\materiallibraries* subdirectory.

4. Select and open **AecTemplates.mat**, as shown in Figure 6–19.

   • In the Material/Map Browser, note that a list of materials is added to the top of with **AecTemplates.mat** listed as the title, as shown in Figure 6–20.

Figure 6–19　　　　　　　　　　**Figure 6–20**

   • You can remove a library by right-clicking on the category heading and selecting **Close Material Library**. Do not close this library.

Double-clicking on a material in the Material/Map Browser also displays the material in the View1 sheet, where you can customize the material, as required. Materials do not have to be placed in the View1 sheet unless they are being customized. General materials can be assigned directly from the Material/Map Browser.

5. In the Material/Map Browser, expand the **Materials>General** category. A list of materials displays. Right-click on the **General** category and select **Display Group (and Subgroups) As>Medium Icons**. All of the materials in the **General** category now display as thumbnail images. Right-click on the **General** category again and select **Display Group (and Subgroups) As>Icons and Text** to display the materials in the icons and name format.

6. The *View1* sheet already displays the materials used in the scene. To create a new view, right-click on the *View1* label and select **Create New View**, as shown in Figure 6–21.

Figure 6–21

*The Autodesk Material Library is not available in the Material/Map Browser when **Scanline**, **VUE File**, or **Arnold** are set as the active renderers.*

7. Accept the default name of **View2** and click **OK**. A new empty sheet named **View2** is added.

8. In the Material/Map Browser, expand the **Autodesk Material Library** category.

9. In the list, expand **Metal** and **Steel** to display the materials listed.

10. Double-click on the **Galvanized** material. The material displays as a node on the *View2* sheet, as shown in Figure 6–22.

Figure 6–22

Hint: Add Materials to Sheets

Add materials to sheets if you want to modify them. If they are simply going to be assigned to an object in the scene, select and drag them directly from the Material Browser list onto the objects.

---

11. In the *View2* sheet, double-click on the title bar of the **Metal/Steel Galvanized** material.

Note that in the active sheet (View2), the material node is surrounded by a dashed white border, indicating that the Parameter Editor for this material displays.

12. The Parameter Editor for this material opens in the Slate Material Editor. In the *Relief Pattern* rollout, note that *Image* displays the map name as **Metals.Metal Fabrications.Metal Stairs. Galvanized.png**. Use the *Amount* slider or enter the value **0.5** directly in the edit box, as shown in Figure 6–23.

Figure 6–23

Hint: Parameter Editor

You can customize the materials by making changes in the Parameter Editor.

---

13. In the *View2* sheet, review the preview icon for the material and note that there is no outline around the icon (as shown in Figure 6–24) indicating that it is not assigned to any object and that it is a cold material.

Figure 6–24

14. Using the drag and drop method from the output socket, assign the **Galvanized** material to the **LP Fixture Housings** (the chamfer cylinders) and **LP Mounting Arms** (the arms holding the fixtures to the post). This method enables you to assign different materials to individual objects in the group.

15. Select the **LP Base Plate** and **LP Pole** and use (Assign Material to Selection) to assign the **Galvanized** material.

16. Review the preview icon for the material. Note that there is now a white outline around the thumbnail, as shown in Figure 6–25. This indicates that the material has been assigned to an object in the scene.

- Note that this new material is also added to the *Scene Materials* list in the Material Map Browser, as shown in Figure 6–26.

| Figure 6–25 | Figure 6–26 |

17. Save the file.

6.4 General Materials

General materials are the most basic materials provided with the Autodesk 3ds Max software. They can be accessed by expanding the **Materials>General** categories in the Material/Map Browser, as shown in Figure 6–27.

Depending on the renderer you are using, the list of the materials might differ from the figure shown.

Figure 6–27

- You can use General materials directly as is or customize them by modifying their parameters to create your own materials, as required.

Physical Material

Physical Material has parameters that create reasonable shading effects and are appropriate for scenes with physically-based lighting. Using Physical Material, you can create materials that are based on the physical properties of a material.

*If the **Physical Material** does not display in the **General** list, in the Main toolbar, use*

*(Render Setup) and select **Scanline Renderer** in the Renderer list.*

- Physical materials are real world materials that are organized in an easy interface that follows a logical layout.

- Materials are comprised of either a base layer that is assigned a diffuse color with dielectric reflections, or a base color with metallic reflections, as shown in Figure 6–28.

- In addition to the diffuse color, the materials have transparency, sub-surface scattering, self-illumination (emission), and a top clear-coat layer, as shown in Figure 6–28.

- These materials contain both standard and advanced parameters that are designed for physically-based material adjustments.

- A number of presets (as shown on the Figure 6–29) are also available with their parameters set for their optimum values. They are provided to be used directly and require minimum modification.

- Physical Material works well with ART (Autodesk® Raytracer) and the Autodesk 3ds Max Arnold renderers.

- Physical Material is not available for **Quicksilver Hardware** and **VUE FIle** renderers.

Figure 6–28

Figure 6–29

Physical Material Parameters

The parameters of the Physical Material are easy and follow a simple workflow. The available parameters are:

- The *Coating Parameters* rollout (shown in Figure 6–30) contains options that are used for applying a clear coat onto the finish of the surface.
    - To create a glossy coating on the material, set the *Clearcoat Weight* to **1.0**.
    - *Coating IOR* sets the reflectivity of a clear coat. The higher the value, more reflective the clear coat is.
    - *Roughness* adds a softer sheen and makes a clear coat less glossy.
    - *Affect Underlying* area adds an affect to the base diffuse color.

Figure 6–30

- In the *Basic Parameters* rollout (shown in Figure 6–28), the *Base Color and Reflections* area enables you to set the base color of the material surface and add the type and amount of reflectivity.
    - A *Weight* of **0** has no color, and a value of **1** is full color.
    - *Metalness* determines how the surface reflects. A value of **0.0** creates standard reflections (such as for plastics), and a value of **1.0** creates a metal surface (such as for steel or aluminum).
    - *Roughness* and *IOR* work in a similar fashion as the Clearcoat settings, but alter the base surface of the material. A value of **0.0** is a hard surface, and **1.0** is a soft surface.

- In the *Basic Parameters* rollout, the *Transparency* area enables you to create clear materials, like glass.
  - A *Weight* value of **0.0** is completely opaque, and **1.0** is fully transparent.
  - *Thin Walled* creates a glass-like appearance to the surface by making the interior hollow.

- In the *Basic Parameters* rollout, *Sub-Surface Scattering* is a feature that causes light to dissipate through the volume of an object.
  - *Scatter Color* sets the color of the scattered light within the volume of the object.
  - *Depth* sets the distance the light scatters through the object in a real-world distance.

- In the *Basic Parameters* rollout, the *Emission* area enables you to create a material that can emit light and illuminate the scene.
  - An *Emission Weight* of **1** sets the material to full emission and defaults to a *Luminance* of 1500 cd/m² (candelas per meter square).

Multi/Sub-Object Materials

Objects might require different materials on each face. For example, a door or window might need different materials for front and back frames, mullions, and glazing. For this, Multi/Sub-Object materials are used, as shown in Figure 6–31.

- They enable you to stack multiple materials into a single *parent* material, each with a material ID number.

- Faces and polygons of individual objects can have a corresponding ID number assigned through modifiers such as **Edit Mesh** and **Edit Poly**.

- Objects brought into the Autodesk 3ds Max software from vertical applications, such as the AutoCAD Architecture software and the AutoCAD Civil 3D software are divided into multiple objects by material and do not require Multi/Sub-Object materials.

- The Slate Material Editor provides a convenient view that enables you to visually identify all of the materials that make up a Multi/Sub-Object material. Initially, when the material is created, the parent material node opens with 10 default slots. You can wire sub-materials to each slot. Each of the sub-materials can be modified or you can add new materials to the view and rewire into any of the slots. Figure 6–31 shows an example of a Multi/Sub-Object material that is wired to five materials. Slots can be added or deleted using the **Add** or **Delete** options in the *Multi/Sub-Object Basic Parameters* rollout.

Figure 6–31

Additional General Materials

Depending on the renderer, the additional General materials available for use are described as follows:

Blend	Combines two materials to create a third.
Composite	Enables multiple materials to be combined into a single, composite material through additive colors, subtractive colors, or opacity mixing.
DirectX Shader	Enables you to shade objects in the viewport to more accurately display how objects look when exported to real-time viewing.
Double Sided	Enables you to have one material assigned to the outside of objects and another to the inside (the back-facing sides).

Ink 'n' Paint	Creates a flat shaded cartoon rendering with the contours or edges as ink lines.
Shell Material	Used with *texture baking*, which is the process of creating replacement color maps that include the scene illumination (illumination is *baked in*).
Shellac	Superimposes two materials together through additive composition.
Top/Bottom	Assigns different materials to faces with normals pointing *up* and *down*.
XRef Material	Assigns a material applied to an object to another Autodesk 3ds Max scene file. As with Xref scenes and objects, you can only change the material parameters in the original source file.

6.5 Scanline Materials

Scanline materials are another set of basic materials included in the Autodesk 3ds Max software and are best used with the **Scanline** renderer. These materials can be accessed by expanding the **Materials>Scanline** category in the Material/Map Browser, as shown in Figure 6–32.

Figure 6–32

*Depending on the current renderer used, the list of the materials might differ. Scanline materials are not available with the **Arnold** renderer.*

Architectural Materials

Architectural materials are a type of Scanline materials (as shown in Figure 6–32) that are appropriate for scenes with physically-based lighting.

Architectural materials are applicable to many different kinds of visualization projects, not only Architectural or Civil/Site projects.

- Architectural materials use a streamlined interface that highlights the parameters and maps that are most likely to change.

- Controls that are not directly available to Standard materials are also available, such as refraction, luminance, and advanced lighting overrides.

Raytrace Material

The Raytrace material is used to create highly configurable, realistic reflections and refractions. These materials support fog, color density, translucency, fluorescence, and other effects. Some Architectural materials (such as ones with the mirror template) automatically generate raytraced results.

Standard Materials

Standard materials are the most basic material and consist of four color components: Ambient color, Diffuse color, Specular color, and Filter color. These materials can be used in most models and can be easily customized.

Advanced Lighting Override Material

The Advanced Lighting Override material is not a regularly used material and is used only to supplement any renderable base material. It is used when there is a need to directly control the radiosity properties of a material.

6.6 Autodesk Materials

The Autodesk 3ds Max software offers a number of **Autodesk** base materials, as shown in Figure 6–33. These can be used as templates to build materials as per your requirements. Their default parameters are already set to produce the optimum effect.

Additionally, there are categories of precreated Autodesk materials present in the *Autodesk Material Library* (as shown in Figure 6–34), which can be used directly in your scene.

Figure 6–33   Figure 6–34

- The Autodesk Materials are only available for use with the **ART** renderer and the **Quicksilver Hardware** renderer.

- The Autodesk materials should be used with physically accurate (photometric) lights.

- The Autodesk materials have a much simpler interface and contain presets that enable faster selection of specific material parameters and preassigned bitmaps.

- You can adjust the reflection, refraction, and transparency of the material.

- It enables you to round corners through a post-production pixel shader and an Ambient Occlusion setting that adds subtle detail enhancement to surface corners, cracks, and crevices.

- The Autodesk Material Library was designed specifically for architectural visualization and includes material categories for *Ceramic*, *Concrete*, *Fabric*, *Finish*, *Flooring*, *Glass*, *Liquid*, *Masonry*, *Metal*, etc.

- These materials are aligned with the latest release of the Autodesk Revit software, which means that the materials applied in the Autodesk® Revit® Architecture software display as Autodesk Material Library materials inside the Autodesk 3ds Max software.

6.7 Assigning Maps to Materials

Maps are often assigned to replace the shader parameters, especially Diffuse Color. Maps can be assigned to various materials through the *Maps* rollout. Figure 6–35 shows the *Maps* rollout for Standard materials and Figure 6–36 shows the S*pecial Maps* and *Generic Maps* rollout for Physical Materials. Maps include Diffuse Color, Bump maps, Opacity etc.

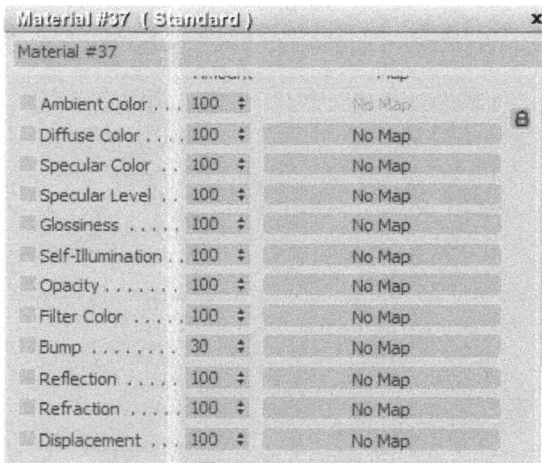

Material #25 (Physical Material)

Material #25

▸ **Anisotropy**
▾ **Special Maps**
Special Maps

✔ Bump Map	0.3 ⬍	No Map
✔ Coating Bump Map: . .	0.3 ⬍	No Map
✔ Displacement	1.0 ⬍	No Map
✔ Cutout		No Map

▾ **Generic Maps**
Generic Maps

✔ Base Weight	No Map
✔ Base Color	No Map
✔ Reflection Weight	No Map
✔ Reflection Color	No Map
✔ Roughness	No Map
✔ Metalness	No Map
✔ Diffuse Roughness	No Map
✔ Anisotropy	No Map
✔ Anisotropy Angle	No Map
✔ Transparency Weight	No Map
✔ Transparency Color	No Map
✔ Transparency Roughness	No Map

Material #37 (Standard)

Material #37

	Amount	Map
Ambient Color . . .	100 ⬍	No Map
Diffuse Color	100 ⬍	No Map
Specular Color . .	100 ⬍	No Map
Specular Level . .	100 ⬍	No Map
Glossiness	100 ⬍	No Map
Self-Illumination . .	100 ⬍	No Map
Opacity	100 ⬍	No Map
Filter Color	100 ⬍	No Map
Bump	30 ⬍	No Map
Reflection	100 ⬍	No Map
Refraction	100 ⬍	No Map
Displacement . . .	100 ⬍	No Map

Figure 6–35   **Figure 6–36**

Clicking **No Map** next to a channel opens the Material/Map Browser (shown in Figure 6–37) where you can select a map and assign it, or change a map and its settings.

Figure 6–37

- **Bitmap:** Enables you to assign an external image as a map. Different types of image formats can be used as maps including Windows Bitmaps, JPEGs, PNGs, Targas, TIFFs, and more.

- **Color Map:** Enables you to make an instance of a solid color swatch. This helps you be consistent in the solid colors that you use in your models. You can also assign a color bitmap instead of creating a color swatch.

- **MutiTile:** Enables you to assign more than one texture maps into a UV editor. The map is designed so that high resolution textures can be opened and displayed. This map type supports patterns created using Mudbox, Zbrush, and Mari.

- The remainder map types are Autodesk 3ds Max **Procedural** maps, which are automatically generated mathematically rather than from image files.

- When you assign (or edit) a map to a material, individual nodes are created and display the maps assigned to the material components. Wires are created automatically between the map and the material component to which the map has been assigned, as shown in Figure 6–38. Maps can also be added individually and wired into a material to establish a link. To edit any of the parameters in the material or maps, double-click on the title bar heading for the item to access its associated Parameter Editor.

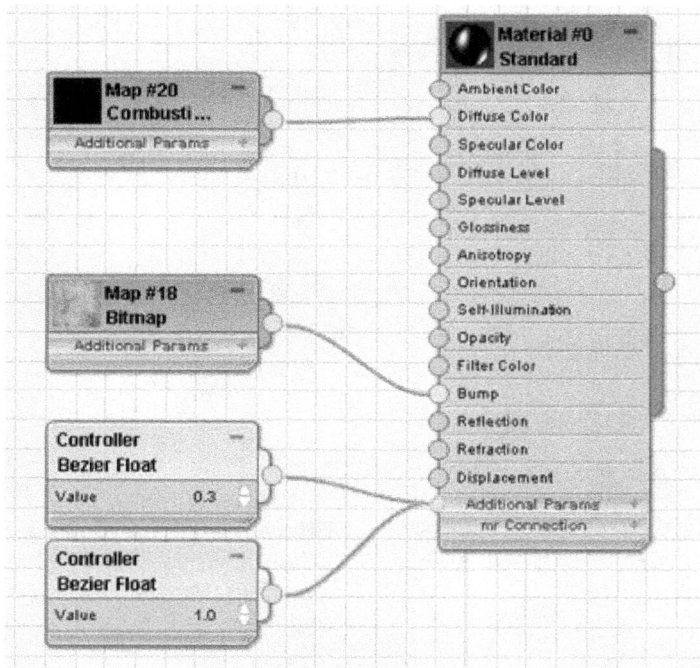

Figure 6–38

Practice 6b

Working with Standard Materials and Maps

Practice Objectives

- Assign a Standard material and modify it.
- Apply an image file and a procedural map to the Diffuse Color of the material.

In this practice, you will assign a Standard material to an object and apply parameter changes to it. You will then apply an image file and a procedural map to an object.

You must set the paths to locate the External files and Xrefs used in the practice. If you have not done this already, return to Chapter 1 and complete Task 1 to Task 3 in *Practice 1a: Organizing Folders and Working with the Interface*. You only have to set the user paths once.

Task 1 - Load Materials into the Material Editor.

*If a dialog box opens prompting you about a Mismatch, click **OK** to accept the default values.*

1. Open **Standard Materials.max**. A model of a guitar displays in the **Perspective** viewport.

2. In the Main Toolbar, click [icon] to open the Slate Material Editor.

3. In the Slate Material Editor, in the Material/Map Browser, expand the **Scene Materials** category. There are currently nine materials available in this scene, as shown in Figure 6–39.

   - Each material name is listed and is followed by its material type, in parentheses ( ). The square brackets [ ] includes the scene object to which the material has been assigned.

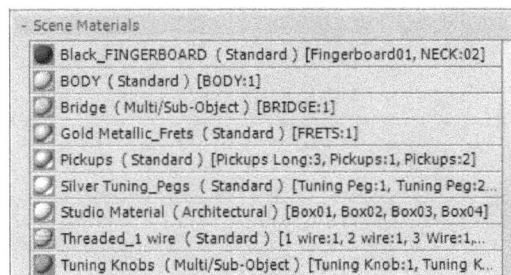

Scene Materials

Black_FINGERBOARD (Standard) [Fingerboard01, NECK:02]
BODY (Standard) [BODY:1]
Bridge (Multi/Sub-Object) [BRIDGE:1]
Gold Metallic_Frets (Standard) [FRETS:1]
Pickups (Standard) [Pickups Long:3, Pickups:1, Pickups:2]
Silver Tuning_Pegs (Standard) [Tuning Peg:1, Tuning Peg:2...
Studio Material (Architectural) [Box01, Box02, Box03, Box04]
Threaded_1 wire (Standard) [1 wire:1, 2 wire:1, 3 Wire:1,...
Tuning Knobs (Multi/Sub-Object) [Tuning Knob:1, Tuning K...

Figure 6–39

4. Note that all of these materials are also displayed in the *View1* sheet and are overlapping each other, as shown in Figure 6–40. In the Slate Material Editor toolbar, click

   (Lay Out All -Vertical) to display the materials vertically in the *View1* sheet.

Figure 6–40

Task 2 - Change the material parameters.

1. In the *View1* sheet, using pan and zoom, locate the **BODY Standard** node (name displayed in the title bar), as shown in Figure 6–41. Double-click on the title bar heading to open its Parameter Editor, as shown in Figure 6–42. Note that a white dashed border displays around the node in the *View1* sheet.

Figure 6–41

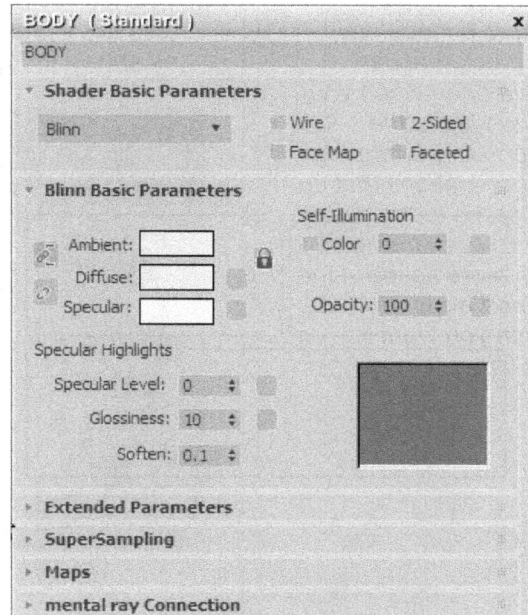

Figure 6–42

2. Note that the **Body** material is a Standard material that uses the Blinn shader. In the *Blinn Basic Parameters* rollout, select the Diffuse color swatch to open the Color Selector dialog box, as shown in Figure 6–43.

Figure 6–43

3. In the Color Selector dialog box you can select a color from the chart or set RGB (red-green-blue) or HSV (hue-saturation-value) levels. Experiment with different colors for the guitar body and click **OK**.

The Slate Material Editor is a modeless dialog box that can remain open when you are working in the viewport or performing other operations that do not pertain to the dialog box. You can minimize it to get more space in the viewport and maximize it when you want to work in it.

4. Change the *Shading Viewport* to **High Quality**. The guitar displays in the viewport with high quality shading and lighting, as shown in Figure 6–44.

[+][Perspective][High Quality][Default Shading]

Figure 6–44

5. In the Parameters editor, in the *Specular Highlights* area, the material's *Specular Level* is set to **0**, which is appropriate for a material that is not shiny. To simulate a shiny coating, increase the *Specular Level* to **100**, as shown in Figure 6–45. Note the shiny coating on the guitar body.

Specular Highlights
Specular Level: 100
Glossiness: 10
Soften: 0.1

Figure 6–45

6. Change the *Glossiness* to **25**. Increasing the glossy value focuses the highlighting in a smaller area.

The current renderer has been set to **Scanline***.*

7. Click (Render Production) in the Main Toolbar to display a more realistic rendered image. Close the Render Window.

Task 3 - Applying a procedural map and image file.

A Procedural Map is generated algorithmically. It is not a digital photo or painting. Procedural Maps are useful for terrains or other objects where the texture should not repeat in a tiled pattern.

1. To replace the Diffuse Color with a procedural map that represents a wood grain, verify that the Body material has a white dashed boundary around it, indicating that its parameters display. In the Parameter Editor, expand the *Maps* rollout, as shown in Figure 6–46. Next to the **Diffuse Color** option, click **No Map**.

Figure 6–46

2. In the separate Material/Map Browser that opens, expand the **Maps>General** categories and select **Advanced Wood**. Click **OK** to assign it as a map to the **BODY** Standard material.

*As with all procedural maps, **Advanced Wood** is defined by parameters and formulas, not by an image file.*

*The **Map Output Selector** replaces **No Map** for the Diffuse color in the Parameter Editor.*

3. A new Map node has been added in the *View1* sheet that represents the **Advanced Wood** map. The node is wired to the Diffuse Color in the **Body** material, as shown in Figure 6–47. Note that the title bar of this node is green, indicating that the node is a Map node.

Figure 6–47

4. Double-click on the title bar heading for the **Advanced Wood** map. Note that a white dashed border surrounds the **Advanced Wood** map node, indicating that its parameters display in the Parameter Editor. In the *Presets* rollout, select **3D Ash-Semigloss** in the Presets list. In the *General* rollout, set *Scale* to **6.00** and change the *Axis* to **X**, as shown in Figure 6–48.

Figure 6–48

5. With the *Shading Viewport* set to **High Quality**, the wood grain might not display in the viewport. Select *Shading Viewport* label and select **Materials>Shaded Materials with Map**, as shown in Figure 6–49. (Note that the *Shading Viewport* displays as **User Defined**.) The wood grain displays on the guitar body in the viewport.

Figure 6–49

You can minimize the Render window such that it does not block the view of other objects on the screen. You can maximize it when required.

6. In the Main Toolbar, click ![Render Production icon] (Render Production) to render. The wood map displays on the body of the guitar, as shown in Figure 6–50. Leave the modeless Render Window dialog box open.

Figure 6–50

7. To replace the **Advanced Wood** map with an image file, in the *View1* sheet, double-click on the title bar heading for the **BODY** material to open its Parameter Editor. Expand the *Maps* rollout, right-click on **Map Output Selector**, and select **Clear**. Alternatively, you can drag any **No Map** onto it. Note that in the *View1* sheet, the wiring between the **BODY** material node and the **Advanced Wood** map node has been deleted.

8. Click **No Map** next to the **Diffuse Color** to open its specific Material/Map Browser.

9. In the Material/Map Browser, double-click on **Bitmap** in the **Maps>General** categories, as shown in Figure 6–51.

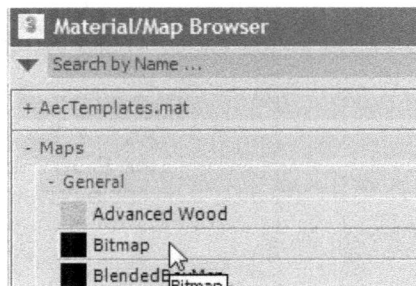

Figure 6–51

You can delete the unused node by clicking its title bar heading and pressing <Delete>. This keeps the active sheet clean. It also removes the material from the active sheet only.

10. The Select Bitmap Image File dialog box opens. Browse to the *...\Maps* folder. Select **GuitarDiffuse.jpg** and click **Open**. A new node for Bitmap is added to the *View1* sheet and its output socket is connected to the Diffuse Color input socket of the **BODY** material node, as shown in Figure 6–52. The new **Bitmap** node and **Advanced Wood** Map node might overlap. Select the header of one of the nodes to move them apart.

Figure 6–52

11. Double-click on the new **Bitmap** node title bar to display its Parameter Editor. In the *Coordinates* rollout, clear the **Use Real-World Scale** and set the *Tiling* to **1.0** in both **U** and **V**, as shown in Figure 6–53.

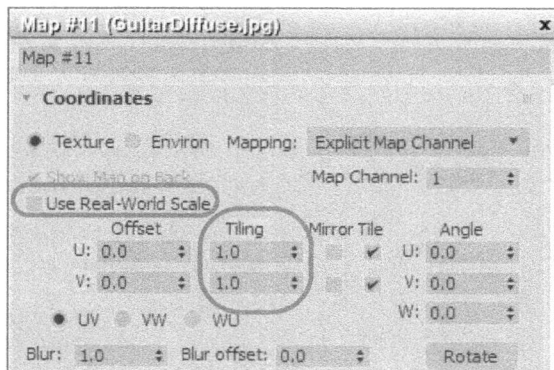

Figure 6–53

• As the *Shading Viewport* is already set to **User Defined**, the **BODY** material with the new map in the viewport displays automatically.

12. If the Render Window is still open, click **Render**, which is located near the top right corner, to display the effect, as shown in Figure 6–54. If you closed the Render Window, open it again from the Main Toolbar by clicking ![Render Production icon] (Render Production). Leave the dialog box open.

Figure 6–54

Hint: Use Mix Map Type

You could also mix the wood grain with the bitmap by selecting a Mix map type. The mix material on the guitar displays as shown in Figure 6–55.

Figure 6–55

---

13. To use a Color Correction map along with the Bitmap, In the Material/Map Browser, open the **Maps>General** categories. Double-click on the **Color Correction** map. A new node for **Color Correction** is added to *View1*, as shown in Figure 6–56. To relocate a node in the active sheet, hold and drag the title bar heading and place it below the **Bitmap** node, as shown in Figure 6–56.

Figure 6–56

14. Select the red wire that connects the **Bitmap** node to the Diffuse Color of the **BODY** material, press <Delete>.

The input socket of Color correction is used for a Map.

15. For the **Bitmap** node (**Map # Bitmap**), select the material output socket ⊙ (right socket) and drag/drop the wire to the material input socket (left socket) for the **Color Correction** node (**Map # Color Correction**), as shown in Figure 6–57. Note that the wired slots display in bright green.

16. Select ⊙ (material output socket) for the **Color Correction** node and drag the wire to the material input socket for the Diffuse Color entry in the **BODY** material node, as shown in Figure 6–58.

Figure 6–57　　　　　　　　　　　　　**Figure 6–58**

17. Double-click on the Color Correction heading to open its Parameter Editor. In the *Color* rollout, change the *Hue Shift* slider and note that the guitar changes color interactively in the viewport. Set the slider at any color (such as a green color hue).

18. In the Render dialog box, click **Render** to render the scene, as shown in Figure 6–59.

Figure 6–59

19. Save your work as **MyGuitar.max**.

Practice 6c

Working with Multi/Sub-Object Materials

Practice Objective

- Create a Multi/Sub-Object material and assign different materials to specific faces of a single object.

In this practice, you will create a Multi/Sub-Object material with various materials on different material ID's. You will assign an instanced scene material to all the faces of the wall system, a Physical material to some of the outside faces, and an accent paint color to other interior faces using material ID numbers of the Multi/Sub-Object material.

You must set the paths to locate the External files and Xrefs used in the practice. If you have not done this already, return to Chapter 1 and complete Task 1 to Task 3 in *Practice 1a: Organizing Folders and Working with the Interface*. You only have to set the user paths once.

Task 1 - Identify and Apply Multi/Sub-Object Materials.

*If a dialog box opens prompting you about a Mismatch, click **OK** to accept the default values.*

1. Open **Interior Model.max**.

2. In the Main toolbar, click ![icon] (Render Setup). In the Render Setup dialog box, open the Renderer drop-down list and select **Scanline Renderer**. The **Scanline Renderer** should display in the *Renderer* category, as shown in Figure 6–60. Close the dialog box.

Figure 6–60

3. In the Main Toolbar, click ![icon] to open the Slate Material Editor.

4. In the Material/Map Browser, expand the **Scene Materials** categories and note that six of the materials in the scene are Multi/Sub-Object materials.

You can leave the modeless Slate Material Editor dialog box open.

5. Click, drag, and drop the **Curtain Wall Doors** material on **PivotDoor07** (door on the left side of the model), as shown in Figure 6–61.

Figure 6–61

6. Select **PivotDoor07** object and click 🔲 (Zoom Extents Selected). The doors have glass panels and solid frames, as shown in Figure 6–62.

Figure 6–62

Task 2 - Create a Multi/Sub-Object Material.

1. In the Material/Map Browser, expand the **Materials> General** category. Double-click on **Multi/Sub-Object** or drag an instance of it to add it to the *View1* sheet, as shown in Figure 6–63.

2. Right-click on the title bar heading for the new material, and select **Rename**, as shown in Figure 6–64.

Figure 6–63

Figure 6–64

3. In the Rename dialog box, enter **Wall Multi** and click **OK**.

4. There are ten default slots in a Multi/Sub-Object material. This material only requires five slots. To set the number of materials, double-click on the Wall Multi material title bar to open its Parameter Editor. Click **Set Number**, enter **5** in the *Number of Materials* edit box and click **OK**. Note that the node has only 5 slots now.

5. You will use an instanced copy of the **Paint – Beige Matte** material present in the scene for your sub-material 3. (This material displays dark brown in this practice but will look more like beige when lights are added to the scene.) In Material/Map Browser, in **Scene Materials** category, locate **Paint – Beige Matte**, which is an Architectural material.

To display all of the materials in the Scene Materials, use its scroll bar.

6. Click and drag the **Paint – Beige Matte** material and place it directly on the input socket 3 in the **Wall Multi** (Multi/Sub-Object material). When you move the cursor on top of the socket, its color changes to green indicating that the socket is selected, as shown in Figure 6–65. Drop the material on this socket.

Figure 6–65

7. In the Instance dialog box, verify that **Instance** is selected and click **OK**.

8. The Paint – Beige Matte material node is wired to slot 3 of **Wall Multi** material. Use the pan and zoom (middle mouse button) to display both the material nodes in the *View1* sheet.

9. Verify that the Wall Multi (Multi/Sub-Object material) node has a white dashed boundary indicating that its Parameter Editor displays. Note that the **Paint – Beige Matte** material displays on the 3 ID slot, as shown in Figure 6–66.

Figure 6–66

10. In the Material/Map Browser, in the **Materials>General** categories, double-click on **Physical Material** to display it in the *View1* sheet.

11. Double click on the **Physical Material** node to display its Parameter Editor.

12. Change the material name to **Paint – Front**, as shown in Figure 6–67.

13. In the *Basic Parameters r*ollout, select the **Base Color and Reflections** swatch. In the Color Selector, set that color to cyan, similar to the one shown in Figure 6–68. Click **OK**.

| Figure 6–67 | Figure 6–68 |

14. In the *Coating Parameters* rollout, set *Clearcot* to **0.2** to add a glossy coating on the material. Then, set the *Roughness* to **0.2** to add a softer sheen.

15. In the *View 1* sheet, click on the output socket of the **Paint – Front** material and drag its wire to connect to the slot 5 of the **Wall Multi** material.

16. Not all the nodes are visible and might be overlapping each other in the active sheet (*View1*). In the Slate Material Editor toolbar, click   (Lay Out All - Vertical) to arrange the sub-materials vertically, as shown in Figure 6–69. Double click on the Wall-Multi material title bar to display its Parameters Editor. Note that in the Parameter Editor of the **Wall Multi** material, the *ID5* slot now displays **Paint – Front (Physical Material)**, as shown in Figure 6–69.

Figure 6–69

17. In the Material/Map Browser, in the **Scene Materials** category, click and drag the **Paint – Beige Matte** material and place it on the input socket for sub-material 4 in the **Wall Multi** material.

18. In the Instance dialog box, select **Copy** and click **OK**.

19. Double-click on the title bar heading for the new **Paint – Beige Matte** material (slot 4) to open its Parameter Editor.

Use ☷ (Lay Out All - Vertical), if required.

20. Change the material name to **Paint – Accent**, as shown in Figure 6–70.

21. In the *Physical Qualities* rollout, select the **Diffuse Color** swatch. In the Color Selector, set *Value* to **255** and press <Enter>. The color changes to light beige, as shown in Figure 6–71. Click **OK**.

Figure 6–70

Figure 6–71

22. Close the Slate Material Editor.

Task 3 - Assign Material ID Numbers to the Wall System.

1. In the **Perspective** viewport, zoom out and pan so that the entire model displays in the viewport.

2. In the Scene Explorer (■ (Display None)> ● (Display Geometry)), select **Layer:VIZ-1-Walls**, which selects all of the walls in the lower floor in the viewport.

3. In the Command Panel, in the Modify panel (⬚), note that it is an Editable Mesh in the Modifier Stack. Select the **Polygon** Sub-object mode, as shown in Figure 6–72.

Figure 6–72

4. In the viewport, select the **Edged Face** *Per-View Preference* label and select **Wireframe Override** in the menu. Use ⬤ (Orbit) until your model displays as shown in Figure 6–73. Right-click in empty space to exit the command and maintain the selection.

5. Using <Ctrl>, select the two front side polygons as shown in Figure 6–73.

Figure 6–73

6. In the Command Panel, in the *Surface Properties* rollout, in the *Material* area, set *Set ID* to **5**, and press <Enter>. *Select ID* also changes to **5**, as shown in Figure 6–74. This sets the selected polygons to ID 5 and will associate the **Paint – Front (Physical Material)** with those two walls.

Figure 6–74

7. Clear the selection of the two walls and select the polygon as shown in Figure 6–75. Set *Set ID* to **4** and press <Enter>. This will associate the **Beige - Accent** material with this wall.

Figure 6–75

8. In the Command Panel, select **Editable Mesh** to exit Sub-object mode.

9. Change the visual display to **Default Shading** and **Edged Faces** by selecting the **Wireframe** *Per-View Preference* label and selecting **Default Shading**. There is no change in the model because the material has not yet been assigned.

10. With the wall object (**Layer:VIZ-1-Walls**) still selected (if not, select it), open the Slate Material Editor, select the Wall Multi material title bar heading in the *View1* sheet. In the Slate

    Material Editor toolbar, click ![icon] (Assign material to Selection).

11. Note that the interior wall displays in light beige (**Paint – Accent**) and the two exterior brick walls display in cyan (**Paint – Front**), as shown in Figure 6–76.

Figure 6–76

12. In the Slate Material Editor, double-click on the **Paint - Front** title node to open its Parameter Editor.

13. In the *Basic Parameters* rollout, select the **Base Color and Reflections** color swatch to open the Color Selector. Change the color to a different one, such as red. In the viewport, note that only the color of the two walls that have ID 5 changes, as shown in Figure 6–77. This indicates that your **Multi-Sub -Object** materials have been applied.

Figure 6–77

14. Save the file as **MyInterior Model MultiMaterials.max**.

6.8 Opacity, Bump, and Reflection Mapping

You can use simple objects with materials and textures applied to them to add detailed effects without adding complex geometry to a scene. For example, leaves on trees or a chain link fence can be generated using a simple model with mapped textures and materials rather that creating it with complex geometry.

Opacity Mapping

Opacity mapping controls the transparency of objects, as shown with the lace curtains in Figure 6–78.

Figure 6–78

To create an Opacity map, add a map to the *Cutout map* channel, under the *Maps* rollout of the material.

- The black to white values are mapped to the transparent state, where black creates a hole (completely invisible), white makes a surface (100% opaque), and grays create a semi-transparent effect, good for clouds and fabrics.

- If a color image is used as an Opacity map, the RGB color is ignored and only the Luminance value is used. Opacity maps are usually created by taking digital photos and manipulating them in other programs.

Hint: Two-sided Opacity Mapped Material

When you create an opacity mapped material, it is recommended to make the material two-sided to see the backsides of faces if looking inside/through an object.

Bump Mapping

Bump mapping gives the illusion of an embossed or pitted surface without geometry being present on the model, as shown for a braided carpet in Figure 6–79. As with Opacity mapping, it uses black to white values to generate the appearance of a raised surface.

The white value raises the surface fully while the black value does not raise it at all.

- When combined with texture mapping, it helps the scene lighting integrate with the textures to place shadows in cracks, and generally add a veneer of three-dimensionality to the surfaces.

Figure 6–79

Reflection Mapping

Reflection mapping gives a surface the ability to mirror the world surrounding the object, as shown on the glass in Figure 6–80.

- Using Standard materials, you can place a bitmap or a reflection map type in the *Reflection map* channel.

- If you add a bitmap to the *Reflection map* channel, the faces reflect the bitmap based on shininess and scene lighting.

- If you add a Reflect/Refract or Raytrace map, the objects in the scene reflect along with the environment.

Figure 6–80

Practice 6d

Texture Mapping with Physical Material

Practice Objective

- Assign a Diffuse Color texture map, Cutout map, and Bump map to an object.

In this practice, you will create a chain link fence using cutout and bump mapping to display the cutouts in a solid piece of geometry. You will then add a map to the *Specular Level* channel to add shininess to the object texture.

You must set the paths to locate the External files and Xrefs used in the practice. If you have not done this already, return to Chapter 1 and complete Task 1 to Task 3 in *Practice 1a: Organizing Folders and Working with the Interface*. You only have to set the user paths once.

Task 1 - Assign the texture map.

*If a dialog box opens prompting you about a Mismatch, click **OK** to accept the default values.*

1. Open **start_chainlink.max**.

2. In the *Shading Viewport* label, select **High Quality**.

3. In the viewport, select the object **Line01** (yellow fence object).

4. In the Main Toolbar, click [icon] to open the Slate Material Editor.

5. In the Material/Map Browser, expand the **Materials>General** categories. In the list, double-click on the **Physical Material** material to add it to the *View1* sheet.

6. Assign the **Physical Material** material to the selected fence object by clicking [icon] (Assign Material to Selection) in the Material Editor toolbar. Verify that the fence object now displays in gray in the viewport.

7. In the *View1* sheet, double-click on the **Physical Material** material title bar heading to open its Parameter Editor. To open a separate Material/Map Browser, in the *Basic Parameters* rollout, next to *Base Color and Reflections* color swatch, click ▨ (None), as shown in Figure 6–81.

*Ensure that you select **None** for the Color Map and not the Weight Map*

Figure 6–81

8. Expand the **Maps>General** categories and double-click on Bitmap, as shown in Figure 6–82.

Figure 6–82

The Autodesk Maps are available in your local drive, generally, C:\Program Files\ Autodesk\3ds Max 2019\maps.

9. In the Select Bitmap Image File dialog box, in the practice files ...\Maps folder, open **Chain-link.bump.jpg**.

   • Note that in the Parameter Editor the icon changes to ▨, as shown in Figure 6–83. Also note that in *View1* sheet, the output socket of the **Bitmap** node is wired to the Base Color Map input socket of the **Physical Material** material, as shown in Figure 6–83.

Figure 6–83

10. In the *View 1* sheet, select the **Map # Bitmap** and then click

    ![icon] (Show Shaded Material in Viewport). The **Chainlink** texture should display on the **Line01** object in the viewport, but does not display correctly because the settings need to be changed.

11. In the *View1* sheet, double-click on the **Map # Bitmap** title bar heading to open its Parameter Editor.

12. In the *Coordinates* rollout, clear **Use Real-World Scale** and set *Tiling* as **U: 6.0** and **V: 3.0**, as shown in Figure 6–84. Press <Enter> for the values to take effect. The **Chainlink** texture should display in the viewport.

    • If it does not display, render the scene once (Main Toolbar> ![icon] (Render Production)). Close the Render Window. If required, click ![icon] (Show Shaded Material in Viewport) twice to toggle it off and on again.

Figure 6–84

You can minimize the Render window such that it does not block the view of other objects on the screen. You can maximize it when required.

13. In the Main Toolbar, click ![icon] (Render Production). The map displays in the Render window. Leave the Render window open.

14. In the menu bar, select **Rendering>Environment**. In the *Background* area, select the color swatch as shown in Figure 6–85. In the Color Selector, select a new color (cyan) and click **OK**. Close the Environment and Effects dialog box.

Figure 6–85

15. In the Render window, click **Render**. The Render window should display as shown in Figure 6–86. Leave the window open.

Figure 6–86

Task 2 - Assign the Opacity map.

1. In the Slate Material Editor, in the *View1* sheet, double-click on the **Physical Material** material title bar heading to open its Parameter Editor.

2. Expand the *Generic Maps* rollout and note that **Chain-link** map has already been applied to the *Base* Color channel.

3. Expand the *Special Maps* rollout and click **No Map** for *Cutout*, as shown in Figure 6–87.

To control the transparency, apply the map to the Opacity channel

Figure 6–87

The Tiling settings for the Diffuse map and the Cutout map should be the same so that they overlap each other for the cutout to display correctly.

4. In the Material/Map Browser, expand the **Maps>General** categories. Double-click on **Bitmap** to open the Select Bitmap Image File dialog box. Open **Chain-link.cutout.jpg** (from the ...\Maps folder). Note that this bitmap is wired to *Cutout Map* for Physical Material. It also replaces **No Map** in the *Special Maps* rollout of the Parameter Editor.

5. In the *View1* sheet, double-click on **Map #1 Bitmap** (cutout) title bar heading to open its Parameter Editor. In the *Coordinates* rollout, clear **Use Real-World Scale** and set the *Tiling* to **U: 6.0** and **V: 3.0**. Press <Enter>.

6. Orbit around in the **Perspective** view so that the fence is facing you. In the Render window, click **Render** to render the scene. Note that the background displays through the fence, as shown in Figure 6–88. This is caused by the map on the *Cutout* channel. The chainlink in your rendering might display a little lighter in color than that shown in Figure 6–88.

Figure 6–88

7. Close the Render window.

Task 3 - Assign the Bump map.

1. In the Slate Material Editor, in the *View1* sheet, double-click on the **Physical Material** material title bar heading to open its Parameter Editor. In the *Special Maps* rollout, for *Bump Map,* click **No Map**.

*You can also drag and drop the map from the Diffuse channel onto the Opacity channel and select **Copy** in the dialog box.*

2. In the Material/Map Browser, in the **Maps>General** categories, double-click on **Bitmap** to open the Select Bitmap Image File dialog box. Open **Chain-link.bump.jpg** (from the *...\Maps* folder). Note that this bitmap displays on **Bump Map**, as shown in Figure 6–89 (the same map was used on the *Base Color* channel). Note that in the *View1* sheet, it is wired to **Bump Map** in **Physical Material** material, as shown in Figure 6–89.

Figure 6–89

If you copied the map, the settings are also copied and you are not required to enter the Tiling values.

3. In the *View1* sheet, double-click on the **Map #2 Bitmap** (*Bump* channel) title bar heading to open its Parameter Editor. In the *Coordinates* rollout, clear **Use Real-World Scale** and set the *Tiling* to **U: 6.0** and **V: 3.0**.

To display the various maps correctly in the viewport, in the View1 sheet, select the **Material # Physical Material** *heading (parent material node) and then click*

⬚ *(Show Shaded Material) to switch it on.*

4. Click ▨ (Render Production) to render the scene.

5. To make the chain link more realistic (smaller cutouts), set the *Tiling* values for all the three map channels to **U: 18** and **V: 11**. Double-click on each map title bar heading to open its Parameter Editor and change the values.

6. Render the scene again. The rendered scene is similar to one shown in Figure 6–90.

Figure 6–90

There is no light on this side, so the rendering display might be dark.

7. Click ▨ (Orbit) and navigate in the viewport to the other side of the chain link fence. Render the scene again. Note that the chain link displays. Leave the Render window open.

8. In the viewport, navigate back to the front side of the fence.

9. Save your work as **MyChainLinkFence.max**.

6.9 Arnold Materials

Solid Angle's MaxtoA (Arnold) renderer offers high quality production rendering capabilities. Along with the renderer, a shader library is also provided. Once you set **Arnold** as the current renderer, the Arnold specific components become available for use.

In the Slate Material Editor, the **Arnold** category (shown in Figure 6–91) contains materials that are meant to be used specifically with the Arnold renderer. You are required to have **Arnold** selected as the production renderer in the Render Setup dialog box for the **Arnold** material category to be displayed.

The materials are grouped into different categories (as shown in Figure 6–92) and can be used directly in your scene.

Figure 6–91

Figure 6–92

AOV

The **AOV** (Arbitrary Output Variables) category enables you to render a scene using different shading components and features and then combine them at a later time. It contains **AOV Write Float**, **AOV Write Int**, and **AOV Write RGB**.

- A new AOV file has to be created before writing an AOV. A custom AOV can be added in the Render Setup dialog box> *AOV Settings* tab when the current renderer is **Arnold**.

Atmosphere

The **Atmosphere** category contains **Atmosphere Volume** and **Fog**. You can use **Atmosphere Volume** when you want to simulate shafts of lights and shadows that are cast from geometric objects. The **Fog** shader causes the far off objects to display dimmer with subdued colors simulating the effects of fog.

Surface

The **Surface** category contain a number of surface shaders, as shown in Figure Figure 6–92.

- The **Standard Surface** material (as shown in Figure 6–93) is the most commonly used shader with Arnold. It is a physically-based shader and enables you to create different types of materials by modifying its parameters. It contains a diffuse layer for color and then using other group of parameters you can create metals, plastics, stone, etc. You can use the *Sub-Surface Scattering* parameters (as shown in Figure 6–93) to create organic materials, such as skin, that do not reflect light at the surface, but scatter or absorb light below the surface.

- The **Standard Hair** material can be used to easily create realistic looking hair and fur. It should be used specifically on curved shapes.

- The **Two-sided** material can be used to apply two different shaders on either side of a two sided surface.

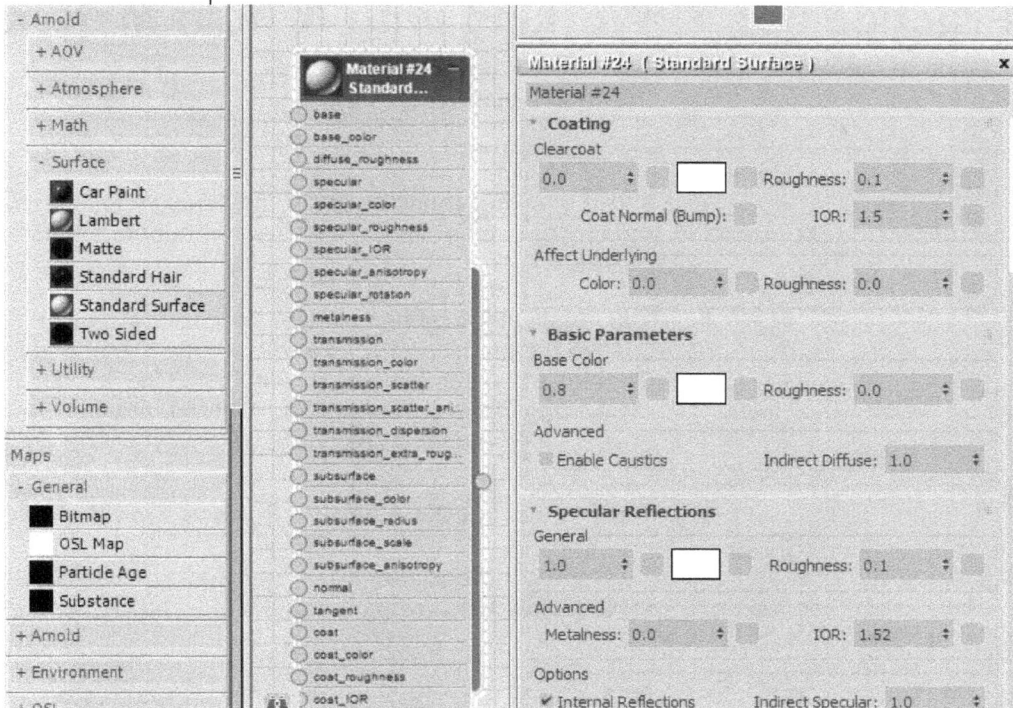

Figure 6–93

Utility

The **Utility** category contains the **Maps to Material** option that enables you to use the Maps directly on the objects in the scene. The map/input shader must to be connected to the input slot of *Texture Map*, as shown in Figure 6–94.

Figure 6–94

Practice 6e

Working with Arnold Materials

Practice Objectives

- Assign and modify Arnold material.

In this practice, you will explore the Arnold shaders. You will modify the Arnold Standard Surface shader to create different materials.

You must set the paths to locate the External files and Xrefs used in the practice. If you have not done this already, return to Chapter 1 and complete Task 1 to Task 3 in *Practice 1a: Organizing Folders and Working with the Interface*. You only have to set the user paths once.

Task 1 - Assign the Standard Surface Arnold shader.

*If a dialog box opens prompting you about a Mismatch, click **OK** to accept the default values.*

1. Open **candleholder.max**. The candle holder displays in the four viewports layout. A camera view has already been set up.

2. In the Main Toolbar, click ⚙ (Render Setup) or select **Rendering>Render Setup**. Note that the current *Renderer* is set to **Arnold**, as shown in Figure 6–95. Click ✖ to close the dialog box.

Figure 6–95

The current renderer used for this practice is the Arnold renderer.

3. In the Main Toolbar, click 🖉 to open the Slate Material Editor. In the Material/Map Browser, expand the **Materials** category and note that **Arnold** category are listed.

Standard Surface material is an Arnold specific material and is similar to Physical Materials.

4. In the Slate Material Editor, expand the **Scene Materials** category at the bottom of the Material/Map Browser. Note that the white **Standard Surface** materials are used in the scene, as shown in Figure 6–96.

Figure 6–96

5. Double-click on each of the white materials (**CandleHolder**, **Countertop**, **Left Wall**, and **Right Wall**) to place them on the *View1* sheet. They are placed on top of each other. In the Material Editor toolbar, click ▪▪ (Lay Out All - Horizontal) to display the four materials horizontally in the *View1* sheet.

6. To change the color on each of these scene materials, double-click on a material node to open its Parameter Editor. In the *Basic Parameters* rollout, select the color swatch for *Base Color* and select a color in the Color Selector, as shown for the **Right Wall** in Figure 6–97. Change the color of all the four objects using any colors (**Countertop** - dark pink, **Right Wall** - cyan, **CandleHolder** - dark blue, and **Left Wall** - green).

7. Verify that the **Camera01** viewport is active (yellow border) and in the Main Toolbar, click 🫖 (Render Production) or press <F9> to render the scene, as shown in Figure 6–98. Note the shadow cast by the candleholder.

   • There are two Arnold lights set up in the scene. Both are illuminating the scene but only one of them is casting a shadow. Leave the Render window open.

Figure 6–97

Figure 6–98

Task 2 - Modify the Standard Surface Arnold shader.

1. In the Slate Material Editor, double-click on the **CandleHolder** shader title bar to open its Parameter Editor. In the *Basic Parameters* rollout, select the color swatch for *Base Color*, and enter **0.926**, **0.721**, **0.504** for the *Red*, *Green* and *Blue* values to get a beige color.

2. In the *Specular Reflections* rollout, select the color swatch for *General* and enter **0.996**, **0.957**, **0.823** for *Red*, *Green* and *Blue* values. Additionally, change the *Metalness* to **0.8** and *Roughness* to **0.4**. as shown in Figure 6–99

Figure 6–99

Verify that the ***Camera01*** *viewport is active before rendering the view.*

3. Click **Render** in the Render Window, or click ![icon] (Render Production) if the Render window was closed, to render the **Camera01** viewport, as shown in Figure 6–100. A brushed metal shader has been created and it reflects the colors of the countertop around it.

The rendering time is a little slower due to the calculations for reflections.

To get a metal looking shader, increase the ***Metalness*** *in the Specular Reflections rollout, whereas increasing the* ***Roughness*** *creates a brushed metal look.*

Figure 6–100

4. Verify that the Parameters of the **CandleHolder** shader display. Then, do the following:

- In the *Basic Parameters* rollout, select the color swatch for *Base Color*, and set it to white.
- In the *Specular Reflections* rollout, select the color swatch for *General* and set it to white as well.
- Increase the *Metalness* to **1.0** and lower the *Roughness* to **0.2**.

5. Render the **Camera** viewport. A chrome looking metal displays, as shown in Figure 6–101.

Figure 6–101

6. To create a glass looking shader, do the following, as shown in Figure 6–102:

   - in the *Basic Parameters* rollout, select the color swatch for *Base Color* and set it to black.
   - In the *Specular Reflections* rollout, set the *Metalness* to **0.2** and the *Roughness* to **0.1**.
   - In the *Transmission* rollout, set the *General* value to **1.0**.

7. Render the **Camera** viewport. A glass candle holder is created, as shown in Figure 6–102. Note that the shadow on the wall has become lighter.

Figure 6–102

8. In the Material/Map Browser, expand **Maps>General** category and double-click on **Bitmap** to open the Select Bitmap Image File dialog box.

9. Open the file **Finishes.Flooring.Tile.Square.Terra Cotta.jpg** from the practice files *.../Maps* folder.

10. Wire the output socket of the bitmap to the input socket of Countertop shaders **base-color**, as shown in Figure 6–103.

11. Render the **Camera** viewport again and note how the countertop has the tile image on it, as shown in Figure 6–103

Figure 6–103

12. Double-click on **Bitmap** to open its Parameter Editor. In the *Coordinates* rollout, select **Use Real-World Scale**. For *Height* and *Width*, in the *Size* column enter **0.4** in each edit box.

13. Double-click on the **Countertop** title heading to open its Parameter Editor. In the *Coating* rollout, set *Clearcoat* to **1.0**.

14. Render the **Camera** viewport and note how the countertop tiles are smaller and shinier.

15. Save your work as **MyCandleholder.max**.

Practice 6f

Materials that Create Lighting

Practice Objective

- Create a self illuminating material.

In this practice, you will learn how to create a self-illuminating material from an Arnold material.

You must set the paths to locate the External files and Xrefs used in the practice. If you have not done this already, return to Chapter 1 and complete Task 1 to Task 3 in *Practice 1a: Organizing Folders and Working with the Interface.* You only have to set the user paths once.

If a dialog box opens prompting you about a File Load: Mismatch, click OK to accept the default values.
The Arnold renderer has been set as the current renderer.

1. Open **LightPole-SelfIllumination.max**.

2. Verify that the **PhysCamera001** viewport is active. In the Main Toolbar, click ![teapot icon] (Render Production) and note the rendered image with all gray materials. Leave the Render Frame Window open and minimize it.

3. In the Main Toolbar, click ![material editor icon] (Material Editor) to open the Slate Material Editor.

4. In the Material/Map Browser, in the **Scene Materials** category, note the two materials. Both of the materials in the scene are **Standard Surface** Arnold materials, as shown in Figure 6–104.

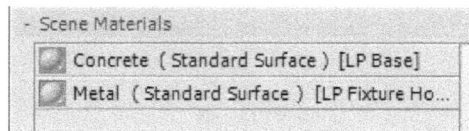

- Scene Materials
    - Concrete (Standard Surface) [LP Base]
    - Metal (Standard Surface) [LP Fixture Ho...

Figure 6–104

5. In the Material/Map Browser, expand the **Materials>Arnold> Surface** categories. Double-click on the **Standard Surface** material to place it on the *View1* sheet.

6. Double-click on the title bar heading of the new node to open its Parameter Editor and set its name to **Illumination**. Minimize the Slate Material Editor.

7. In any viewport, select one of the globes and in the menu bar, select **Group>Ungroup** to ungroup the objects. Similarly, ungroup the second globe group.

8. In the **PhysCamera001** viewport, select the two globes (inverted hemispheres). In the Slate Material Editor, click ⬚ (Assign Material to Selection) to apply the **Illumination** material to the globes.

9. In the Render Frame Window, click **Render** or in the Main Toolbar, click ⬚ (Render Production) to render the **PhysCamera001** viewport.

10. In the Slate Material Editor, verify that the **Illumination** materials Parameter Editor is open. Scroll down and in the *Emission* rollout, change the value to **0.5**, as shown in Figure 6–105.

11. Render the **PhysCamera001** viewport again. The globes are glowing, as shown in Figure 6–106.

Figure 6–105   **Figure 6–106**

12. In the Slate Material Editor, in the Parameter Editor, change the *Emission* value to **1.0**. Click on the color swatch in the *Emission* rollout. In the Color Selector, change the color to medium pink (as shown in Figure 6–107) or any other color. In the *Basic Parameter* rollout, set the *Base Color* value to **0.0**

13. Render the **PhysCamera001** viewport again. The globes have a pink glow, as shown in Figure 6–108.

Figure 6–107   **Figure 6–108**

14. Close the Render window and the Slate Material Editor.

15. Save your work as **MyIlluminatedMaterials.max**.

6.10 The Material Explorer

The Material Explorer enables you to manage all of the materials used in a scene. It displays the material's *Name*, *Type*, *Show in Viewport* setting, and *Material ID*, as shown in Figure 6–109.

- You can open the Material Explorer dialog box by selecting **Rendering>Material Explorer**, as shown in Figure 6–109.

Figure 6–109

- Selecting the various headings sorts the materials in various ways. For example, if you select the *Type* heading, materials of the same type are listed alphabetically according to the material type (such as Architectural, Standard, Arch & Design, etc.).

- The bottom panel of the interface displays information on the maps or other properties of the material. This panel has its own menu that enables you to manipulate each material's properties.

- From the Material Explorer, you can save directly to a new material library (as shown in Figure 6–110) or perform a variety of tasks depending on the type of the material.

Figure 6–110

6.11 Scene Converter

With many feature changes in the Autodesk 3ds Max 2019 software, the Scene Converter has become a valuable tool for enabling legacy scenes to work with the modern renderers (**ART** and **Arnold**) provided with the software. Since the scenes are based on the renderer used, the materials, lights, cameras and other objects used therein are specific to that renderer. These legacy components are not physically accurate and they are not compatible with the latest renderers. To take advantage of the newer realistic and physically accurate components and renderers, you must update those scenes. The Scene Converter provides an easy and an efficient method of converting the scenes.

- You can open the Scene Converter (as shown in Figure 6–111) by selecting **Rendering>SceneConverter**.

Figure 6–111

- Scene Converter uses a conversion script file to convert the specified legacy materials maps, cameras, lights and various render elements.

- The 3ds Max software provides you with existing scripts. Note that the *File Name* is set to **ART.ms**, which is the default script provided with the software. This is also used to convert the legacy scene elements to ART renderer elements.

- In the *Conversion rules* area, you can expand the various categories to check the conversion details. For example, in the **Materials** category, this script is designed to convert all the *mental ray Arch and Design* materials, *Autodesk materials,* and *Standard materials* to the physically based modern **Physical Material**, as shown in Figure 6–112.

Figure 6–112

- The *Editor* tab enables you to create a new script file and set all the conversion details as per your requirements. In the *Source* area, you can select the elements that you want to convert and then select what you want that element converted into in the *Destination* area. For example, you can convert the *Autodesk Generic* material into a **Physical Material**, as shown in Figure 6–113.

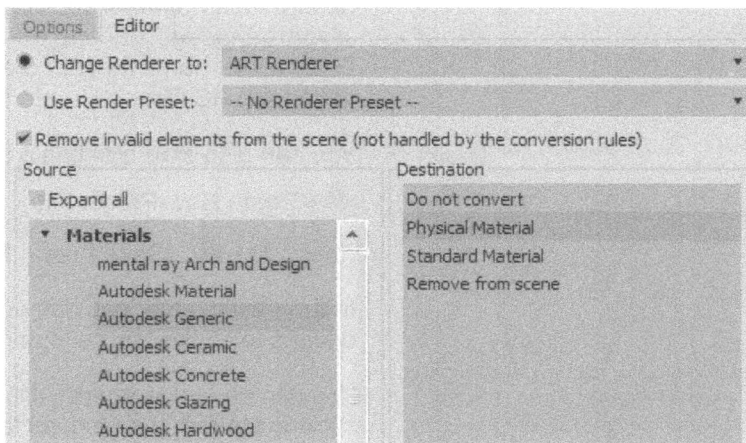

Figure 6–113

- After selection, click **Add rule** to accept the conversion rule and note that it is added to the *Conversion rules* area, as shown in Figure 6–114.

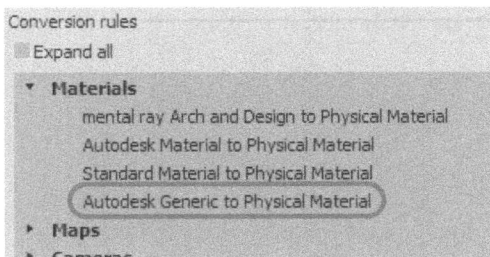

Figure 6–114

- You can also remove the rules that are not relevant for your scene by selecting the rule in the *Conversion rules* area and clicking **Remove Selected Rules**.

- After all the conversion rules are set, click (Save Preset File as) to open the Save Conversion Preset As dialog box to the path where the Autodesk 3ds Max script files are saved (*users\<username>\AppData\Local\Autodesk\3ds max 2019 -64bit\<language>\Scene Converter\ConversionPresets*). Enter a new name for your created preset. The script files are saved as .MS files.

- You can also start creating a script file from scratch by using (Create New Preset File). After setting all the conversion rules, click (Save Preset File).

- In the *Options* tab, you can use the **Batch Conversion** options to convert more than one scene file at the same time.

- You can save a temporary file that can be fetched later by clicking **Hold** in the *Options* tab.

Chapter Review Questions

1. What are the three color channels in Standard materials that determine the color applied to an object?

   a. *Ambient, Bump, Specular*

   b. *Bump, Diffuse, Opacity*

   c. *Specular, Opacity, Diffuse*

   d. *Ambient, Diffuse, Specular*

2. The materials and maps listed in the Material/Map Browser are dependent on...

   a. the active scene.

   b. the active renderer.

   c. the active viewport.

   d. the active material editor.

3. In the active view sheet of the Slate Material Editor, the green color (title bar) of a node indicates that it is a...

   a. Material

   b. Map

   c. Controller

   d. Material with the **Show Map In Viewport** option applied.

4. In the active view sheet of the Slate Material Editor, a dashed white border around a material node indicates that the...

   a. Material is being used in the scene.

   b. Map is assigned to one of the channels (socket) of the material.

   c. Parameters of the material display in the Parameter Editor.

   d. Material is a customized material.

5. The Phong shader generates softer, smoother (often more realistic) highlights than the Blinn shader.

   a. True

   b. False

6. Which type of general material enables you to stack multiple materials into a single parent material, each with a material ID number.

   a. Multi/Sub-Object material

   b. Architectural material

   c. Raytrace material

   d. Shell material

7. Which type of mapping gives the illusion of an embossed or pitted surface without actual geometry having to be present on the model?

   a. Opacity mapping

   b. Bump mapping

   c. Reflection mapping

   d. Cutout mapping

Command Summary

Button	Command	Location
	Compact Material Editor	• **Main Toolbar** • **Rendering:** Material Editor>Compact Material Editor
N/A	Material Explorer	• **Rendering:** Material Explorer
	Render Production	• **Main Toolbar**: Render flyout • **Rendering:** Render
	Render Setup	• **Main Toolbar** • **Rendering:** Render Setup
	Slate Material Editor	• **Main Toolbar** • **Rendering:** Material Editor>Slate Material Editor

Mapping Coordinates and Scale

When creating a realistic representations of a model, both materials and image texture maps can be used. They can be incorporated in a Material or you can use specific Map Modifiers and Scaling controls to further control how these elements look in a model.

Learning Objectives in this Chapter

- Work with mapping coordinates required for objects with texture maps.
- Assign mapping coordinates using various tools.
- Adjust the size of the image maps using the various map scaling options.
- Assign spline mapping to a curved object.

7.1 Mapping Coordinates

Most of the sample materials provided with the Autodesk® 3ds Max® software are assigned image texture maps, especially the Diffuse Color and Bump maps. Objects that are assigned materials with maps require mapping coordinates to control how the map is projected onto the object. For example, a rectangular sign can use planar or box mapping and a cylindrical can uses cylindrical mapping.

UVW is used instead of XYZ to indicate that the mapping does not need to be aligned with the world XYZ coordinates.

- Mapping is referenced by its own local coordinate system, described by UVW coordinates.

- Many objects (including primitives) are automatically assigned mapping coordinates. This is controlled by **Generate Mapping Coords** in the Command Panel, in the object's *Parameters* rollout, as shown in Figure 7–1.

- Linked or imported objects with materials assigned in AutoCAD® automatically have mapping coordinates if the **Generate coordinates for all objects** is selected in the import or link preset options, as shown in Figure 7–2.

Figure 7–1	**Figure 7–2**

- The Autodesk 3ds Max software provides a number of different modifiers (such as **UVW Map**, **Unwrap UVW**, and **MapScaler**) that can be used to reassign mapping manually.

- Mapping is often disturbed by editing (as through an Edit Mesh modifier) and by Boolean operations. The Edit Poly modifier has a Preserve UVW's feature that can be toggled on to prevent the need for remapping.

- If you select to render an object without mapping coordinates, you receive a warning message that the maps might not render correctly.

Mapping Controls in Slate Material Editor

At the map level of the Slate Material Editor, in the Parameter Editor of the map (shown in Figure 7–3), the **Use Real-World Scale** option manipulates the positioning of a map with mapping coordinates.

Use Real-World Scale On

The **Use Real-World Scale** attempts to simplify the correct scaling of textures by specifying the actual height and width (as shown in Figure 7–3) as represented by the 2D texture map. This option requires that the object use UV texture mapping set to **Real World Map Size** and that the Material also have **Use Real-World Scale** selected. It replaces the *Tiling* fields with a Size value for **Width** and **Height**.

Figure 7–3

Hint: Importing with Use Real-World Scale

Using the **Use Real-World Scale** option when importing from earlier versions of the Autodesk 3ds Max software might cause textures to display incorrectly. It can be due to **Real World Map Size** and **Use Real-World Scale** trying to create an extreme texture. If you leave these on, you need to reset *Tiling* to a different value. You can use **0.01** or a similar small value before you can see the bitmap texture, or go larger and use **10** or **20**. If the texture does not display correctly, it might be easier to toggle off **Use Real-World Scale** and set *Tiling* to **1.0** x **1.0**.

Use Real-World Scale Off

When the **Use Real-World Scale** is toggled off, the map texture is placed with respect to the UV values, as shown in Figure 7–4.

Figure 7–4

Offset	Enable you to move the map on an object relative to the mapping coordinates.
Tiling	Enables you to specify whether the map is repeated or tiled across the surface, in either the U (often width) or V (often height) direction.
Mirror	Causes tiled maps to be mirrored end-to-end as they tile.
Angle (W-rotation field)	Controls rotation of the map about the W (local Z) axis. For 2D maps (such as with an image file) this value typically is used to rotate the map on the surface of an object.

MapScaler Modifier

You can use the MapScaler Modifier (Modifier List in the Modify panel ( )) to project a map perpendicular to each face of an object. There are two MapScalers:

- **MapScaler World Space Modifier (WSM)** (shown in Figure 7–5) keeps the map scale constant if the object size changes with the Scale transform.

- **MapScaler Object Space Modifier (OSM)** (shown in Figure 7–6) scales the map proportionally.

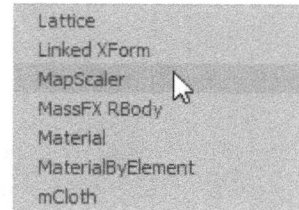

WORLD-SPACE MODIFIERS	
Camera Map (WSM)	
Displace Mesh (WSM)	Lattice
Hair and Fur (WSM)	Linked XForm
MapScaler (WSM)	MapScaler
PatchDeform (WSM)	MassFX RBody
PathDeform (WSM)	Material
PFlow Collision Shape (WSM)	MaterialByElement
Point Cache (WSM)	mCloth

Figure 7–5   **Figure 7–6**

MapScalers do not always project well on curved surfaces.

- MapScalers enable automatically generated, continuous tiling across complex geometry that might be difficult with UVW Maps. They tend to work well with geometry imported from the AutoCAD Architecture and the Autodesk Revit software.

- One method of repositioning a map on an object assigned a MapScaler is to adjust the U- and V-offset settings in the *Bitmap Parameters* rollout in the Material Editor. Otherwise, apply a UVW XForm modifier to the object and apply the offsets there instead.

- MapScaler modifiers are generally used on objects that have tiling material maps but do not have a defined beginning or end point, such as concrete pads, metals, asphalt, grass, and sometimes brick.

UVW Map Modifier

The UVW Map modifier (Modify panel (⬚)>Modifier List) enables you to apply a map to an object, where you select a specific shape and location to project the map onto.

- The UVW Map modifier has a gizmo for transforming in Sub-object mode.

- UVW Maps might not project as well as MapScalers on geometry that does not lend itself to the standard projection shapes (planar, box, cylinder, etc.).

> **Hint: Unwrap UVW**
>
> The **Unwrap UVW** modifier is another commonly used mapping method. For more information on *Unwrap UVW*, see the Autodesk 3ds Max Help files.

Practice 7a

Applying Mapping Coordinates

Practice Objective

- Adjust the placement of a map on an object.

In this practice, you will adjust the material mapping using the UVW Map and MapScaler (WSM) modifiers.

You must set the paths to locate the External files and Xrefs used in the practice. If you have not done this already, return to Chapter 1 and complete Task 1 to Task 3 in *Practice 1a: Organizing Folders and Working with the Interface*. You only have to set the user paths once.

*If a dialog box opens prompting you about a File Load: Mismatch, click **OK** to accept the default values.*

1. Open **Light Pole Mapping.max**.

2. In the viewport or in the Scene Explorer, select the concrete **LP Base** object and then click (Zoom Extents Selected) to zoom into the base object as shown in Figure 7–7. When this cylinder was created, the mapping coordinates were generated automatically.

Figure 7–7

*You need to scroll down the list to select the **UVW Map** modifier.*

3. With the **LP Base** object selected, in the Command Panel> Modify panel (   ), expand the Modifier list. In the *OBJECT-SPACE MODIFIERS* group, select **UVW Map**, as shown in Figure 7–8.

Turn to Poly
Twist
Unwrap UVW
UVW Map
UVW Mapping Add
UVW Mapping Clear

Figure 7–8

4. In the *Parameters* rollout, in the *Mapping* area, select **Box,** as shown in Figure 7–9. Scroll down and select **Real World Map Size** to display the map in the viewport. Note that the Box mapping projects the concrete map onto the object from all six sides of an imaginary box, causing a seam to form in places, as shown in Figure 7–10.

Parameters
Mapping:
   Planar
   Cylindrical   Cap
   Spherical
   Shrink Wrap
   ● Box
   Face
   XYZ to UVW

Figure 7–9

Figure 7–10

5. Change the projection to *Cylindrical* and then *Planar*, noting the differences.

   • The Cylindrical projection is not handling the beveled top very well, as shown in Figure 7–11.

   • The Planar projection is not displaying the cylindrical base correctly, as shown in Figure 7–12.

Figure 7–11   **Figure 7–12**

6. Remove the UVW Map modifier from the Modifier Stack by selecting it and clicking 🗑 (Remove modifier from the stack), as shown in Figure 7–13.

Figure 7–13

7. In the Modifier drop-down list, in the WORLD-SPACE MODIFIERS, select **MapScaler (WSM)**. The MapScalers are automatically projected perpendicular to each face of an object.

8. Change the *Shading Viewport (User Defined)* label to **High Quality**.

9. In the *Parameters* rollout, adjust the *Scale* spinner down (or enter **0'0 6/8"**) to visually improve the look of the map, as shown in Figure 7–14.

Figure 7–14

10. Save your work as **MyLight Pole Mapping.max**.

Practice 7b

Mapping a Large Scale Image

Practice Objective

- Assign a map to a model and apply mapping coordinates.

In this practice, you will apply a scanned image to a terrain model and map it accurately. You will use the Slate Material Editor and the **UVW Map** modifiers to assign a map to a model, apply mapping coordinates, and adjust the map.

You must set the paths to locate the External files and Xrefs used in the practice. If you have not done this already, return to Chapter 1 and complete Task 1 to Task 3 in *Practice 1a: Organizing Folders and Working with the Interface*. You only have to set the user paths once.

*If a dialog box opens prompting you about a File Load: Mismatch, click **OK** to accept the default values.*

1. Open the file **Mapping a large scale image.max**.

2. If your Units setup is maintained for Imperial, a Units Scale Mismatch dialog box opens. Click **OK** to accept the defaults. The units for this file are set to **Meters** and the *System Unit Scale* is **1 Unit=1 Meter**. This is required because the map that will be used is set for Metric units.

3. In the Main Toolbar, click (Material Editor) to open the Slate Material Editor. In the Material/Map Browser, expand the **Materials>Scanline** categories. Double-click on the **Standard** material to add it to the *View1* sheet. Double-click on the title bar heading for this new material to open the Parameter Editor. Change the material name to **Quad Map**.

4. Expand the *Maps* rollout and for *Diffuse Color*, click **No Map**. The separate Material/Map Browser opens.

5. In the Material/Map Browser, expand the **Maps>General** categories. Double-click on **Bitmap** to open the Select Bitmap Image File dialog box. Open the image **q257938.tif** from the ...*Maps* folder in the practice files folder.

Depending on the number of maps opened so far, the current number for the map might vary.

6. In the *View1* sheet, note that the **Map # Bitmap** is wired to the Input socket of *Diffuse Color* of the Quad Map material. Double-click on the Bitmap title bar heading to open its Parameter Editor. In the *Bitmap Parameters* rollout, in the *Cropping/Placement* area, click **View Image** to open the bitmap. Close the Specify Cropping/Placement window.

7. In the *Coordinates* rollout, clear **Use Real-World Scale**. Clear *Tile* for both **U** and **V** (as shown in Figure 7–15) because you want this map to display only once and in a specific location.

Figure 7–15

8. In the viewport, select the **Terrain01** object. In the *View1* sheet, select the **Quad Map** material and in the Material Editor toolbar, click ⬚ (Assign Material to Selection). The material does not preview in the viewport.

9. In the viewport, right-click on the **Terrain01** object and select **Object Properties**. In the *Display Properties* area, clear **Vertex Channel Display** and click **OK**. Now the gray color of the material is visible on the terrain, and no texture map indicates a mapping issue.

10. In the Main Toolbar, click 🫖 (Render Production) to render the scene and note the warning message of missing map coordinates. Click **Cancel** in the Missing Map Coordinates dialog box and close the Render window.

11. In the viewport, select the **Terrain01** object, if required. In the Command Panel, select the Modify panel ($\mathscr{C}$), and in the Modifier List, select **UVW Map**. Since the diffuse map is not meant to tile, in the *Parameters* rollout, verify that **Planar** is selected and clear **Real-World Map Size**, as shown in Figure 7–16.

12. In the Command Panel, in the *Parameters* rollout, note that the map was automatically scaled to the correct coordinates displayed in the *Length* and *Width* values, as shown in Figure 7–16.

Figure 7–16

13. In the Main Toolbar, click (Render Production) to render the scene. The terrain model should now resemble a 3D map, as shown in Figure 7–17.

Figure 7–17

- Without any direct manipulation, it appears that this texture map is being applied correctly. This is because the contours used to create the surface were trimmed very close to the geographic boundary of the image file.

14. Close the Render window. If the map does not display in the viewport, in the Slate Material Editor toolbar, click ▣ (Show Shaded Material in Viewport) to display the map in the viewport.

15. In the Modifier Stack, expand UVW Map and select **Gizmo** to enter Sub-object mode, as shown in Figure 7–18.

Figure 7–18

16. In the Main Toolbar, click ✛ (Select and Move) and move the image map on the terrain object. You can adjust the map more precisely using the UVW Map gizmo.

17. In the Command Panel, select **UVW Map** to exit the sub-object level mode. Clear the selection in the viewport.

18. Save your work as **MyLargeScaleProjectMapped**.

7.2 Mapping Scale

Mapping Scale is directly related to mapping coordinates and both are often addressed at the same time. Objects that use materials with image maps need to have them sized appropriately.

- Procedural maps also need to be scaled, but they are normally controlled by scale parameters at the Map level of the Material Editor.

Explicit Map Scaling

The size parameters of the UVW Map modifier enables you to control the number of times a map displays. Examples of this include maps used in materials for 3D models of signs, billboards, computer screens, paintings, etc.

- These kinds of maps are not assigned a real-world scale since they often require to be sized manually for each object. In these situations, clear the **Use Real-World Map Scale** option in the *Map Coordinates* rollout and clear the **Real-World Map Size** in the **UVW Map** parameters, as shown in Figure 7–19.

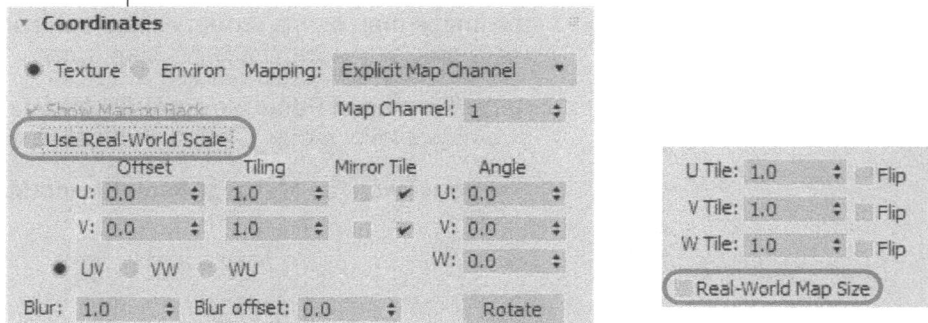

Figure 7–19

- To display the map once, the U and V tile values should be set to **1.0** in both the *Map Coordinates* rollout of the Material Editor and the **UVW Map** modifier parameters.

- To display the map in the V-direction twice, for example (the map's local Y-direction), set the V tile value to **2** in one of these locations, but not both.

Continuous Map Scaling

When material maps are meant to tile continuously across an object, a continuous approach can be used. The size of these maps can be controlled by a Real World scale that affects all objects using the map, or they can be sized directly using **UVW Map** or **MapScaler** size parameters for each object. Setting a Real World scale makes it easier to affect a global map scale change to multiple objects. You might need to determine the physical size you want to display an image file map in your scene.

Calculating Real World scales

U is the map's local X-axis and V is the local Y.

The **Brick** material uses an image file for a diffuse color map, as shown in Figure 7–20. This image map represents a section of wall that is five bricks wide (measured along the long edges) and 16 courses tall. If you want to use this material to represent bricks that are 11" on center laid in 4" courses, this brick map should be scaled to exactly **4'7" (11" x 5)** in the U direction and **5'4" (4" x 16)** in the V direction.

Figure 7–20

You can set this scale in various ways:

- At a global scale, enable **Use Real-World Scale** and assign appropriate size values in the map's *Coordinates* rollout, as shown in Figure 7–21.

Figure 7–21

- If mapping coordinates are required, apply UVW Maps or Map Scalers to objects displaying this map. UVW Maps should have the **Real World Map Size** option enabled as shown in Figure 7–22. The Map Scalers should be set to a size of one scene unit (such as 1"), as shown in Figure 7–23, in the *Parameters* rollout of WSM modifier.

U Tile: 1.0 ☐ Flip	**Parameters**
V Tile: 1.0 ☐ Flip	Scale: 0'1"
W Tile: 1.0 ☐ Flip	U Offset: 0'0"
☑ Real-World Map Size	V Offset: 0'0"
	☑ Wrap Texture
	Wrap using Smoothing Groups
	Channel: 1

Figure 7–22   Figure 7–23

- If you want to control map scaling of individual objects through a UVW Map, clear the **Use Real-World Scale** option in the *Coordinates* rollout and set the *Tiling* values to **1.0**, as shown in Figure 7–24.

- Objects showing map can be assigned sizes directly through the UVW Map modifier's **Length**, **Width** and **Height** parameter values. Clear **Real-World Map Size** in the **UVW Map** parameters.

- If you want to control map scaling on individual objects with a Map Scaler, clear the **Use Real-World Scale** option, set the *U-Tiling* value to **1.0** and the *V-Tiling* value equal to the ratio of the U-scale divided by the V scale, as shown in Figure 7–25.

Figure 7–24   Figure 7–25

- Objects showing this map can be assigned MapScaler modifiers with the **Scale** parameter value set to the U scale.

Practice 7c | Assigning Map Scales

Practice Objectives

- Assign a material that contains an image map.
- Adjust the size of the image maps.

In this practice, you will assign a material containing an image map to an object in a scene. You will then use the **MapScaler (WSM)** modifier to adjust the image map and the scaling options to position it correctly in the scene.

You must set the paths to locate the External files and Xrefs used in the practice. If you have not done this already, return to Chapter 1 and complete Task 1 to Task 3 in *Practice 1a: Organizing Folders and Working with the Interface*. You only have to set the user paths once.

Task 1 - Position and Scale the Brick Maps.

If a dialog box opens prompting you about a File Load: Mismatch, click OK to accept the default values.

1. Open the file **Interior Mapping.max**. If you completed the Terrain Mapping practice, the *Units* were changed to **Metric**, and a Units Scale Mismatch dialog box now opens. Click **OK** to accept the defaults and adopt the file's units (Imperial).

2. In the Scene Explorer, ■ (Display None) and ● (Display Geometry). Select **Layer:VIZ-1-Walls**, to select all of the walls in the lower floor in the viewport.

3. In the Main Toolbar, click ✦ (Material Editor) to open the Slate Material Editor.

4. In the *Scene Materials*, double-click on the **Wall Multi (Multi/Sub-Object)** material to open it on the *View1* sheet. Locate the **Masonry** material, wired to input socket 5 of the **Wall Multi** material, as shown in Figure 7–26. Note that this material has bitmaps wired to the *Diffuse* and *Bump* channels.

Figure 7–26

The Slate Material Editor is a modeless dialog box and can remain open while you are working in the viewport or other commands. You can minimize or maximize it, as required.

5. Verify that **Layer:VIZ-1-Walls** is still selected. In *View1* sheet, select the **Masonry Architect** material, click ⬚ (Assign Material to Selection), and click ⬚ (Show Shaded Material in Viewport). The **brick** material is assigned to the walls but it does not display. Minimize the Slate Material Editor. With the **Layer:VIZ-1-Walls** still selected, in the Modify panel (⬚), select **MapScaler (WSM)** from the Modifier List. In the *Parameters* rollout, set the *Scale* value to one system unit **0'1"**, as shown in Figure 7–27. Note that the bricks become visible. If the brick texture is not visible, click on the *Viewport Shading* label and select **Materials>Shaded Materials with Maps**.

Figure 7–27

6. In the **Perspective** viewport, use the various navigation tools, such as 🔍 (Zoom), ✋ (Pan), and 🪐 (Orbit), to zoom into and obtain the required orientation of one of the brick walls. The brick texture displays as shown in Figure 7–28.

Figure 7–28

7. Maximize the Slate Material Editor. Double-click on the **Masonry Bitmap** wired to the **Masonry** material's *Diffuse Map* to open its Parameter Editor.

8. In the *Coordinates* rollout, verify that **Use Real-World Scale** is selected and set the following, as shown in Figure 7–29:
   - *Width, Size:* **4'7"**
   - *Height, Size:* **5'4"**

Figure 7–29

*You can also move the texture along the wall with the **U-** and **V-** offset parameters in the map's Coordinates rollout, or with a UVW XForm modifier.*

- Note that the brick size is bigger and the brick texture terminates in acceptable positions along the wall edges, as shown in Figure 7–30.

Figure 7–30

9. For images in a material to be aligned, all of their mapping coordinates' parameters should also match. In the Slate Material Editor, double-click on the title bar heading for the **Masonry.Unit** bitmap, wired to the Bump Map of the **Masonry** material. In the *Coordinates* rollout, set the *Width* and *Height Size* values that were used for the Diffuse Map. This makes the bitmap texture display more realistic.

Hint: Multiple Sets of Mapping Coordinates

In the example, you scaled a Multi/Sub-Object material map with a single MapScaler Modifier. What if another material's map in Wall Multi required a **UVW Map** or different **MapScaler Scale** parameter?

Material maps can be assigned to separate channels in the Material Editor, so that each can be controlled by separate UVW Maps or MapScaler Modifiers. In such a case, you can apply multiple UVW Maps or MapScaler Modifiers to the same object and assign each the applicable channel identified in the **Map** parameters, as shown in Figure 7–31.

Figure 7–31

Task 2 - Assign the Ceiling Material.

1. Change your current view to the **Camera - Lobby1** camera view, by selecting the **Perspective** *POV* label and selecting **Cameras>Camera - Lobby1**.

2. Change the *Shading Viewport (User Defined)* label to **High Quality**.

*To display the Autodesk Material Library, the production renderer should be the **ART Renderer** or the **Quicksilver Hardware Renderer**.*

3. To use a material from the Autodesk Material Library, set the *Renderer* to **ART Renderer**. In the Main Toolbar, click

    (Render Setup) to open the Render Setup dialog box. In the Renderer drop-down list, select **ART Renderer** and close the Render Setup dialog box.

4. Maximize or open the Slate Material Editor. A Render Message dialog box displays that certain Scanline Architectural materials that are not supported by the ART renderer will be changed to use relevant ART renderer supported materials. Click **Close** to accept those changes.

5. In the Slate Material Editor, right-click on the *View1* label and select **Create New View**. Accept the default view name (**View2**) and click **OK**. The *View2* sheet, which is empty, is the now active sheet.

6. Expand the Autodesk Material Library and the **Miscellaneous** category. Double-click on the **Acoustic Tile - 2x2 White Pebbled** material to display it in *View2* sheet, as shown in Figure 7–32.

Figure 7–32

7. In the viewport, select the ceiling object and note that **Layer:VIZ-1-Ceiling** displays in the Command Panel. In the Command Panel, apply a **MapScaler (WSM)** modifier by selecting it from the Modifier List. In the *Parameters* rollout, set the *Scale* to **0'1"**.

8. In the Slate Material Editor, in the *View2* sheet, select **Miscellaneous** material by clicking on its title bar and click

   ![icon] (Assign Material to Selection).

9. Note that the ceiling displays in white/gray in the viewport. In the Slate Material Editor toolbar, click ![icon] (Show Shaded Material in Viewport) to preview the diffuse map in the viewport, as shown in Figure 7–33. The ceiling tiles have been sized using the Real-World Map Size that was defined for this material in the Autodesk Material Library (to a 2'x2' grid).

Figure 7–33

10. You can reposition the ceiling texture through the *Offset* fields in the MapScaler modifier. In the Command Panel, in the *Parameters* rollout, change the *U Offset* and *V Offset* spinner arrows and observe the change in the viewport. Move it so that the left ceiling tile edge coincides with the corner of the ceiling and the left curtain wall window, as shown in Figure 7–34.

Figure 7–34

11. Save your work as **MyInterior Mapping.max**.

7.3 Spline Mapping

Generating mapping coordinates that follow the path of extrusion is useful when a texture needs to follow the curvature of the lofted object. The **Unwrap UVW** modifier enables you to apply spline mapping and to select a spline for the basis of the mapping coordinates. You can use the Mapping gizmo to modify the mapping along the cross-section.

- It is applied at a sub-object level (Polygon or Face), as shown in Figure 7–35.

- It is present in the *Wrap* rollout of the **Unwrap UVW** parameters, as shown in Figure 7–36.

Figure 7–35

Figure 7–36

Practice 7d

Spline Mapping

Practice Objective

- Apply spline mapping to a curved object.

In this practice, you will apply spline mapping to a curved object using the **Unwrap UVW** modifier and adjust the scale and position to place it appropriately.

You must set the paths to locate the External files and Xrefs used in the practice. If you have not done this already, return to Chapter 1 and complete Task 1 to Task 3 in *Practice 1a: Organizing Folders and Working with the Interface*. You only have to set the user paths once.

Task 1 - Position and Scale the Checker Map.

*If a dialog box opens prompting you about a File Load: Mismatch, click **OK** to accept the default values.*

1. Open **Spline Mapping.max**. There is a curved object that needs to be mapped to display the correct road texture.

2. Select the object **Roadshape01**. A spline has already been prepared in this file and it runs (yellow line) through the center of the curved object. You can change the *Per-View Preference* to **Wireframe Override** to display the spline more clearly and then change it back to **Default Shading**.

3. Expand the Modify panel ( ) and in the Modifier Stack verify that a Line object and an Extrude modifier are listed.

4. In the Main Toolbar, click (Material Editor) to open the Slate Material Editor.

5. In the Material/Map Browser, in the **Scene Materials** category, double-click on **02 - Default** (Physical Material) to place it in the *View1* sheet. This material has already been assigned to the **Roadshape01** object.

6. Double-click on the **02 - Default** title bar to open its Parameter Editor. In the *Basic Parameters* rollout, click (None) for the *Base Color* channel, as shown in Figure 7–37.

Depending on the number of maps opened so far, the current number for the Checker map might vary.

7. In the Material/Map Browser that opens, in the **Maps> General** categories, double-click on **Checker**. In the *Generic Maps* rollout, note that the **Map # (Checker)** displays for the **Base Color** slot. Click to put a checkmark next to the **Base Color**, as shown in Figure 7–38. In the *View1* sheet, note that the **Checker** node is wired to the input socket of Base Color Map of the **02- Default** material.

Basic Parameters

Base Color

1.0   Roughness: 0.0

Reflections

Figure 7–37

Generic Maps

Generic Maps

✔ Base Weight . . . .   No Map

✔ Base Color . . . .   Map #3 (Checker)

Reflection Weight . . . .   No Map

Reflection Color . . . .   No Map

Figure 7–38

A checker board mapping material is useful for identifying map scaling and orientation issues, which can then be corrected before applying the actual texture map so that it displays correctly.

8. In the Slate Material Editor toolbar, click ⬛ (Show Shaded Material in Viewport). The checker map does not show in the viewport. In the *View1* sheet, double-click on the **Map # Checker** title bar to open its Parameter Editor. Verify that the **Use Real-World Scale** option is cleared. For the *Tiling* values, enter **0.03** in both *U* and *V* edit boxes, as shown in

Figure 7–39. Click ⬛ (Show Shaded Material in Viewport) again. Note that the checker texture displays on the road shape in the viewport, as shown in Figure 7–40.

Figure 7–39

Figure 7–40

• Note that the checker map is projected as a single sheet on top of the rectangular object and not generated to follow the curvature of the spline.

You can minimize the Slate Material Editor so that it is not in the way while you are working in the Command Panel and the viewport and maximize it when you need it again.

9. In the Command Panel>Modify panel ( ), in the Modifier List, select **Unwrap UVW**. Note that the **Unwrap UVW** is listed above **Extrude** in the Modifier Stack.

10. In the Modifier Stack, expand **Unwrap UVW** and select **Polygon**, as shown in Figure 7–41.

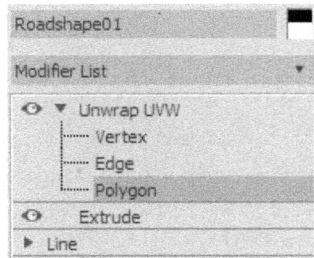

Figure 7–41

11. In the viewport, select the top face along the curve of the **Roadshape01** object. Note that the top checker face displays in a red hue indicating that the face is selected.

12. In the Command Panel, pan down to the *Wrap* rollout. Click

 (Spline Mapping), as shown in Figure 7–42.

Figure 7–42

*Apply **Planar** for roads and planar surfaces with a line cross-section. Use **Circular** Mapping for objects with a circular cross-section.*

13. In the Spline Map Parameters dialog box, set *Mapping* to **Planar** and click **Pick Spline**, as shown in Figure 7–43.

14. In the viewport, hover the cursor on the spline (yellow line), which displays at either end of the **Roadshape01** object. The spline is highlighted and visible through the object, as shown in Figure 7–43. Select this spline.

Figure 7–43

15. In the Spline Map Parameters dialog box, click **Commit**.

16. In the Modifier Stack, select **Unwrap UVW** to clear the selection and exit Sub-object mode. The checker texture is lost, indicating that the position and scale need to be corrected.

If the checker map does not display as required, use the spinner for the Size Width to increase or decrease the value and note the interactive changes in the viewport. The checker line should pass through the center, following the curve line.

17. In the Slate Material Editor, in the *View1* sheet, double-click on the **Map # Checker** title bar to display its Parameter Editor. In the *Coordinates* rollout, select the **Use Real-World Scale** and set the following, as shown in Figure 7–44:

- *Size Width*: **0'0.8"**
- *Size Height*: **0'0.1"**

Press <Enter> and verify that the *Offset* values are **0'0.0"** for both *Width* and *Height*. It is recommended to use the spinners to increase and decrease the *Size Width* while checking the interactive display of checker in the viewport.

Figure 7–44

- The checker map displays as shown in the Figure 7–45. This is the correct position and scale of the **checker** material as it follows the spline path.

Figure 7–45

Task 2 - Assign the Road Material.

1. In the Material/Map Browser, expand the **Maps>General** categories. Double-click on **Bitmap** to open the Select Bitmap Image File dialog box. Open **TextureForRoad.jpg** (from the ...\Maps folder in the practice files).

   • Note that a new node for this bitmap is added in the View1 sheet but is not associated with any material.

2. Delete the wire that currently exists between the **Checker** Map and the Base Color Map of **02 Default** material by selecting the wire and pressing <Delete>.

3. Draw a new wire linking the input socket of the Base Color Map for **02 Default** material to the output socket of the road texture Bitmap (**Map #4 Bitmap**), as shown in the Figure 7–46.

Figure 7–46

4. In the viewport, the road texture should display on the face of the **Roadshape01** object. If it does not display, click on the road bitmap node **Map # Bitmap (TextureForRoad)** and then select 🔲 (Show Shaded Material in Viewport) in the Slate Material editor toolbar.

5. Double-click on the road bitmap node **Map # Bitmap (TextureForRoad)** to open its Parameter Editor. In the *Coordinates* rollout, clear **Use Real-World Scale**, if required.

6. Set *Tiling* for **U: 2** and **V: 8**. Use the **Offset U** and **V** sliders to center the road. Increasing the **Tiling V** brings the dashes closer to the middle of the road while decreasing it makes the dashes longer and farther apart along the center curve. Use the **Offset U** spinner to increase or decrease the value so that the dashed line is placed along the center of the road, as shown in Figure 7–47.

Figure 7–47

7. Save your work as **MyStartSplineMapping.max**.

Chapter Review Questions

1. Which option manipulates the positioning of a map with mapping coordinates at the map level of the Slate Material Editor?

   a. Generate coordinates for all objects.

   b. Generate Mapping Coords

   c. Unwrap UVW

   d. Use Real-World Scale

2. The MapScaler in the World Space Modifier keeps the map scale constant if the object size changes with the Scale transform.

   a. True

   b. False

3. The **UVW Map** modifier enables you to.... (Select all that apply.)

   a. Explicitly apply a map to an object by selecting a shape and location.

   b. Use a gizmo for transforming in Sub-object mode.

   c. Perfectly project on geometry with non-standard projection shapes.

   d. All of the above.

4. Which of the following is the correct method for controlling map scaling of individual objects using a UVW Map? These options are accessed in the Parameter Editor of the map in the Slate Material Editor.

   a. Select **Use Real-World Scale** and assign the appropriate size (*Width* and *Height*) values.

   b. Select **Use Real-World Scale** and assign both the *Width* and *Height Size* values to the U-scale value.

   c. Clear **Use Real-World Scale** and set the *Tiling U* and *V* values to **1.0**.

   d. Clear **Use Real-World Scale** and set the *U-Tiling* value to **1.0** and the *V-Tiling* value equal to the ratio of the U-scale divided by the V scale.

5. Which mapping modifier is used to generate a map to follow the curvature of the spline along which the object was extruded (Spline mapping)?

   a. UVW Map

   b. Unwrap UVW

   c. MapScaler (WSM)

   d. MapScaler (OSM)

Introduction to Lighting

Once materials have been added to an Autodesk® 3ds Max® project, lighting can be used to further enhance and create a realistic representation of the model. Projects automatically include default illumination that can be further enhanced or modified to create local or global illumination. Illumination can be accomplished using photometric, Arnold, or standard lights.

Learning Objectives in this Chapter

- Work with various lighting strategies such as default lighting, local illumination, and global illumination.
- Work with standard lights and control the various parameter settings.
- Control the specific settings of various types of standard lights.
- Work with different types of shadow casting methods available in the software.
- Control the common parameters and set the specific parameters for each type of shadow casting method.

8.1 Local vs. Global Illumination

The Autodesk 3ds Max software provides several different kinds of scene lighting and enables you to add lighting objects that simulate real lights.Commonly used lighting methods provide either local or global illumination.

Default Illumination

By default, the Autodesk 3ds Max software automatically adds light to unlit scenes with invisible, unselectable light objects referred to as default lighting.

- A key light is located in the front and left of a scene and a fill light behind and to the right. These lights act as omni lights that illuminate in all directions. When user-defined light objects are added to a scene, the default lighting is automatically disabled for rendering.

Local Illumination

With a traditional local illumination approach, light sources only affect those objects that they can directly illuminate. They do not account for the diffuse light that bounces off of one surface to illuminate another nor do the effects of this reflected light become mixed together.

- Using a local illumination strategy, also referred to as Standard Lighting, requires arbitrary fill or ambient lights to simulate indirect lighting.

- Using Ray traced materials in a scene lit by standard lighting permits for the calculation of specular reflections between surfaces, which create mirrored effects and highlights on shiny surfaces.

- When a scene is illuminated with standard lighting (local illumination), without ambient or indirect light, the ceiling and shadows are dark as there are no lights pointed directly at those areas, as shown in Figure 8–1. When the ambient lights are added with standard lighting, the ceiling and shadows become softer, as shown in Figure 8–2.

Figure 8–1   **Figure 8–2**

Global Illumination

Global Illumination (GI) algorithms describe how light interacts with multiple surfaces. The illumination and rendering methods that take into account GI include radiosity and raytracing.

- Ray tracing is not used as a stand-alone rendering method but rather to compliment the other rendering methods.

- Radiosity is a lighting/rendering strategy that calculates diffuse inter-reflections of light, automatically generates ambient illumination and light mixing, producing realistic results, especially when daylight is involved.

- Radiosity is designed to work with physically based (photometric) lights that have parameters derived from real-world lighting properties.

Figure 8–3 was created with global illumination, showing an interior scene with night time lighting. Figure 8–4 was created with global illumination, showing an interior scene with daytime lighting.

Figure 8–3   **Figure 8–4**

Hint: Global Illumination vs Standard Lighting

Although longer to generate, Global Illumination (GI) approaches results are often more realistic. Standard lighting is less time consuming than the GI approaches (although there are exceptions), especially when working with simple scenes that contain a small number of objects or surfaces.

GI approaches are very popular in architecture, interior design, and related fields. However, standard lighting still has a place in these industries for conceptual tasks, projects with short timeframes, or projects that do not require extreme photorealism.

Types of Lights

Three types of lights are provided with the software:

- **Standard** lights: Work best with the Scanline renderer.

- **Photometric** lights: Best used with the ART and Arnold renderers.

- **Arnold** lights: Similar to Photometric lights and are meant to be used with the Arnold renderer.

Photometric and Arnold lights are discussed later in the learning guide.

There are many different parameters available when you create these types of lights. They can be created using the Command Panel. In the Create panel (+), click (Lights), and select the type of light in the drop-down list, as shown in Figure 8–5. Alternatively, you can select **Create>Lights** and then select the type you want to create, either **Photometric, Arnold**, or **Standard**. The Photometric lights are the default type available.

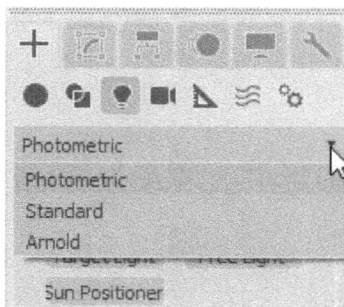

Figure 8–5

8.2 Standard Lighting

*In the Command Panel, select **Create>Lights> Standard**.*

Standard lights (as shown in Figure 8–6) are objects based on computer calculations, which imitate lights used in everyday life. The following specifics apply to working with a standard lighting strategy.

Figure 8–6

- Standard lighting strategies use standard light objects, such as **Spot**, **Directional**, **Omni**, and **Skylight**. They are highly configurable, but are not based on real-world lighting parameters and require arbitrary adjustments to achieve the required effect.

- Objects illuminated with standard lighting can use any material type.

- Scenes lit by standard lighting almost always require additional ambient (fill) lights, either through a global ambient value or ambient light objects.

Exposure control is a method of balancing illumination levels in rendered output. It is essential to work with global illumination, using radiosity.

- Lighting results are calculated at render time and are not stored on the objects. Processing standard lights does not increase file size and mesh subdivision is not required (as with radiosity).

- Standard lighting does not require exposure control. In standard lighting, ensure exposure control is not toggled on as it might result in differences between the viewport display and the rendering result

Photometric lights are the preferred lighting technique when working with the ART and Arnold Renderer.

- Standard lighting is designed for use with the Scanline Renderer.

- All of the standard lights except for directional lights, are considered Point lights, which cast light from a single point rather than along a line or from an area.

Common Parameters

All standard lights share common General Parameters and Intensity/Color/Attenuation settings. These parameters can be set while creating each type of standard light, as shown in Figure 8–7. Once the lights have been created, you can access these parameters in the Modify panel ( ) in the Command Panel.

Figure 8–7

General Parameters

Lights cast illumination even if they are on a hidden layer.

The *General Parameters* rollout enables you to toggle the light on and off in the scene, select to work with a target, and select shadow settings.

> **Hint: Target Lights**
>
> Several types of lights (and some cameras as well) can have a target object. A light always points directly at its target, enabling you to change the direction of the light by moving the target. Target lights are lights with targets and Free lights are lights without targets.

Intensity/Color/Attenuation Parameters

The *Intensity/Color/Attenuation* rollout provides you with following options:

Multiplier	Controls brightness for standard lights. This is an arbitrary value that needs to be evaluated by trial. Start with a **1.0** value and adjust, as required. Avoid using high Multiplier values, which creates overly bright lighting. The color swatch enables you to select a color to filter the light with.
***Decay* area**	Offers techniques for simulating how light fades over distance.
***Far Attenuation* area**	Provides a similar kind of fading based on explicitly set distances. The *Start* value is where fading begins and the *End* value is the point at which the light fades to zero illumination. Typically you would use either the options in the *Decay* or *Far Attenuation* areas, not both.
***Near Attenuation* area**	Enables you to define a distance from the light where the light starts casting faint illumination and then end with full illumination. Near attenuation does not occur in the real world and is included here as a computer graphics lighting effect
Show (Attenuation option)	Enables a graphical representation of the attenuation distances to remain visible after the object is cleared.

8.3 Types of Standard Lights

The type of standard light objects that can be created are **Spot**, **Directional**, **Omni**, and **Skylights**. They can be selected in the *Object Type* rollout, as shown in Figure 8–8.

Figure 8–8

Omni Lights

Omni lights (shown in Figure 8–9) are used to represent point lights that cast light equally in all directions, such as an idealized light bulb. Omni lights are also commonly used for ambient fill lights. A single omni light requires six times the computational effort of a single spotlight, so use spotlights in place of omni lights whenever possible.

Figure 8–9

Spotlights

Spotlights are used to represent point light sources that cast focused beams of light in a cone with a circular or square base. Figure 8–10 shows an example of a spotlight with a circular base in 2D, and Figure 8–11 shows an example in 3D. Most real world lighting fixtures are more appropriately represented by spotlights rather than omnis or directional lights.

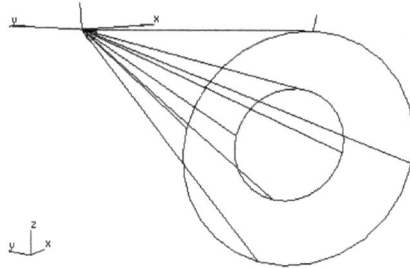

Figure 8–10   **Figure 8–11**

Two types of spotlight objects are available:

- **Target Spot:** Light objects cast focused beams of light pointing directly at a target.

- **Free Spot:** Light object casts focused beams of light pointing anywhere without a target object.

In addition to the Common Standard Parameters, spotlights have specific parameters (as shown in Figure 8–12) to control the distribution of the light they cast.

Figure 8–12

- The *Hotspot/Beam* value is the angle over which the full lighting intensity is projected. It is represented as the inner cone, as shown in Figure 8–11.

- The *Falloff/Field* value is the outer angle that illumination projects. It is represented as the outer cone, as shown in Figure 8–11.

- The light fades from full intensity to zero intensity between these two angles. Therefore, when these angles have similar values, the light creates a sharp, defined pool of light. Widely separated angles create a soft, gradual fade.

- The **Overshoot** option enables a spotlight to cast light in all directions (as an omni). However, spotlights only cast shadows within their falloff angle. Overshoot generally looks unnatural and should be used with care.

- The **Aspect** option enables you to define the width and height ratio through a numeric value.

- **Bitmap Fit** enables you to match the rectangular proportions of the lighting area to those of an image bitmap file directly.

Directional Lights

Directional lights are used to represent light sources that cast parallel rays, as shown in Figure 8–13. The best example of parallel light would be the light cast from the sun to an Architectural-scale project or smaller. (The sun could be considered an omni light when dealing with massive visualizations at the continental or global scale.)

Figure 8–13

Two types of directional light objects are available:

- **Target Direct**

- **Free Direct**

In addition to the Common Standard Parameters, directional lights have specific options available through the *Directional Parameters* rollout, as shown in Figure 8–14. The *Directional Parameters* options are nearly identical to those in the *Spotlight Parameters* rollout options. The only difference is the *Hotspot/Beam* and *Falloff/Field* values. These are measured in terms of a width parameter rather than an angle.

Figure 8–14

Fill Lights

Any light can be used to approximate indirect lighting, which is referred to as a fill light. Fill lights can act as normal lights or they can be specifically set to cast ambient light, by selecting the **Ambient Only** option in the *Advanced Effects* rollout in the **Standard lights** parameters, as shown in Figure 8–15.

Figure 8–15

- Standard materials have an **Ambient color** parameter that can be used when illuminated using ambient lights. This color can be different from the diffuse color produced by normal (non-ambient) lights. The Ambient color is normally locked to the diffuse or it can be set darker than the diffuse color for emphasis.

- Setting a fill light to cast ambient light automatically disables shadow casting because only real-world light sources (the sun and lighting fixtures) are normally permitted to cast shadows.

- If you want your fill lights to cast normal light (which illuminates a material's diffuse color instead of ambient), do not select the **Ambient Only** option, but rather manually disable shadow casting.

- Architectural materials were designed for radiosity and do not have an **Ambient color** parameter. Otherwise, they function similar to Standard materials with standard lighting.

Skylight

The Standard light category also includes a Skylight object, which is used to provide scattered atmospheric light in addition to the direct sunlight.

Practice 8a

Standard Lighting for an Interior Scene

Practice Objectives

- Create standard lights and adjust their parameters.
- Create ambient fill lighting to brighten the dark areas.

In this practice, you will model interior lighting conditions by creating a spot light and array it to position it at various locations around the room. You will adjust the parameters to make the scene realistic and add ambient lighting to brighten areas that are not directly illuminated by your standard light objects.

You must set the paths to locate the External files and Xrefs used in the practice. If you have not done this already, return to Chapter 1 and complete Task 1 to Task 3 in *Practice 1a: Organizing Folders and Working with the Interface.* You only have to set the user paths once.

Task 1 - Create, Array, and Instance Light Objects.

*If a dialog box opens prompting you about a File Load: Mismatch, click **OK** to accept the default values.*

1. Open **Standard Lighting – Interior.max**.

2. You will add lights in the **Top** viewport such that they point toward the floor. Maximize the **Top** viewport, by selecting it from the overlay (Hold <Win> and press <Shift>).

3. Zoom into the foyer area (leftmost area). Open the *Per-View Preference* label and select **Wireframe Override**.

4. In the Create panel (✛), click 💡 (Lights). In the drop-down list, select **Standard** and in the *Object Type* rollout, click **Free Spot**, as shown in Figure 8–16.

Figure 8–16

The small yellow circles represent the opening for recessed lighting.

5. Click near the approximate center of the upper left circle. A free spotlight is added at that location, as shown in Figure 8–17. You will position it accurately in the next step.

Figure 8–17

6. With the light object still selected, click ![icon] (Select and Move).

7. In the Status Bar, verify that ![icon] (Absolute Mode Transform Type-In) displays. Set the following, as shown in Figure 8–18:
   - X: **84'7"**
   - Y: **126'10"**
   - Z: **9'11"**
   - Press <Enter>.

Figure 8–18

In addition to placing the light at the exact center of the recessed fixture, it places the light at a height of 9'11", which is 1" below the ceiling height.

8. With the light object selected, in the Command Panel, select the Modify panel (![icon]) and name the light **Ceiling Downlight 00**.

*You can also select **Array** in the Extras toolbar, which is hidden, by default. Use the right-click Interface Item menu to display the Extras toolbar.*

*The exact coordinates, were determined using the **Measure** tool in the **Utilities** Command Panel. The six lights in the foyer area are 12' apart along the world X-direction and 6' apart along the world Y-direction.*

9. You will use the **Array** command to locate your light objects at the center of the circles representing the recessed fixtures, With the light selected, select **Tools>Array**.

10. In the Array dialog box, click **Preview** to enable the previewed display in the scene.

   - For the first dimension of the array, in the *Array Transformation* area, set the *X Incremental* value to **12'0"**.

   - In the *Array Dimensions* area, set *1D Count* to **2** to create two columns of lights.

   - Select **2D**, set *2D Count* to **3**, and *Incremental Row Offset, Y* to **-6'0"** to create three rows of lights.

   - In *Type of Object* area, verify that **Instance** is selected so that the parameters of all of the lights can be adjusted at the same time.

   - Note that *Total in Array* is automatically set to **6** (two lights in each of the three rows), as shown in Figure 8–19. Also note that the six lights display in the viewport because **Preview** is selected.

Figure 8–19

11. If the lights preview is in the correct positions (as shown in Figure 8–20), click **OK** in the dialog box.

Figure 8–20

When arraying the objects, the software automatically increments the name by 1.

12. Select the light in the upper right corner in foyer (**Ceiling Downlight 001**). Using ⊕ (Select and Move), and holding <Shift>, drag along the Transform gizmo's X-axis to locate the light over the desk area, almost on top of the chair in the yellow circle provided, as shown in Figure 8–21. In the Clone Options dialog box, select **Instance** and click **OK**.

Figure 8–21

13. With the light still selected, in the Status Bar, set the *X* value to **104'7"** and ensure that the *Y* value is set to **126'10"** and the *Z* value is set to **9'11"**, as shown in Figure 8–22:

Figure 8–22

14. Continue to <Shift> + click and drag to instance the remainder of the Ceiling Downlights, to the circles provided for the locations of the recessed lighting, as shown in Figure 8–23. In the interest of time, approximate their positions. You should have 14 lights with the last one named as **Ceiling Downlight 013**.

Figure 8–23

Task 2 - Adjust Standard Light Parameters.

In Task 1, you made instances of each of the lights so that their parameters can be adjusted together. You will now adjust lighting levels through light object parameters, avoiding exposure control.

1. Select **Rendering>Exposure Control**. In the Environment and Effects dialog box, in the *Exposure Control* rollout, clear **Active**, as shown in Figure 8–24. Close the Environments and Effects dialog box.

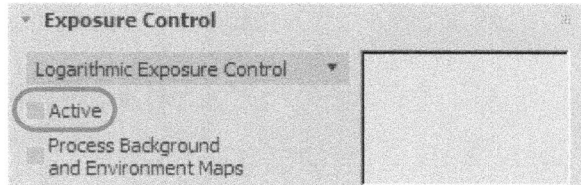

Figure 8–24

2. Select any of the instanced lights. In the Command Panel,

   verify that the Modify panel ( ) is open and that the **Ceiling Downlight** (any number) name displays (i.e., selected). In the *Spotlight Parameters* rollout, set *Hotspot/Beam* to **45**, press <Enter> and verify that **Circle** is selected. Verify that the *Falloff/Field* is set to **47.0**, as shown in Figure 8–25.

Figure 8–25

3. Change to the **Camera – Lobby1** view by selecting the **Top** *POV* label and selecting **Cameras>Camera - Lobby1**. Additionally, change the *Per-View Preference* to **Default Shading.**

4. In the Main Toolbar, click ![icon] (Render Production). Verify that the *Renderer* is set to **Scanline Renderer**. Open the *Raytracer* tab, and in the *Global Raytrace Engine Options* area, clear the **Enable Raytracing** option, as shown in Figure 8–26. Close the dialog box.

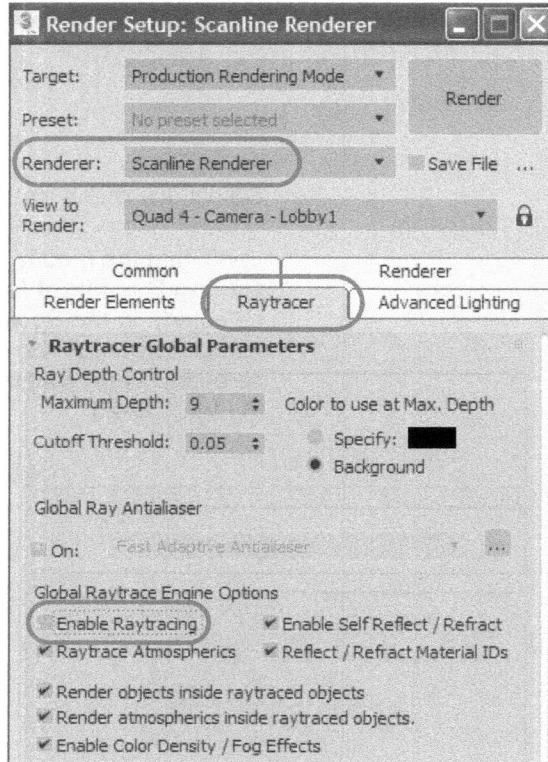

Figure 8–26

5. In the Main Toolbar, click ![icon] (Render Production). Due to their current hotspot and falloff values, the light objects are only illuminating small pools of light on the floor, as shown in Figure 8–27.

Figure 8–27

- The **Layer:VIZ-1-Ceiling Lights** object is formed from extruded circles representing the openings for your recessed lighting. They have been assigned a self-illuminated material to make the openings display brightly lit. The light objects you have just added to the scene do not render.

6. In the viewport, select one of the instanced lights, if not already selected. In the *Spotlight Parameters* rollout, set the *Falloff/Field* value to **170** degrees and press <Enter>.

*If you need to change some of the parameters and render again, you can leave the Rendered Frame Window open because it is a modeless dialog box. After changing a parameter, click **Render** in the Rendered Frame Window to render the viewport again.*

7. Click ![icon] (Render Production) if you closed the Rendered Frame Window or click **Render** if the Rendered Frame Window is open. The illumination now spreads out, but the floor is being lit too brightly and has lost all of its contrast (sometimes referred to as being washed out), as shown in Figure 8–28. Leave the Rendered Frame Window open.

Figure 8–28

8. In the *Intensity/Color/Attenuation* rollout, in *Far Attenuation* area, select **Use**. Set the following, as shown in Figure 8–29:
   - *Start*: **0'0"**
   - *End*: **16'0"**

Figure 8–29

9. Click **Render**. The washed out effect is removed but the overall render looks dark, as shown in Figure 8–30.

Figure 8–30

*As with most **Standard Lighting** parameters, attenuation settings are arbitrary and require trial and error to achieve the best result.*

10. Adjust the overall brightness of the lights using the Multiplier. In the *Intensity/Color/Attenuation* rollout, set *Multiplier* to **2.0**. Click **Render** in the Rendered Frame Window. The surfaces under direct illumination should now become brighter.

Task 3 - Add Ambient Fill Light.

Next use ambient fill lighting to approximate the indirect illumination that would be present in the real world. With a standard lighting approach, fill light is required to brighten areas that are not directly illuminated by your light objects.

1. Add the ambient light globally. Select **Rendering> Environment** to open the Environment and Effects dialog box.

2. In the *Environment* tab, in the *Common Parameters* rollout, in the *Global Lighting* area, select the **Ambient** color swatch, as shown in Figure 8–31.

Figure 8–31

3. In the Color Selector dialog box, change the *Value* to **25**, and press <Enter>, as shown in Figure 8–32. Leave both the Environment and Effects dialog box and Color Selector dialog box open.

Figure 8–32

4. In the Rendered Frame Window, click **Render** to render the scene. In this rendering many areas have become lighter but the ceiling is still too dark. In the Color Selector dialog box, change the *Value* to **50** and render again. The ceiling is brighter but objects under direct illumination have lost some contrast, as shown in Figure 8–33. The front of the half-wall behind the stairs looks flat because the ambient lighting is so uniform. (This is a pitfall of adding too much global ambient light.)

Figure 8–33

5. This scene might respond better with manually configured ambient light rather than the global settings. In the Color Selector dialog box, set the ambient color *Value* to **0** and press <Enter>. Close all dialog boxes.

6. In the viewport, change to the **Top** viewport by pressing <T> and zoom out to see the floorplan. In the Create panel (+), click 💡 (Lights). Verify that **Standard** displays and then click **Omni** to create an omni light.

7. Click once in the center of the six lights in the foyer to add an omni light. In the *Name and Color* rollout, enter **Lobby Fill Light 00** as the name of the light.

8. Click ✛ (Select and Move) and in the Status Bar, change its absolute Z-elevation to **2'0"**.

9. Hold <Shift>, and drag and click to create two instances of the omni light, as shown in Figure 8–34.

Figure 8–34

10. With one of the omni lights selected, in the Modify panel

(⬛), in the *Advanced Effects* rollout, select **Ambient Only**, as shown in Figure 8–35. This setting causes the light to illuminate the ambient color of Standard materials and not to cast shadows.

Figure 8–35

11. Change to **Camera – Lobby1** viewport and render the scene. Note that everything is washed out. Ambient lights can wash out a scene with their default settings. Leave the Rendered Frame Window open.

12. With the omni light still selected, in the *Intensity/Color/Attenuation* rollout, set *Multiplier* as **0.75** and in the *Far Attenuation* area, select **Use**. Additionally, set the following, as shown in Figure 8–36:
- *Start*: **0'0"**
- *End*: **16'0"**

Figure 8–36

Your rendering might not be exactly the same because of your monitor display. You can adjust your Gamma and LUT correction (Preference Settings dialog box> Gamma and LUT tab) to get a similar rendering.

13. Render the scene. The ambient lighting does not look flat, but the floor and desk lamp are illuminated too brightly, as shown in Figure 8–37.

Figure 8–37

14. To resolve the brightness issue, you can exclude these objects from the ambient light. With one of the omni lights (Lobby Fill Light) still selected, in the Modify panel ( ), in the *General Parameters* rollout, click **Exclude**. The Exclude/Include dialog box opens.

15. Verify that **Exclude** is selected. In the list on the left, select **1-Desk Lamp** and **Layer:VIZ-1-Floor-Tile**. Click **>>** to add them to the Exclude list on the right, as shown in Figure 8–38.

Figure 8–38

16. Click **OK** to close the dialog box.

17. Render the scene. The brightness of the lamp and the floor is removed, as shown in Figure 8–39. Close the Rendered Frame Window.

Figure 8–39

18. Save your work as **MyStandard Lighting – Interior.max**.

8.4 Shadow Types

Autodesk 3ds Max lights are able to cast realistic shadows from opaque objects. There are several shadow-casting methods available, such as Shadow Mapped, Ray Traced, Area, etc. While creating light objects, you can set the type and aspect of shadow by selecting it in the drop-down list (as shown in Figure 8–40), in the *Shadows* area of *General Parameters* rollout. Alternatively, after creating the light objects, you can control or change them using the Modify panel ( ) parameters of light objects. Individual lights might cast different kinds of shadows in the same scene and shadow casting can be disabled for specific lights.

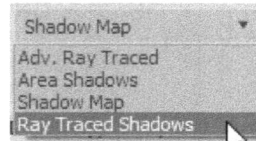

Figure 8–40

Figure 8–41 shows the shadow-casting methods available.

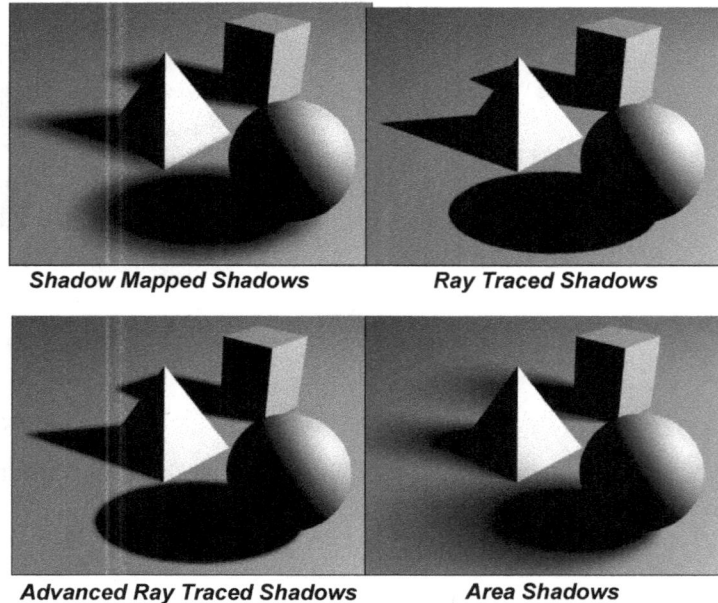

Shadow Mapped Shadows	**Ray Traced Shadows**
Advanced Ray Traced Shadows	**Area Shadows**

Figure 8–41

Shadow Type	Description, Advantages	Disadvantages
Shadow Map	Traditional approach, shadow mapping is relatively fast and creates soft-edged shadows. **Animation:** Shadows only need to be calculated once when scene geometry is not animated. Most efficient shadow type for omni lights.	Not as accurate as other methods; might not be appropriate for shadow studies. Uses a lot of RAM. Does not support materials with transparency or opacity maps.
Ray Traced Shadows	More accurate than shadow maps, supports transparency and opacity mapping. **Animation:** Shadows only need to be calculated once when scene geometry is not animated. In these cases, RT might be best for animations (including animated shadow studies) in terms of rendering time.	Slower than shadow maps, and shadows have sharp edges. Avoid omni lights with Ray Traced shadows whenever possible, as they require 6x the processing time of spot and directional lights.
Advanced Ray Traced	A good, general-purpose shadow type that is an improvement on RT shadows. It is more accurate than Shadow Maps, supports transparency and opacity mapping. Uses less RAM than standard raytraced shadows, therefore is generally faster for producing still renderings. Offers several parameters that can help soften and smooth shadows.	Slower than shadow maps. **Animation:** Shadows must be calculated at every frame, regardless of whether scene geometry is animated or not. Avoid omni lights with Advanced Ray Traced shadows whenever possible, as they require 6x the processing time of spot and directional lights.
Area Shadows	Enables a simulation of shadows cast from an area light (the other methods assume point light sources). Supports transparency and opacity mapping, uses relatively little RAM.	Generally slower than shadow maps, Ray Traced and Advanced Ray Traced. **Animation:** Shadows must be calculated at every frame, regardless of whether scene geometry is animated or not.

Common Shadow Parameters

The most commonly used shadow parameters in the Autodesk 3ds Max software are:

General Shadow Parameters

All lights have certain general parameters (*Shadows* area in *General Parameters* area) common to all shadow types, as shown in Figure 8–42.

Figure 8–42

On	Enables you to select whether to cast shadows from this light or not and the type of shadows to use.
Use Global Settings	Controls whether the scene's global shadow generator or the light's own individual shadow generator is used.
Drop-down list	Contains all the types of shadows available in the software. Selecting the type provides a shadow specific rollout that can be used to control the advanced settings in the selected shadow type.

Shadow Parameters Rollout

The *Shadow Parameters* rollout (shown in Figure 8–43) contains settings that are common to all types of shadows.

Figure 8–43

Color	Use this swatch to set a shadow to display as a color other than black.
Density	Controls the overall darkness of the created shadows. A density below 1.0 makes shadows lighter, greater than 1.0 makes them darker.
Map	Use this option to have an image map project inside your shadow.
Light Affects Shadow Color	Enables colored light to blend with the assigned shadow color when generating shadows.
Atmosphere Shadows	Enables atmospheric effects to cast shadows.

Shadow Map Parameters

In the *General Parameters* rollout, in the *Shadows* area, selecting **Shadow Map** in the drop-down list provides a *Shadow Map Params* rollout, as shown in Figure 8–44. Lights set to cast shadow mapped-shadows have additional controls that are specific to the Shadow Map type of shadow.

Figure 8–44

Bias	A relative adjustment that can move the shadow closer to or further away from the objects casting them. This value sometimes needs to be adjusted with large scenes.
Size	The height and width (in pixels) of the image map used to create the shadows. Shadow detail and computation time increase as the size increases.
Sample Range	Controls the amount of blending and smoothing. If shadow mapped-shadows appear grainy, increase this value.
Absolute Map Bias	Enables the Bias to be fixed to a value measured absolutely in scene units rather than a relative, normalized value. This option should normally not be used unless shadows flicker and disappear during an animation.
2 Sided Shadows	Enables both sides of a face to cast shadows. Double-sided mode is discussed in the rendering information.

Ray Traced Shadows

In the *General Parameters* rollout, in the *Shadows* area, selecting **Ray Traced Shadow** in the drop-down list provides a *Ray Traced Shadow Params* rollout, as shown in Figure 8–45. This rollout contains additional settings for lights set to cast (standard) ray traced shadows.

Figure 8–45

Ray Bias	Similar to shadow map bias, ray bias is a relative adjustment to move a shadow closer or further away from an object casting them. This value might need to be adjusted for large scenes.
2 Sided Shadows	Enables both sides of a face to cast shadows.
Max Quadtree Depth	Controls ray-tracing performance. Increasing the quadtree depth can speed up ray-tracing time but requires more RAM. You need to experiment to determine the most efficient quadtree settings for individual scenes (default = 7).

Advanced Ray-Traced Shadows

In the *General Parameters* rollout, in the *Shadows* area, selecting **Adv. Ray Traced** in the drop-down list provides an *Adv. Ray Traced Params* rollout, as shown in Figure 8–46 and the *Optimizations* rollouts, as shown in Figure 8–47. Both rollouts contains additional settings for lights set to cast advanced ray-traced shadows.

Figure 8–46   **Figure 8–47**

Adv. Ray Traced Params Options

Basic Options	The menu assigns either a mode without antialiasing (simple), a single or double-pass antialiasing mode. Antialiasing is an additional calculation made to smooth pixilated edges of shadows.
2 Sided Shadows	Enables both sides of a face to cast shadows.
Shadow Integrity and Quality	Controls the number of rays cast in the calculation. Increasing these values can enhance the final result at the expense of longer calculation time.
Shadow Spread	A parameter to blur or soften shadows, measured in pixels.
Shadow Bias	The minimum distance required to cast a shadow. This parameter should be increased as shadow spread is increased.
Jitter Amount	Blurred shadows sometimes cause artifacts to form. Increasing jitter can help break up the patterns of these artifacts and make them less noticeable.

Optimizations Options

Transparent Shadows	When enabled, transparent objects cast colored shadows based on their transparency and diffuse color.
Antialias Suppression	When using supersampling, reflections or refractions, this option disables the second pass in two-pass antialiased mode. This is a good idea to save time since the second pass often adds little in these situations. (Supersampling is discussed in the rendering and animation material.)
Skip Coplanar Faces	Prevents coplanar faces from shading each other (those that lie overlapped in the same plane).

Practice 8b

Working with Shadow Parameters

Practice Objective

- Understand the different types of shadows casting methods.

In this practice, you will adjust parameters to refine the shadows in a scene.

You must set the paths to locate the External files and Xrefs used in the practice. If you have not done this already, return to Chapter 1 and complete Task 1 to Task 3 in *Practice 1a: Organizing Folders and Working with the Interface*. You only have to set the user paths once.

*If a dialog box opens prompting you about a File Load: Mismatch, click **OK** to accept the default values.*

1. Open **Shadow Parameters.max**.

2. In the Scene Explorer, (![icon](Display None) and ![icon](Display Lights)), select one of the Ceiling Downlight objects, such as **Ceiling Downlight 06**.

3. In the Command Panel, select the Modify panel (![icon]), and examine its parameters. These lights use the default Advanced Ray Traced shadow type (**Adv. Ray Traced** in *General Parameters* rollout), as shown in Figure 8–48.

Figure 8–48

4. In the Main Toolbar, click (Render Production) to render the scene. In the Rendered Frame Window, zoom and pan to the desk area, as shown in Figure 8–49. The edges of the shadow under the desk display jagged. Leave the Rendered Frame Window open.

Figure 8–49

5. In the Modify panel ( ), expand the *Adv. Ray Traced Params* rollout and in the *Basic Options* area, select **2-Pass Antialias** in the drop-down list. In the *Antialiasing Options* area, set the following, as shown in Figure 8–50:

- *Shadow Integrity*: **2**
- *Shadow Quality*: **3**

Figure 8–50

6. In the Rendered Frame Window, click **Render**. The shadow edges display less jagged than before, but the rendering time has increased.

When soft shadows are required or speed is critical, Shadow maps make a good alternative.

7. In the *General Parameters* rollout, in the *Shadows* area, change the type from *Adv. Ray Traced* to **Shadow Map** by selecting **Shadow Map** in the drop-down list, as shown on the left in Figure 8–51.

8. Render the scene. These shadows are fuzzier and less accurate (as shown on the right in Figure 8–51) but significantly faster to render.

Figure 8–51

There might not be a huge difference in shadows under the desk.

9. To make the shadow-mapped shadows better defined, increase the map size. In the *Shadow Map Params* rollout, double the *Size* from 512 to **1024**, as shown in Figure 8–52.

Figure 8–52

10. Render the scene. The shadows are now better defined under the desk.

11. Adjust the Shadow map by setting the following:
    - *Size*: **2048**
    - *Bias*: **0.01**

12. Render the scene again. Note that the shadows have become more significant and less jagged under the desk.

13. Save your work as **MyShadow Parameters.max**.

Chapter Review Questions

1. Which of the following is not required to be used with Standard lighting?

   a. Near Attenuation options

   b. Exposure control

   c. Decay options

   d. Shadow options

2. Which type of standard lights are used to represent light sources that cast parallel rays?

   a. Omni lights

   b. Spotlights

   c. Directional lights

   d. Skylight

3. In the *Intensity/Color/Attenuation* rollout (shown in Figure 8–53), which has common parameters for all of the standard lights, which option does not occur in the real world and is only included as a computer graphics lighting effect?

   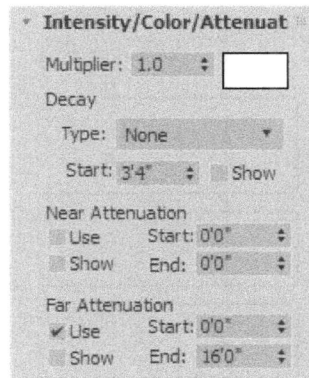

   Figure 8–53

   a. Multiplier

   b. Decay options

   c. Near Attenuation options

   d. Far Attenuation options

4. In the *Spotlight parameters* rollout (shown in Figure 8–54),
    which option enables a spotlight to cast light in all directions
    and behave like an omni light? (Hint: Setting this option
    generally looks unnatural and it should be used with care.)

Figure 8–54

a. Show Cone

b. Overshoot

c. Hotspot/Beam

d. Falloff/Field

5. In the Shadow Map type of shadows, a density value below
    1.0 makes the shadow darker and a density value of greater
    than 1.0 makes the shadow lighter.

a. True

b. False

Command Summary

Button	Command	Location
	Array	• **Extras toolbar** • **Tools:** Array
	Lights	• **Command Panel:** *Create* panel • **Create:** Lights
	Render Production	• **Main Toolbar** • *Rendering:* Render

Lighting and Cameras

Photometric lights are generally used to accurately represent real-world lighting. Once added, their parameters can be further modified to create realism in a design. Although photometric lights work well with the Arnold renderer, Arnold specific lights are also provided. Additionally, the use of cameras and background images can enhance the scene.

Learning Objectives in this Chapter

- Create photometric lights and modify them by changing their parameters.
- Create Arnold lights and modify them by changing their parameters.
- Create different types of cameras and control their parameters.

9.1 Photometric Light Objects

Photometric light objects are based on quantitative measurements of light levels and distribution. They provide a real-world lighting and accurate scene illumination when used with ART Renderer, Arnold Renderer, and other global illumination solutions. In the Autodesk® 3ds Max® software, photometric lights are the default choice for creating lights.

- Photometric lights take advantage of physically-based color, intensity, and distribution properties. They can be defined with real-world lighting parameters in engineering units.

- Since photometric lights are based on real-world calculations of light energy, they are **scale-specific**. Scenes using photometric lights and radiosity should have an appropriate system unit scale.

- All photometric lights automatically decay (attenuate) with an inverse-square relationship. Far attenuation can be controlled manually, to save calculation time and energy.

- Photometric lights work for Scanline, ART, and Arnold renderers.

- Exposure control should be used with Photometric lights objects to adjust the brightness of the scene, the Shadow/Midtones, and Highlight areas of the image.

Photometric Light Types

In the Command Panel's Create panel (➕)> 💡 (Lights), **Photometric** is the default light type, as shown in Figure 9–1. The object types for photometric lights are:

- **Target Light**

- **Free Light**

Figure 9–1

While creating a Target Light or a Free Light, you can set different parameters to illuminate the scene accurately and effectively. Once the lights have been created, you can modify the parameters using the Modify panel in the Command Panel.

Templates Rollout

With the Target or Free photometric lights, there are templates to select from, as shown in Figure 9–2. Selecting a template controls the intensity and color temperature of the light.

Figure 9–2

General Parameters Rollout

The *General Parameters* rollout controls some of the basic settings for toggling the light on/off in the scene and the different shadow casting methods (Ray Traced, Adv. Ray Traced, Area shadows, and Shadow Map). The options found in the *Light Properties* area and *Shadows* area are similar to the options found in Standard Lights, and can be used in the same manner.

Any Free Light can be changed into a Targeted Light (and vice-versa) by using the **Targeted** option in the *Light Properties* area. When the Targeted option is enabled, a tool tip displays as you move the target indicating the illumination, as shown in Figure 9–3.

Int. at Target: 37.57 fc

| Figure 9–3 | Figure 9–4 |

*In the General Parameters rollout, many options (Light Properties area options, Shadows area options, and **Spotlight** parameters) are identical or similar to the options used when creating Standard Lights.*

The *Light Distribution* area (shown in Figure 9–4) contains a list of the photometric light distribution types available in the software. These control the way the light illuminates the surrounding space. The options are described as follows:

Uniform Spherical	Casts light in all directions, like a standard Omni light.
Uniform Diffuse	Casts light in one hemisphere only and mimics the way light emits from a surface.
Spotlight	Provides hotspot and falloff parameters identical to standard spotlights.
Photometric Web	Casts light according to a 3D representation of light intensity as determined by a lighting file format, such as IES, LTLI, or CIBSE. These are files provided by lighting manufacturers, usually available via the Internet.

Distribution (Photometric Web) Rollout

If you select Photometric Web in the Light Distribution type list, the *Distribution (Photometric Web)* rollout displays, as shown in Figure 9–5. Real-world luminaries (lighting fixtures) nearly always cast light in varying amounts in different directions. The Web distribution method enables the Autodesk 3ds Max software to simulate the laboratory-determined light distribution of specific lighting fixtures.

- Photometric lights can make use of web distribution information from IES, LTLI, or CIBSE photometric web data files that can be obtained from lighting manufacturers for specific light fixture models. They are often available directly from manufacturers' web sites.

- Lights with Web distributions are indicated with photometric web icons (as shown in Figure 9–6) that graphically represent the 3D distribution of light cast from the light fixture.

Figure 9–5

Figure 9–6

Web Distribution in Viewports

You can see the web distribution in the viewport. Select the *Shading Viewport* label (such as **High Quality**) and select **Lighting and Shadows>Illuminate with Scene Lights** (as shown in Figure 9–7) to see the lights in the viewport. You can add shadows by selecting **Shadows** and toggle on **Ambient Occlusion** in the viewport to add subtle detail enhancement. These options only take effect in viewport and have no effect on the actual renderings.

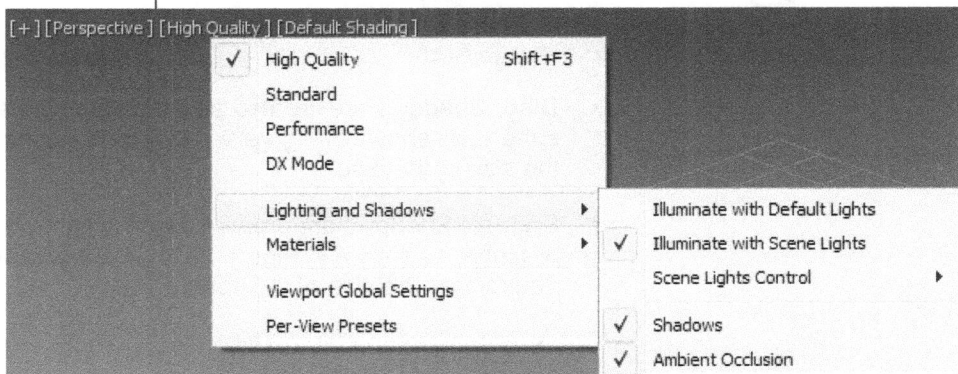

Figure 9–7

Shape/Area Shadows Rollout

The Shape/Area Shadow controls are used to generate a shadow casting shape and to calculate shadows based on a particular shape. The various shapes have different parametric controls and the shapes can be selected in the *Shape/Area Shadows* rollout, as shown in Figure 9–8.

Figure 9–8

- **Point:** Shadows are created as if the light was one single point, as shown in Figure 9–9.

- **Line:** Shadows are created as if the light was one single line, as shown in Figure 9–10. The size of the line is controlled with the **Length** parameter.

Use this for fluorescent tubes or rectangular ceiling lights.

- **Rectangle:** Shadows are created as if the light was a rectangular area (as shown in Figure 9–11) governed by **Length** and **Width** parameters.

Figure 9–9   **Figure 9–10**   **Figure 9–11**

- **Disc:** Shadows are created as if the light was a flattened sphere, as shown in Figure 9–12. A radius control determines the size of the disc.

- **Sphere:** Shadows are created as if the light was a round ball or globe, as shown in Figure 9–13. Again a radius control determines the size of the sphere.

- **Cylinder:** Shadows are created as if the light emitter is cylindrical, as shown in Figure 9–14. **Radius** and **Length** are the two parameters to control the cylinder proportions.

Figure 9–12   **Figure 9–13**   **Figure 9–14**

In the *Shape/Area Shadows* rollout, in the *Rendering* area, you can also select the **Light Shape Visible in Rendering** option. This permits the Cylinder, Disc, Sphere, and Rectangle light shapes (as shown on the top in Figure 9–15) to render as objects in the viewport (as shown on the bottom in Figure 9–15). The Point and Line objects do not work with this feature.

Figure 9–15

Intensity/Color/ Attenuation Rollout

Photometric light color can be assigned through a lamp specification (such as fluorescent, halogen, incandescent, etc.) or through a temperature specified in degrees Kelvin. This color can also be filtered (tinted) through a color swatch. All of these options can be selected in the *Color* area of the *Intensity/Color/ Attenuation* rollout, as shown in Figure 9–16.

Figure 9–16

The overall brightness of Photometric lights can be specified as one of three intensity values (*Intensity* area):

Luminous flux	The overall output strength of the lamp, measured in lumens (lm).
Luminous intensity	The light energy that is released over time, measured in candelas (cd).
Illuminance	A measurement of how much illumination reaches a surface a set distance away from a lamp with a certain facing. Illuminance is measured in foot-candles (fc, lumens/ft2) or lux (lumens/m2). When using this option, specify both the Luminous flux (lumens) and the distance at which that brightness occurs

> **Hint: Photometric Lights Data**
>
> The Autodesk 3ds Max software ships with a host of sample lighting templates that you can use out-of-the-box.
>
> The Autodesk 3ds Max Help lists a number of sample fixtures in the **Common Lamp Values for Photometric Lights** section.
>
> Lights that combine the geometry of a light fixture with the correct photometric light distribution model are referred to as luminaries. These are assemblies with a hierarchy created so that the photometric light is linked to the geometry. You can obtain luminaries from manufacturer websites (such as ERCO). You can also import lighting fixtures from the Autodesk® Revit® software using FBX import.

The *Far Attenuation* area controls the end location of the Photometric light and the area that is graduated as the end of the range is approached, as shown in Figure 9–17.

Figure 9–17

Practice 9a

Working with Photometric Lights

Practice Objectives

- Create photometric lights and modify their parameters.
- Use preset lamps and their provided data.

In this practice, you will create and adjust photometric lights. You will use different lamp presets to apply realistic lighting to the lobby model.

You must set the paths to locate the External files and Xrefs used in the practice. If you have not done this already, return to Chapter 1 and complete Task 1 to Task 3 in *Practice 1a: Organizing Folders and Working with the Interface*. You only have to set the user paths once.

Task 1 - Create free photometric lights.

If a dialog box opens prompting you about a File Load: Mismatch, click OK to accept the default values.

1. Open **Photometric Lighting start.max**.

2. Maximize the **Top** viewport and click (Zoom Extents) to display the floorplan. Verify that the scene displays in Wireframe mode.

3. In the Create panel ( ), click (Lights) and verify that **Photometric** displays in the drop-down list. In the *Object Type* rollout, select **Free Light**, as shown in Figure 9–18.

Figure 9–18

You can zoom into the area where the yellow circles are placed, which indicate the slots for lights.

4. Click approximately over the upper left light fixture circle to place a light, as shown in Figure 9–19. You will position it accurately in the next step.

Figure 9–19

Alternatively, right-click on ✛ *(Select and Move) in the Main Toolbar to open the Transform Type-In dialog box. You can also enter the values in the Status Bar.*

5. In the viewport, right-click on the new light and in the quad menu, next to **Move**, select ▢ (Settings). In the Move Transform Type-In dialog box, in the *Absolute:World* area, set the following, as shown in Figure 9–20:
   - *X:* **84'7"**
   - *Y:* **126'10"**
   - *Z:* **9'11"** (elevation)

Figure 9–20

6. Close the dialog box. With the light object selected, in the Modify panel (🖊), rename the light object as **Light – Downlight A 00**.

7. In the *General Parameters* rollout, set *Light Distribution (Type)* to **Spotlight**. Note that the shape of the light object changes in the viewport.

8. In the *Intensity/Color/Attenuation* rollout, set *Color* to **HID Quartz Metal Halide**, as shown in Figure 9–21.

Figure 9–21

Hint: Accessing Photometric Lights Data

When using metal halide lamps, you can find suggestions for their photometric light parameters in the Help system. Select **Help>Autodesk 3ds Max Help**. In the *Search* box, enter **Common Lamp Values**. Select **Common Lamp Values for Photometric Lights** and scroll down to **Par38 Line Voltage Lamps**. The **Medium Beam** has intensities between 1700-4000 candelas, as shown in Figure 9–22. The values for beam and field angles are also displayed.

Par38 Line Voltage Lamps

Class.	Watts	Type	Intensity	Beam	Field
Narrow Beam	45	Spot	4700	14	28
Narrow Beam	75	Spot	5200	12	25
Narrow Beam	150	Spot	10500	14	28
Medium Beam	45	Spot	1700	28	60
Medium Beam	75	Spot	1860	30	60
Medium Beam	150	Spot	4000	30	60

Figure 9–22

9. With the new light still selected, click ✛ (Select and Move) and then use <Shift> + click and drag the light to the right on the next yellow circle. Select **Instance** in the Clone Options dialog box to instance the light.

10. Using the method used in Step 9, instance the lights such that they correspond to the rest of the symbols for Ceiling Lights (circles provided for the locations of the recessed lighting). You can approximate their positions and have 14 lights with the last one named **Light - Downlight A 013**.

11. Select the [**Top**] *Point of View* label and select Cameras> **Camera - Lobby1** to display the **Camera - Lobby1** viewport. Change the *Shading Viewport* to **Standard** and [Wireframe] *Per-view Preference* viewport to **Default Shading + Edged Faces** to display the 14 spotlights, as shown in Figure 9–23.

Figure 9–23

12. Select **Rendering>Exposure Control** to open the Environment and Effects dialog box. Note that the **Logarithmic Exposure Control** option is selected in the *Exposure Control* rollout.

13. In the *Exposure Control* rollout, select **Active**. Click **Render Preview** and note the render preview.

14. In the *Logarithmic Exposure Control Parameters* rollout, increase the *Brightness* to **70**, press <Enter>, and watch the render preview update. Close the dialog box.

*The Production Renderer is set to **ART Renderer**. It might take a few minutes to complete the render.*

15. In the Main toolbar, click ![Render Production icon] (Render Production) to render the viewport. In the Rendering dialog box, note the progress of the rendering. When the Rendering dialog box closes, indicating that the rendering is complete, note the rendered scene and leave the Rendered Frame Window open.

Task 2 - Adjust the light parameters.

1. In the viewport, select any one of the lights. In the Command Panel, Modify panel (![icon]), in the *Distribution (Spotlight)* rollout, note that *Hotspot/Beam* and *Falloff/Field* have default values of **30°** and **60°**.

When changing the Light Distribution Type, the shape of the light object (in the viewport) changes accordingly.

2. If you have access to a photometric data file for a light fixture, you can use it for this light. In the *General Parameters* rollout set *Light Distribution (Type)* to **Photometric Web**, as shown in Figure 9–24.

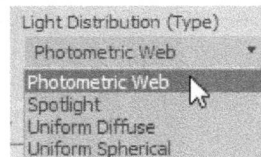

Figure 9–24

3. In the *Distribution (Photometric Web) Parameters* rollout, click **< Choose Photometric File >** and in the Practice Files folder, in the ...\sceneassets\photometric folder, open **sample_downlight.ies**. The thumbnail diagram of the selected web file displays as shown in Figure 9–25.

The red shape displays the beam.

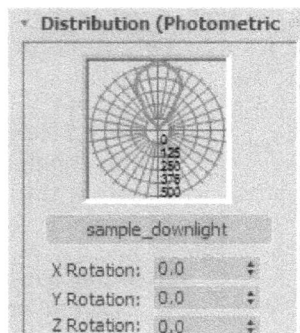

Figure 9–25

The **Dimming**
parameter should be
cleared to control the
intensity of light.

4. Note that in the *Intensity/Color/Attenuation* rollout, in the *Intensity* area, the intensity of the light has been updated to **3298.0 cd**.

5. In the *General Parameters* rollout, in the *Shadows* area, select **On** and **Use Global Settings**. Select **Shadow Map** in the drop-down list, as shown in Figure 9–26.

Figure 9–26

6. Click **Render** in the Rendered Frame Window. Note that the dark areas have been removed but the scene looks washed out.

7. In the *Intensity/Color/Attenuation* rollout, in the *Intensity* area, set the intensity to **1100** cd and render the scene again. The rendering has slightly improved, as shown in Figure 9–27. Close the Rendered Frame Window.

Figure 9–27

8. The photometric lights representation displays in the viewport and you can control their effects individually. Select the *Shading Viewport* label to display the label menu and select **Lighting and Shadows** and **Illuminate with Scene Lights**. Expand the label menu again and select **Lighting and Shadows>Scene Lights Control>Auto Display Selected Lights**, as shown in Figure 9–28.

Figure 9–28

9. In the viewport, select one of the lights to enable it. You will see the effect of that light in the viewport. Select another light and see its effect in the viewport. Using <Ctrl>, select a few more lights to activate them together and visually see the effects.

10. In the *Shading Viewport* label menu, select **Lighting and Shadows>Shadows** to display the shadows that are cast along with the lighting effect of the light selected.

11. With one of the lights selected, in the Command Panel, Modify panel ( ), in the *Templates* rollout, select **75 W Bulb** as shown on the left in Figure 9–29. Note the changes in the viewport, as shown on the right in Figure 9–29.

Figure 9–29

12. With one of the lights selected, in the Command Panel,

Modify panel ( ), in the *Templates* rollout, select **Recessed 75W Lamp (web)**. This uses a different IES file.

13. Click (Render Production) to render the scene. Once the rendering is complete, note that the lighting is dark and moody, as shown in Figure 9–30.

Figure 9–30

14. (Optional) This might take longer to render the scene: In the Command Panel, Modify panel ( ), in the *Templates* rollout, select **75 W Bulb** and render the scene. Once the rendering is complete, note that the lighting now illuminates differently and the reflections and shadows add realism, as shown in Figure 9–31.

Figure 9–31

15. Save your work as **MyPhotometricLighting.max**.

Hint: Using Light Lister

The Autodesk 3ds Max software includes a Light Lister utility (as shown in Figure 9–32) (**Tools>Light Lister**) that enables you to view and change light properties without having to select them first. You can change the settings for all lights together or for the selected lights.

Figure 9–32

Hint: Standard Lights Considerations

Standard lights can also be used instead of photometric light objects, but since they are not physically-based, the results achieved are not accurate. For better accuracy, it not is recommended to mix standard and photometric lights in the same scene. The following should be considered:

- The luminous intensity of standard lights is equal to the light's multiplier parameter times the Physical Scale value in Logarithmic Exposure Control. (The default *Physical Scale* value is **1500** candelas in the *Logarithmic Exposure Control Parameters* rollout in the Environments and Effects dialog box.) You can make drastic changes to the P*hysical Scale* value to compensate for scale problems in lighting a scene. Change this value to **80,000** or **150,000** to brighten a scene.

- To limit the effects of exposure control (i.e., not have the exposure control affect the direct lighting) use the **Affect Indirect Only** option.

9.2 Arnold Lights

Although the Photometric lights work very well with the Arnold renderer, the 3ds Max software provides you with Arnold lights that are specifically meant to be used with this renderer. It has parameters that are geared towards rendering using Arnold.

You can open the Arnold lights from the Command Panel's Create panel (✛)> 💡 (Lights) by selecting **Arnold** from the list, as shown in Figure 9–33. In the *Object Type* rollout, click **Arnold Light**, as shown Figure 9–34.

Figure 9–33   **Figure 9–34**

- In the *General Properties* rollout, you can toggle the light on or off, as shown Figure 9–34. You can also set the light as either free or targeted. By default, **Targeted** is cleared, which automatically creates the light as a free light.

- In the *Shape* rollout, you can select the shape of the light, as shown in Figure 9–35. The shape selected controls how the light is emitted. By default, the **Quad** option is selected, which illuminates a rectangular area and emits the light only in one direction. The parameters in the *Shape* rollout are based on the type of light selected.

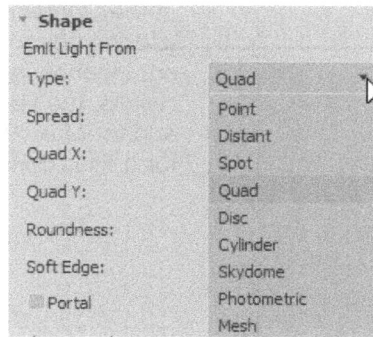

Figure 9–35

- In the *Color/Intensity* rollout (shown in Figure 9–36), you can set the color of the light source. Typically, you are required to adjust the **Intensity** or **Exposure** of the light source to get a good render of a scene. Exposure is an intensity multiplier and increases the intensity in multiple jumps.

- In the *Rendering* rollout (shown in Figure 9–37), you can adjust the quality of specular highlight and shadows. Increasing the **Samples** value reduces the noise in shadow areas, but increases the render time.

- In the *Shadow* rollout (shown in Figure 9–37), you can toggle the casting of shadows from the light on or off. The **Atmospheric Shadows** option controls the calculations of volumetric shadows.

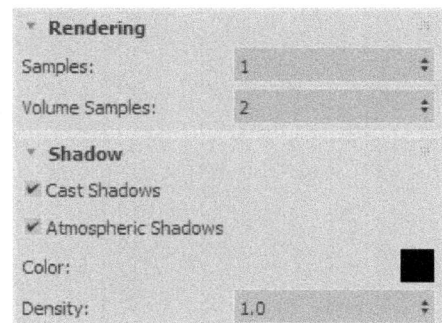

Figure 9–36   **Figure 9–37**

- In the *Contribution* rollout (shown in Figure 9–38), you can use the advanced options to control the aspects of light contribution in the final rendering. For physically accurate results, the various values should be left as a default of 1.0 and for *Max. Bounces* as 999. You can change those options for artistic control.

Figure 9–38

Practice 9b

Working with Arnold Lights

Practice Objective

- Create Arnold lights and modify their parameters.

In this practice, you will create and adjust Arnold lights. You will use different lamp presets to apply realistic lighting to the lobby model.

You must set the paths to locate the External files and Xrefs used in the practice. If you have not done this already, return to Chapter 1 and complete Task 1 to Task 3 in *Practice 1a: Organizing Folders and Working with the Interface*. You only have to set the user paths once.

Task 1 - Create Arnold Lights.

*If a dialog box opens prompting you about a File Load: Mismatch, click **OK** to accept the default values.*
*The Production Renderer is set to **Arnold**.*

You will first configure an Environment Map to serve as a viewport and rendering background.

1. Open **Arnold Lights.max**.

2. Verify that the **Camera01** viewport is active and in the Main Toolbar, click ![teapot icon] (Render Production) to render the viewport. Note that the rendered scene has no shadows as the scene is illuminated by default lights. Leave the Rendered Frame Window open.

3. In the Create panel (![+]), click ![light icon] (Lights), and in the drop-down list, select **Arnold**. In the *Object Type* rollout, select **Arnold Light**, as shown in Figure 9–39.

Figure 9–39

4. In the **Top** viewport, click to place a light at the approximate center of the candle holder. Note that you might not be able to see the light because it is placed at the bottom of the candle holder, which is not visible in the **Top** view. Do not click again as another light will be created.

5. In the Command Panel, name the light as **Light Top**.

6. Verify that the Arnold Light is still highlighted in blue. In the **Top** viewport, click under the bottom horizontal line, as shown in Figure 9–40.

Figure 9–40

7. In the Command Panel, name this light as **Light Front**. Press <Esc> to exit the light creation tool.

8. Activate the **Camera** viewport and render it. Note that the rendering is dark (black).

9. In the Scene Explorer, select **Light Top** and in the **Left** viewport, note the vertical line below the light object (as shown in Figure 9–41), which indicates that the direction of the light is pointing below the countertop.

Figure 9–41

10. With the **Light Top** selected, select (Select and Move). In the Status Bar, enter **500.0** in the *Z Transform Type* to move the light up.

11. Render the **Camera** viewport (activate it) and note that the rendering is still all dark.

Task 2 - Modify the Light parameters.

1. With the **Light Top** selected, in the Modify panel ( ), in the *Color/Intensity* rollout, increase the *Intensity* to **10.0** and the *Exposure* to **16.0**, as shown in Figure 9–42.

2. Render the **Camera** viewport and note that the scene has light, but the candle holder is not very crisp, as shown in Figure 9–43.

| **Figure 9–42** | **Figure 9–43** |

3. In the Scene Explorer, select **Light Front**. Using (Select and Move), in the Status Bar, enter **500.0** in the *Z Transform Type* to move the light up. In the *Color/Intensity* rollout, increase the *Intensity* to **10.0** and *Exposure* to **16.0**.

4. Render the **Camera** viewport and note that the scene has become brighter and the shadows are being cast on the wall and on the tiles, as shown Figure 9–44.

Figure 9–44

5. Verify that the **Light Front** is still selected. In the *Shadow* rollout, clear the **Cast Shadows** option. Render the **Camera** viewport and note that the shadow on the wall has been removed. Select **Cast Shadows** again.

Quad is the default type when a light is created.

6. With the **Light Front** still selected, in the *Shape* rollout, open the Type drop-down list and select **Point**. In the *Color/Intensity* rollout, in the *Color* area, select **Kelvin** and enter a value of **4500.0**. Render the **Camera** viewport and note that a warmth (more yellow) has been added and the shadow has become sharper, as shown in Figure 9–45.

Figure 9–45

7. With the **Light Front** selected, in the *Rendering* rollout, increase the *Samples* to **3**. Render the **Camera** viewport and note that shadow has become more sharp but the rendering time has increased.

8. Save your work as **MyArnold Lights.max**.

9.3 Cameras

Cameras are created using ■ (Cameras) in the Command

Panel, in the Create panel (+), as shown in Figure 9–46.

- Target cameras have a target object that can be selected and transformed separately from the camera itself.

- Free cameras do not have a target object.

- Physical cameras includes exposure control and other effects while framing the scene.

*Alternatively, you can create a camera by selecting **Create> Cameras**.*

Figure 9–46

- Cameras can also be created on the fly to match a **Perspective** viewport using **Views>Create Standard Camera From View** or **Views>Create Physical Camera From View.**

Physical Camera

The **Physical Camera** (shown in Figure 9–47) is the best option for setting up photorealistic, physically based scenes. The Physical Camera integrates framing the scene with per-camera exposure control, perspective control, distortion, depth of field, and motion blur. The options that can be incorporated while using the Physical camera is dependent on the active renderer. The Physical Camera works well with both ART and Arnold renderers.

The **Physical Camera** parameters (shown in Figure 9–48) are described as follows:

Figure 9–47

Figure 9–48

Basic **rollout**	When **Targeted** is selected, it defines properties for a target camera, and viewport display options.
Physical **Camera rollout**	Contains properties to define the scene view using real world camera values for accurate reproduction of a camera shot scene. Presets are available for common camera types which define *Lens* properties, focus, and shutter speed.
Exposure **rollout**	Defines exposure properties to be used with the physical camera. These properties do not affect the *Global Exposure* settings in the Physical Camera Exposure Control in the Environment settings.
Bokeh (Depth of **Field) rollout**	Properties to create a blurring effect in areas of the image that are out of focus. This effect is most apparent when the out-of-focus areas of the scene have small points of high contrast, typically from light sources or bright objects.
Perspective **Control rollout**	Properties to shift the perspective of the camera scene without changing the location or orientation of the camera.
Lens Distortion **rollout**	Settings to apply a camera distortion effect to the rendered image using cubic or texture distortion.
Miscellaneous **rollout**	Enables clipping planes and modifies near and far environment ranges.

Target and Free Camera Parameters

As with any other object, the **Target** and **Free Camera** parameters are available in the Command Panel, in the Modify panel (⬚), as shown in Figure 9–49.

Figure 9–49

The Camera parameters found in the *Parameters* rollout for the Target and Free camera are:

- The focal length of real-world cameras is the distance between the focus point (the film or light-sensitive media) and the optical center of the lens. The *Lens* option available governs how much of the scene is visible to the camera. This corresponds to the focal length of real-world cameras.

- The camera focal lengths are directly related to that camera's field of view (*FOV*), which is an angular measurement of how much of the horizon can be seen by the camera. The field of view can be measured horizontally, vertically, or diagonally using the different field of view options, as shown in Figure 9–50.

Figure 9–50

- Human vision is often approximated with a 45° field of view and it varies from 60 degrees above to 75 degrees below the horizontal meridian. A focal length of 50mm is very commonly used in real-world cameras, which relates to about a 40° field of view in the Autodesk 3ds Max software.

- Other stock focal lengths are provided in the Autodesk 3ds Max software as button presets. Focal lengths below 50mm are considered short or wide-angle lenses, while those above 50mm are called telephoto lenses.

- The **Orthographic Projection** option (shown in Figure 9–51) causes a camera view to display as an orthographic or user view (axonometric rotated) rather than a three-point perspective.

- The camera's cone of vision is visible when the camera is selected, as shown in Figure 9–52. The **Show Cone** option causes it to remain visible even after the camera is no longer selected.

- The **Show Horizon** option (shown in Figure 9–53) displays a dark gray line in the camera viewport, representing the horizon in the camera view. It is helpful when aligning a camera to a background image.

Figure 9–51 **Figure 9–52**

Figure 9–53

Hint: Two-Point Perspectives Through Cameras

By default, camera and perspective viewports show three-point perspective views. You can display a two-point perspective by adding a Camera Correction modifier to the camera object. To do so, select **Camera Correction** in **Modifiers>Cameras**, as shown in Figure 9–54. Two-point perspective causes vertical lines to remain vertical rather than converge over distance.

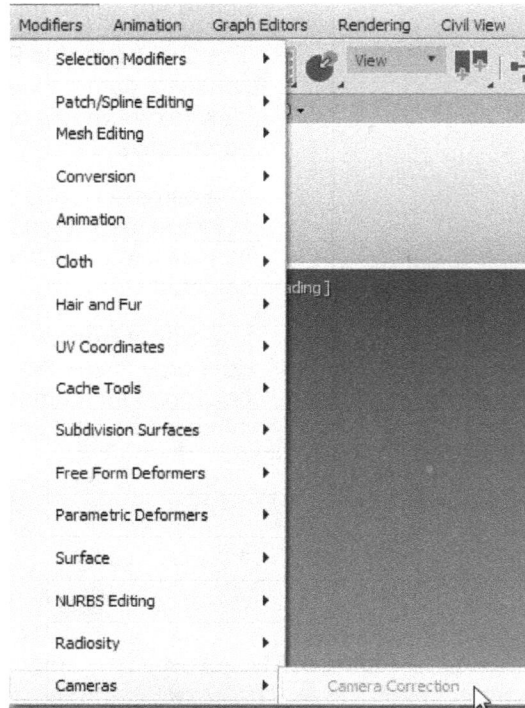

Figure 9–54

Some additional **Target** and **Free Camera** parameters are shown in Figure 9–55.

Figure 9–55

- The *Environment Ranges* are contains the near and far range distances measured from the camera for the atmospheric effects. You can set the atmospheric effects in the *Atmosphere* rollout in the *Environment* tab in the Environment and Effects dialog box (**Rendering> Environment**).

- The *Clipping Planes* area contains the cutoff distances for the geometry that displays in the camera. When enabled, only the geometry between the clip distances is visible.

Depending on the selected effect, a Parameters rollout specific to that effect (Depth of Field Parameters or Motion Blur Parameters) opens below the Cameras Parameters rollout.

- The *Multi-Pass Effect* area (default option is **Depth of Field**) is a camera-specific rendering effect that causes distance blurring, where only a certain point is in focus. This effect simulates how areas away from the focal point display blurred in human vision and photography. You can select **Depth of Field** or **Motion Blur** (as shown in Figure 9–56).

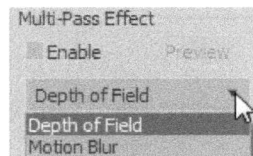

Figure 9–56

9.4 Background Images

The Autodesk 3ds Max software can use image files as viewport and rendering backgrounds. Background images are used to add detail to a scene or show a proposed construction project in its real-world context. You can load an image into the viewport background, independent of the rendering background (the environment map) or load it to both the viewport and rendering backgrounds.

How To: Enable a Background Image to Viewports

1. Select **Views>Viewport Configuration>**_Background_ tab (<Alt>+<B>). The _Background_ tab options display as shown in Figure 9–57.

Figure 9–57

*If any option other than the **Use Files** option is selected, the Setup area will be grayed out.*

2. Select **Use Files** to make the *Setup* area available for use.
3. In the *Aspect Ratio* area, select **Match Bitmap** to keep the aspect ratio of the image file constant.
4. Click **Files...** to browse for the image file and open it.
5. Click **Apply to Active View** to only display the image in the active viewport or click **Apply to All Views in Active Layout Tab** to display it in all of the viewports.
6. Click **OK**.

How To: Assign an Environment Map

*Select **Rendering> Environment** to open the Environment and Effects dialog box.*

1. To enable an environment map to display in a viewport, you need to select the **Use Map** option and load a map using the *Environment Map* slot in the Environment and Effects dialog box, as shown in Figure 9–58. You can adjust the map parameters using an Instance of the map in Slate Material Editor, and opening its Parameter Editor.

Figure 9–58

*Select **Views>Viewport Configuration** or press <Alt>+<B>.*

2. Select the viewport in which you want to display the map.
3. In the Viewport Configuration dialog box (*Background* tab), select **Use Environment Background** and click **OK**.

Hint: Updating a Background Image

Certain changes (e.g., change in resolution or aspect ratio) do not update the background image automatically. You should use <Alt>+<Shift>+<Ctrl>+<B> to update the background image in the active viewport. This command is not available if the active viewport does not display a background image.

Hint: Assign Background Image from Windows Explorer

You can also assign a background image directly from Windows Explorer by dragging and dropping the image file onto a viewport. A Bitmap Viewport Drop dialog box opens prompting you to select it as a viewport background, an environment map, or as both, as shown in Figure 9–59.

Figure 9–59

Aspect Ratio

The Autodesk 3ds Max software uses an aspect ratio to describe image proportions, which is the relationship between length and width of images, renderings, and viewports. For example, an HDTV video can be created at a resolution of 1920 x 1080 pixels (1080p), which has an aspect ratio of 1.78 (1920 / 1080 = 1.78).

It is recommended to match the aspect ratio of a background image to the aspect ratio of a viewport and the rendered output. This enables you to see a more accurate representation of the final output in the viewports. The composition of a massing study displays different in the viewport (as shown in Figure 9–60) than it does in the rendered output (as shown in Figure 9–61), when their aspect ratios do not match.

Figure 9–60

Figure 9–61

You can maintain the aspect ratio of the viewport background using the options in the *Aspect Ratio* area in the Viewport Configuration dialog box, in the *Background* tab, as shown in Figure 9–62.

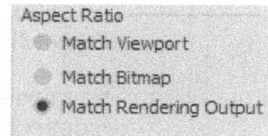

Aspect Ratio
- Match Viewport
- Match Bitmap
- Match Rendering Output

Figure 9–62

Match Viewport	Enables you to match the aspect ratio of the image to the aspect ratio of the viewport.
Match Bitmap	Enables you to lock the original aspect ratio of the image.
Match Rendering Output	Enables you to match the aspect ratio of the image to the active rendering output device.

Safe Frames

Safe Frames is a viewport display option that defines the portions of the viewport for rendered display. To enable this option, select the *Viewport* **+** label, and select **Configure Viewports** or select **Views>Viewport Configuration**. When the Viewport Configuration dialog box opens, select the *Safe Frames* tab, as shown in Figure 9–63.

Figure 9–63

The *Safe Frames* tab offers setup options that relate to safe areas for animated action and titles when creating graphics for television. When set, these display as rectangles in the active view, as shown in Figure 9–64:

- The outer rectangle is the *Live* area, the limits of what is rendered.

- The middle rectangle is the *Action safe* area, the recommended area for any animated action when creating graphics for television.

- The inner rectangle is the *Title safe* area, the recommended area for titles when creating graphics for television.

Figure 9–64

- The *User Safe* frame can be enabled, if required. It can be toggled on and customized to any proportion.

- The *12-Field Grid* frame displays a grid of cells (or fields) in the viewport. The 12-field grid yields either 12 (4x3) or 108 (12x9) cells and is used mainly by directors to reference specific areas of the screen.

Assigning Size and Aspect Ratio for Rendered Output

The rendering size (in pixels) and the aspect ratio of rendered output can be assigned in the *Output Size* area of the Render Setup dialog box, as shown in Figure 9–65 (**Rendering> Render Setup**>*Common* tab). There are several different presets available for output size.

Figure 9–65

The pixel aspect ratio is determined by the image width and height.

Do not confuse the *Image Aspect* ratio with the *Pixel Aspect* ratio. You can define the proportions of the pixel rectangle independent from the image. Consider the pixels to be individual tiles in a mosaic, where the tiles can be narrow, long, or short and wide.

> **Hint: Use Standard Aspect Ratios**
>
> Be cautious about selecting random width and height values. Most outputs have a required width and height value for a particular media type. Problems occur when non-standard choices are made for the rendering aspect ratio.

Practice 9c

Cameras and Background Images

Practice Objectives

- Apply a bitmap image as a background for the scene.
- Create a Physical Target Camera and modify the parameters.

In this practice, you will apply a bitmap image as an Environment Map in a rendered scene and as a Background Image in a viewport. You will then create a Physical Camera and modify its parameters to correctly display scene objects on top of the background image.

You must set the paths to locate the External files and Xrefs used in the practice. If you have not done this already, return to Chapter 1 and complete Task 1 to Task 3 in *Practice 1a: Organizing Folders and Working with the Interface*. You only have to set the user paths once.

Task 1 - Apply an Environment Map.

You will first configure an Environment Map to serve as a viewport and rendering background.

If a dialog box opens prompting you about a File Load: Mismatch, click OK to accept the default values.

1. Open **Camera Background.max**.
   - This is the retail exterior scene with standard exterior lighting.

2. In the menu bar, select **Rendering>Environment**. The Environment and Effects dialog box opens.

3. In the *Environment* tab, in the *Common Parameters* rollout, in the *Background* area, click **None** for *Environment Map*.

4. In the Material/Map Browser, open the **Maps>General** categories and double-click on **Bitmap**.

5. In the Select Bitmap Image File dialog box, open **Background.jpg** (from the *...\Maps* folder of the Practice Files folder).

- Note that *None* is replaced with **Map # (Background.jpg)** and **Use Map** is automatically enabled, as shown in Figure 9–66.

Background:

Color: Environment Map: ✔ Use Map

Map #9 (Background.jpg)

Figure 9–66

6. Close the Environment and Effects dialog box.

The Production renderer has been set to Arnold for this practice.

7. Activate the **Perspective** viewport and click 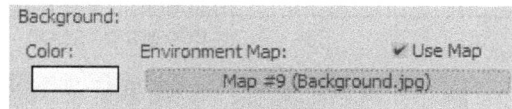 (Render Production). The background with trees displays behind the model, as shown in Figure 9–67.

Figure 9–67

- Note that the image file only displays in the rendering as a background and not in the viewport.
- The position of the background image is not correct.

8. Close the Rendered Frame Window.

You can also press <Alt>+<B> or select Views>Viewport Configuration to open the Viewport Configuration dialog box.

9. Ensure that the **Perspective** viewport is active and then select the *General* viewport label (+)>**Configure Viewports**. In the Viewport Configuration dialog box, select the *Background* tab.

10. Select **Use Environment Background**, as shown in Figure 9–68. Click **OK**.
   - Note that the background image displays behind the scene in the **Perspective** viewport, but it is not in the correct position.

Figure 9–68

11. To modify the image, open the Slate Material Editor.

Depending on the number of maps you have opened so far, the map number might vary.

12. In the Material/Map Browser, in the **Scene Materials** category, double-click on **Map # (Background.jpg) [Environment]**, **to** place its node on the *View1* sheet, as shown in Figure 9–69.

Figure 9–69

13. Double-click on the **Map # Bitmap** title bar to open its Parameter Editor.

14. In the *Bitmap Parameters* rollout, click **View Image**, as shown in Figure 9–70.

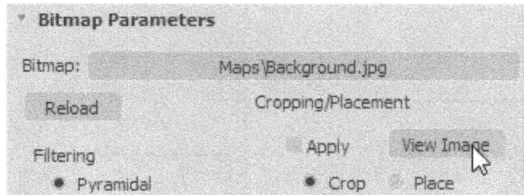

Figure 9–70

You can use programs such as Adobe Photoshop to remove features that are not required in a background image.

- The Specify Cropping/Placement viewer displays a grassy field with the top of a trailer, as shown in Figure 9–71.

Figure 9–71

- In the viewer, you can specify the image cropping (the limit of the area to be displayed) by re-sizing the red rectangle around the image. When required, cropping is enabled in the *Bitmap Parameters* rollout, in the *Cropping Placement* area, using the **Apply** option.

The Aspect value indicates if the image is being stretched or not.

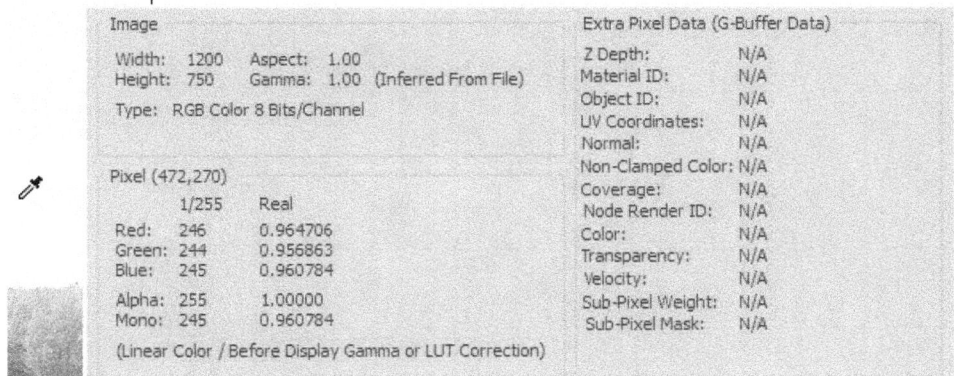

15. Right-click and hold over the image to access the color and other image data information, as shown in Figure 9–72. The image is currently 1200 pixels wide by 750 pixels high. An Aspect value of 1.00 means that this image is displaying normally. Close the Specify Cropping/Placement viewer.

Figure 9–72

*The **Spherical Environment** is the default mapping option*

16. In the Map Parameter Editor (Slate Material Editor), in the *Coordinates* rollout, verify that the **Environ** is selected. This indicates that the map is used as a 2D backdrop. In the Mapping drop-down list, select **Screen**, as shown in Figure 9–73. Close the Slate Material Editor.

Figure 9–73

- In the **Perspective** viewport, note that the background image has updated and that a small portion of the tree line displays behind the right side of the building.

17. Render the **Perspective** viewport. The tree line in the image should display partially behind the model, as shown in Figure 9–74 (although the image is not yet in the correct position). Close the Rendered Frame Window.

Figure 9–74

Task 2 - Create a Camera.

The background photograph was taken from about the center of the westerly end of the proposed parking lot curb island location. The camera was approximately eleven feet above the proposed first floor elevation (on a ladder) and pointed horizontally towards a proposed interior wall corner and vertically to the level of the horizon. In this task you will create a camera approximately lined up with the background image. This type of approximation is required when exact measurements of camera position and other existing features are not available.

1. Activate the **Top** viewport and maximize it. Zoom into the building and parking lot area.

2. In the Command Panel>Create panel (✛), click

   ◼️ (Cameras), and click **Physical**. Start with the approximate camera location (to the left of the middle double parking lot), click and drag to locate the target approximately over the model's back wall, and release to place the target, as shown in Figure 9–75.

Figure 9–75

3. Maximize to the four viewports. Press <Esc> to exit the **Cameras** command and then activate the **Perspective** viewport.

4. Select the **[Perspective]** *POV* label and select **Cameras> PhysCamera001**. Note that the background image is visible in the viewport with the building being viewed at an angle from the bottom up, and that the top of the trailer might be visible in the front.

5. In the Scene Explorer, select the camera object by selecting

   PhysCamera001. In the Main Toolbar, click ✥ (Select and Move). In the Status Bar, note that the *Z* elevation is **0.0**. Set Z to **11'0"**. Note that the tree lining is now visible behind the building along the left side and the trailer top is not visible.

6. You can now adjust the camera to display the image with respect to the building. In the **Top** Viewport, move the Camera object back and keep looking in the **PhysCamera001** viewport until you get the scene similar to that shown in Figure 9–76.

Figure 9–76

Task 3 - Approximately Match the Camera to the Background.

The background image has an aspect ratio of 1.6 (1200 pixels wide/750 pixels high). You will match the viewport and rendering to this aspect ratio.

1. In the Main Toolbar, click ![icon] (Render Setup) or select **Rendering>Render Setup**.

2. In the Render Setup dialog box, in the *Common Parameters* rollout, in the *Output Size* area, set *Image Aspect* to **1.6.** Click

   ![icon] next to it to activate it. Then, set the *Width* to **600** pixels and press <Enter>, as shown in Figure 9–77. Note that the *Height* is automatically adjusted to **375** because the *Image Aspect* is locked at **1.6**.

Figure 9–77

3. Close the dialog box.

4. Select the **PhysCamera001** *POV* label and select **Show Safe Frames**. Note the safe frames in the viewport, as shown in Figure 9–78.

Figure 9–78

Real-world 35mm cameras are named because of the diagonal measurement of their film, not their focal length.

5. Select the camera object in any viewport or Scene Explorer, and in the Command Panel, select the Modify panel (![icon]). In the *Physical Camera* rollout, note that in the *Film/Sensor* area, the *Preset* is set to **35mm** (Full Frame). This indicates that the photo was taken with a 35mm camera that had an adjustable lens.

6. In the *Exposure* rollout, verify that the **Exposure Control** has been installed (grayed out). If it is not installed, click **Install Exposure Control.**

7. Render the **PhysCamera001** viewport and note that the rendering is washed out.

8. In the *Exposure* rollout, change the *Target* to a value between **8.5** to **9.0** EV, as shown in Figure 9–79. Render the scene and note that the rendering is no longer washed out.

Figure 9–79

9. In the *Basic* rollout, in the *Viewport Display* area, select **Show Horizon Line**, as shown in Figure 9–80. In the **PhysCamera001** viewport, note that a horizontal black line displays across the viewport. It represents the horizon of the 3D model as seen by the camera.

Figure 9–80

10. To adjust the position of the horizon, in the *Perspective Control* rollout, in the *Lens Shift* area, set the *Vertical* value to **-10** %, as shown in Figure 9–81. Note that the tree line is now visible behind the building.

Figure 9–81

11. Verify that the **PhysCamera001** viewport is active and render the scene. Note that, with the help of some assumptions, you have reasonably located the model over an existing photograph, as shown in Figure 9–82.

Figure 9–82

12. Save your work as **MyCamera Background.max**.

Chapter Review Questions

1. Which photometric light distribution type only casts light in one hemisphere and mimics the way light emits from a surface?

    a. Uniform Spherical

    b. Uniform Diffuse

    c. Spotlight

    d. Photometric Web

2. Since photometric lights are based on real-world calculations of light energy, they are not scale-specific.

    a. True

    b. False

3. Which of the following parameters in the Arnold light source is an Intensity multiplier?

    a. **Exposure**

    b. **Samples**

    c. **Volume Samples**

    d. **Diffuse**

4. What is the most commonly used focal length in real-world cameras?

    a. 30mm

    b. 50mm

    c. 70mm

    d. 90mm

5. For background images, which keys do you press to update the active viewport with the specific changes made to the image (the changes that do not update automatically)?

    a. <Alt>+<B>

    b. <Alt>+<Ctrl>+<B>

    c. <Alt>+<Shift>+<B>

    d. <Alt>+<Ctrl>+<Shift>+<B>

Command Summary

Button	Command	Location
	Cameras	• **Command Panel:** *Create* panel • **Create:** Cameras
	Lights	• **Command Panel:** Create panel • **Create:** Lights
	Render Production	• **Main Toolbar** • **Rendering:** Render
	Render Setup	• **Main Toolbar** • **Rendering**: Render Setup
	Systems	• **Command Panel:** Create panel

Exposure Control, Daylight, and Rendering

The Autodesk® 3ds Max® software is set so that the default rendering options provide excellent rendering results; however, understanding the different rendering options and presets that you can use to customize and save rendering settings will help you further control the results obtained in your renderings. Additionally, the use of Sun positioner in a daytime scene and the use of exposure controls can help to add realism.

Learning Objectives in this Chapter

- Work with various Exposure Control methods and control the method specific parameters.
- Create Sun Positioner and modify the parameters to enhance the lighting in a scene.
- Set the common options available in all of the renderers.
- Control specific options for Arnold Renderer, Scanline Renderer, and ART Renderer.
- Create scene states and render pass states using the State Sets feature.
- Set the print resolution, paper size, and other options for a rendering.

10.1 Exposure Control

Lighting, Materials, and Exposure Control are all used together to produce a real-world rendered image.

- **Exposure Control** parameters are a global adjustment used to modulate the output levels and color range of renderings and viewport displays to expected values. The exposure control methods are optional when using scanline renderer.

- The Autodesk 3ds Max software can incorporate exposure control in the viewport but is dependant on the driver used. To display exposure control in the viewport and modify it interactively, use the Nitrous or Direct 3D display drivers.

- The Autodesk 3ds Max software calculates real-world illumination values through ART and Arnold. Computer monitors (and printed media) are only able to show a small fraction of the total brightness range visible to your eyes.

- Exposure control enables you to adapt the often large dynamic range (the variation of lighting levels) into the relatively small dynamic range that can be displayed on a computer screen or printed on paper.

Exposure Control Methods

The various exposure control methods are available in the *Environment* tab in the Environment and Effects dialog box (**Rendering>Environment** or **Rendering>Exposure Control**). In the *Exposure Control* rollout, select an exposure control method in the drop-down list, as shown in Figure 10–1.

- Exposure Control is used when the **Active** option is enabled.

Figure 10–1

- **Automatic Exposure Control:** Attempts to automatically adjust the sample range of lighting levels. It is appropriate for still renderings with very large dynamic ranges. This method can cause flashing when animating, because different frames could be modulated differently.

- **Linear Exposure Control:** Interprets and adjusts the lighting levels linearly, which might provide better results when working with low dynamic ranges (small variations in lighting levels).

- **Logarithmic Exposure Control:** Interprets and adjusts the lighting levels with a logarithmic distribution and provides additional controls that can be used effectively for animations. It enables you to control the *Brightness*, *Contrast*, *Midtones*, and *Color Correction*. Presets automatically adjust the settings, but if a rendering is overly bright or too dark, you can adjust the *Physical scale* setting.

- **Physical Camera Exposure Control:** Interprets and adjusts the exposure value and uses color-response curve to set exposure for physical cameras. This is the recommended exposure control to use with ART and Arnold renderers.

- **Pseudo Color Exposure Control:** Generates a lighting analysis rendering colorized by luminance (light source brightness) or illuminance (the amount of illumination that arrives at a surface). The different colors in the render (shown in Figure 10–2) give a representation of lighting levels, red for overlit areas, blue for underlit areas, and green for good lighting level areas.

Figure 10–2

Logarithmic Exposure Control Parameters

When **Logarithmic Exposure Control** is selected as the *Exposure Control* method, a corresponding rollout with parameters specific to this method displays, as shown in Figure 10–3.

Figure 10–3

Brightness/ Contrast	Adjusts the overall brightness and contrast of the rendered image. • Brightness: Controls the perceived illumination of surfaces. • Contrast: Used to adjust the difference between light and dark portions of the image. Images that look washed out (with only a small difference in brightness levels) often benefit from increasing contrast.
Mid Tones	Enables you to shift the brightness levels of the middle portion of the color range. Increasing the midtones value brightens the middle tones of an image, while lowering the value darkens them.
Physical Scale	Sets the real-world luminous intensity value of standard lights measured in candelas. This value has no effect on scenes that only have Photometric or IES lights.
Color Correction	Enables you to adjust the color caste of an image so that the color in the swatch displays as white in the final rendering. This adjustment takes place automatically in human vision and is manually adjusted in some real-world cameras using balancing.
Desaturate Low Levels	Converts dark colors to shades of gray, simulating what happens to human vision under dim lighting.
Affect Indirect Only	Enables you to apply exposure control only to indirect lighting, not the direct lighting of your light objects. When working with standard lights this is a helpful option that enables you to manipulate the light object's direct illumination separate from the calculated ambient light.

Exterior daylight	Indicates that you are working with outdoor illumination values, which are much higher than is normally used indoors. When rendering with a camera outside in daylight this option is essential to avoid over exposure.

Physical Camera Exposure Control

When working with ART and Arnold rendering workflow, it is recommended to use the **Physical Camera Exposure Control**. When it is selected as the Exposure Control method, a corresponding rollout with parameters specific to this method displays, as shown in Figure 10–4.

Figure 10–4

Physical Camera Exposure	Controls the settings of a specific physical camera rendering. The *EV Compensation for Physical Cameras* sets the exposure value for the physical camera.
Global Exposure	Controls the settings of all the physical camera renderings. The *Exposure Value* has a default value of 6.0.
Image Control	Enables you to adjust the color response curve for *Highlights*, *Midtones* and *Shadows* which have default values of 0.25, 1.0 and 0.2 respectively.
Physical Scale	Sets the real-world luminous intensity value of non-photometric lights (standard lights). This value has no effect on scenes that have only Photometric or IES lights.

10.2 Daytime Lighting

Lights can be used to illuminate a nighttime interior scene or a scene that does not have openings to allow in daylight. Nighttime exterior scenes can be lit similarly, with outside light sources such as light fixtures and dim fill lights. Both interior and exterior scenes can be lit with specialized light objects during daytime.

Sunlight represents the direct illumination of the sun, as shown in Figure 10–5 (thick parallel arrows). The light that reflects off of the earth's surface and back down from the atmosphere (and the light that diffuses through the atmosphere on overcast days) is represented as skylight. Skylight illuminates a scene as if it were cast down from a hemispherical dome, as shown in Figure 10–5 (smaller, solid white arrows).

Figure 10–5

In Autodesk 3ds Max, you can create a **Daylight System** using either of the following methods:

- Sun Positioner and Physical Sky

- Sunlight and Skylight systems

Sun Positioner Daylight System

A Sun Positioner enables you to create a light system that provides realistic sunlight with a full sky environment. This system uses a simple and intuitive workflow to create a geographically correct positioning and movement of the sun.

How To: Create a Sun Positioner Object

1. In the Create panel (+), click 💡 (Lights).
2. In the drop-down list, ensure that the **Photometric** option is selected.
3. Click **Sun Positioner**, as shown in Figure 10–6.

- The **Sun Positioner** option enables you to create a compass rose and a light source that mimics the sun. You can modify the settings of the sunlight system using the sun positioner parameters.

- The *Display* rollout (shown in Figure 10–7) enables you to control the display of the *Compass Rose* and set its radius. Using the *North Offset* option, you can set the cardinal direction and place the sun based on the date and time. In the *Sun* area, you can set the distance of the sun from the compass rose.

Figure 10–6

Figure 10–7

- The *Sun Position* rollout (shown in Figure 10–8) enables you to set the position of the sun. The *Date & Time* area enables you to set the time, day, month, and year. You also have the option of using daylight savings time and setting the range of days to be used. The *Location on Earth* area (shown in Figure 10–9) enables you to set the location using a database file, or set the *Latitude* and *Longitude* coordinates.

Figure 10–8

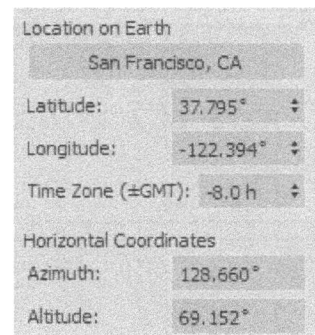

Figure 10–9

Sunlight and Skylight System

The Daylight system can be created by combining both Sunlight and Skylight systems.

Sunlight System

Sunlight can be modeled with a Sunlight system that includes a sun object (a direct light) and a compass object that is used to orient the sun in the scene. The angle of the sun's light can be controlled through the date, time, and location parameters. You can also animate the position of the sun over time for shadow studies.

Sunlight and **Daylight** objects are created as System objects, by selecting the Create panel ($+$) and clicking $\overset{\circ}{\circ}$ (Systems), as shown in Figure 10–10.

When creating a Sunlight system, locate the compass over the center of your site at an approximate ground elevation and control the sun's position using the Control Parameters, as shown in Figure 10–11. Once a sun object has been created, these Control Parameters become available in the Command Panel's Motion panel (●).

Figure 10–10

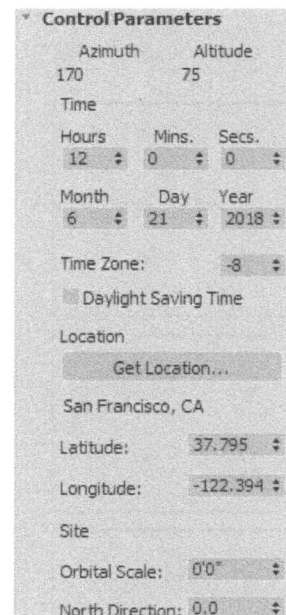

Figure 10–11

- Parameters in the *Time* and *Location* areas enable you to interactively position the sun in the correct location.

- The angle that indicates north in the current coordinate system can be entered in the *North Direction* field. This is used to orient the sunlight to your project geometry.

- The *Orbital Scale* value is the distance from the sun object to the compass (and the ground). The orbital scale should be large enough so that there are no objects behind the sun.

Sun objects are directional lights. Their Modify panel (⌐)
parameters are similar to those for directional lights. To generate shadows correctly, it is sometimes required to clear the **Overshoot** option in *Directional Parameters* rollout and increase the *Hotspot/Beam* value until it encompasses the entire site.

Skylight System

A Skylight object is not part of the Sunlight system, and is an entirely separate object. With a standard lighting approach, the illumination of a skylight object is not controlled by the date, time, or location settings of the sunlight system. The skylight's brightness (multiplier) parameter can be set manually and animated to change over time.

To create a **Skylight** object as a standard light object, in the

Create panel (+), click 💡 (Lights), and then click **Standard**, as shown in Figure 10–12. Skylight objects have special controls available in the *Skylight Parameters* rollout, as shown in Figure 10–13.

Figure 10–12

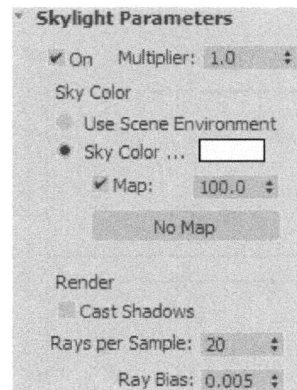

Figure 10–13

- The light cast from skylights can be colored based on the scene environment map. The **Use Scene Environment** option uses the environment that has been set up in the *Environment* tab in the Environment and Effects dialog box (**Rendering>Environment**).

- The **Sky Color** option enables you to use a single color or a map and it comes with the illumination capabilities in all renderers.

Skylight creates complex shadows that can be realistic and enhance scenes lit with natural lighting. The following settings help control the overall quality (and calculation time) of sky shadows:

Rays per Sample	The number of illuminated rays collected at each sampling point. Lower values result in faster renderings but grainier shadows. Set this value low for test renderings but increase it for the final product (use 15 for still images, but animations might need as much as 20 or 30 to avoid flickering).
Ray Bias	This is the minimum distance between two points for one to cast sky shadows on the other. Increasing this value in scenes with a lot of small detail might speed up rendering time without significantly lowering rendering quality.

Sun and Skylight Options

The following table displays the scene with different sun and skylight options:

	Scene with default lighting (no light objects or shadow casting).
	Scene with Sun (no skylight or ambient light). Note the pitch black shadows.

	Scene with Sun and Skylight; no ambient fill lights or radiosity calculations have been added. Number of Rays = 4.
	Scene with Sun and Skylight; no ambient fill lights or radiosity calculations have been added. Note that the shadows here are less grainy than the ones rendered above. Number of Rays = 10.
	Scene with Sun and Skylight; no ambient fill lights or radiosity calculations have been added. Note that the shadows here are even less grainy than the ones rendered above. Number of Rays = 30. This result took 10x longer to render than the 4 Rays sample.

Practice 10a	Lighting with Sun Positioner

Practice Objective

*   Create a Daylight system using Sun Positioner for Arnold renderer.

In this practice, you will create an Sun Positioner daylight system and modify the parameters to get a realistic rendering of the scene.

You must set the paths to locate the External files and Xrefs used in the practice. If you have not done this already, return to Chapter 1 and complete Task 1 to Task 3 in *Practice 1a: Organizing Folders and Working with the Interface*. You only have to set the user paths once.

If a dialog box opens prompting you about a File Load: Mismatch, click OK to accept the default values.

1. Open **Retail Exterior-Daylight.max**.

2. In the Main Toolbar, click (Render Setup) or select **Rendering>Render Setup** to open the Render Setup dialog box. In the upper area of the dialog box, in the Renderer drop-down list, verify that **Arnold** is set as the renderer, as shown in Figure 10–14. Close the Render Setup dialog box.

Figure 10–14

3. Maximize the **Top** viewport and zoom to the extents.

4. In the Create panel (+), click 💡 (Lights). In the *Object Type* rollout, click **Sun Positioner**, as shown in Figure 10–15.

Figure 10–15

The first click is the location of the compass rose. The second click is for the direction. Keep holding the cursor and drag the mouse to resize the compass rose.

5. Near the center of the **Top** viewport, click, hold, and drag out to create a compass rose similar to the size shown in Figure 10–16. The north and south points of the compass should approximately touch the top and bottom horizontal lines of the white layout area rectangle. Release the mouse button to complete the creation. You are still in the **SunPositioner** command.

6. Verify that the North (N) (if the direction has changed, move the cursor till the compass is North facing) is still pointing towards the top horizontal line of the rectangle, as shown in Figure 10–16. Click again to position the direction of the compass. Continue using the **Sun Positioner** command.

Figure 10–16

You will set the exact distance in the Parameters area of the Command Panel.

7. Note that the sun object is attached to the cursor while in the **Sun Positioner** command (Do not click). Press <L> to change to a **Left** view. Move the cursor up and down to graphically set the initial orbital scale of the sun object. Click when the sun is at a position similar to that shown in Figure 10–17.

Figure 10–17

8. Sun objects should be placed back from the scene for the shadows to be generated correctly. With the Sun positioner object still selected, in the Modify panel ( ), in the *Display* rollout, in the *Sun* area, set the *Distance* to **300'0"**, as shown in Figure 10–18.

Your Radius value might be different. Do not change it.

Figure 10–18

9. In the *Sun Position* rollout, in the *Location on Earth* area, click the default **San Francisco, CA** location. In the Geographic Location dialog box, select **Portland, ME** and click **OK**. Note the changes in *Latitude* and *Longitude*. The *Time Zone* is set to **-5.0 h**, as shown in Figure 10–19.

10. In the *Date & Time* area, set the following, as shown in Figure 10–20:

- *Time:* **7h** and **0 min**
- *Day:* **21**
- *Month:* **3**
- *Year:* **2018**

The location of the sun object changes based on the time and date.

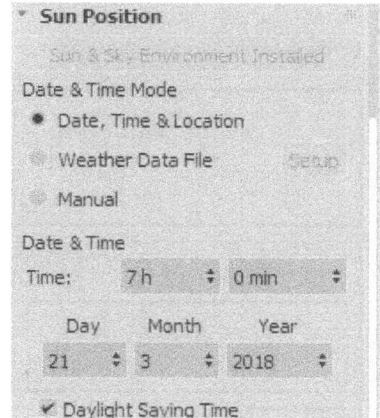

Figure 10–19   **Figure 10–20**

11. Activate the **Camera - Southeast View** viewport. Click

    (Render Production) to render the view.

- Note that not much displays in the rendering and that it is completely washed out.

12. In the Rendered Frame Window, click (Environment and Effects (Exposure Control)). Alternatively, select **Rendering>Exposure Control** to open the Environment and Effects dialog box. In the Environment and Effects dialog box, in the *Exposure Control* rollout, note that **Physical Camera Exposure Control** is selected and is set to **Active**.

13. In the *Physical Camera Exposure Control* rollout, in the *Physical Camera Exposure* area, set the *EV Compensation for Physical Camera* to **-5.0**. In the *Exposure Control* rollout, click **Render Preview** and note the dim light and an early morning sky, as shown in Figure 10–21. Close the dialog box.

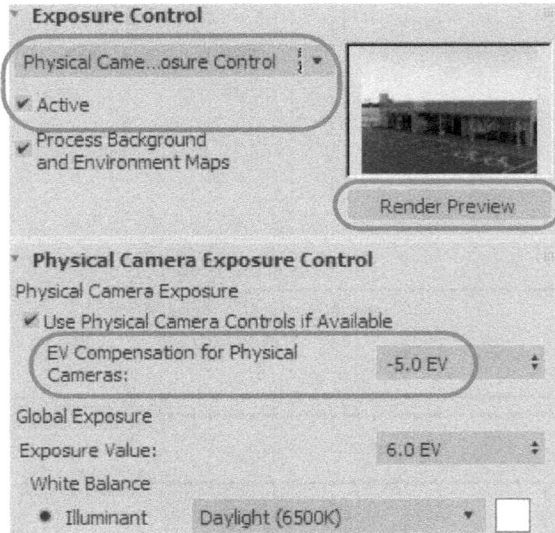

Figure 10–21

14. In the Rendered Frame Window, click **Render**. Note the lighting is based on **7 a.m** in the month of **March**, as shown Figure 10–22.

Figure 10–22

15. With the **Sun Positioner** selected, in the *Sun Position* rollout, in the *Date & Time* area, change the *Time* to **12h** and render the **Camera** viewport again. Note the bright light and a mid day sky as the rendering is for 12 noon in the month of March, as shown Figure 10–23.

Figure 10–23

16. Change the *Time* to **7h** and the *Month* to **7**, and then render the **Camera** viewport again. Note the bright morning sky and long shadows in the month of July, as shown Figure 10–24.

Figure 10–24

17. Save your work as **MyDaylight.max**.

10.3 Rendering Options

You can set, modify, and change the different options in the Render Setup dialog box, as shown in Figure 10–25. The various ways to open the Render Setup dialog box are as follows:

To quickly re-render the last rendered viewport (regardless of the active viewport) press <F9>. This eliminates the use of the Render Setup dialog box.

- Select **Rendering> Render Setup**.
- Press <F10>.
- In the Main Toolbar, click ⚙ (Render Setup).

- In the Rendered Frame Window, click ⚙ (Render Setup).

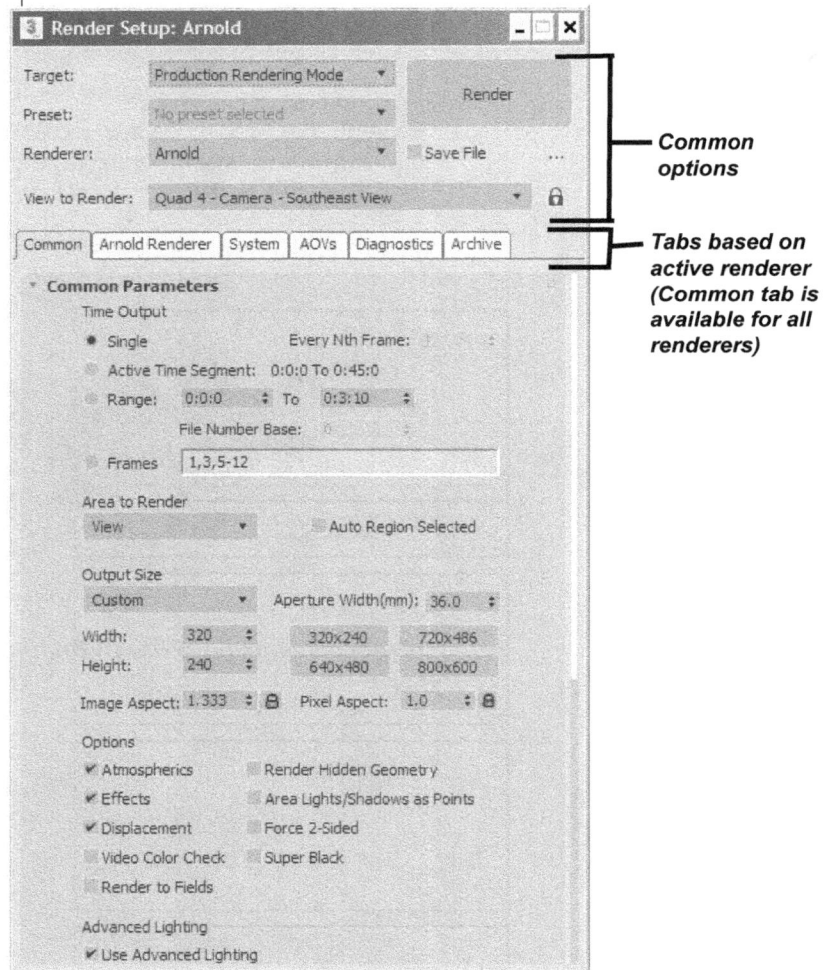

Figure 10–25

Common Options

Common options are available for all the renderers and are located at the top of the dialog box. These include:

- The **Target** drop-down list enables you to select the rendering options such as, Production, Iterative, A360 Cloud etc, as shown in Figure 10–26.

Figure 10–26

- The **Preset** drop-down list (as shown in Figure 10–27) enables you to swap between the available preset files or create, load, and save presets as RPS files using **Load Preset** and **Save Preset**. These presets are also accessed from the Render Shortcuts toolbar, as shown in Figure 10–28. When using the toolbar, you can save the current rendering settings as preset A, B, or C by selecting one of the corresponding buttons in the toolbar while holding <Shift>.

Figure 10–27

Figure 10–28

You can also select the rendering system in the Assign Renderer rollout in the Common tab of the dialog box.

- The Renderer drop-down list enables you to select the required rendering system, as shown in Figure 10–29.

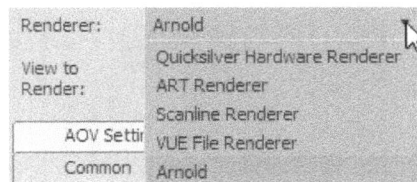

Figure 10–29

Quicksilver Hardware Renderer	Uses the system's graphics hardware (GPU) to quickly produce high-quality images. In order to use this renderer your graphics hardware must support Shader Model 3.0 (SM3.0) or a later version.
ART Renderer	A physically based renderer that uses the CPU only and renders the scene quickly.
Scanline Renderer	Intended to be used with both standard lighting (local illumination) and radiosity-based lighting.
VUE File Renderer	A legacy functionality that is not a graphical renderer. It uses ASCII text files to describe the position and transformation of objects, lighting, etc.
Arnold Renderer	A separate lighting and rendering system that accurately renders ray tracing light paths to create physically based renderings.

The tabs in the Render Setup dialog box change according to the active renderer.

- Clicking **Render** in the Render Setup dialog box or clicking

  (Render Production) in the Main Toolbar, renders the active viewport based on the settings in the Render Setup dialog box. A Rendered Frame Window opens, displaying the rendering as it is being calculated, as shown in Figure 10–30.

Figure 10–30

- A Rendering dialog box also opens displaying the status of the rendering along with other information, as shown in Figure 10–31. Once the Rendering dialog box closes, it indicates that the rendering is complete. You can also abort the rendering process by clicking **Cancel**.

Figure 10–31

Common Tab

The *Common* tab contains settings applicable to all rendering systems. Some of the options are described as follows:

Common Parameters rollout

- The *Time Output* area designates whether you are rendering a still frame (Single) or an animation. When rendering an animation you can specify to render the entire animation (Active Time Segment), a certain range (Range) or specify individual frames (Frames).

- The *Area to Render* area enables you to define what portion of the scene is rendered, such as View, Selected, Region, Crop, or Blowup.

- The *Output Size* area contains the render size options.

- The *Options* area enables you to select the objects and effects to render (**Atmospherics**, **Render Hidden Geometry**, etc.). You can also select the overrides (**Area Lights/Shadows as Points**, **Force 2-Sided**).

- The *Advanced Lighting* and *Bitmap Performance and Memory Options* areas provide additional options to further customize the rendering.

- The *Render Output* area enables you to specify a filename before rendering. Some of the commonly used file formats in which the rendering images are saved are as follows:

JPEG	The JPEG is a lossy format, which sacrifices quality in exchange for a smaller file size.
BMP	Windows Bitmap (24 bit, 16.7 Million Colors).
TGA	Targa (as 24 or 32 bit uncompressed).
PNG	Portable Network Graphics (as 24 or 48 bit color, no interlacing). This has the best file size to quality ratio as it offers the highest color depth with a smaller compression.
TIFF	Tagged Image File Format (24 bit color without compression).

Assign Renderer Rollout

In this rollout, you can switch rendering systems and select the **ActiveShade** renderer that you want to use.

Alternatively, they can be changed using the Renderer drop-down list in the Common area near the top of the Render Setup dialog box.

Email Notifications Rollout

In this rollout, you can set the option of having an email notification sent to you or another user whose email address has been specified. This is useful when the render is run without being monitored, in the case of lengthy renders.

Scripts Rollout

In this rollout, you can enable the software to run a selected script before a rendering process has begun or after the process has been completed. The valid scripts that can be run are MAXScript file (.MS), macro script (.MCR), batch file (.BAT), and executable file (.EXE).

Renderer Tab

The *Renderer* tab displays renderer-specific options. It is provided for all of the renderers with render-specific options.

10.4 Arnold Renderer

The Arnold renderer is a physically accurate renderer that renders by tracing the light paths and by progressively refining the image until it has completed the rendering process. It is a CPU based render that does not take into consideration the graphics or video card of the computer. Setup is minimal and simple, similar to a point and shoot camera.

- It supports both physical materials and advanced Arnold materials. In physical material, the custom reflection curve feature is not supported by Arnold. In addition to the above materials, other materials supported by Arnold are Multi/Sub-object, Double Sided, Direct X, and Shell.

- It supports Photometric lights and Sun Positioner Daylight system.

- When Arnold is selected as the active renderer, the *Common* tab, *Arnold Renderer* tab, *System* tab, *AOV Settings* tab, *Diagnostics* tab, and *Archive* tab become available in the Render Setup dialog box.

Arnold Renderer Tab

The *Arnold Renderer* tab contains options that are easy to set and quite intuitive to work with.

- In the *Samples and Ray Depth* rollout (shown in Figure 10–32), you can control the quality of the rendered image and the noise in the rendering. In the *General* area, increasing the number of **Samples** improves the render quality but it also increases the rendering time. **Camera (AA)** is a multiplier for all other values. Increasing its value extends the rendering time.

Figure 10–32

- The *Filtering* rollout (shown in Figure 10–33) contains filters that are used for legacy purposes. It is recommended to use the **Gaussian** (default) or the **Blackman-Harris** filter types. While the type of filter used has no effect on the render time, the filter width can affect it slightly.

- In the *Environment, Background & Atmosphere* rollout (shown in Figure 10–34), you can control how the image based lighting is being used. The **Physically-Based** setting provides automatic and optimized image-based lighting. In this case, the software automatically uses a hidden Skydome to provide IBL. To manually control the settings, use the **Advanced** mode.

Figure 10–33

Figure 10–34

- In the *Motion Blur* rollout (shown in Figure 10–35) you can control the **Motion Blur** option to apply it to objects in a scene. You can respect the settings that were defined in the Physical Camera. You can also control the motion blur shape as a **Box** (default), **Triangle**, or a **Curve** that can be adjusted manually.

Figure 10–35

- The *Geometry, Subdivision & Hair* rollout (shown in Figure 10–36) contains global settings for tessellation of subdivision surfaces. The *Displacement Default Subdivision* area enables you to set the subdivision rule that is used for the polymesh at the time of rendering. You can use **None** (ignores any subdivision), **Linear** (places vertices in the middle of each face), or **Catmull-Clark** (creates a mesh of quadrilateral faces). The *Hair (Curves) and Points* area controls how the curves are rendered. To create hair, fur, or grass, set the *Type* to **Ribbon**. To create spaghetti like hair, select **Thick**.

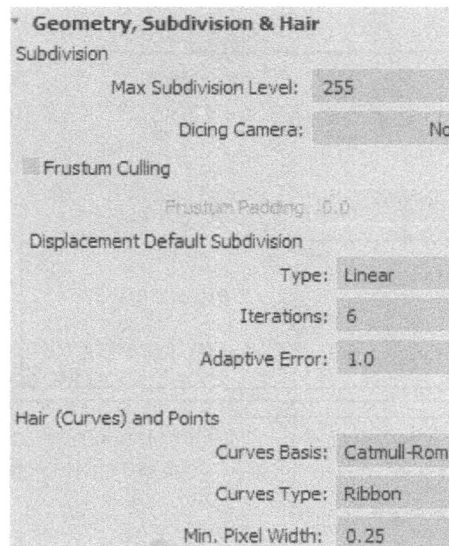

Figure 10–36

System Tab

The *System* tab (as shown in Figure 10–37) contains options to control the Arnold rendering settings.

- Arnold uses Bucket rendering that enables you to see different portions being rendered. If they are not rendered correctly, you can cancel the process, make the required modifications, and start the rendering again. The *General* area enables you to control how the image buckets are processed (as shown in Figure 10–37). By default, the **Spiral** method in used, which renders from the center, outwards in a spiral pattern. You can also set the size of the bucket for rendering. To process legacy maps, select **Legacy 3ds Max support**.

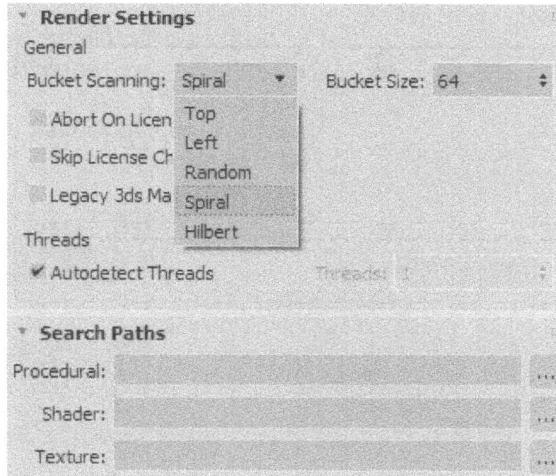

Figure 10–37

Archive Tab

The 3ds Max scenes can be stored as an .ASS (Arnold Scene Source) file that are saved and rendered outside of the 3ds Max software. From the *Archive* tab (shown in Figure 10–38), you can export the scene as a .ASS file. You can also select the node types that are included in this type of file.

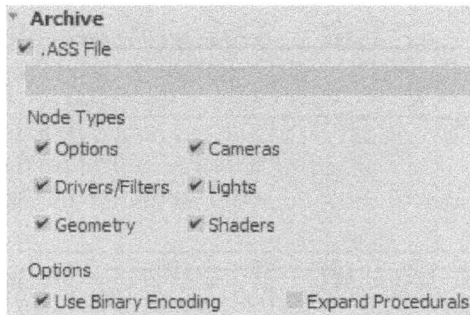

Figure 10–38

Diagnostics Tab

In the *Diagnostics* tab (as shown in Figure 10–39), Arnold generates a log file providing you with errors encountered, other information, and warnings. This file is a great tool for debugging and improving the render. In the *Error Handling* rollout, you can set how the information is provided when an error is encountered.

Figure 10–39

AOV Settings Tab

In the *AOV Settings* tab, you can set the various AOV's (Arbitrary Output Variables) for a scene. AOV's are separate image files for various elements of the rendered image, such as a separate image for a diffuse pass or an image for the Specular pass. You can check the AOV files for issues and make modifications to that element only to improve the final renders. You can also use these AOV files for creating compositing workflows which can reduce the need to rerender the complete scenes multiple times.

Image Based Lighting

Image Based Lighting (IBL) is a rendering technique that involves a scene representation of real-world light information as a photographic image. The image used is typically in a high dynamic range file format, such as, .HDR or .EXR. In the Autodesk 3ds Max software, this image displays as an environment map and is used to simulate the lighting for the objects in the scene. This enables detailed real-world lighting to be used to light the scene.

Image Based Lighting is available when **ART** or **Arnold** are the active Production renderers. When using **Arnold** as the active renderer, you can control the IBL settings in the *Arnold Renderer* tab, in the *Environment, Background & Atmosphere* area, as shown in Figure 10–40. The *Environment Lighting & Reflective (IBL)* should be set to **Enabled**. Increasing the *Samples (Quality)* creates sharper images but increases render times. In the *Background (Backplate)* area, you can set the *Source* to use the default **Scene Environment** or you can use the **Custom Color** or **Custom Map** options.

Figure 10–40

Practice 10b

Working with Arnold Renderer

Practice Objective

- Set various rendering options to improve the rendering of a scene.

This practice uses the Arnold Renderer as the active renderer. In this practice, you will set some of the Arnold Rendering parameters to enhance the rendered image.

You must set the paths to locate the External files and Xrefs used in the practice. If you have not done this already, return to Chapter 1 and complete Task 1 to Task 3 in *Practice 1a: Organizing Folders and Working with the Interface*. You only have to set the user paths once.

Task 1 - Setting Exposure Control.

*If a dialog box opens prompting you about a File Load: Mismatch, click **OK** to accept the default values.*

1. Open **Arnold Render Start.max**.

2. Verify that the **Camera-Lobby1** viewport is active.

3. In the Main Toolbar, click (Render Setup) or select **Rendering>Render Setup** to open the Render Setup dialog box. Near the top of the dialog box, in the common options, note that the *Renderer* is set to **Arnold**, as shown in Figure 10–41. Also note that the *View to Render* displays **Quad 4 - Camera-Lobby1** (the active viewport).

4. In the *Common* tab, in the *Common Parameters* rollout, in the *Output Size* area, select **320X240** to render a smaller image to reduce rendering time. Note that the *Width* and the *Height* changes to **320** and **240** respectively, as shown in Figure 10–41.

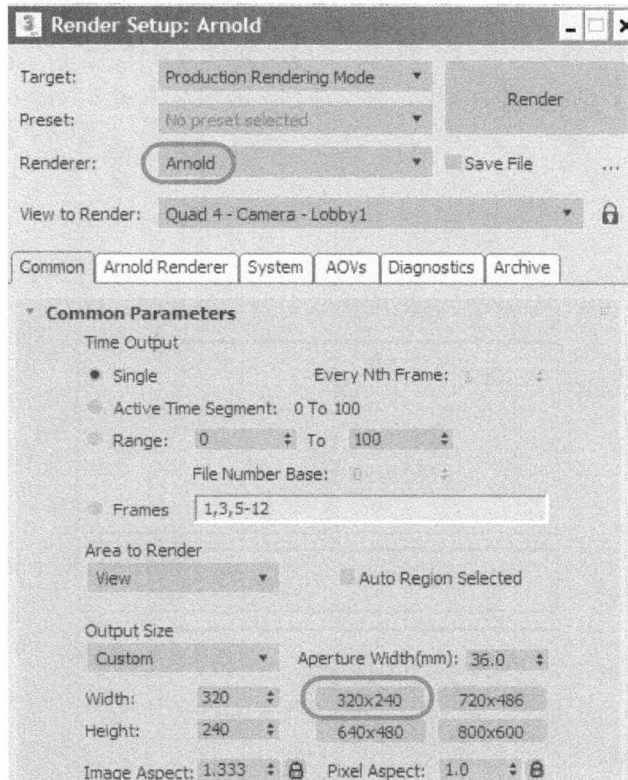

Figure 10–41

5. In the *Common* tab, in the *Common Parameters* rollout, in the *Advanced Lighting* area, verify that the **Use Advanced Lighting** option is enabled and clear the **Compute Advanced Lighting when Required** option, if required.

6. Click **Render**. A Rendering dialog box displays the status of the rendering. Note that the rendering is fast but the rendered image is washed out with black specs (noise) throughout. Close the Rendered Frame Window and the Render Setup:Arnold dialog box.

7. Select **Rendering>Exposure Control** to open the Environment and Effects dialog box. In the *Exposure Control* rollout, note that no exposure control is being used. Change this to **Physical Camera Exposure Control** (as shown in Figure 10–42) and click **Render Preview**. Note that there is no change in the image.

Figure 10–42

8. In the *Physical Camera Exposure Control* rollout, set the *EV Compensation for Physical Cameras* to **-5.0**, and click **Render Preview**. Note that the washing out effect has been removed, as shown in Figure 10–43. Close the dialog box.

Figure 10–43

9. In the Main Toolbar, click (Render Production) to render the **Camera-Lobby1** view. The rendered image is not washed out but has a lot of noise and is overall dark (although the sun light is coming through the windows), as shown in Figure 10–44. Leave the Rendered Frame Window open.

Figure 10–44

Task 2 - Setting Arnold Render Parameters.

1. Open the Render Setup dialog box (Main Toolbar>

    ![icon] (Render Setup) or Rendered Frame Window> ![icon]).

2. Open the *Arnold Renderer* tab and expand the *Sampling and Ray Depth* rollout. In the *General* area, set *Camera (AA)* to **4** (as shown in Figure 10–45) and click **Render**. A Rendering dialog box displays the status of the rendering. Note that the rendering time has increased but the noise is substantially removed, as shown in Figure 10–46.

Figure 10–45

Figure 10–46

3. Set the *Diffuse Samples* to **4** (as shown in Figure 10–47) and render the scene again. The noise is further reduced, but it is still dark inside. Note that the doors at the back of the room are not visible.

4. Set the *Diffuse Ray Depth* to **4** and render again. Note that the doors at the back have become slightly visible as more light is reflected around the space, as shown in Figure 10–47.

Figure 10–47

5. Note that you still cannot see outside of the windows. Set the *Transmission Ray Depth* to **4** and render again. Note that it takes more time to render but the outside is visible through the curtain wall windows, as shown in Figure 10–48.

Figure 10–48

With the increased Camera (AA) value, it might take a few minutes to render.

6. Increasing the **Camera (AA)** value removes the noise but significantly increases the render time. Set the *Camera (AA)* to **7** and render the viewport. Note the significant noise reduction and brightening of the interior areas, as shown in Figure 10–49.

Figure 10–49

7. Save your scene as **MyArnold_Render.max**.

Note that this render might take a significant amount of time to complete.

8. (Optional) When possible, open the **MyArnold_Render.max** and open the Render Setup dialog box. In the *Common* tab, increase the *Output Size* to **640X480**. In the *Arnold Renderer* tab, set *Diffuse Samples* to **6** and *Camera (AA)* to **10** and render the scene, as shown in Figure 10–50.

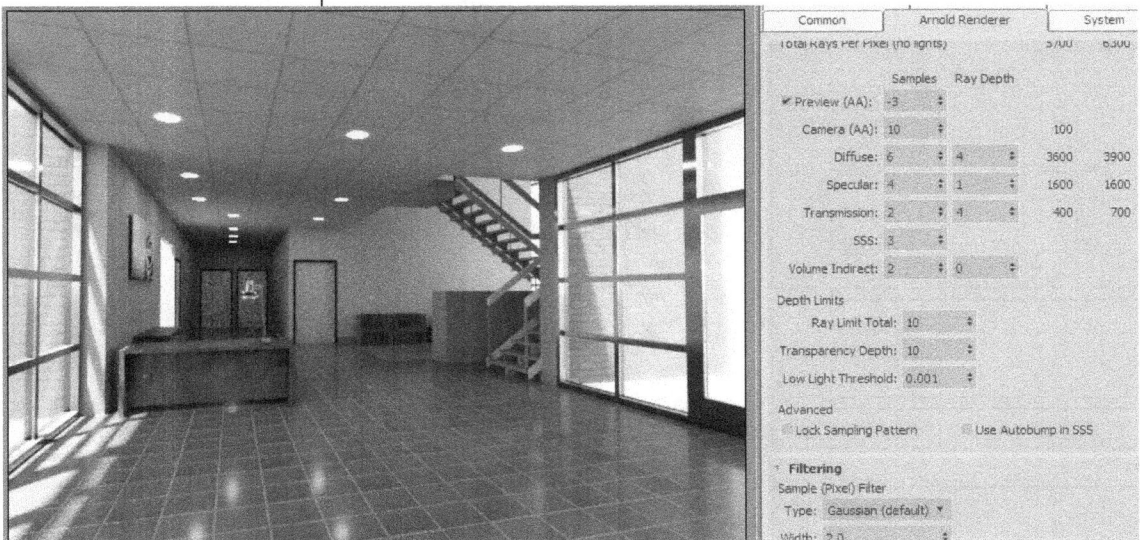

Figure 10–50

Practice 10c

Image Based Lighting in Arnold Renderer

Practice Objective

- Light a scene using the light in an environment map image.

In this practice, you will learn to light an exterior scene using an HDR image in the Image Based Lighting (IBL) technique using the Arnold renderer.

You must set the paths to locate the External files and Xrefs used in the practice. If you have not done this already, return to Chapter 1 and complete Task 1 to Task 3 in *Practice 1a: Organizing Folders and Working with the Interface*. You only have to set the user paths once.

*If a dialog box opens prompting you about a File Load: Mismatch, click **OK** to accept the default values.*

1. Open **Retail Exterior.max**.

2. In the Main Toolbar, click [   ] (Render Setup) or select **Rendering>Render Setup**. In the Renderer drop-down list, verify that **Arnold** is set as the renderer. Close the Render Setup dialog box.

3. Select **Rendering>Environment** or press <8> to open the Environment and Effects dialog box.

4. In the *Common Parameters* rollout, in the *Background* area, select **None** for *Environment Map*.

5. In the Material/Map Browser, expand the **Maps>General** categories and double-click on **Bitmap**.

6. In the Select Bitmap Image File dialog box, navigate to the ...*sceneassets\images* folder of the practice files folder and open **CountryRoad.hdr**. This image will provide the lights for the scene.

7. In the HDRI Load Settings dialog box, in the *Internal Storage* area, verify that **Real Pixels** and **Def. Exposure** are selected, as shown in Figure 10–51. Click **OK**.

Figure 10–51

8. In the Environments and Effects dialog box, note that **None** has been replaced with **Map #9 (CountryRoad.hdr)**. Do not close the dialog box.

9. In the Main Toolbar, click ⬚ (Material Editor) to open the Slate Material Editor.

10. From the Environments and Effects dialog box, drag and drop **Map #9 (CountryRoad.hdr)** onto the *View1* sheet in the Slate Material Editor.

11. In the Instance (Copy) dialog box, verify that **Instance** is selected and click **OK**. The **Map # Bitmap** node is placed on the *View1* sheet.

12. In the *View1* sheet, double-click on the **Map # Bitmap** title bar to open its Parameter Editor.

13. In the Parameter Editor, in the *Coordinates* rollout, note that **Spherical Environment** is selected for *Mapping*, as shown in Figure 10–52. The light from the image illuminates the scene from all directions.

Figure 10–52

14. Close the Slate Material Editor and the Environments and Effects dialog box.

15. Open the Render Setup dialog box ((Render Setup)). In the Render Setup dialog box, open the *Arnold Renderer* tab. Expand the *Environment, Background & Atmosphere* rollout. Verify that **Enable (using scene environment)** is selected in the *Environment Lighting & Reflections (IBL)* area and that *Source* is set as **Scene Environment** in the *Background (Backplate)* area, as shown in Figure 10–53. Do not close the Render Setup dialog box.

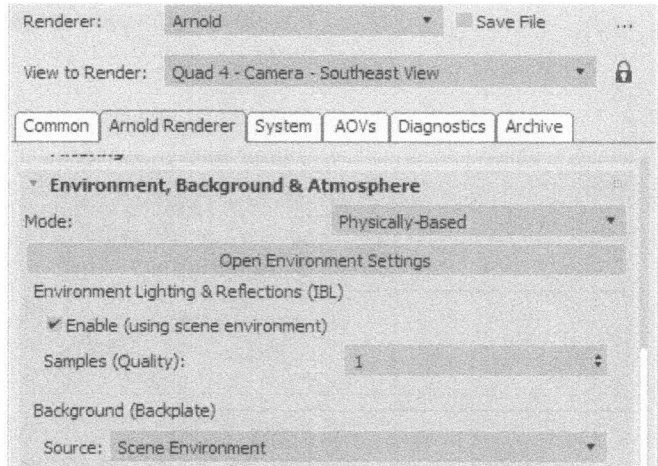

Figure 10–53

The Rendering dialog box shows the rendering progress.

16. Verify that Camera - Southeast View is active. Click **Render** in the Render Setup dialog box (you can also use

    ![teapot icon] (Render Production)) to render the scene, as shown in Figure 10–54. Once the rendering is complete, note that the environment background is used and that it lights the scene.

Figure 10–54

You can minimize the Rendered Frame Window when not in use and maximize it later.

17. In the Rendered Frame Window, using the mouse wheel, zoom into the portion of one of the door and window front, as shown in Figure 10–55. Note that the image is not sharp. Leave the Render Frame Window open.

Figure 10–55

18. In the Render Setup dialog box, in the *Arnold Renderer* tab, in the *Environment, Background & Atmosphere* rollout, set the *Samples (Quality)* to **2** and click **Render**. Note the image has improved slightly. Close the Render Setup dialog box.

19. In the Render Frame Window, zoom out to see the complete view and leave the Rendered Frame Window open.

20. Select **Rendering>Environment** or **Rendering>Exposure Control** to open the Environment Effects dialog box. In the *Environment* tab, in the *Exposure Control* rollout, note that the **Logarithmic Exposure Control** is already set, but it is not currently used because **Active** is not checked. Keep the dialog box open.

21. In the Scene Explorer, select the **Camera - Southeast View** object. In the Modify panel ( ), in the *Exposure* rollout, click **Install Exposure Control** and click **OK** to install the Physical Camera Exposure Control. In the Environment and Effects dialog box, note that the **Physical Camera** is the exposure control used and is also set as **Active**. Close the dialog box.

22. In the Render Frame Window, click **Render**. Note that the scene brightens up as it permits more light into the camera.

23. In the *Exposure* rollout, in the *Exposure Gain* area, increase the *Target* to **6.5 EV**, as shown. Render the **Camera - Southeast View** again and note how the brightness is slightly lowered, as shown in Figure 10–56.

Figure 10–56

24. Close the Rendered Frame Window and save the file as **MyIBL.max**.

10.5 Scanline Renderer

The Scanline renderer generates a render by calculating a series of lines starting at the top and moving down. It is intended to be used with both standard lighting and radiosity based lighting.

Renderer Tab

The *Renderer* tab for the Scanline Renderer displays its specific options, as shown in Figure 10–57.

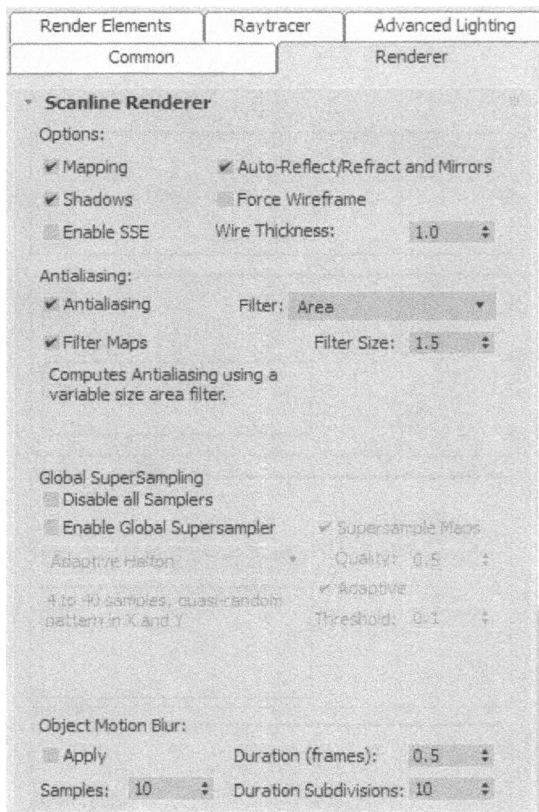

Figure 10–57

- The *Options* area enables you to globally enable or disable the use of all image maps (**Mapping**) or the calculation of all shadows (**Shadows**). The **Force Wireframe** option causes the scene geometry to render as wireframe objects with the **Wire Thickness** parameter listed below.

- The *Antialiasing* area contains options for antialiasing that smooths the jagged diagonal lines and curves in renderings but at a reduced quality, as shown on the left in Figure 10–58.

Antialiasing On   *Antialiasing Off*

Figure 10–58

- SuperSampling (*Global SuperSampling* area) is an additional antialiasing pass applied to material textures. SuperSampling cuts down on noise, flickering, and moire patterns caused by dense material maps, as shown in Figure 10–59.

Supersampling Off   *Supersampling On*

Figure 10–59

Raytracer Tab

Raytracing is a rendering method used to calculate accurate reflections, refractions, and shadows. Raytracing is used for raytrace materials and some Architectural materials with shiny, transparent, or mirrored templates (e.g., glass, mirrors, etc.). Raytraced and area shadows cause raytracing to take place and for Scanline Renderer these are managed by the options in *Raytracer* tab, (as shown in Figure 10–60).

Figure 10–60

Several of these options relate to rendering performance. In many ways, these are black box parameters that need to be adjusted through trial and error for individual scenes.

Shadow types such as Advanced Raytraced also have antialiasing options.

- The **Maximum Depth** option is a measurement of how many reflections of reflections you want to permit. The default value of **9** might be excessive, while **3** might be as effective and requires much less rendering time.

- The **Cutoff Threshold** option is a percent value that causes the software to ignore rays that only contribute that percent or less of a pixel's color in the final rendering. Increasing this value reduces rendering time at a cost of lower accuracy.

- If you find that your raytraced reflections or shadows have jagged diagonal lines or curves, you can enable **Global Ray Antialiasing** to add smoothness.

- When cleared, the **Enable Raytracing** option disables all raytracing in the scene.

Single vs. Double-Sided in Scanline Rendering

When using the Scanline renderer, Autodesk 3ds Max 3D objects are treated as surface models rather than solids, to make calculations faster. 3D geometry is resolved into triangular faces when rendered.

Figure 10–61 displays two identical Box objects, with the one on the right displaying all of its edges as triangular faces. To display triangular faces, right-click on the object and select **Object Properties**. In the *General* tab, in the *Display Properties* area, clear the **Edges Only** option. If the viewport is set to **Edged Face** mode (<F4>), the triangular faces display.

*In the Object Properties dialog box, in the Display Properties area, all of the options are grayed out if it is set to **By Layer** Change it to **By Object** for the options to be available.*

Figure 10–61

Working in single-sided mode is a more efficient way to render. It is recommended to use single-sided mode whenever possible.

- In single-sided rendering mode, the faces only display in the viewport and in renderings from the outside of the object. Therefore, no time is spent on calculating the inner faces of the object.

- When using the scanline renderer, rendering in double-sided mode forces the Autodesk 3ds Max software to determine what the inside and the outside of each face looks like, adding significant rendering time.

- In single-sided mode, the Scanline renders faces whose vectors point towards the camera even if at very oblique angles, as shown in Figure 10–62.

- 3D objects such as primitives like these boxes automatically have their face normals pointing to the outside.

- Single-sided rendering mode can cause problems when object normals are inconsistent (inverted). In Figure 10–63, the box on the right has its top face normals pointing down instead of up. This can cause the box to have missing faces. (The back-facing edge lines are shown here for clarity but normally, they would not be visible.)

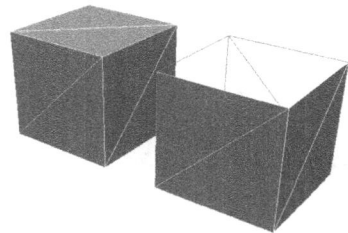

Figure 10–62   Figure 10–63

The viewport behavior might vary depending on your video driver.

- Faces with inverted face normals display in black in the viewport, but are invisible in the scanline rendering. To see through the faces that point away, right-click on the object, select **Object Properties** and in the *Display Properties* area, select **Backface Cull**.

- CAD software packages generally do not assign surface normals to 3D geometry. When you import this data into the Autodesk 3ds Max software, surface normals are automatically assigned to faces based on the order in which the vertices were created, which can result in inconsistent facings.

- When linking or importing 3D blocks and drawing from other software, there might still be inconsistent or inverted face normals, which need to be corrected.

- If the data was imported or linked (.DWG or .DXF file), delete, re-import or reload the linked file, and in the Import Options dialog box, select **Orient normals of adjacent faces consistently**, as shown in Figure 10–64. This option should not be selected unless face-normal issues are present.

Figure 10–64

- If reimporting or reloading data is not feasible (or the data was not imported/linked), the Normal modifier can be used to unify faces. This object-space modifier has the ability to flip all of the face normals when an object is completely inside out.

- If you have a small number of faces with normals pointing the wrong way (or a large number and some time to spare) you can manually flip and unify face normals. Using the **Edit Mesh** and **Edit Poly** modifiers, select the inverted polygon and then in the *Surface Properties* rollout, use the **Flip** and **Unify** options, as shown in Figure 10–65.

Figure 10–65

Enabling Double-Sided Mode

If you only have certain objects with face-normal issues that
cannot be easily fixed, use **2-sided** materials. This renders the
objects as double-sided, while rendering the rest of the scene
geometry as single-sided. Different scanline materials have the
2-sided options in different rollouts in the Parameter Editor.

- **Scanline>Standard** materials have the **2-Sided** option in the
  Shader Basic Parameters rollout, as shown in Figure 10–66.

- **Scanline>Architectural** materials have the **2-Sided** option
  in the *Physical Qualities* rollout, as shown in Figure 10–67.

Figure 10–66

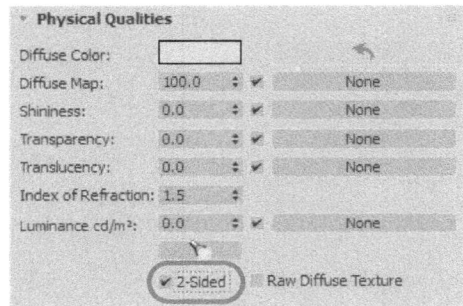

Figure 10–67

- To render a scene double-sided, in the Render Setup dialog
  box, in the *Common* tab, in the *Options* area, enable the
  Force 2-Sided option, as shown in Figure 10–68.

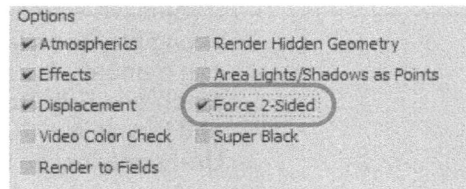

Figure 10–68

10.6 ART Renderer

The Autodesk Ray Trace (ART) renderer is a path tracing renderer which generates fast and accurate renderings using few settings. ART is a physically based renderer and uses the computers CPU only. It supports photometric lights, the Sun Positioner, and physical material. ART is compatible with the Autodesk® Revit® software and is capable of creating highly accurate renderings of architectural scenes due to ART's support of the photometric and day lighting features in the Autodesk Revit software.

When you select **ART Renderer** as the active renderer, the *Common* tab, *ART Renderer* tab, and *Render Elements* tab are available in the Render Setup dialog box, as shown in Figure 10–69.

ART Renderer Tab

The *ART Renderer* tab displays the renderer-specific options, as shown in Figure 10–69.

Figure 10–69

- The *Rendering Parameter* rollout enables you to set the *Target Quality,* which is measured in decibels (dB). A lower value is lower quality with more noise in the final image. A higher quality reduces the amount of noise in the final image, but the image takes longer to render.

- You can limit the time or number of iterations for a rendering in the *Stop rendering even if quality is not attained* area. This would prevent an image from taking too long to complete, but the resulting image might not have the desired quality.

- The *Lighting and Material Fidelity* area options are used to create image renderings. You can use the **Fast Path Tracing** method to render high fidelity, indirect illumination, or use the **Advanced Path Method** to generate final renders for true high fidelity images.

- The *Filtering* rollout enables you to activate **Noise Filtering** on final renderings. The **Anti-Aliasing** option sets the *Filter Diameter* in pixels and determines how the ART Renderer anti-aliases the edges in the image.

- The *Advanced* rollout has options to set the size of point lights in scene lighting using the **Point Light Diameter** value. You can also use the **Animate Noise Pattern** option to keep the noise pattern from being static in the final rendering.

Practice 10d

Working with Scanline Rendering Options

Practice Objective

- Set various rendering options to improve the rendering of the scene.
- Render an object as double-sided using a double-sided and single-sided material.

This practice uses the Scanline Renderer as the active renderer. In this practice, you will set various Rendering options render an object as double-sided using a double-sided and single-sided material.

You must set the paths to locate the External files and Xrefs used in the practice. If you have not done this already, return to Chapter 1 and complete Task 1 to Task 3 in *Practice 1a: Organizing Folders and Working with the Interface*. You only have to set the user paths once.

Task 1 - Setting Rendering Options.

*If a dialog box opens prompting you about a File Load: Mismatch, click **OK** to accept the default values.*

1. Open **Rendering Options.max**.

2. In the Main Toolbar, click (Render Setup) or select **Rendering>Render Setup** to open the Render Setup dialog box.

   - Note that the *Renderer* is set as **Scanline Renderer**, as shown in Figure 10–70.

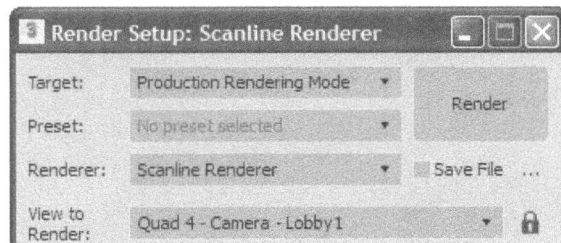

Figure 10–70

If this option is enabled, the software will recalculate radiosity for the material adjustments you make. They are very subtle, so you can ignore the recalculations for this practice.

You can also click

(Render Production) in the Main Toolbar.

3. In the *Common* tab, in the *Common Parameters* rollout, in the *Advanced Lighting* area, verify that **Use Advanced Lighting** is enabled, as shown in Figure 10–71. Clear **Compute Advanced Lighting when Required**, if required.

Advanced Lighting
☑ Use Advanced Lighting
☐ Compute Advanced Lighting when Required

Figure 10–71

4. Ensure that the **Camera – Lobby1** viewport is active. In the Render Setup dialog box, in the *View to Render* edit box, ensure that **Quad 4 - Camera - Lobby1** is selected. Click **Render** in the Render Setup dialog box.

5. In the Rendered Frame Window, use the mouse wheel to zoom into the floor. Note the moire pattern on the tile floor and on the windows, as shown in Figure 10–72.

Figure 10–72

This tab contains settings specific to Scanline rendering.

6. In the *Renderer* tab, in the *Scanline Renderer* rollout, in the *Global SuperSampling* area, ensure that **Enable Global Supersampler** is cleared (as shown in Figure 10–73) to avoid calculating Supersampling for all materials.

Global SuperSampling
☐ Disable all Samplers
☐ Enable Global Supersampler   ☑ Supersample Maps
Adaptive Halton   Quality: 0.5

Figure 10–73

7. Open the Slate Material Editor. In the Material/Map Browser, expand Scene Materials and double-click on **Finishes. Flooring.Tile.Square.Terra Cotta** to display it in *View1* sheet, as shown in Figure 10–74.

Figure 10–74

8. Double-click on the title bar of the material to open its Parameter Editor.

9. Expand the *SuperSampling* rollout and clear **Use Global Settings**, as shown in Figure 10–75. Use the default parameters including **Adaptive Halton** as the local supersampler.

Figure 10–75

10. Render the **Camera – Lobby1** viewport and note that the moire pattern is somewhat reduced, but that the rendering time has increased. The visible edges of the sun's highlight area are also much better defined and antialiased. Some jaggedness displays along the rails in the curtain wall, as shown in Figure 10–76.

Figure 10–76

Clearing Raytraced self-reflections prevents the rails and mullions from reflecting in the glass.

11. Part of this jaggedness is caused by reflections of the shadows being cast near the glass. In the Render Setup dialog box, in the *Raytracer* tab, clear **Enable Self Reflect / Refract**, as shown in Figure 10–77.

Global Raytrace Engine Options

✔ Enable Raytracing   Enable Self Reflect / Refract
✔ Raytrace Atmospherics   ✔ Reflect / Refract Material IDs

✔ Render objects inside raytraced objects
✔ Render atmospherics inside raytraced objects.
✔ Enable Color Density / Fog Effects

Acceleration Controls   Exclude...

Figure 10–77

12. Render the scene. Note that the outside wall is jagged, and half of it is turned dark (as shown in Figure 10–80) as there is a significant refraction of the outside walls through the glass.

13. In the Slate Material Editor, in the Material/Map Browser, in the Scene Materials, double-click on Curtain Walls and Curtain Wall Doors to display in the *View1* sheet. Click

(Lay Out All - Vertical) to arrange the materials vertically, as shown in Figure 10–78.

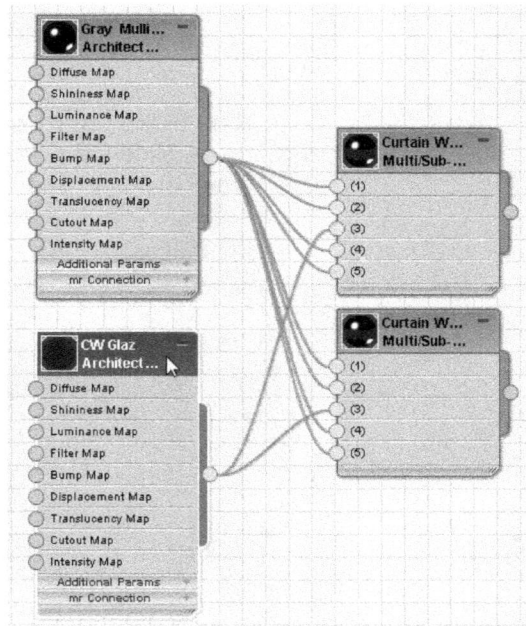

Figure 10–78

With a Raytrace material you could disable refraction, whereas for an Architectural material reduce the Index of Refraction.

14. Double-click on the title **CW Glaz** (Architectural material) to open its Parameter Editor. In the *Physical Qualities* rollout, set the *Index of Refraction* to **1.0** (as shown in Figure 10–79) which results in no refraction.

Figure 10–79

15. Render the scene again, as shown in Figure 10–80. The outside wall and rails are less jagged and the glass is less shiny than before.

Index of Refraction: 1.5   *Index of Refraction: 1.0*

Figure 10–80

16. Save your scene file as **MyRendering Options.max**.

At the university of Utah in 1975, Professor Martin Newell developed the teapot object. It was used for testing rendering algorithms. Today, the (Newell) teapot still exists in many 3D applications, including the Autodesk 3ds Max software.

Task 2 - Assign a double-sided material.

1. Reset the scene.

2. In the Command Panel>Create panel,(+), click

   ● (Geometry), and in the *Object Type* rollout, click **Teapot**. In the **Perspective** viewport, click and drag to create the teapot object of any size.

3. With the teapot selected, select the Modify panel ( ) and in the *Teapot Parts* area in the *Parameters* rollout, clear the **Lid** option, as shown in Figure 10–81. In the **Perspective**

   viewport, use (Orbit) to change the orientation of the teapot so that the inside displays, as shown in Figure 10–82. The faces on the inside of the teapot are visible because the **Backface Cull** option is not set by default. You can change the *Viewport Shading* to **High Quality** to see the inside of the teapot clearly.

Figure 10–81   **Figure 10–82**

4. Select the teapot, if required, right-click, and select **Object Properties**. In the *General* tab, in the *Display Properties* area, click **By Layer** to change it to **By Object**, if required. Select **Backface Cull** (as shown in Figure 10–83) and click **OK**. The inside faces of the teapot become invisible.

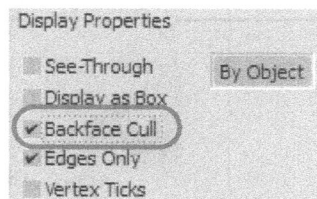

Figure 10–83

In the Object Properties dialog box, in the Display Properties area, all of the options are grayed out if it is set to **By Layer***. Change it to* **By Object** *for the options to become available.*

You can also click

(Render Production) to render the scene

5. Click to open the Render Setup dialog box and ensure that the *Renderer* is set to the **Scanline Renderer**. Click **Render** to render the **Perspective** view. Note that the inside of the teapot is black, due to the black background (as shown in Figure 10–84) indicating that the inside faces of the teapot are missing. Leave the Rendered Frame Window open.

Figure 10–84

6. Open the Slate Material Editor. In **Materials>General** categories, double-click on the material **Double Sided**. Both the **Facing** and the **Back** materials are gray. Double-click on the **Facing** material node and assign a blue color to the **Diffuse** swatch. Similarly, double-click on the **Back** material node and assign a red color to the **Diffuse** channel. Drag and drop, or use to assign the material to the teapot.

7. Render the scene. The inside faces are now visible in the rendering, as shown in Figure 10–85. The Object properties are overridden by the double-sided material.

Figure 10–85

Task 3 - Use the double-sided rendering option.

1. In the Slate Material Editor, double-click on **Standard** in the *Materials>Scanline* list. The **Standard** material is not double-sided. Double-click to open the Parameter Editor and assign the color red to its **Diffuse** channel. Assign this material to the teapot. Close the Slate Material Editor.

2. Render the scene. The faces inside the teapot are missing and display as black because of the background color.

*To open the Render
Setup dialog box, click*

 *(Render Setup) in
the Main Toolbar, or
select **Rendering>
Render Setup**.*

*The background has
been changed to white
for printing clarity.*

3. Open the Render Setup dialog box. In the *Common* tab, in
   the *Common Parameters* rollout, in the *Options* area, select
   Force 2-Sided, as shown in Figure 10–86.

Options
- ✔ Atmospherics   Render Hidden Geometry
- ✔ Effects   Area Lights/Shadows as Points
- ✔ Displacement   ✔ Force 2-Sided
- Video Color Check   Super Black
- Render to Fields

Figure 10–86

4. Render the scene. The teapot renders double-sided, as
   shown in Figure 10–87.

Figure 10–87

5. Save your work as **MyTeapot.max**.

10.7 State Sets

State Sets is a scene management/render pass manager in the Autodesk 3ds Max software. The State Sets dialog box enables you to record the changes made to the scene at different intervals and saves them in an hierarchical form. Select

Rendering>State Sets or click {◎} in the State Sets toolbar to open the State Sets explorer, as shown in Figure 10–88. It opens in the tree view called *States* in which the states are recorded and managed.

Some of the changes, such as using transforms, are not recordable by State Sets. See the Autodesk 3ds Max Help for a list of properties that can be used with the State Sets.

- The tree view opens with the master state at the top, which displays as ▣ ⊞ State Sets , and contains the **State01** state.

- You can add a new state by clicking ⊞ next to the master state or by selecting **States>Add State**. A new state with the name **State02** is added in the tree view, as shown in Figure 10–88.

Figure 10–88

- To make a state current, click on the gray arrow. An active state is indicated by a green arrow.

- To record changes to a state, click ⊚ (gray circle) next to the state. The ⊚ (gray circle) changes to ◉ (black circle), indicating that the state is being recorded, and that you can start making changes to the scene. Once you have made your changes, click ◉ (black circle) to stop recording. The recorded changes display as a children for this state, as shown in Figure 10–89.

Figure 10–89

- You can add states and record changes in those states.

- To render all of the recorded states, in the State Sets menu bar, select **States>Render All States**, as shown in Figure 10–90. The states are rendered to files and saved in the path and filename specified in the Render Outputs panel.

Figure 10–90

- To set a name and path for the output files, select **States>Render Outputs** to display the render outputs panel where you can browse and set the path for the files.

State Sets can bi-directionally interoperate with the Adobe After Effects CS4 (32-bit) and Adobe After Effects CS5/CS5.5 (64-bit). This requires that the files are copied from the Autodesk 3ds Max install folder into the After Effects install folder.

Compositer View

You can display the Compositor View by selecting **Compositor> Compositor View** in the dialog box menu bar with similar functionality to the View sheet in the Slate Material Editor, as shown in Figure 10–91.

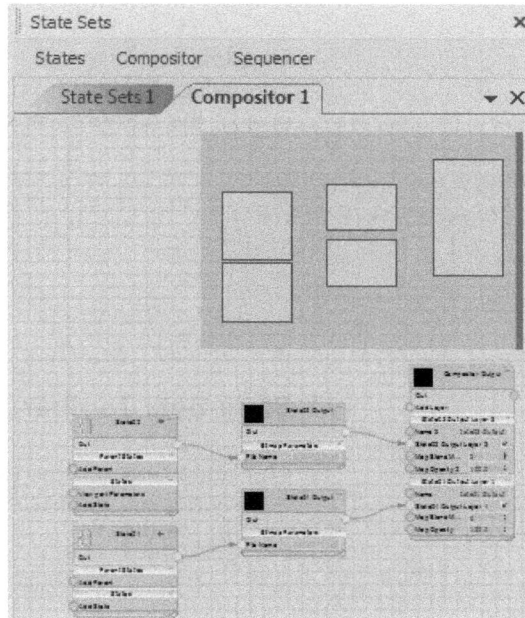

Figure 10–91

Note that in the Compositor View, all of the wired states display. You can modify the composition by modifying the nodes. You can select **Compositor>Compositor Link** to output the composition to the After Effects software or select **Compositor>Create PSD** to output the composition to an Adobe Photoshop .PSD file, as shown in Figure 10–92.

Figure 10–92

Camera Sequencer

You can use the Sequencer mode to set up an animation using multiple camera views. Select **Sequencer>Sequencer Mode** to activate a window along the bottom of the viewports with a track window indicating the cameras that are in use along with the range of frames for active cameras, as shown in Figure 10–93.

To add a camera, use to add a state and then click on **None** and select camera from the menu. Click on the check box to enable the camera track.

Figure 10–93

State Sets Toolbar

The State Sets toolbar (shown in Figure 10–94) enables you to quickly access the State Sets features.

Figure 10–94

- Click to open or close the State Sets explorer. When you toggle it on and then select **Render All States** from the **States** menu in the State Sets dialog box, the state is rendered with the changed properties.

- Click to toggle the render output for the state on or off. When you toggle it on and then select **Render All States** from the **States** menu in the State Sets explorer, the state is rendered.
- Use the drop-down list to activate a state or access other controls.

- Click to open the Select Composite Link File dialog box where you can browse and use the selected .SOF (state output file).

10.8 The Print Size Wizard

When you create renderings for print, the Print Size Wizard (shown in Figure 10–95) can help you select an appropriate rendering based on a required output resolution. To access the wizard, select **Rendering>Print Size Assistant**.

Figure 10–95

Trial and error might be required to determine an appropriate resolution.

- A rendering's print resolution describes how many pixels show per printed inch, often referred to as pixels-per-inch on screen (ppi) or dots-per-inch on paper (DPI). Select the required dpi in the *Choose DPI Value* options.

- Rendering time increases exponentially with size, so select the lowest resolution that provides an acceptable result.

- Many laser printers and plotters output between 300-600 DPI, however, when rendering values such as 72-150 DPI you can also get good results. High-end equipment plotting at 1200 DPI or better creates outstanding prints at 200-300 dpi and on high-quality paper.

- Higher quality paper can get better results than increasing resolution.

Practice 10e

Using the Print Size Wizard

Practice Objective

- Set the print resolution, paper size, and other options for a rendering.

In this practice, you will prepare a rendering for an A-size, 8.5"x11" print at 72 DPI. You want at least a 1/2" border around all sides and the aspect ratio of 1.6. Using the Print Size Wizard, you will set all the options to get the required print.

You must set the paths to locate the External files and Xrefs used in the practice. If you have not done this already, return to Chapter 1 and complete Task 1 to Task 3 in *Practice 1a: Organizing Folders and Working with the Interface*. You only have to set the user paths once.

*If a dialog box opens prompting you about a File Load: Mismatch, click **OK** to accept the default values.*

1. Open **Print Wizard.max**.

2. Open the Print Size Wizard by selecting **Rendering>Print Size Assistant**. Verify that the printing units (*Choose Unit*) are set to **inches** and the orientation is set to **Landscape**.

3. In the Paper Size drop-down list, select **A – 11x8.5in**. Note in the viewport that this setting changes the aspect ratio (11"/8.5" = 1.29). Change the Paper Size back to **Custom**.

4. Set the *Paper Width* to **10** (11" minus a half-inch border on each side). When printing, the 1/2" border displays along both sides as long as you print this image centered on an 8.5" x 11" page at 72 DPI.

On a hand-calculator, work out the required rendered height 10"/1.6 = 6.25".

5. Set the *Paper Height* to **6.25** and select the *DPI* value of **72**, as shown in Figure 10–96. Press <Enter>. Note that the rendering size changes to 720 x 450 pixels, as shown in Figure 10–96.

Figure 10–96

6. Click **Render**.

- Once rendered, you save the image and open it in an image editor or layout program to add your company logo, titles, labels, and other additional details.

- You can also print directly to the current system printer by clicking 🖶 (Print Image) in the Rendered Frame Window.

7. Save the file as **MyPrint Wizard.max**.

Chapter Review Questions

1. Which exposure control is recommended to used with ART and Arnold renderers?

   a. Automatic Exposure Control

   b. Linear Exposure Control

   c. Physical Camera Exposure Control

   d. Pseudo Color Exposure Control

2. Which of the following statements is correct?

   a. The angle of the sun's light cannot be controlled using date, time, and location parameters.

   b. The illumination of a skylight object is controlled by date, time, and location settings of the sunlight system.

   c. Skylight objects are directional lights and their modify parameters are similar to those for directional lights.

   d. Sunlight objects are directional lights and their modify parameters are similar to those for directional lights.

3. Which of the following is not supported by Arnold renderer?

   a. Standard lights

   b. Photometric lights

   c. Physical materials

   d. Sun Positioner

4. Which Production renderer must be active for the Image Based Lighting (IBL) rendering technique to become available?

   a. Scanline Renderer

   b. Arnold Renderer

   c. VUE File Renderer

   d. Quicksilver Hardware Renderer

5. Which renderer in the Autodesk 3ds Max software is not a graphical renderer and uses ASCII text files to describe the position and transformation of objects, lighting, etc.?

   a. Scanline Renderer

   b. VUE File Renderer

   c. Quicksilver Hardware Renderer

   d. ART Renderer

6. When saving a rendering as an image file, which of the following format offers highest color depth with a smaller compression? In other words, this image file format is the best choice regarding file size to quality ratio.

   a. JPEG

   b. BMP (Bitmap)

   c. TGA (Targa)

   d. PNG (Portable Network Graphics)

   e. TIFF (Tagged Image File Format)

7. In rendering, which of the following is used to calculate accurate reflections, refractions, and shadows?

   a. Antialiasing

   b. SuperSampling

   c. Motion Blur

   d. Raytracing

Command Summary

Button	Command	Location
	Effects and Environment dialog box	• **Rendered Frame Window** • **Rendering:** Environment
	Render Setup	• **Main Toolbar** • **Rendering:** Render Setup
	State Sets	• **State Sets Toolbar** • **Rendering:** State Sets
N/A	**Viewport Configuration dialog box> *Background* tab**	• **Views:** Viewport Background> Configure Viewport Background • **Keyboard:** <Alt>+<B>

Animation

Animations created in the Autodesk® 3ds Max® software involve the use of Animation and Time Controls. These enable you to animate and keyframe a camera to create a walkthrough animation or to create single-frame images and then assemble them to create a movie.

Learning Objectives in this Chapter

- Work with Animation and Time Controls and set various options.
- Create animation output using the various approaches available.

11.1 Animation and Time Controls

Animations in the Autodesk 3ds Max software are created by playing back a number of still frames in rapid succession using desktop animation files such as .AVIs and .MOVs.

- Traditional movies play back a sequence of still images in rapid succession.

- Computer movie formats compile a sequence of still images into a compressed format, keeping track of the changes from frame to frame at the pixel level.

- Animations are based on Key Frames (or keys), which are time indexes at which objects change their position, rotation, scale, and/or a limited number of object parameters.

- The Autodesk 3ds Max software generates animations by interpolating between a small number of user-defined key frames – smoothly or otherwise.

- The Autodesk 3ds Max animation system offers powerful controls to create animations, ranging from simple camera movements to extremely complex sequences.

- The animation controls enable you to create and play back a preview animation in one or more viewports.

Time Slider and Track Bar

The time slider and the track bar (shown in Figure 11–1) are found below the viewports and enable you to advance and reverse along an animation forward or backwards in time.

- The numbers below the time slider indicate the current time or frame number. Use the greater than (>) and lesser than (<) keys as shortcuts for moving the time slider a frame at a time.

- The shortcut menu in the Track bar contains the key properties and the controller properties. Selecting a key and then right-clicking displays all of the values for that key. Using the shortcut menu, you can also delete keys and use filter options for the display of the track bar.

Figure 11–1

- On the left side of the track bar, clicking ![icon] (Open Mini Curve Editor) opens the Mini Curve Editor (as shown in Figure 11–2), which replaces the track bar and the time slider. The Curve Editor contains a menu bar, toolbar, controller window, and the key window. You can collapse the Curve Editor by clicking **Close** at the left end of the Curve Editor toolbar.

Figure 11–2

Hint: Track View: Using the Curve Editor and Dope Sheet

The Curve Editor and Dope Sheet are two animation data editors which graphically display and enable you to modify the animation controllers that are used to interpolate the objects in a scene.

- To open the Track View - Curve Editor, in the Main toolbar,

  click ![icon], or in the Menu Bar, select **Graph Editors>Track View- Curve Editor**.

- In the Curve Editor, the animation displays in the form of function curves, as shown in Figure 11–3. You can visualize and modify the motion by controlling the curves (i.e., tangent handles) at various keys.

Figure 11–3

- To open the Track View - Dope Sheet, in the Menu Bar, select **Graph Editors>Track View- Dope Sheet**.

- In the Dope sheet, the animation displays in the form of a spread sheet displaying keys and ranges, as shown in Figure 11–4. You can visualize and modify the motion by controlling the keys directly.

Figure 11–4

Animation and Time Controls

The Animation and Time Controls (shown in Figure 11–5) are found at the bottom right corner next to the Navigation Controls.

Figure 11–5

The various Animation and Time controls are described as follows:

<table>
<tr><td></td><td>Enables you to manually add an animation key at the time shown in the time slider.</td></tr>
<tr><td>**Auto Key/ Set Key**</td><td>Activates either **Auto Key** or **Set Key** Animation Modes.

• When **Auto Key** mode is active all movement, rotation, and scale changes are automatically stored as keys at the current frame. This method is more widely used by design visualizers. Press <N> as a shortcut to toggle on the mode.

• The **Set Key** mode enables you to create keys, set key information, and offers more control over the kinds of keys you create through filters by using

. Its functionality was added primarily for character animators who used this methodology in other packages. Press <'> (single apostrophe) as a shortcut to toggle on the mode.</td></tr>
<tr><td>Previous/ Play/ Next</td><td>Enable you to play an animation in your viewport(s) and advance to the next or previous frame/key.

• When you click (Play Animation), the software plays the animation in the active viewport and replaces this icon with (Stop Animation).

• (Play Animation) is a flyout and contains (Play Selected), which only plays the selected objects in the active viewport.</td></tr>
</table>

*When either **Auto Key** mode or **Set Key** mode is active, their corresponding buttons display in red, indicating that you are in the animation mode.*

◀▶ (Key Mode Toggle)	Enables you to move between frames or keys. • When you are in Key mode (active), the Previous and Next icons display as ◀ ▶ ▶◀ and enable you to jump to the previous or next keyframe. • Keyframes are set in the Time Configuration dialog box (Key Steps area). When Key mode is off, the Previous and Next icons display as ◀❙❙ ▶ ❙❙▶ and you can jump to the previous and next frame.
❙◀◀ (Go to Start)/ ▶▶❙ (Go to End)	Enable you to move directly to the beginning or end of an animation. The time slider jumps to the selected location.
86 ▲▼ (Current Frame)	Enables you to advance to a specific frame or time in the animation.
Key Filters...	Opens the Set Key Filters dialog box, which enables you to select the tracks on which the keys can be created. The track sets are created with the **Set Key** mode. The Selected drop-down list contains the created track sets and selection sets and enables you to select the required one quickly.
(Default In/Out Tangents for New Keys)	Contains a list of tangent types.
(Time Configuration)	Opens the Time Configuration dialog box.

Time Configuration

Clicking (Time Configuration) opens the Time Configuration dialog box (as shown in Figure 11–6) where you assign an animation, its length, playback rate, and other critical parameters. It is recommended to adjust these parameters before you start configuring an animation.

Figure 11–6

The *Frame Rate* area provides options to define how many still frames to show per second (FPS). When setting a frame rate, the goal is to create an animation that flows smoothly without rendering additional frames. The best choice for frame rate depends on the medium where you intend to play your animation.

NTSC	**National Television Standards Committee:** the standard television frame rate used across most of the Americas and Japan: 30 FPS.
PAL	**Phase Alternate Line:** the standard used across Europe: 25 FPS.
Film	Assigns the frame rate used in film production: 24 FPS.
Custom	Enables you to select a specific frame rate. Animations created for desktop and web-based presentations are often set 12-25 FPS.

The *Time Display* area provides options to select how you want to measure time during your animation.

Frames	Measures time in the number of frames that have elapsed since the beginning of the animation.
SMPTE	The time measurement standard used by the Society of Motion Picture Technical Engineers for video and television productions. This standard measures time in minutes, seconds, and frames separated by colons (such as 1:22:43).
FRAME:TICKS	Measures time in frames and ticks only. A tick is a unit of animated time that equals 1/4800 of a second.
MM:SS:TICKS	Measures time in minutes, seconds and ticks.

The *Playback* area provides options to control how the animation is played back in the viewports.

Real Time	Plays the animation at the real world playback rate, skipping frames, if required. Clearing this option displays all frames in sequence, even if it slows down the animation preview. This is used by most animators to inspect every frame for problems.
Speed	When **Real Time** is enabled, speed up or slow down the animation using this option or continually play using the **Loop** option.
Direction	When not using **Real Time** you can select to play the animation forwards, backwards, or ping-pong (forwards and backwards again) using the **Direction** option.
Active Viewport Only	Limits the animation preview to the active viewport, which might be required if system resources are taxed by the animation playback.

The options in the *Animation* area define the active time segment (the current animation length) between the starting and ending time.

Start Time	Can be equal to 0, a positive, or negative time value as required.
End Time	Can be equal to 0, a positive, or negative time value as required.
Length	The calculated time between the starting and ending points.

| Frame Count | A value equal to the animation length + 1 frame, to account for the rendering of frame 0. |
| Current Time | Provides the frame you are on in the animation. Use this field to change to a different frame without exiting the dialog box. |

When animation times are changed in this dialog box, the existing keys do not automatically scale to the new time. For example, if you lengthen an existing animation by increasing the end time, the current animation still stops at the old end time (unless you then manually adjust the keys).

To expand or contract an animation's overall length, click **Re-scale Time**, to open the Rescale Time dialog box, as shown in Figure 11–7. Changing the animation times spaces the existing keys along the new animation length.

Figure 11–7

The *Key Steps* area provides options to limit how and which animation keys are created in Key mode. Leave the **Use TrackBar** option enabled to not limit key creation.

Progressive Display and Adaptive Degradation

The Progressive Display (only for Nitrous drivers) and Adaptive Degradation is a display option that can be very useful when playing animations in the viewport or when navigating large files in the viewport. When enabled (in the Status Bar, click ⬡ , or use <O> to toggle it on/off) it degrades an animation preview to a simpler display method to display the correct playback rate. It enables you to play a complex animation in a viewport at the correct speed, even if it means simplifying the display to a less detailed display mode, such as wireframe.

If you are using one of the legacy display drivers (Direct3D or Open GL), the Adaptive Degradation tab replaces the Display Performance tab in the Viewport Configuration dialog box.

In the Status Bar, right-click on ⬡ (Adaptive Degradation) to open the Viewport Configuration dialog box in the *Display Performance* tab, as shown in Figure 11–8. You can also open this dialog box by selecting **Views>Viewport Configuration** and then selecting the *Display Performance* tab. Alternatively, in the *Viewport* label, click [+] to display the label menu and select **Configure Viewports**. Using the menu bar or the *Viewport* label menu opens the dialog box in the *Visual Style & Appearance* tab. Select the *Display Performance* tab.

Figure 11–8

Improve Quality Progressively

This option (only available for Nitrous display drivers) enables you to improve the viewport quality through successive iterations. Once the iterations have been completed, a high quality rendered image displays in the viewport. You can also activate or clear this option in the menu bar (**Views> Progressive Display**).

Viewport Images and Textures Display Resolution

This area contains the following options:

Baked Procedural Maps	Enables you to set the resolution, in pixels, that is used to display the procedural maps in the viewports.
Texture Maps	Enables you to set the resolution in pixels, that is used to display the texture maps in the viewports.
Viewport Background / Environment	Enables you to set the resolution in pixels, that is used to display the environment and background maps.

Adaptive Degradation

The *Adaptive Degradation* area has the following options:

- When **Draw Backfaces during Degrade** is toggled on, the software draws the backface polygons while degrading the objects.

- When **Never Degrade Selected** is toggled on, the software does not degrade the selected objects.

- When **Degrade to Default Lighting** is toggled on, the software toggles off all of the lights in the viewport with only the default lighting toggled on.

- When **Never Redraw after Degrade** is toggled on, the software degrades the object display as is and does not redraw.

- When **Never Degrade Geometry** is toggled on, the geometry in the viewport is not degraded.

- The **Maintain Frames Per Second** option enables you to set the frame rate. The software maintains this frame rate through degradation.

- The **Delay Complete Viewport Redraw** option enables you to set a time in seconds, during which the viewports are not redrawn when degradation is complete.

Hint: Bitmap Proxy Images

Using Proxy images enables you to reduce the memory required for the 2D texture and increase the rendering speed. Expand the **File** menu, select **References**, and select **Asset Tracking** to open the Asset Tracking dialog box. Use **Bitmap Performance and Memory>Global Settings** to set the proxy resolution.

Antialiasing Quality

Enables antialiasing in the viewport, which attempts to soften the rough edges in 3D Geometry. Note that higher quality settings can reduce system performance.

Hardware Shaders Cache Folder

The folder, along with the complete path where the hardware shaders are saved, displays. Click **...** (as shown in Figure 11–9) to open the Configure System Paths dialog box, which enables you to modify the location for saving the hardware shaders.

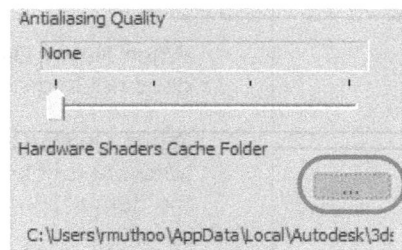

Figure 11–9

11.2 Walkthrough Animation

When animating cameras, it is often easier to have a camera follow a linear path than to configure the camera's position manually. For example, in Figure 11–10, you can animate a camera following a path going up a street to the house.

Figure 11–10

- To animate a target camera following a path, you create a helper object called a Dummy object, as shown in Figure 11–11. While a Dummy object is not required, it provides more control.

- The path can be a spline (shown in Figure 11–11) created in the Autodesk 3ds Max software or a linked/imported object. You then create a target camera and Dummy object and align them so they share a similar orientation. Multiple paths can be assigned and weighted during an animation.

Figure 11–11

- To create a Dummy object, in the Command Panel>Create panel (✛), click ◣ (Helpers). In the *Object Type* rollout, click **Dummy**, as shown in Figure 11–12.

- A Dummy object (white square object) is usually drawn in the **Top** viewport to ensure orientation with world space, as shown on the right in Figure 11–12. Dummies have no parameters in the Modify panel and do not render in your final animation.

Dummy object drawn in Top viewport

Figure 11–12

- In the Main Toolbar, use ⌀ (Select and Link) to link the Camera and Dummy.

- To animate the Dummy object and Camera, define a Path Constraint. Select **Animation>Constraints>Path Constraint**, as shown on the left in Figure 11–13. A dotted line displays in the viewport, as shown in Figure 11–13. Select the spline to be used as the path. If you cannot see the path, you can press <H> to select the path by name from the Select From Scene dialog box.

Figure 11–13

- Alternatively, the target object can be positioned over the subject and left unanimated. In this case, the target stays fixed over the building and the Dummy and Camera back animate along the path.

Practice 11a

Creating a Turntable Animation

Practice Objective

- Animate a building by rotating a camera around it at keyframe intervals.

In this practice, you will animate a camera rotating around the retail exterior building. You will add a dummy object on the building and set the key frames. Then apply rotation at the keyframes. You will then add interpolation to the keys using the dialog box and the Curve Editor. This creates the illusion that the viewer is standing still and the building is revolving as if on a turntable.

You must set the paths to locate the External files and Xrefs used in the practice. If you have not done this already, return to Chapter 1 and complete Task 1 to Task 3 in *Practice 1a: Organizing Folders and Working with the Interface*. You only have to set the user paths once.

Task 1 - Add a Dummy object and Keyframe it.

*If a dialog box opens prompting you about a File Load: Mismatch, click **OK** to accept the default values.*

1. Open **Turntable_Animation_Start.max**.

2. Verify that the **Top** viewport is active and maximize it.

3. Select the camera (**Turntable camera** is the only camera object) in the viewport. Click (Zoom Extents All Selected) to display the camera, its target, and the entire building, as shown in Figure 11–14.

Figure 11–14

4. In the Command Panel>Create panel (⊞), click ◥ (Helpers).

5. In the *Object Type* rollout, click **Dummy**. Starting from the camera target, click and hold on the target (the small blue square in the center of the building, as shown in Figure 11–15). Then, drag to create a dummy object (a square box) large enough to approximately extend beyond the two side (vertical) walls of the building, as shown in Figure 11–15.

Dummy box

Target (starting point

Figure 11–15

6. In the Main Toolbar, click ⬚ (Select and Link). In the viewport, select **Turntable camera** (camera object). Note that the cursor displays as two linked squares when you hover it over the selected camera. Starting from the camera object, click and drag the cursor to the Dummy object (box). A white dotted line displays between the camera and the dummy, as shown in Figure 11–16. Release the mouse to link the camera to the dummy.

Figure 11–16

7. To test it, click ⬚ (Select and Move) and move the Dummy object. The camera should move with it. Undo the move after the test and click ⬚ (Select Object) to exit the **Move** command.

8. In the Animation playback controls, click ⬚ (Time Configuration) to open the dialog box. Set the following:

   • *Time Display*: **Frames**
   • *Animation* area - *End Time*: **99**

9. Click **OK**. Near the bottom of the viewport, note that the Time Slider displays as **0/99**.

10. Using the layout overlay (holding <win> and pressing <Shift>), maximize the **Turntable camera** viewport.

*When clicked, the **Auto Key** displays in red, indicating that you are in the **Auto Key** animation mode. The slider bar area displays in red and a red border surrounds the current viewport.*

11. In the Animation controls, click **Auto Key** (it displays in red) and drag the Time Slider to **frame 33**. The Track Bar displays a blue rectangle at frame 33, as shown in Figure 11–17.

Figure 11–17

*You can also use the Rotate gizmo to rotate the dummy object horizontally until the values on the screen display as [**0.00, -0.00, -120.00**].*

12. In the Scene Explorer, using ▣ (Display None) and ◹ (Display Helpers), select **Dummy001**. Verify that **Dummy001** displays in the *Name and Color* rollout of the Command Panel.

13. Click ↻ (Select and Rotate). In the Status Bar, in the *Z* field, enter **-120**, and press <Enter>, so that the building is rotated as shown in Figure 11–18.

Figure 11–18

14. Drag the Time Slider to frame **66** and rotate the dummy object (along with the building) another 120 degrees, by entering **-240** in the Z field of the Status Bar and press <Enter>, as shown in Figure 11–19.

Figure 11–19

15. Drag the Time Slider to frame **99** and rotate the dummy object another 120 degrees, by entering **-360** in the Z field. Press <Enter>.

16. In the Animation controls, click ![play] to play the animation. Note that there is a pause with each revolution of the camera.

   Stop the animation by clicking ![pause].

17. If your animation has a lag, in the Status Bar, click

   ![icon] (Adaptive Degradation). If your animation plays without a lag, move to Step 21.

The working of the Adaptive degradation depends on your system configuration. You might not see the wireframe model while using Adaptive Degradation.

18. In the Animation controls, click ▶. Note that over time, the objects change into a wireframe model and animate smoothly. Stop the animation by clicking ⏸. Note that the model is redrawn as shaded almost immediately.

19. Right-click on ⬢ (Adaptive Degradation) to open the Viewport Configuration dialog box in the *Display Performance* tab. In the *Adaptive Degradation* area, set *Delay Complete Viewport Redraw in* to **5.0** seconds. Click **OK** to close the dialog box

20. Click ▶. Let the animation play in the viewport until the complete model has been degraded to a wireframe model and then click ⏸. Note that the model remains a wireframe for 5 seconds before it is redrawn as a shaded model.

If the animated object is not selected, the modified keys (green) is not displayed in the timeline.

21. Verify that the Dummy object is still selected. To fix the pause at each revolution, right-click on the green key in the timeline at frame 99 and select **Dummy001: Z Rotation**, as shown in Figure 11–20. You can Pause the animation, if it is still running.

22. In the dialog box that opens, expand the *In* interpolation to display the interpolation tools flyout, as shown in Figure 11–21. Click ⟋ (Linear interpolation).

Figure 11–20   **Figure 11–21**

23. Similarly, change the *Out* interpolation to 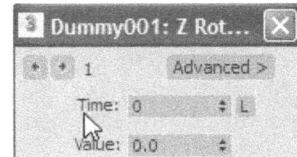 (Linear interpolation), as shown in Figure 11–22.

- This sets the interpolation to Linear at frame 4 (99).

24. You will set the interpolation to Linear for the other three frames (0, 33, 66). In the upper left corner of the dialog box, click ⬦ (left arrow) (as shown in Figure 11–22) three times such that you advance to key **1**, which is the key number. The *Time* displays as **0** and the *Value* displays as **0.0**, as shown in Figure 11–23. Set the *In* and *Out* Interpolation to **Linear** for key 1.

Figure 11–22	**Figure 11–23**

25. Repeat for the remaining keys **2** and **3** (frames 33 and 66), using ⬦ (right arrow) to move to the required key. Close the dialog box.

26. Click ▶ to play the animation. It should rotate in a loop without any pause.

27. Click ❙❙ to stop the animation.

Task 2 - Use the Curve Editor.

Use the scroll bar to display the animation line.

1. In the Main toolbar, click 🔲 (Track View) to open the Curve Editor. It displays the key window (right side) containing keys (small gray squares) and the linear slanting line (blue line) that displays the animation, as shown in Figure 11–24. You might have to zoom and pan inside the key window for the keys to display.

2. Hover the cursor over the Controller window (left side). It displays as a **Hand** icon. If required, hold and drag it until the dummy object is listed with its applied Transforms, as shown in Figure 11–24.

3. In the Rotation node of the dummy object, select **X Rotation**, **Y Rotation**, and **Z Rotation**, if not already selected, as shown in Figure 11–24.

Figure 11–24

The selected key in the Curve Editor is represented as white in color.

4. In the Key window, on the blue line, select the key (small gray square) at frame 33. It displays in white indicating that it has been selected. In the Curve Editor toolbar, click ⟍ (Set Tangents to Slow), as shown in Figure 11–25.

• Note that a slight curve is added at this frame 33.

Figure 11–25

5. Click ▶ to play the animation and note that the animation slows down slightly when it reaches frame 33. Click ⏸ to stop the animation.

6. Add **Set Tangents to Slow** to the keys at frame 0, 66, and 99. Slight curves are added to these frames, as shown in Figure 11–26.

Figure 11–26

7. Click ▶ to play the animation and click ⏸ to stop.

8. Close the Curve Editor.

9. Save your work as **MyTurntable_Animation.max**.

Practice 11b

Keyframing a Camera Animation

Practice Objective

- Animate a camera to fly over the site.

In this practice, you will add a camera to the scene and set the animation for the camera. You will then modify the animation by creating a new key and modifying the camera position at this key. This approach is similar to manually configuring a walkthrough or driveby animation.

You must set the paths to locate the External files and Xrefs used in the practice. If you have not done this already, return to Chapter 1 and complete Task 1 to Task 3 in *Practice 1a: Organizing Folders and Working with the Interface*. You only have to set the user paths once.

Task 1 - Save the Previous Render Options as a Preset.

*If a dialog box opens prompting you about a File Load: Mismatch, click **OK** to accept the default values.*

1. Open **Presets.max**.

2. Before you configure the animation you should save all of the rendering settings for the still rendering. In the Render Shortcuts toolbar, in the Presets drop-down list, select **Save Preset**, as shown in Figure 11–27.

*To display the toolbar, right-click anywhere in the blank area of the Main Toolbar and select **Render Shortcuts** and detach it from the Main toolbar.*

Figure 11–27

3. In the Render Presets Save dialog box, in the *File name* edit box, enter **Retail_Exterior_with_Background** to save your current render settings and click **Save**.

4. In the Select Preset Categories dialog box that opens, leave all of the preset categories as highlighted and click **Save**.

Task 2 - Configure the Camera Animation.

1. Maximize the **Top** viewport and zoom out till the building, parking lot, and the end of the road on the left side displays.

2. In the Command Panel>Create panel (+), click

   ■◀ (Cameras). In the *Object Type* rollout, click **Target**. Create a camera and the target in the approximate positions, as shown in Figure 11–28.

Figure 11–28

For the Target Camera to work well, the **Scanline** *renderer should be used.*

3. Click ◀ (Render Setup) to open the Render Setup dialog box and verify that **Scanline Renderer** is the current renderer used.

4. With the new camera selected, select the Modify panel

   (◀). Leave the camera with the default parameters but change its name to **Camera - Flyover**.

5. Maximize to display all four viewports. Right-click on the **Front** viewport to activate it. Change that view to show the **Camera - Flyover** view (as shown in Figure 11–29) by selecting the **Front** *Point of View* label and selecting **Cameras>Camera – Flyover**.

Figure 11–29

6. In the Animation controls, click ⬭ (Time Configuration). In the *Frame Rate* area, select **Custom**, set *FPS* to **20**, and in the *Animation* area, set *End Time* to **0:30:0**, as shown in Figure 11–30. Verify that all of the other values match the values in Figure 11–30. Your animation is 30 seconds long and intended for desktop playback at 20 FPS. Click **OK**.

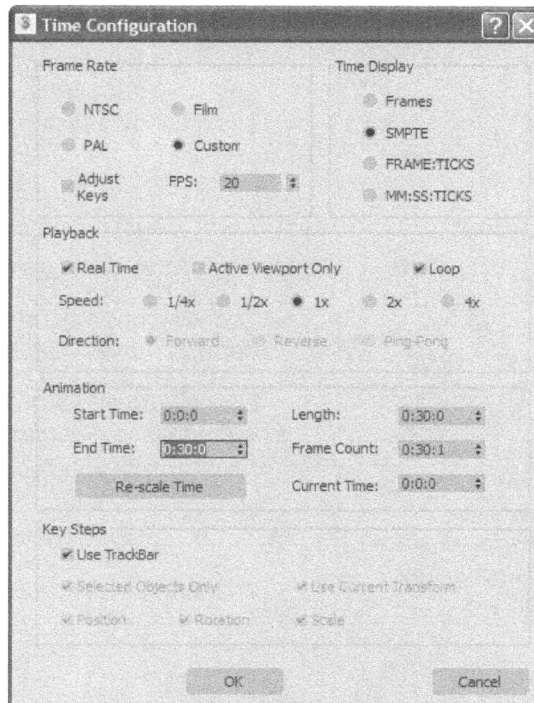

Figure 11–30

7. Verify that the Time Slider is currently located at time **0:0:0**, as shown in Figure 11–31.

Figure 11–31

8. Click **Auto Key**. It displays in red. Note that the Time Slider and outline of **Camera - Flyover** viewport also display in red.

9. Drag the Time Slider all of the way to the *end time* of **0:30:0**, as shown in Figure 11–32. Note the blue marker on the scale.

Figure 11–32

10. Verify that the **Camera - Flyover** object is selected (note the name in the Modifier Stack. Click ✛ (Select and Move) and in the Status Bar, in the *Transform Type-In* area enter **X = 300'0"**, **Y = 0'0"**, and **Z = 0'0"**, as shown in Figure 11–33. The roundoff error might change your X-coordinate to a value just below 300' (this occurs sometimes, but does not significantly affect this animation).

Figure 11–33

*If you do not click **Auto Key** again to toggle the mode off, you create an unintended animation. The camera's animation keys are visible along the time slider as colored boxes (as long as the camera is selected). Right-click to modify or delete a key.*

11. Click **Auto Key** again to toggle off Auto Key mode.

12. Slide (scrub) the Time Slider left and right and watch the camera move. With the **Camera - Flyover** viewport active, click ▶ to see a preview of the animation. Note that the camera is low and there are times in the animation when the camera views through the ground.

13. ▶ is changed while the animation is playing. Stop the animation by clicking ▮▮. Move to the beginning by clicking |◀◀ .

Task 3 - Modify the Animation by Adding a New Key.

You are currently skimming at elevation 0 which makes you fly directly through some slopes of the terrain. To make the animation look more like a flyover you will add another key in the middle of the animation and raise the camera up in the Z-direction at that point.

1. Verify that the **Camera – Flyover** camera is selected.

2. Move the Time Slider to exactly **0:15:0** (the midpoint of the animation) and click (Set Keys). A new key is created at this point.

3. In the Time Slider, right-click on this new key and select **Camera – Flyover: Z Position** (as shown in Figure 11–34). Set the *Value* to **30'0"** (as shown Figure 11–35) press <Enter>, and close the dialog box. This raises the camera higher.

Figure 11–34   **Figure 11–35**

4. Click ◄◄ (Go to Start) to return to the beginning and click

   ▶ (Play) to preview the animation. Note the vertical change has been adjusted but now at around the midpoint the camera is too close to the building. You will pull the camera back from the building at the midpoint. Stop the animation by

   clicking ❚❚

5. Drag the Time Slider to exactly **0:15:0** and click **Auto Key**.

If done without being in Auto Key mode you would move the camera at frame 0 and at all other keys.

6. Right-click in the **Top** viewport and verify that the **Camera – Flyover** camera is still selected (if not, then select it). Click

    (Select and Move) and in the Status Bar, in the *Transform Type-In* area, set the following, as shown in Figure 11–36:

    - *X:* **15'0"**
    - *Y:* **-120'0"**
    - *Z:* **30'0"**

    This moves the **Camera – Flyover** camera away from the building. Since this is done in **AutoKey** mode the camera's existing key at 0:15:0 is updated with this new position.

    X: 15'0"   Y: -120'0"   Z: 30'0"

    Figure 11–36

7. Click **Auto Key** to toggle it off. Click �again to return to the beginning and click ▶ to preview the animation. Note how the camera has been moved away from the building. Stop the animation by clicking ❚❚.

8. Click (Render Setup) to open the Render Setup dialog box. In the *Common* tab, in the *Common Parameters* rollout, in the *Time Output* area, select **Active Time Segment** (entire animation), as shown in Figure 11–37. Normally, you select a filename and location to render to.

9. In the *Common Parameters* rollout, in the *Output Size* area, set the *Width* to **300** and press <Enter>, as shown in Figure 11–37. With the aspect ratio locked at 1.6, a rendering *Height* of **188** is automatically calculated.

Figure 11–37

10. Near the top of the dialog box, in the Preset drop-down list, select **Save Preset** and save the rendering settings as **RetailExteriorAnimation.rps**. Save all preset categories.

11. Save the file as **MyCameraAnimationFlyover.max**.

Practice 11c

Creating a Walkthrough Animation

Practice Objective

- Animate a camera object along a path in a scene.

In this practice, you will merge a .MAX file, which has a hemispherical dome with a simple sky texture and ground color applied to be used as a background for the current scene. You will also merge a file in which the path has been created.

You must set the paths to locate the External files and Xrefs used in the practice. If you have not done this already, return to Chapter 1 and complete Task 1 to Task 3 in *Practice 1a: Organizing Folders and Working with the Interface*. You only have to set the user paths once.

*If a dialog box opens prompting you about a File Load: Mismatch, click **OK** to accept the default values.*

1. Open **Camera Animations.max**.

2. Maximize the **Top** viewport.

3. In the **Top** viewport, zoom into the parking lot area and the road leading into it. Note that there is no path (line) on the road that goes into the parking lot area.

4. In the Menu Bar, select **File>Import>Merge,** select **Animation Path.max**. Click **Open**.

5. In the Merge dialog box, select **Animation Path 3D** and click **OK**. This 3D path is located along the proposed ground surface of the access road to the parking lot area, as shown in Figure 11–38.

Figure 11–38

6. Using the Scene Explorer, select the object group **_Site Model** (■ (Display None) and ▣ (Display Groups)).

7. Right-click in the viewport and select **Freeze Selection** in the quad menu. The Site model geometry displays in a dull gray color and you can easily see the blue path that travels along the street. If required, use **Zoom** and **Pan** to display the complete path in the viewport.

8. In the Command Panel>Create panel (✛), click

   ■ (Cameras). In the *Object Type* rollout, click **Target**. Click near the left end of the path to place the camera, hold and drag to the center of the building and release to set the target, as shown in Figure 11–39. In the *Name and Color* edit box, enter the name of the camera as **Walkthrough_Cam01**.

Figure 11–39

9. In the viewport, zoom into the Camera object. Click in the viewport to clear any selection.

10. In the Command Panel>Create panel (✛), click

   ◸ (Helpers). Click **Dummy**.

If you were flying a camera through the interior of a design you would align the camera to the dummy at this point. In this animation it is not required for this type of exterior flyby.

11. Click and drag to create the Dummy object around the Camera by starting at the beginning of the animation path spline, as shown in Figure 11–40.

Figure 11–40

12. In the Main Toolbar, click (Select and Link).

13. In the viewport, select and hold the newly created **Walkthrough_Cam01** object to define it as the child object. Drag the cursor to the outline of the **Dummy**. A dotted line displays between the cursor and the object, and the dummy object turns yellow, as shown in Figure 11–41. Release to link the camera to the **Dummy**.

Figure 11–41

14. To check it, in the Main Toolbar, click and move the Dummy object. You should see the Camera move with it. This confirms that the linkage is correct. Undo the move.

When you hover the cursor over the path, it should turn yellow to show that it is going to be selected. Once it turns yellow, click to select it.

15. Now you will constrain the dummy to the path. Select the Dummy object in the viewport and select **Animation> Constraints>Path Constraint**. The cursor is connected with a dotted line to the pivot point of the Dummy object. Click anywhere over the blue spline (Animation Path 3D) to select it as the animation path, as shown in Figure 11–42. The pivot point of the dummy automatically shifts to coincide with the start point of the path.

Figure 11–42

16. Zoom out till the entire blue path displays. Click ▶ to play the animation. The Dummy and the camera animates along

the path, as shown in Figure 11–43. Click ❚❚ to stop the animation.

Figure 11–43

17. Maximize to display all four viewports. Activate the **Camera01** viewport and change it to the **Walkthrough_Cam01** viewport (select the *POV* label and select **Cameras>Walkthrough_Cam01**).

18. Click ► to play the animation. The animation might be improved if the camera was higher off the ground.

19. Click |◄◄ to go to the start of the animation, at frame zero.

Use the Scene Explorer,

*use ■◄ (Display Cameras) and select **Walkthrough_Cam01**, child of **Dummy001**.*

20. Since the Camera is a child of the Dummy you can add transforms to the Camera without affecting the Dummy's animation. Select **Walkthrough_Cam01** object (as shown in Figure 11–44) and rename it as **Camera_Flyby**.

Figure 11–44

21. With the **Camera_Flyby** object selected, in the Main Toolbar, right-click on ✛ (Select and Move) to open the Move Transform Type-In dialog box.

22. In the *Absolute:World*, change the *Z* value to **6'0"** and press <Enter>. Close the dialog box. Since **Auto Key** is off this lifts the Camera for the entire animation.

23. Play the animation in the **Camera_Flyby** viewport. Stop the animation.

24. Right-click on the viewport and select **Unfreeze All**. The Site model displays with full color. Play the animation again.

25. Save your work as **MyCameraAnimationFlyby.max**.

11.3 Animation Output

There are two strategies for creating animation output:

- Render directly to a single, composite animation file such as a .MOV or .AVI. This is generally recommended for previews.

- Render each still image (such as .PNG, .JPEG, .BMP, .TIFF, etc.) and later combine the stills into a composite animation using the Autodesk 3ds Max RAM Player, Video Post, or 3rd party post-production software.

You can select an animation output option in the Render Output File dialog box. To open this dialog box, open the Render Setup dialog box and expand the *Common Parameters* rollout in the *Common* tab. In the *Render Output* area, click **Files...**, as shown in Figure 11–45.

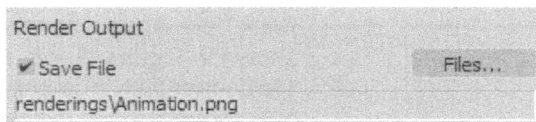

Figure 11–45

The Render Output File dialog box opens. In the Save as type drop-down list (shown in Figure 11–46), you can select to render to a single, compressed animation file (.MOV or .AVI) or to individual frames (such as .PNG, .JPEG, .BMP, .TIFF, etc.). If you select to render as individual frames, you need to provide the name once and the software automatically creates individual files for each frame, which are numbered sequentially.

Figure 11–46

Assembling Animations

It is recommended to render files individually and then combine them into an animation. The Autodesk 3ds Max RAM player is a utility used for comparing two images side-by-side, or for previewing and compiling animations.

The RAM player (shown in Figure 11–47) can be opened in the menu bar by selecting **Rendering>Compare Media in RAM Player**.

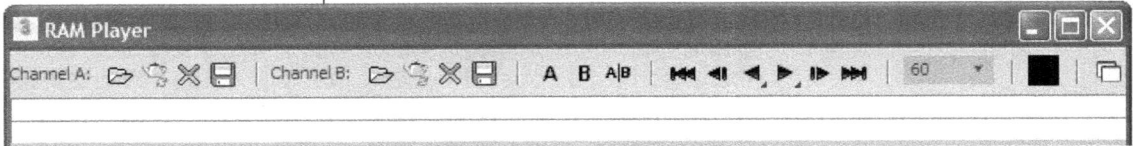

Figure 11–47

Click (Open Channel A) to open the Open File dialog box, shown in Figure 11–48. Enter the path and the first filename of the sequentially numbered image files. Selecting the **Sequence** option opens all of the files, which are named as specified in the *File name* field.

Figure 11–48

An image file list (.IFL) is an ASCII list of which files were used and in which order.

Once you open the specified image file, the Image File List Control dialog box opens (as shown in Figure 11–49), which displays the folder where the image file list (.IFL) is being created. The dialog box also provides you with options to limit the animation to certain frames.

Figure 11–49

Use the various playback options in the RAM Player to play the created animation.

Rendering files individually and then combining them into an animation later has various advantages, such as:

- A lot of time is spent calculating the information to create a rendered frame. Instead of compressing the frames, save them as a sequence of still images for access to all of the information later.

- When rendering individual frames, all of the previously saved frames remain available after a catastrophic error such as a system crash, disc error, power outage, etc. Therefore, you only need to re-render the missing frames required to complete your animation.

- When rendering animations, material, lighting or geometry, errors might occur in certain frames. Unlike compressed animation files, rendering to frames enables you to easily adjust, fix errors, and re-render the affected frames.

- When rendering to an animation file you need to first select the compression or video quality settings. If you do not like the results, select another value and re-render the entire animation.

- When rendering to stills, select a quality value after rendering is complete to try different settings and save out another composite file from the same still renderings.

- Rendering to a still image file format that supports an alpha channel (transparency) enables you to use a compositing package such as Combustion or Adobe After Effects for post-production processing and assembly.

Practice 11d

Creating Animation Output

Practice Objective

- Create an animation preview and create single-frame file images.

In this practice, you create single-frame file images at 5 frame intervals and save them as .PNG file format. You will then assemble the individual frame images to create a movie using the RAM Player.

You must set the paths to locate the External files and Xrefs used in the practice. If you have not done this already, return to Chapter 1 and complete Task 1 to Task 3 in *Practice 1a: Organizing Folders and Working with the Interface*. You only have to set the user paths once.

Task 1 - Create Still Frames.

If a dialog box opens prompting you about a File Load: Mismatch, click OK to accept the default values.

1. Open **Camera_Animation_Start_Render.max**.

2. Make the **Camera - Flyover** viewport active.

3. Click (Time Configuration) to open the Time Configuration dialog box. Change the *Time Display* to **Frames**.

4. In the *Animation* area, note that the *End Time* is set to **600** indicating that you have a 600 frame animation. Click **OK**.

5. Note that the *Time slider* should display as **0/600**, but it does not. Open the Time Configuration dialog box again ( ) and click **Re-scale Time** in the *Animation* area. The Re-scale Time dialog box opens. Click **OK** in both of the dialog boxes, and note that the *Time slider* is updated to display **0/600.**

*Rendering 600 frames might take a long time. You can select a shorter range and set the **Every Nth Frame** option to make it manageable.*

6. Click (Render Setup) to open the Render Setup dialog box. In the *Common* tab, verify that the *Common Parameters* rollout is expanded and do the following, as shown in Figure 11–50:

   • In the *Time Output* area, select **Range**.

   • Set a *Range* of **200** to **600**.

   • Set *Every Nth Frame* to **5**.

   This renders every 5th frame between 200 and 600, which is a total of 81 frames of animation.

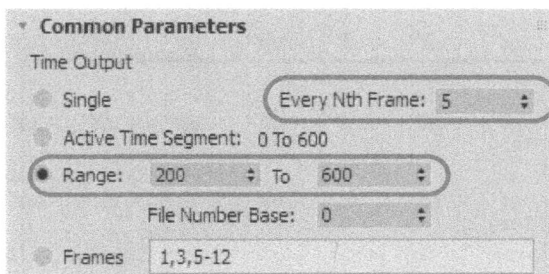

Figure 11–50

7. In the *Render Output* area, click **Files...**.

8. The Render Output File dialog box opens. Locate the *...\renderings* folder in the practice files folder. Set the *Save as type* to **PNG Image File (*.png)**, and in the *File name* enter the name **Animation**. Click **Save**.

In the Render Output File dialog box, in the Save as type drop-down list, you can select to render to a single, compressed animation file (.MOV, .AVI), or to individual frames. If you select a single-frame file format (such as .PNG, .JPEG, .BMP, .TIFF, etc.), you will then automatically create individual files for each frame, numbered sequentially.

9. In the PNG Configuration dialog box, select **RGB 24 bit** and leave **Alpha channel** enabled. Click **OK**. Note that the folder location is set and the **Save File** option is checked in the *Render Output* area of the Render Setup dialog box, as shown in Figure 11–51.

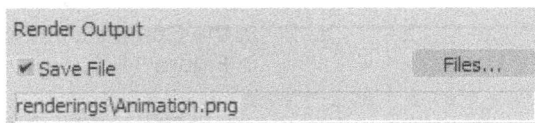

Figure 11–51

10. In the Render Setup dialog box, click **Render** to begin creating individual renderings for every fifth frame.

11. The Rendered Frame Window opens with each fifth frame being rendered and the Rendering dialog box opens (as shown in Figure 11–52), displaying information about the renderings, number of files to be rendered, estimate of the remaining rendering time, render settings, etc.

- It might take some time to complete the 81 frames of the animation, so you can stop the process with some frames completed or let it continue until all of the frames have completed.

Figure 11–52

12. Close the Rendered Frame Window and Render Setup dialog box.

Task 2 - Assemble the Final Animation.

It is called a RAM player because it loads these images into RAM.

1. In the menu bar, select **Rendering>Compare Media in RAM Player** to open the RAM player. The RAM player is a utility used for comparing two images side-by-side or previewing and compiling animations.

2. In the *Channel A* area, click 🗁 (Open Channel A), as shown in Figure 11–53.

Figure 11–53

*The **Sequence** option enables the system to open all of the PNGs named **Animation*.png**.*

3. In the Open File, Channel A dialog box, browse to the ...\renderings folder in the practice files folder. Note that there are 81 still images, such as Animation0200.png, Animation0205.png, Animation0210.png etc. Select **Animation0200.png** and verify that **Sequence** is enabled, as shown in Figure 11–54. Click **Open**.

Figure 11–54

4. The Image File List Control dialog box opens, as shown in Figure 11–55. It displays the folder where the image file list (.IFL) is being created. Click **OK**.

Figure 11–55

5. The RAM Player Configuration dialog box opens. It enables you to change the image size or aspect ratio on import, to limit the number of frames to use and the maximum amount of RAM you want to dedicate to the process. Click **OK**.

The lesser frame rate plays slows down the animation whereas the higher frame rate plays it faster.

6. After the animation has loaded into the RAM player you can play back the animation at different frame rates by selecting a number in the drop-down list, as shown in Figure 11–56.

   Click ▶ (Playback Forward) to play the animation. Select different frame rates and play the animation to see the effect.

Figure 11–56

7. To save a desktop animation file, click 🖫 (Save Channel A).

8. In the Save File, Channel A dialog box, browse to the ...\renderings folder. Set *Save as type* to **AVI File (*.avi)**. Save the animation as **FlybyAnimation**.

9. In the AVI File Compression Setup dialog box, for the *Compressor*, select **MJPEG Compressor**, set the *Quality* to **60**, and click **OK**.

10. Save your work as **MyCameraAnimation.max**.

If the quality of the animation is not as required, you could try other methods or qualities until you have an acceptable result.

11. In your Windows Explorer, navigate to your renderings folder and play **Flyby Animation.avi** file to watch the animation.

Chapter Review Questions

1. Activating (toggling on) which option in the Animation Controls changes **Previous**, **Play**, **Next Frame** ( ) to **Previous**, **Play**, and **Next Keyframe** ( )?

   a. **Auto Key** animation mode

   b. **Set Key** animation mode

   c. (Key Mode)

   d. (Set Keys)

2. A frame rate of 30 frames per second (FPS) is best suited for which medium?

   a. NTSC

   b. PAL

   c. Film

   d. Custom

3. When animation times are changed in the *Animation* area in the Time Configuration dialog box, the existing keys automatically scale to the new time.

   a. True

   b. False

4. Which category in the Create panel ( ) contains **Dummy** as its Object Type?

   a. (Geometry)

   b. (Shapes)

   c. (Cameras)

   d. (Helpers)

5. If you render each still image (such as .PNG, .JPEG, etc.), which utility can you use to combine the stills into a composite animation?

   a. Media Player

   b. RAM Player

   c. Batch Render

   d. Panorama Exporter

Command Summary

Button	Command	Location
Auto Key	Auto Key animation mode	• **Animation Controls Toolbar**
	Cameras	• **Command Panel:** *Create* panel • **Create:** Cameras
	Curve Editor	• **Main Toolbar** • **Graph Editors:** Track View - Curve Editor
	Default In/Out Tangents for New Keys	• **Animation Controls Toolbar**
N/A	Dope Sheet	• **Graph Editors:** Track View - Dope Sheet
	Go to End	• **Animation Controls Toolbar**
	Go to Start	• **Animation Controls Toolbar**
	Helpers	• **Command Panel:** *Create* panel
	Key Mode	• **Animation Controls Toolbar**
	Mini Curve Editor	• **Track bar**
	Previous, Play, Next Frame	• **Animation Controls Toolbar**
	Progressive Display	• **Status Bar**
	Render Setup	• **Main Toolbar** • **Rendering:** Render Setup
	Select and Link	• **Main Toolbar**
Set Key	Set Key animation mode	• **Animation Controls Toolbar**
	Set Keys	• **Animation Controls Toolbar**
	Time Configuration	• **Animation Controls Toolbar**

Optional Topics

There are some additional tools available in the Autodesk® 3ds Max® software that you can use when creating and rendering models. This appendix provides details about several additional tools and commands.

Learning Objectives in this Appendix

- Access Autodesk 3ds Max Help and use the various Help tools.
- Work with Architectural materials and the Compact Material Editor.
- Replace objects in a scene with AutoCAD® blocks or other Autodesk 3ds Max objects.
- Create hierarchies by collecting objects together with parent/child relationship.
- Customize the user interface elements.

A.1 Getting Help with Autodesk 3ds Max

The Help menu contains an extensive list of help options, which are organized as submenus so that finding information is easy. Some of the available help options are described as follows:

You can also press <F1> to access the help.

- The **Autodesk 3ds Max Help** is robust, well illustrated, and often the fastest way to find what an option or parameter controls and how to use it. This help is in the form of HTML files at autodesk.com website and you are required to have a working internet connection to access Help. To access help, in the menu bar, select **Help>Autodesk 3ds Max Help**. The 3ds Max Help screen opens with all the help topics listed in a tree structure along the left side of the page, as shown in Figure A–1. The topics are in the form of links. Click on the topic to display the related help along the right side of the Help screen, as shown in Figure A–1.

🏠 Help Home   Renu Muthoo ▾

3 AUTODESK® **3DS MAX®** 2019   🔍 Enter a keyword

➕ What's New

➖ 3ds Max Installation

  — <u>Installing and Licensing 3ds Max</u>

   ➕ 3ds Max Installation

   3ds Max Licensing

➕ Installation Administrator's Guide

➕ Installation Basics

➕ Getting Started

Installing and Licensing 3ds Max

These pages cover the installation and uninstallation of the Autodesk® 3ds Max® 3ds Max components, tools, and utilities that ship with the software product, and from the online Help to the local version of the Help.

Certain items are unique to the 3ds Max installation process.

Autodesk Software Installation, Licensing, and Deployment

Before you choose to install an Autodesk software product, verify your system me minimum system requirements and your hardware meets the minimum requireme product.

Figure A–1

- You can also search for a specific help topic by entering a keyword and selecting from the list of available related topics, as shown in Figure A–2.

X 2019   Q Materials ← *Search Keyword*

Showing 1-15 of 2889 results for **Materials**

<u>Managing Materials with the Slate Material Editor</u>

To get a **material** from the scene: On the Slate **Material Editor** toolbar, click Object).

Product Documentation | 2018-03-22

Related Help Topics

Managing Materials with the Compact Material Editor

To make a copy of a preview **material** : On the Compact **Material Editor** tool **Material** Copy).

Product Documentation | 2018-03-22

To Manage a Material with the Material Explorer Material Panel

To change a **material** assignment, do one of the following: Drag the **materia** icon (to the left of its name) from the **Material** Explorer **Material** panel onto viewport.

Product Documentation | 2018-03-22

Material Editor

Figure A-2

- The **Autodesk 3ds Max Tutorials** (select **Help> Tutorials**) offer thorough and comprehensive learning materials to get you started with almost all of the features in the Autodesk 3ds Max software. The tutorials are in the HTML format at autodesk.com website. You can download the Tutorials and the files required for the tutorials from http://www.autodesk.com/3dsmax-tutorials-scene-files-2016. Install the files on your local hard drive for use as you are completing the tutorials.

- **3ds Max Communities:** Select **Help>3ds Max Communities>Autodesk AREA, Student Community,** and **3ds Max Facebook** community provides a single location for users to closely interact. In addition to the Autodesk 3ds Max forum, the AREA contains forums for other entertainment products, such as Mudbox, Motionbuilder, FBX, Maya. You can also connect with other Autodesk 3ds Max users and share information using the Autodesk 3ds Max Facebook page.

- **3ds Max Resources and Tools:** Select **Help>3ds Max Resources and Tools** (as shown in Figure A–3) to link you to the following:

  - **App Store:** Enables you to download various applications for 3ds Max.
  - **Creative Market:** Enables you to download digital content
  - **Keyboard Shortcut Map:** Enables you to download a printable PDF of the keyboard shortcuts, etc.

- **Feedback:** The Autodesk 3ds Max software provides various **Speak Back** options, as shown in Figure A–4. Selecting an option connects you to web pages for reporting a bug in the software or making a request for small enhancements and new features, as shown in Figure A–4. It also enables you to activate the **Desktop Analytics Program**.

Figure A–3

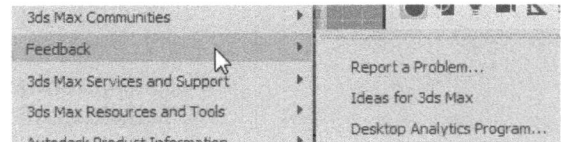

Figure A–4

- **3ds Max Services and Support**: Select **Help>3ds Max Services and Support>Support Center** (as shown in Figure A–5) to connect to the support site. It has many frequently updated technical support articles available. There might also be documents describing how to fix commonly occurring problem. Autodesk Subscription customers also have access to email support directly from Autodesk.

- **Arnold Help**: You can access the Arnold for 3DS Max User Guide at the Solid Angle website by selecting **Arnold>Help> User Guide**, as shown in Figure A–6. Information about the Arnold renderer for 3DS Max has been provided to guide you through the various features of the Arnold renderer.

Figure A–5

Figure A–6

A.2 Compact Material Editor

The Autodesk 3ds Max software contains two editors for working with materials:

- Slate Material Editor: Used to design and build materials where the material components display graphically.
- Compact Material Editor: Used when the materials have already been created and you just need to apply them.

- The Compact Material Editor can be opened by clicking

  ▣ (Compact Material Editor) in the Main Toolbar (Material Editor flyout), or by selecting **Rendering>Material Editor> Compact Material Editor**.

You can also use

🖉 *(Pick Material from Object) in the Material Editor and select the object in the viewport.*

- It is possible to have a material in the scene that has not been loaded into the editor. You can add a scene material to

  the editor by using 🗔 (Get Material).

- **Options>Options...** in the Material Editor offers controls that can help speed up performance when several large or complex materials are present in the editor.

- A material shown in a sample slot is previewed as applied to a 3D object. A map previewed in a sample slot is shown as a flat 2D rectangle.

*It is recommended that the sample material contain a scene material for the **Select by Material** option to be available. The Highlight Assets in ATS dialog is available if the material contains a map.*

- Figure A–7 shows the various options available in the shortcut menu. The options enable you to copy the materials from one slot to another, rotating and resetting the rotation of the material sample, and set the number of slots.

Figure A–7

*   The Material Editor toolbars (shown in Figure A–8) work in the same way as the tools present in the Slate Material Editor.

Figure A–8

The Material/Map Browser is embedded in the Slate Material Editor.

*You can also open the Material/Map Browser independently by selecting **Rendering> Material/Map Browser** in the menu bar.*

- The Material/Map Browser can be accessed by clicking

  (Get Material). Once you have located a required material in the browser, drag it from the browser to a scene object or to a sample slot in the Material Editor.

- Previews of the materials can be shown in a list, or as buttons. The display can be changed in the shortcut menu, as shown in Figure A–9.

Figure A–9

A.3 Architectural Materials

Architectural materials are used with the Scanline renderer and offer a simplified interface over Standard materials because they have limited control (directly selecting a shader, some specular parameters, etc.). Architectural materials offer additional, built-in controls for translucency, refraction, and global illumination renderers.

Architectural Material Parameters

Architectural materials use Templates to assign shaders, which are predefined with many common material types (such as metals, paint, plastic, masonry, etc.). Selecting a template automatically populates other values in the *Physical Qualities* rollout, as shown in Figure A–10.

Figure A–10

Diffuse Color/ Diffuse Map	Located at the top of the *Physical Qualities* rollout, which are identical to those for Standard materials.
Shininess	Similar controls to the Specular Level of Standard materials. Architectural material highlights are generated through the **Shininess** and **Index of Refraction** parameters.

Transparency	The overall percentage that a material is transparent. For example, clear glass materials could be assigned transparencies between 90 and 100%.
Translucency	A measure of how much light is scattered as it passes through the object.
Index of Refraction (IOR)	Controls refraction and reflection. Typical values include 1.0 for air (effectively no refractive distortion), 1.33 for water, 1.5-1.7 for thick glass, and 2.5 for diamond.
Luminance	The amount of physically-based light the material emits. Unlike the Self-Illumination parameter of Standard materials, objects assigned Architectural materials can actually add light to scenes through this parameter as if they were light objects. (For example, illuminated materials are often used to represent neon tubes.)
Bump Maps	Can be assigned in the *Special Effects* rollout.

Architectural materials do not have Ambient Color controls because these materials are designed to work with radiosity, which directly calculates ambient illumination.

Architectural materials indicate when a reflectance value is out-of-range by colorizing the value in the Material Editor (based on the selected material template). Values that are too low are shown in blue and those that are too high are shown in red. Reflectance values that are out-of-range can be adjusted in a number of ways:

- When using a simple diffuse color (no diffuse image map), lower the overall value (V) of the color.

- The reflectance of Architectural materials can be reduced by entering a lower value for the *Reflectance Scale* in the *Advanced Lighting Override* rollout, as shown in Figure A–11.

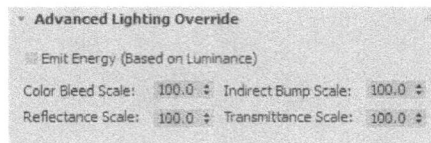

Figure A–11

A.4 Object Substitution

Linked or imported AutoCAD Blocks can be automatically replaced with 3D objects using the **Substitute** modifier.

- The Objects to be replaced (such as linked AutoCAD blocks) should be located with the correct 3D coordinates (including elevation) and rotation for the replacing object.

- The substituting object needs to be one object. For example, the light pole could be used if it was collapsed to a single mesh object. (To do so, right-click on the base object in the Modifier Stack and select **Convert to Editable Poly or Mesh**. Then use the object's **Attach** in the Command Panel to join the other parts to the mesh. Materials and mapping can be preserved during this operation).

- The substitute object can be present in the same scene as the object to be replaced or it can be XRefed in from another scene.

- Although this is commonly used for AutoCAD blocks, other Autodesk 3ds Max objects can be substituted as well with this modifier.

Practice A1

Substituting the Parking Lot Light Poles

Practice Objective

- Replace 2D symbol based objects with 3D photorealistic object blocks.

In this practice, you will substitute completed 3D light pole objects for 2D blocks in a scene using the **Substitute** modifier.

You must set the paths to locate the External files and Xrefs used in the practice. If you have not done this already, return to Chapter 1 and complete Task 1 to Task 3 in *Practice 1a: Organizing Folders and Working with the Interface*. You only have to set the user paths once.

1. Open **Substitution_Start.max**.

2. Switch the viewport to **Wireframe shading** by pressing <F3>.

*If a dialog box opens prompting you about a File Load: Mismatch, click **OK** to accept the default values.*

3. Zoom out on the area of the parking lot to display the flat, circular, and square symbols joined by a line (green), as shown in Figure A–12. These objects in the parking area are 2D light pole blocks. The parking lot surface has been hidden so that you can see the lamp symbols.

Figure A–12

4. In the Scene Explorer, use ■ (Display None)> ▣ (Display Shapes) and expand any one of **Block:Light Pole - Single**. Select the **Layer:LIGHTPOLE_SINGLE**, as shown in Figure A–13.

Figure A–13

5. In the Command Panel, select the Modify panel (⌒) and then select **Substitute** in the Modifier List. Only one 2D object is required to be selected because AutoCAD blocks link in as instances of each other, as indicated by the bold type in the Modifier Stack, as shown in Figure A–14.

6. Verify that the **Substitute** parameters match the parameters, as shown in Figure A–15 (default). Click **Select XRef Object...**.

Figure A–14

Figure A–15

7. In the Open File dialog box, open the source file, **Light Poles for Substitution.max** from the practice files folder.

8. In the XRef Merge dialog box, select the object named **LP_Single** and click **OK**.

9. In the Warning message dialog box, select **Apply to All Duplicates** to keep both materials, and click **Auto-Rename Merged Material**.

10. In the Substitution Question dialog box, click **Yes** to enable the substitute object's material to be used in this scene. Note that the 2D light pole blocks are replaced by the 3D single lightpole objects.

11. Repeat this process for one of the **Layer:LIGHTPOLE_ DOUBLE** objects (expand **Block:Light Pole - Double**), substituting **LP_Double** from **Light Poles for Substitution.max**.

12. In the viewport, change to **High Quality** in the *Shading Viewport* and **Default Shading** in the *Per-View Preference* label menu. Both the single light poles and double light poles display as shown in Figure A–16.

    *   The **Substitute** modifier enables you to take a 2D symbol on an instanced object and replace it with a 3D photorealistic one several times in a scene, thus saving memory.

Figure A–16

13. Save your work as **MyCivilBaseSubstitution.max**.

A.5 Creating Hierarchies

Autodesk 3ds Max Hierarchies are collections of objects linked together with parent/child relationships. When used, transforms applied to a parent are automatically passed to its children. Once you have created linkages between objects, you can animate them using forward kinematics where you move/rotate the parent, which in turn moves/rotates the children. Connecting multiple objects in a hierarchical chain can enable sophisticated animations such as the motion of jointed robotic arms.

Most modifiers (such as Substitute) must be applied to the objects in the hierarchy rather than the parent.

In the case of the hierarchy file link options, incoming AutoCAD blocks are brought in as multiple objects so that they can maintain multiple material assignments from AutoCAD. They display together with a Block/Style Parent object, enabling you to transform the block as a unit by selecting the parent. The parent object itself does not have any geometry and does not render.

Practice A2

Create Hierarchies

Practice Objective

- Create hierarchical relationships between objects.

In many animations you will want to create hierarchical relationships so that objects move together when moved. Once you have linkages, you can animate them using forward kinematics in which you move the parent and rotate the children.

You must set the paths to locate the External files and Xrefs used in the practice. If you have not done this already, return to Chapter 1 and complete Task 1 to Task 3 in *Practice 1a: Organizing Folders and Working with the Interface*. You only have to set the user paths once.

*If a dialog box opens prompting you about a File Load: Mismatch, click **OK** to accept the default values.*

1. Open **Lamp Start Linking.max**. This is a model of a desk lamp, as shown in Figure A–17.

Figure A–17

2. In the Scene Explorer, use ■ (Display None) and

   ● (Display Geometry) and note the six geometry objects in the scene. The names are not indented, indicating that there are no linkages.

3. In the viewport, move the Base object that is at the bottom of the lamp. Note that it moves by itself and the other objects are unaffected. Undo the move and clear the selection.

4. In the Main Toolbar, click ✇ (Select and Link). Starting at the top, select and hold each object and drag a dotted line to its parent. You will repeat the process five times as follows:

   • Select **Lampshade** and link it to **Upper Arm - Lamp**, as shown in Figure A–18.
   • Select **Upper Arm - Lamp** and link it to **Lower Arm**.
   • Select **Lower Arm** and link it to **Lower Hub**.
   • Select **Lower Hub** and link it to **Stand**.
   • Select **Stand** and link it to **Base**.

Figure A–18

5. In the Main Toolbar, click ▨ (Select Object) to end the linking process.

6. In the Scene Explorer, note that only **Base** is visible. Expand Base to display its dependent, **Stand**. Expand all of the children to display the dependencies, as shown in Figure A–19.

Figure A–19

7. Move the **Base** and note that the entire lamp moves with it. The base is the parent object and other objects are children and descendants. Undo the move.

8. Rotate the **Lower Arm** and note that the **Upper Arm - Lamp** and **Lampshade**, also rotates along with it. The Lower Hub, Stand, and Base are not part of the rotation. Undo the rotations.

9. Save your scene file as **MyLampStartLinking.max**.

Practice A3

Create an Assembly Animation

Practice Objective

- Create animation assembly to bring the different parts of an object together.

It is common to create an animation of a design that builds up over time. In this practice, you will create an animation of the assembly of a lamp.

You must set the paths to locate the External files and Xrefs used in the practice. If you have not done this already, return to Chapter 1 and complete Task 1 to Task 3 in *Practice 1a: Organizing Folders and Working with the Interface*. You only have to set the user paths once.

In this kind of animation, you will add keyframes to the end of the animation and then adjust the start and end ranges for each component.

1. Open **Lamp Start Linking Animation.max**.

*If a dialog box opens prompting you about a File Load: Mismatch, click **OK** to accept the default values.*

2. In the Animation Controls, click 🕘 (Time Configuration). In the Time Configuration dialog box, in the *Animation* area, set the *End Time* to **200** and click **OK**.

3. Press <Ctrl>+<A> to select all objects in the viewport at once.

4. In the Time Slider, right-click on the **0/200** slider bar to open the Create Key dialog box. Clear **Rotation** and **Scale** leaving **Position** selected and set the *Destination Time* to **160**, as shown in Figure A–20. Click **OK**.

Figure A–20

- A Position key for all objects is placed at frame 160. Note that in the Track Bar, a red box is set at 160, as shown in Figure A–21.

Figure A–21

5. Click **Auto Key** to activate it (it will display in red).

If all of the objects are selected, click in empty area in the viewport to clear the selection and then select each object separately.

6. Verify that your slider bar is located at **0** (0/200). Clear the object selection, and move each individual object randomly on the screen, similar to that shown in Figure A–22. (The placement of the objects can be different to that shown in the image.)

Figure A–22

7. Click ▶ (Play) and note that starting from frame 0, the components start drifting towards their original position and complete their original position at frame 160. Stop the animation.

8. Save your scene file as **MyLampAnimation.max**.

> **Hint: Set the Selection Range**
>
> To have the components assemble one after another, using <Ctrl> select both keys in the Time Slider. Right-click and select **Configure>Show Selection Range**. A bar is added below the track bar indicating the duration of movement for the selected component. You can now move the ends of the range to control when the object starts to move and when it finishes. The shorter the line, the quicker the movement of the object.

A.6 Customizing the User Interface

The Autodesk 3ds Max software has a flexible and highly customizable user interface that can be modified using the Customize User Interface dialog box, as shown in Figure A–23. Select **Customize>Customize User Interface**.

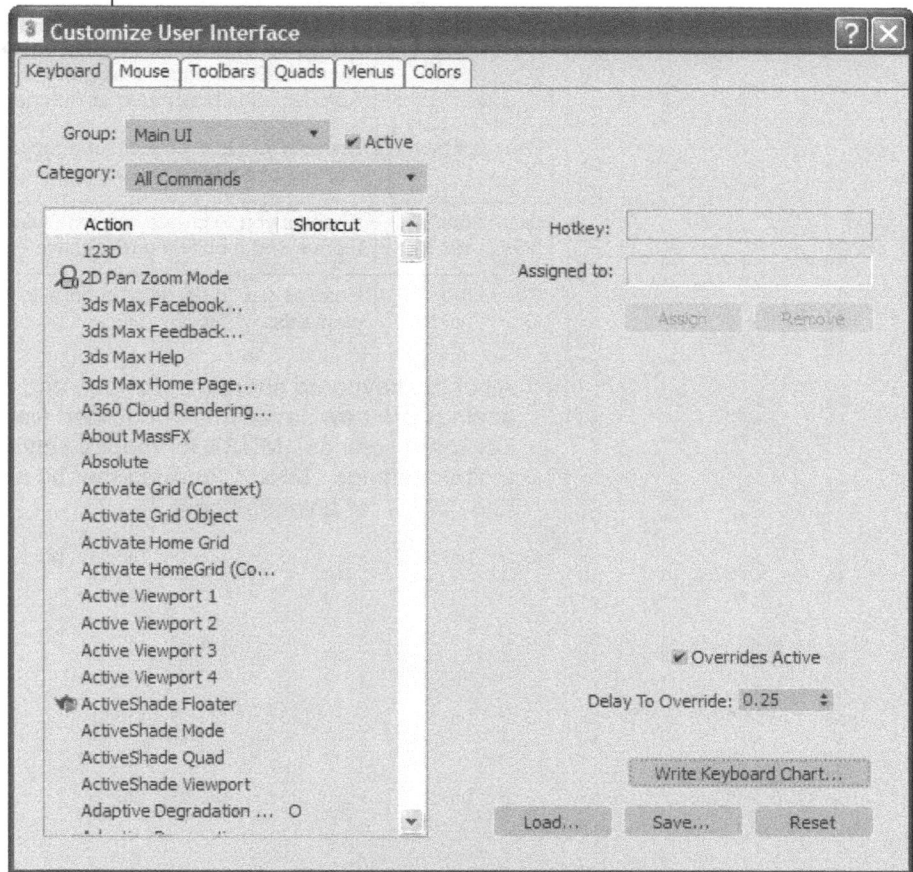

Figure A–23

- The settings located in each tab can be saved or swapped out independently with **Load...** and **Save...**.

- All of the interface settings can be loaded and saved at once using **Customize>Load/Save Custom UI Scheme**.

Keyboard tab	Enables you to assign shortcuts or hotkeys.
Write Keyboard Chart...	Can be found in the *Keyboard* tab. It enables you to save a .TXT file showing all of the current hotkeys. A hotkey is a keyboard stroke or combination assigned to launch a specific option. It is good practice to develop your own set of keyboard shortcuts to improve your productivity.
Mouse tab	Enables you to load and save the mouse settings. The mouse settings are dependent on the interaction mode set in the Preferences dialog box in which you can set the Autodesk 3ds Max mode or Autodesk Maya mode
Toolbars tab	Enables you to create custom toolbars and modify the existing one based on your requirements.
Quads tab/ *Menus* tab	Enables you to create custom Quad sets and custom menus and modify the respective existing ones.
Colors tab	Enables you to set color options for the interface elements.

- All of the keyboard shortcuts, toolbar, and menu custom settings are now saved in an upgraded file format (.KBDX for keyboard settings, .MUSX for mouse settings, .CUIX for toolbar settings, .MNUX for quad menus and menu settings, and .CLRX for color settings).

Practice A4 | Customizing the User Interface

Learning Objectives

- Customize the User interface.

In this practice, you learn to customize the User interface by adding different commands in the quad menu. You will then add different icons for a command to the Main Toolbar.

1. Reset the file so that you have a blank file open.

2. Right-click in any viewport to open the quad menu. Note that the **Clone** option displays after **Place Pivot Surface**, as shown in Figure A–24.

Figure A–24

3. Select **Customize>Customize User Interface** to open the Customize User Interface dialog box.

4. Select the *Quads* tab. Click on any item in the *Action* list and press <O>.

5. Locate **Orbit View Mode**. Click and drag it to the Quad list on the right, placing it just above **Clone**, under the line, as shown in Figure A–25. This enables you to select **Orbit View Mode** with a right-click quad menu. Also note that its position is between **Place Pivot Surface and Clone**.

Figure A–25

6. Open the Group drop-down list and select **ViewCube**, as shown in Figure A–26.

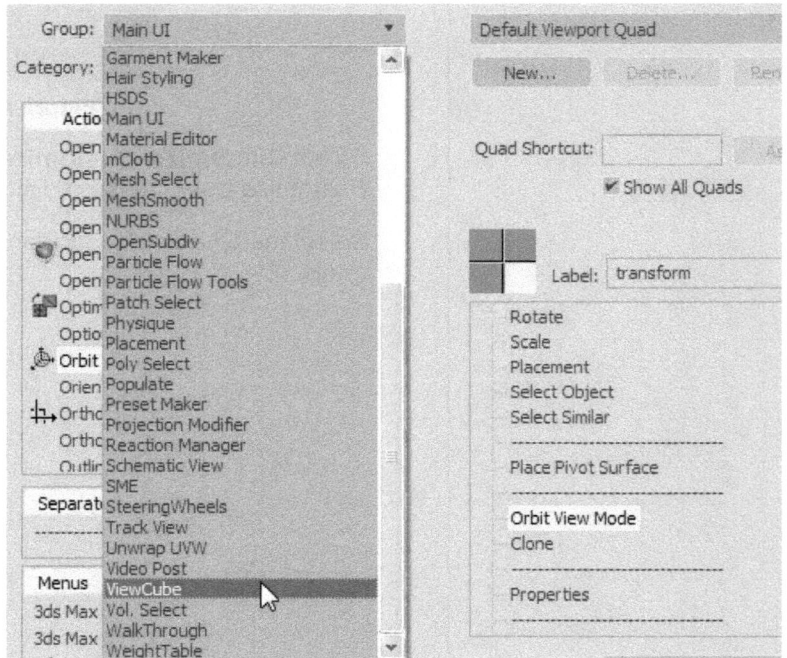

Figure A–26

*You can delete or edit the names of the listed commands by right-clicking on the command in the Action list and selecting **Delete Menu Item** or **Edit Menu item Name**.*

7. In the Action list, select **Toggle ViewCube Visibility**, drag it to the Quad list on the right, and place it just below **Orbit View Mode**, as shown in Figure A–27.

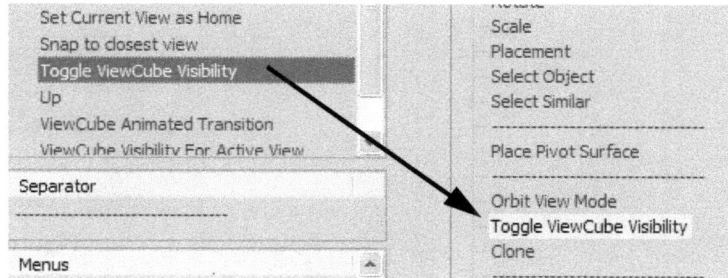

Figure A–27

8. Close the dialog box. Right-click on any viewport and note the new commands between **Place Pivot Surface** and **Clone**, as shown in Figure A–28.

Figure A–28

9. Select **Toggle ViewCube Visibility** to toggle it off. Note that the ViewCube is not visible anymore. Toggle it back on.

10. Select **Customize>Customize User Interface**.

11. In the dialog box, select the *Toolbars* tab. In the *Action* list, click **Ortho Snapping Mode**. Drag this entry to the Main Toolbar, and drop it before the **3D Snaps** icon, as shown in Figure A–29. The **Ortho Snap** tool is now available in the Main Toolbar. Close the dialog box.

Figure A–29

12. In the Main Toolbar, right-click on the newly placed **Ortho Snap** tool and select **Delete Button**, as shown in the Figure A–30. In the Confirm dialog box, click **Yes**. The button is removed.

Figure A–30

13. In the Main Toolbar, right-click on **Move**. No shortcut menu displays, indicating that you cannot delete it or modify it. Only the added buttons and some of the toggle buttons can be deleted.

Command Summary

Button	Command	Location
N/A	**3ds Max Help**	• **Help**: Autodesk 3ds Max Help
	Compact Material Editor	• **Main Toolbar:** Material Editor flyout • **Rendering:** Material Editor>Compact Material Editor
N/A	**Customize User Interface**	• **Customize:** Customize User Interface

Optional Practices

This appendix contains additional practices that can be worked on to provide further practice using the Autodesk® 3ds Max® software.

Practice B1

Create Additional Extrusions

Practice Objective

- Create 3D objects from 2D shapes.

In this practice, you will create extrusions that define a lobby area using the **Extrude** modifier and its various options, as shown in Figure B–1. You will extrude a part of the second floor that connects to the lobby area.

Figure B–1

1. Open **Extruded Walls with Openings.max**.

2. Select **High Quality** in the *Shading Viewport* label menu.

Press <Enter> after entering a value in the edit box.

3. Select each of the 2D shapes listed in the following table individually (use the Scene Explorer with ⬛ (Display Shapes)). For each selected object, use the **Extrude** modifier (Modify panel (⬛)>Modifier List) and extrude them as described in the table. For each object, set the rest of the parameters (Select **Generate Mapping Coords.**, **Real-World Map Size** and clear **Generate Material IDs**) as shown for **Layer:VIZ-1-Ceiling**, in Figure B–2. For the objects that are required to be moved up (elevation), click

⬛ (Select and Move) and then, in the Status Bar, enter the Z value for elevation, as specified in the table.

Figure B–2

Autodesk 3ds Max Shape	Extrusion Amount	Notes
Layer:VIZ-1-Ceiling	1'0"	Cap only the start (not end) Move up to elevation 10'0"
Layer:VIZ-1-Ceiling Lights	0'0"	Cap only the start (not end) Move up to elevation 9'11 7/8"
Layer:VIZ-1-Floor-Carpet	0'0"	Cap only the end (not start)
Layer:VIZ-1-Floor-Tile	0'0"	Cap only the end (not start)
Layer:VIZ-2-Ceiling (Partial)	1'0"	Cap only the start (not end) Move up to elevation 20'0"
Layer:VIZ-2-Walls (Partial)	9'0"	Cap only the end (not start) Move up to elevation 11'0"

4. When using **Cap Start** and **Cap End**, note that the ceilings are visible from the top and bottom of the model. To manipulate the display so that you can still see inside the lobby when looking down at the model but see the ceilings when looking up, you can set the **Object Properties**. Select the two ceiling layers (**Layer:VIZ-1-Ceiling** and **Layer: VIZ-2-Ceiling (Partial)**) and select **Edit>Object Properties**. The Object Properties dialog box opens. In the *General* tab, in the *Display Properties* area, click **By Layer** to change it to **By Object**. Once **By Object** is enabled, select the **Backface Cull** option. This enables you to see inside the model when looking down from the top.

5. Save the file as **MyAdditional Extrude.max**.

Practice B2	# Making a Chair Base by Lofting Objects

Practice Objectives

- Loft 2D shapes along a 2D path to create a 3D object and apply deformations to the shapes.

In this practice, you will create a loft object to represent the base of a chair. The extrude and sweep modifiers both use a single shape that sweeps along a path to create a 3D object. The Loft Compound Object modifier places multiple shapes along a spline path. It also gives you additional deformations to twist, tweeter, scale, and otherwise fit to shape on a graph

1. Open the file **airport_chair_startLoft.max**. The chair seat and four shapes display in the viewport, as shown in Figure B–3.

Figure B–3

2. In the viewport, select the straight line shape directly under the chair. This shape is used at the path for the loft.

   - In the viewport, there are three more shapes: a **Circle**, a **Star** with three points, and a six sided **NGon**. You will blend from shape to shape along the path.

3. In the Command Panel>Create panel (➕), click

   ⬤ (Geometry), expand the drop-down list, and select **Compound Objects**.

Hovering the cursor over a valid shape, changes it to a Get Shape cursor.

4. In the *Object Type* rollout, click **Loft**.

5. In the *Creation Method* rollout, click **Get Shape**. In the viewport, select the large circle object named **Circle01**. The circle is lofted along the selected straight line, as shown in Figure B–4.

Figure B–4

6. Press <F3> to toggle to wireframe shading.

7. With the **Loft** object selected, in the Command Panel, select the Modify ( ). In the *Path Parameters* rollout, set *Path* to **40**. In the viewport, a small yellow **X** indicator moves up the path, as shown in Figure B–5.

Figure B–5

The **Zoom** and **Orbit** commands were used to display the complete loft object.

8. In the *Creation Method* rollout, click **Get Shape**. In the viewport, select **NGon01** (blue **Ngon** inside the loft object). Change the *Per-view Preference* to **Default Shading**. The circular base shape now tapers to a post, as shown in Figure B–6.

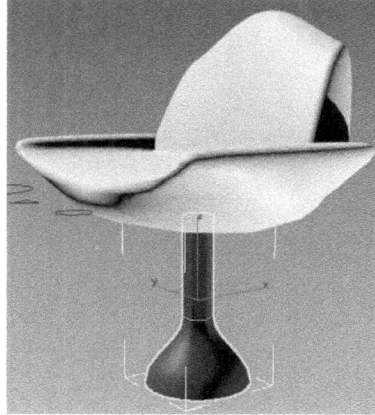

Figure B–6

9. In the *Path Parameters* rollout, set the *Path* value to **60**.

10. Verify that **Get Shape** is still selected (blue) otherwise select it. Select the **NGon01** again. The NGON is placed at the new location.

11. In the *Path Parameters* rollout, set the *Path* value to **100**. Verify that **Get Shape** is still selected and select the **Circle01**. In the viewport, note that the loft flares up before touching the seat, as shown in Figure B–7.

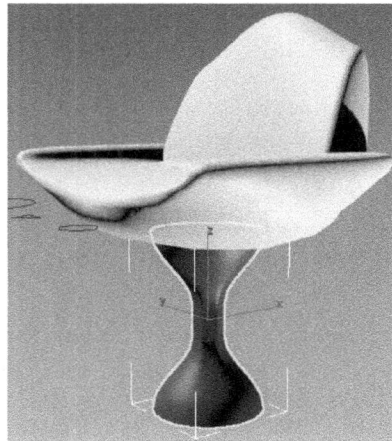

Figure B–7

12. In the *Path Parameters* rollout, set the *Path* value to **50**.

13. Verify that **Get Shape** is still selected (or select it) and select the **Star01** shape. Note that in the center of the loft, the geometry does not look very good. You need to add more points to the star. Click **Get Shape** again to clear its selection.

14. In the Scene Explorer, ((Display Shapes)), select **Star01**.

In the Modify panel ( ), in the *Parameters* rollout, set the following values for the Star (*Radius 1*: **9'0"**, *Radius 2*: **7'0"**, *Points*: **9**), as shown in Figure B–8. In the viewport, note that both the loft object and the star shape have been modified, as shown in Figure B–9.

Figure B–8

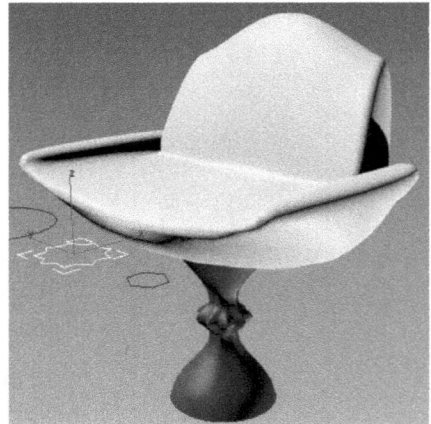

Figure B–9

15. Select the loft object and press <F4> to display in Edged Face mode, as shown in Figure B–10. Note that the mesh looks pretty dense.

Figure B–10

16. With the base selected (Loft001), verify that the Modify panel ( ) is open in the Command Panel.

17. Expand the *Skin Parameters* rollout, and in the *Options* area, set the *Shape Steps* and *Path Steps* to **2**. Increase the *Path Steps* to **4** and leave the *Shape Steps as* **2**, as shown in Figure B–11.

Figure B–11

18. For sculpting the final shape of the Loft object, expand the *Deformations* rollout and click **Scale**. The Scale Deformations graph displays.

19. In the Scale Deformations toolbar, click (Insert Corner Point). When you hover the cursor over the red line, note that it displays as a plus sign. Click on the red line under 20 to set the control point at an approximate position. In the *Text* edit box, at the bottom of the dialog box, enter **20** and press <Enter> (as shown in Figure B–12) to move the control point to the exact position.

Figure B–12

20. Similarly add new control points at **40**, **50**, and **60**.

21. In the dialog box, click ✛ (Move Control Point) to move the points on the graph. Right-click on the points and change them to **Bezier Smooth** or **Bezier Corner**, then adjust the handles, as shown in Figure B–13. Review the object in the viewport as the points are moved and modified.

Figure B–13

22. Play with the handles and scale points while watching the interactive results in the viewport.

23. You can use other deformation tools, such as **Twist**, **Teeter**, **Bevel**, and **Fit** and note how they effect the base of the chair.

24. Save the file as **Myarmchair_withBase.max**.

Practice B3 | Shadow Study Animation

Practice Objective

- Animate the Daylight System to create a shadow study.

In this practice, you will animate the movement of the daylight throughout a day in the exterior scene to create an animated shadow study. This study will provide an accurate representation of how daylight will cast shadows in the scene.

1. Open **Shadow Study.max**.

2. Activate the **Camera01** viewport. This is the non-animated camera view.

3. In the Animation controls, click ⏰ (Time Configuration). Set the settings as shown in Figure B–14. Click **OK**.

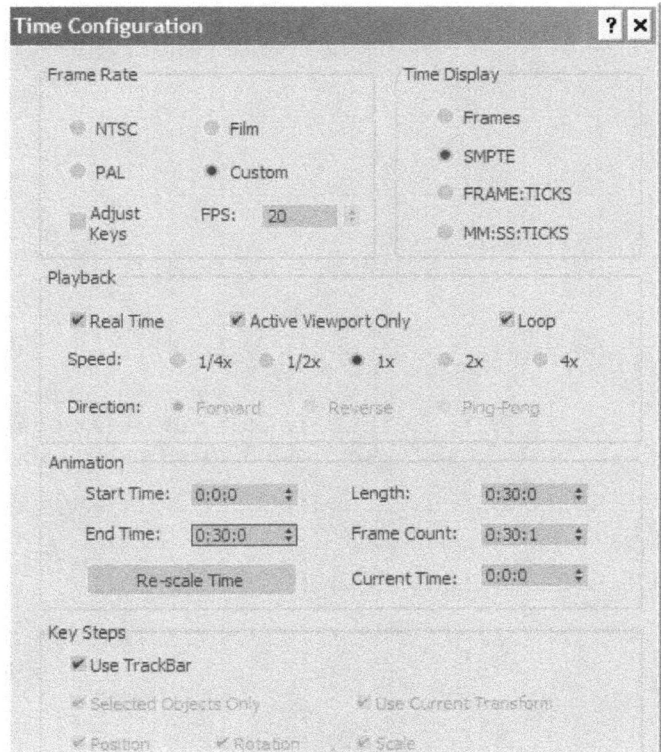

Figure B–14

4. In this shadow study you will animate the **SunPositioner001** object using keyframing. Select the **SunPositioner001** object in the Scene Explorer, using **Display Lights** tool.

5. Verify that the Time Slider is located at a time of **0:0:0** (frame 0), as shown in Figure B–15.

Figure B–15

6. In the Command Panel, select the Modify panel ( ). Start the shadow study animation at frame 0, representing **6:00 AM**. In the *Sun Position* rollout, set the current time to **6h** and date as shown in Figure B–16.

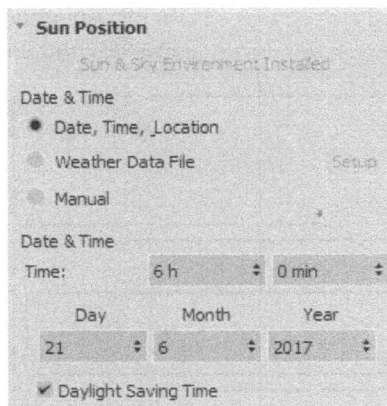

Figure B–16

7. In the Animation Controls, click **Auto Key** (displays in red). While in **Auto Key** mode, drag the time slider to the end time of **0:30:0**, as shown in Figure B–17.

Figure B–17

8. At this time (**0:30:0**) change the sun's position to 7:00 PM by entering **19** in the *Hours* edit box in the Command Panel.

9. Click **Auto Key** again to clear it and end Auto Key mode.

10. Slide the Time Slider left and right (scrub) and in the viewports, watch the **SunPositioner001** object progress across the sky during the animation.

11. Open the Render Setup dialog box by clicking ((Render Setup)). Verify that the active renderer is set to **Arnold**.

12. In the *Time Output* area, select **Active Time Segment** and set *Every Nth Frame* to **20**, as shown in Figure B–18.

This enables you to always render Camera01 even if another viewport is active.

13. In the *View to Render*, set the current viewport to **Quad 4 - Camera01** and click , as shown in Figure B–18.

Target:	Production Rendering Mode ▼	Render
Preset:	No preset selected ▼	
Renderer:	Arnold ▼	Save File ...
View to Render:	Quad 4 - Camera01 ▼	🔒

Common | Arnold Renderer | System | AOVs | Diagnostics | Archive

▾ **Common Parameters**
  Time Output
  ○ Single   Every Nth Frame: 20 ⬍
  ● Active Time Segment: 0:0:0 To 0:30:0
  ○ Range: 0:0:0 ⬍ To 0:3:6 ⬍

Figure B–18

14. In the *Render Output* area, click **Files....** Render the animation to still frames named **shadow study.jpg** (select **JPEG File** from the *Save as type* drop-down list) in the *...\renderings* folder. In the JPEG IMage Control, specify *Quality* as **Best** option and click **OK**.

15. Click **Render** to begin animating the individual frames of the animation through the course of a day from 6.00 a.m. to 7.00 p.m. Note the change in brightness of the daylight and the movement of the shadows from one frame to another

16. In the Windows Explorer, locate the *renderings* folder in the practice files folder and note the rendered images for **Shadow Study** at different frames, as shown for frame 1 and frame 21 in Figure B–19.

Shadow study at Frame 1

Shadow study at Frame 21

Figure B–19

17. Save the scene file as **My Shadow Study.max**.

Autodesk 3ds Max Certification Exam Objectives

The following table will help you to locate the exam objectives within the chapters of the *Autodesk® 3ds Max® 2019: Fundamentals* learning guide to help you prepare for the Autodesk 3ds Max Certified Professional exam.

Exam Topic	Exam Objective	Learning Guide	Chapter & Section(s)
Animation	Create a path animation and evaluate an object along the path	• Autodesk 3ds Max Fundamentals	• 11.2
	Identify Controller types		
	Identify playback settings	• Autodesk 3ds Max Fundamentals	• 11.1
	Locate the value of keys in the Time Slider	• Autodesk 3ds Max Fundamentals	• 11.1
	Use a Dope Sheet	• Autodesk 3ds Max Fundamentals	• 11.1
Cameras	Differentiate camera types	• Autodesk 3ds Max Fundamentals	• 9.3
	Edit FOV (Field of View)	• Autodesk 3ds Max Fundamentals	• 9.3
Data Management/Int eroperability	Differentiate common file types and usages	• Autodesk 3ds Max Fundamentals	• 1.1 • 3.1 & 3.2
	Use the import feature to import model data	• Autodesk 3ds Max Fundamentals	• 3.1
Effects	Identify Space Warp types		
	Use atmosphere effects		
	Use particle system		

Exam Topic	Exam Objective	Learning Guide	Chapter & Section(s)
Lighting	Compare Attenuation and Decay	• Autodesk 3ds Max Fundamentals	• 8.2 • 9.1
	Identify parameters for modifying shadows	• Autodesk 3ds Max Fundamentals	• 8.4 • 9.1 & 9.2
	Add a volumetric effect		
Materials/ Shading	Identify standard materials	• Autodesk 3ds Max Fundamentals	• 6.4, 6.5, 6.6, 6.9
	Use the Slate Material Editor	• Autodesk 3ds Max Fundamentals	• 6.3 • 7.1
Rigging	Use Character Studio for Rigging		
	Create simple Bipeds		
	Use the Skin modifier		
Modeling	Differentiate reference coordinate systems	• Autodesk 3ds Max Fundamentals	• 4.4
	Differentiate workflow	• Autodesk 3ds Max Fundamentals	• 1.2
	Identify Clone types	• Autodesk 3ds Max Fundamentals	• 4.5
	Differentiate standard versus extended primitives	• Autodesk 3ds Max Fundamentals	• 4.1
	Identify and use line tool creation methods	• Autodesk 3ds Max Fundamentals	• 5.1
	Identify Vertex types	• Autodesk 3ds Max Fundamentals	• 4.3 • 5.1
	Use object creation and modification workflows	• Autodesk 3ds Max Fundamentals	• 4.3, 4.6 • 5.2 to 5.5, 5.7
	Use polygon modeling tools	• Autodesk 3ds Max Fundamentals	• 4.6
	Use ProBoolean	• Autodesk 3ds Max Fundamentals	• 5.5
Rendering	Differentiate Renderers	• Autodesk 3ds Max Fundamentals	• 10.3, 10.4, 10.5, 10.6
	Identify rendering parameters	• Autodesk 3ds Max Fundamentals	• 10.3, 10.4, 10.5, 10.6
UI/Object Management	Describe and use object transformations	• Autodesk 3ds Max Fundamentals	• 4.2
	Identify Selection Regions and methods	• Autodesk 3ds Max Fundamentals	• 2.3
	Use Viewports	• Autodesk 3ds Max Fundamentals	• 1.7 • 2.1 & 2.2
	Set up and use Scenes	• Autodesk 3ds Max Fundamentals	• 1.4 • 2.4

Index

#

2019 Enhancements
  Arnold Materials **6-71**
  Project Folder **1-34**
    Create Active Project **1-35**
    Create Default **1-35**
    Create Empty **1-35**
    Create from Current **1-35**
    Recent Projects **1-35**
  Scene Converter **6-85**
2D Boolean **5-14**
2D Shapes **5-2**

A

Adaptive Degradation **1-26**, **11-10**
Animation **11-2**
  Assembling **11-38**
  Curve Editor **11-3**
  Dope Sheet **11-4**
  Hierarchies **A-15**
  Key frames **11-2**
  Output **11-37**
  Path Constraint **11-15**
  RAM Player **11-38**
  Shadow Study **B-11**
  Time Configuration **11-6**
  Time Controls **11-5**
  Time Slider and Track Bar **11-2**
  Turntable **11-16**
  Walkthrough **11-13**
Arnold Lights **9-20**
Arnold Materials **6-71**
Arnold Renderer **10-23**
ART Renderer **10-49**
Aspect Ratio **9-36**
Asset Tracking **3-38**
Attach Operation **5-14**
Autodesk Materials **6-36**
AutoGrid Mode **4-34**

B

Backface Cull **10-46**

Background Images **9-34**
Bezier **5-3**
Boolean **5-23**
  2D Operations **5-14**
  3D Operations **5-23**
  Explorer **5-24**

C

Caddy Display **4-27**
Camera **9-27**
  Navigation Tools **2-4**
  Physical **9-28**
  Target and Free **9-30**
Civil View **3-4**
Clone **4-37**
Command Panel **1-17**
  Create **1-18**
  Display Panel **2-35**
  Modify **1-18**
  Utilities **1-20**
Compact Material Editor **A-6**
Compound Objects **5-23**
Create Geometry **4-2**
Create New Scenes **1-30**
Curve Editor **11-3**
Customize User Interface **A-21**

D

Daytime Lighting **10-6**
  Sun Positioner **10-6**
  Sunlight and Skylight **10-8**
Design Workspace **1-23**
Direct3D **1-38**
Directional Lights **8-10**
Display Driver **1-38**
Dolly Camera **2-4**
Dope Sheet **11-4**
Dummy Object **11-13**

E

Edit Mesh **4-25**, **4-47**
Edit Poly **4-25**, **4-47**
Edit Spline **5-14**

© 2018, ASCENT - Center for Technical Knowledge®

Environment Map **9-35**
Exposure Control **10-2**
   Logarithmic **10-4**
   Physical Camera **10-5**
   Pseudo Color **10-3**
External References **3-38**
Extrude Modifier **5-20**, **B-2**

F

Feedback **A-4**
File Commands **1-30**
File Linking **3-13**
File Menu Bar **1-30**
Fill Lights **8-11**

G

Gamma and LUT Settings **1-34**
General Materials **6-28**
Gizmo **4-11**
Global Illumination **8-3**
Global Menu Search **1-11**
Grouping Objects **4-38**

H

Help **A-2**
   3ds Max Communities **A-3**
   Resources and Tools **A-4**
   Services and Support **A-4**
   Tutorials **A-3**
Hierarchies **A-15**
Home Grid **4-34**

I

Image Based Lighting (IBL) **10-28**
Importing **3-2**
Input Data Files **1-2**
Interface **1-7**
   Alt Menu Bar **1-11**
   Command Panel **1-17**
   Main Toolbar **1-13**
   Menu Bar **1-8**
   Quad Menu **1-12**
   Ribbon **1-20**
   Scene Explorer **1-24**
   Status Bar **1-26**
   Toolbars **1-15**
   User Account Menu **1-8**
   Workspace Selector **1-16**
Interface Item Customize Menu **1-29**

L

Lathe Modifier **5-11**
Layer Explorer **2-30**
   Tools **2-31**
Layers Toolbar **2-30**
Lighting
   Arnold **9-20**

Basic Concepts **8-2**
Default Illumination **8-2**
Directional Lights **8-10**
Fill Lights **8-11**
Global Illumination **8-3**
Image Based Lighting (IBL) **10-28**
Intensity/Color/Attenuation **9-8**
Lister Utility **9-18**
Local Illumination **8-2**
Omni Lights **8-8**
Photometric **9-2**
Photometric Lights Data **9-12**
Skylight **8-11**
Spotlights **8-8**
Standard Lighting **8-5**
Types **8-4**
Web Distribution **9-5**
Linear Exposure Control **10-3**
Linking
   AutoCAD File **3-13**, **3-16**
   Files **3-13**
   Revit and FBX Files **3-22**
Local Illumination **8-2**
Loft Object **B-5**
   Deformations **B-9**
Logarithmic Exposure Control **10-4**

M

Main Toolbar **1-13**
   Dock/Float **1-13**
   Modular **1-14**
   Modular-mini **1-14**
Manage Links **3-14**
Maps
   Assigning maps **6-38**
   Basic concepts **6-4**
   Bump **6-63**
   Mapping coordinates **7-2**
   Mapping scale **7-14**
   Opacity **6-62**
   Reflection **6-63**
Material Explorer **6-83**
Material/Map Browser **6-10**
Materials **6-3**
   Architectural Materials **A-9**
   Arnold Materials **6-71**
   Autodesk Materials **6-36**
   Compact Material Editor **A-6**
   General **6-28**
   Material/Map Browser **6-10**
   Multi/Sub-Object **6-31**
   Physical Materials **6-28**
   Scanline **6-34**
   Shaders **6-6**
   Slate Material Editor **6-10**
Maximize Viewports **2-3**

Menu Bar **1-8**
Merge **3-4**
Modeling Ribbon **1-20, 4-47**
Modifier Stack **1-18**
Modifiers
    Edit Mesh **4-25**
    Edit Poly **4-25**
    Edit Spline **5-2**
    Extrude **5-20, B-2**
    Lathe **5-11**
    Map Scaler **7-4**
    Substitute **A-11**
    Sweep **5-46**
    Unwrap UVW **7-23**
    UVW Map **7-5**
    XForm **4-11**
Modular Main Toolbar **1-14**
Move **4-10**
Multi/Sub-Object Materials **6-31**
MultiRes **4-62**

N

Nested splines **5-22**
New All **1-30**
New from Template **1-31**
Nitrous Direct3D 11 **1-38**
Nitrous Direct3D 9 **1-38**
Nitrous Software **1-38**

O

Object Properties **2-33**
Omni Lights **8-8**
Open **1-31**
OpenGL **1-38**
Optimize **4-62**
Orbit **2-3**
Orbit Camera **2-4**

P

Pan **2-2**
Per-View Preference **2-9**
Photometric Lights **9-2**
Physical Camera **9-28**
Physical Camera Exposure Control **10-5**
Physical Materials **6-28**
Place **4-10**
Polygon Modeling **4-47**
Preferences **1-32**
Primitive Objects **4-2**
Print Size Wizard **10-63**
ProBoolean **5-23**
ProCutter **5-23**
Progressive Display **11-10**
Pseudo Color Exposure Control **10-3**

Q

Quad Menu **1-12**

R

RAM Player **11-38**
Raster Graphics **1-3**
Raytracing **10-44**
Reference Coordinate Systems **4-34**
Rendering
    Arnold Renderer **10-23**
    ART Renderer **10-49**
    Common Options **10-19**
    Common Tab Options **10-21**
    Double Sided Scanline **10-45**
    Material Concepts **6-2**
    Options **10-18**
    Scanline Renderer **10-42**
Reset **1-31**
Rotate **4-10**

S

Safe Frames **9-37**
Save **1-32**
Scale **4-10**
Scanline Materials **6-34**
Scanline Renderer **10-42**
Scene Converter **6-85**
Scene Explorer **1-24, 2-17**
Select Objects **2-16**
Selection
    Edit Menu **2-19**
    Edit Named Selection Sets **2-19**
    Methods **2-16**
    Object **2-18**
    Scene Explorer **2-17**
    Select by Name tool **2-18**
    Window/Crossing **2-19**
Set Project Folder **1-34**
Shadows
    Animation Study **B-11**
    Parameters **8-28**
    Ray traced **8-30**
    Types **8-26**
Slate Material Editor **6-10**
    Active View **6-12**
    Map controls **7-3**
    Menu Bar **6-18**
    Parameter Editor **6-16**
    Toolbar **6-16**
Smoothing **4-26**
Snaps **5-36**
Spline Mapping **7-23**
Splines **5-2**
Spotlights **8-8**
Standard Lighting **8-5**
State Sets **10-59**
    Camera Sequencer **10-62**
    Composer View **10-61**
Statistics **4-63**

Status Bar **1-26**
Steering Wheel **2-5**
Sub-object Mode **4-24**
Substitute Modifier **A-11**
Sun Positioner **10-6**
Sunlight and Skylight systems **10-8**
Sweep Modifier **5-46**
System Paths **1-36**

T
Target and Free Camera **9-30**
Transform Centers **4-36**
Transforms **4-8**
    Gizmo **5-7**
    Select and Move **4-10**
    Select and Place **4-10**
    Select and Rotate **4-10**
    Select and Scale **4-10**
Truck Camera **2-4**

U
Units Setup **2-27**
User Account Menu **1-8**
User Paths **1-37**

V
Vector Data **1-2**
Vertices
    Bezier **5-3**
    Corner **5-3**
ViewCube **2-4**
Viewport Layouts Tab Bar **1-27**
Viewports
    Display **1-39**
    Labels **1-39**
    Layouts **1-27**
    Maximize **2-3**
    Per-View Preference **1-42**
    Point of View **1-40**
    Safe Frames **9-37**
    Statistics **4-63**
Viewports Configuration
    Layout **2-6**
    Statistics **2-8**
    Steering Wheels **2-7**
    ViewCube **2-8**
Visualization Workflow **1-4**

W
Welcome Screen **1-6**
Windows and Doors **5-41, 5-45**
Workspace Selector **1-16**

X
XRefs **3-38**

Z
Zoom **2-2**